THE KENTUCKY ABOLITIONISTS
IN THE MIDST OF SLAVERY
1854-1864

Exiles for Freedom

THE KENTUCKY ABOLITIONISTS IN THE MIDST OF SLAVERY 1854-1864

Exiles for Freedom

Richard Sears

The Edwin Mellen Press
Lewiston/Queenston/Lampeter

Library of Congress Cataloging-in-Publication Data

This book has been registered with The Library of Congress.

ISBN 0-7734-9309-3

A CIP catalog record for this book
is available from the British Library.

The Edwin Mellen Press
Box 450
Lewiston, New York
USA 14092

The Edwin Mellen Press
Box 67
Queenston, Ontario
CANADA L0S 1L0

Edwin Mellen Press, Ltd.
Lampeter, Dyfed, Wales
UNITED KINGDOM SA48 7DY

Printed in the United States of America

FOR MY SONS,
ROBERT AND ALDEN

Table of Contents

PREFACE

From about 1844, when the friendship of Cassius M. Clay and John G. Fee began, until 1864, when abolitionism *per se* was rendered obsolete, this work tells the story of the men and women who conducted the antislavery campaign in Kentucky.

In some cases, the text presents individual biographical (and genealogical) details, but it also deals with the ideas and incidents of a whole social movement, relating that movement to currents across the United States. "Berea" is too small a category, even for Kentucky, since the abolitionist movement from 1844 to 1864 directly affected many areas in the state, including the counties of Madison, Rockcastle, Estill, Jackson, Clay, Laurel, Fleming, Mason, Bracken and Lewis. Indirectly, the work of the abolitionists led by John G. Fee stirred the entire state, mostly in reaction and opposition. By 1859, every Kentuckian who could read a newspaper knew about the threatening doctrines and actions of those "radical insurrectionaries" and "incendiaries" centered in Berea. In abolitionist circles throughout the North and East, John G. Fee and his fellow workers were well-known, and their views and work were influential.

What Fee started in Kentucky was a genuine movement, involving many people—both citizens of the state and "interlopers," both rich and poor, educated and illiterate, famous and infamous—over a long period of time, stretching all the way to the present day. It is true that John G. Fee and his followers were virtually the *only* abolitionists in Kentucky in the period under consideration; however, the manifold connections of Fee's antislavery work with earlier and concurrent movements gives it a broader importance than one man's labors might be expected to have. Through Fee the ideas, reforms, resources and controversies of evangelical abolitionism in the North and East poured into Kentucky before the Civil War. In addition, the work of Fee and his colleagues bore fruit after that conflict ended. The town of Berea, founded as part of the abolitionist mission in Kentucky, remains; Berea College, chartered to promote social equality among the races, still marks the spot where Fee and his workers defied the entire system of slavery. It might be argued that John G. Fee was the only abolitionist in the South whose mission left visible signs.

The reformers who were the last abolitionists to work in Kentucky, who founded Berea, also left a rich legacy of correspondence—literally thousands of letters detail their struggles. Their reports to the American Missionary Association cover virtually every month of their work in Kentucky for the decade from 1854 to 1864; sometimes their lives can be studied on a *daily* basis. As I read in the archives of Berea College and of the AMA, I realized that the story of early Berea had actually never been told—not as it could be told: the abolitionist mission in central Kentucky was an incredible drama, and the principle actors had all recorded their experiences, thoughts and impressions *at the time*. First-hand, contemporary accounts exist for every phase of the last decade of the antislavery movement in Kentucky, and virtually every incident of importance is detailed from many different points of view. Although this is not a documentary history, many events are described in the actual words of the participants, rather than interpreted from the later reports by historians. I have systematically preferred narratives by people involved in the events they are describing; in the many cases where a writer has related the same incident both at the time and again years later, I have emphasized the earlier version. When many people have presented the same event, I have used *all* versions to some extent.

Since much of this book is based on letters, I should explain how I have treated these sources. Many 19th century letter writers produced spelling and punctuation we consider incorrect or substandard. John G. Fee punctuates very erratically and spells only moderately well: his characteristic errors are obvious without editorial interjection. Some mountain people produced letters which are significant because of what their errors reveal. In most cases, my corrections would have spoiled the writer's own "voice"; so I have used *sic* only in instances where a mistake is so peculiar that readers could scarcely credit it (when Fee spells 'daily' as 'dily,' for example). Nineteenth century letter writers employed underlining for emphasis much more than we we do. Quite often they underlined twice for even more dramatic effect. Where double underlining occurs, I have indicated it by the abbreviation [d.u.] following the underlined words. Occasionally a really vehement writer, such as William E. Lincoln in one of his diatribes or William Goodell in a fervent outpouring, uses triple or quadruple underlining, as well as exclamation points. I have sometimes found it desirable to describe the actual handwriting in a given letter since some epistles are *visibly* out of control. Fee's letters, hundreds of which close with the words, "In haste, John G. Fee," are frequently vivid images of the pressing demands of his life as an abolitionist, hasty scrawls, punctuated with long dashes, words flying across the page with splutters of ink marking the rapid passage of his pen. I hope this book conveys some of the excitement and sheer energy of the multitude of letters Kentucky's abolitionists wrote.

The antislavery movement was much more complex and diverse than most people realize. Abolitionists came in many varieties. In Kentucky, they were men, women and *children:* old and young, religious and non-religious, rich and poor, from the North, from the South, from the Bluegrass, from the mountains. They were from Boston, Massachusetts, and from McKee, Kentucky, from Oberlin, Ohio, and London, England. And there were scores of them, all involved in opposing slavery right in the middle of a slave state.

I found this story incredible while I was discovering it: I still think it incredible, after almost ten years of involvement. My intention has been to tell the story of late abolitionism and early Berea, to present what happened as thoroughly and accurately as possible. Theoretical questions have not engaged me as much as the tale itself. Assessing John G. Fee's contribution to the overthrow of slavery, deciding whether his mission was effective or *valuable* by someone else's standards has not concerned me. I have tried to allow Fee and his colleagues to present their own case in their own way.

In the course of my research I traveled many miles and incurred many debts (mostly owing thanks rather than money). I worked in the National Archives, the Library of Congress and the D.A.R. Library in Washington, D.C.; in the Sterling Library at Yale; the New Haven Historical Society, Connecticut Historical Society and the Connecticut State Library; in the New England Historic Genealogical Society Library in Boston; the Ohio State Historical Society in Columbus; Oberlin College Archives and Special Collections; the Missouri Historical Society in Columbia; the Kansas City, Missouri, Public Library; the Filson Club in Louisville; Lexington Public Library, Lexington, Kentucky; Kentucky Archives and Kentucky Historical Society in Frankfort; the King Library at the University of Kentucky; the

Crabbe Library at Eastern Kentucky University; in courthouses in Madison County, Rockcastle County, Garrard County, Bracken County, Jackson County and Estill County, all in Kentucky. I traveled to Cornwall, Connecticut, to see John Rogers' birthplace, to Bracken County, Kentucky, to see John Fee's, to White Hall to Cassius M. Clay's. A number of individuals kindly allowed me to use their family papers, including Dean Warren Lambert, Brenda Harrison, Ray Durham, Marjorie Hylton, Mary Gay Walker, Louise Scrivener and Frances Moore, all of Berea, Kentucky. Joanne Tarbox, great-granddaughter of John and Elizabeth Rogers, and Anne Pirkle, great-grandniece of John G. Fee, were very gracious with information about their particular family traditions.

But my primary resources were the Berea College Archives and the American Missionary Association Archives. The latter contains the Berea correspondence in the Kentucky and Ohio Collections, thousands of letters written by Fee, Rogers, Candee and others—the original documents are housed in the Amistad Research Center in New Orleans, but I used a microfilm copy (in the Hutchins Library, Berea College) made by Fisk University when that institution held the collection. In addition, Berea College Archives contains hundreds of letters and other papers, a complete run of the *American Missionary* and many other primary sources for Berea history.

Everywhere I worked, people were courteous and helpful, but I should mention a few for special thanks: Sidney Farr and Gerald Roberts in Special Collections in the Hutchins Library, Berea College; my former secretary, Jack Gill, who faithfully transcribed the journals of John A. R. Rogers; the entire staff of the Berea College Computer Center, without whose expertise and patience I could not have continued this work; and the secretary of Draper Building, Phyllis Gabbard, who enables whole academic departments to function efficiently. Throughout my labors I was supported by the administration of Berea College, which provided both encouragement and financial assistance. Finally, my wife and children, who did more than endure my work, deserve my warmest thanks. Without Grace's encouragement this book could never have been written.

Berea, 26 Jan 1993

CHAPTER ONE

CASSIUS CLAY AND JOHN G. FEE

The Beginning: An Invitation
"Let us not despise the day of small things, [for] God can take the weak things of this world & confound the wise." John G. Fee.

In 1853, Cassius M. Clay invited Reverend John Gregg Fee to reside in southern Madison County, Kentucky, in the region which would become Berea. A small antislavery group which supported Clay's political ambitions had formed the Glade Church; Clay proposed that Fee become their minister and offered him a homestead, part of some 600 acres Clay owned in a neighborhood called the Glade. Fee could have the land if he would live on it, and he was free to choose the exact site and even the number of acres for himself.[1]

At Clay's urging, Fee visited the Glade and nearby Rockcastle County; beginning in the spring of 1853, he held a series of "protracted" meetings, resulting in the organization of three or four congregations as free churches along new abolitionist lines. As far as Fee was concerned, he was only paying a ministerial visit—his real work was established in Bracken and Lewis Counties on the Ohio River. But many of the people who had heard Fee preach urged him to return and settle among them.[2]

By the spring of 1854, Fee had very reluctantly accepted Clay's proposal "without any reference to salary or spot for a home." When the surveyor came to mark off his land, Fee was preaching at a revival which he had initiated almost instantly upon his arrival in Madison County. He refused to leave his pulpit to accompany the surveyor, but asked two local men, Hamilton Rawlings and William B. Wright, to choose a spot for him. Wright wanted Fee to live near him, and, on that basis, Fee's surrogates picked the extreme corner of Clay's tract, the least valuable corner, and marked off ten acres. "Mr. Clay," Fee complained, "would have been quite as well pleased if they had marked off ten times as much land, and in the best part. . . . " His tract was deep in the woods, covered with dense undergrowth and with "a frog pond in the midst." When Fee examined his plot he was terribly disappointed and saw neither "desirableness [nor] wisdom in the choice."[3]

Nevertheless, he would go, virtually penniless, to his new mission field. He had to clear the land and build a house, doing "a large part of the work with his own hands." Later, he was to see his home-site, which would soon determine the placement of church, town and school, as providentially selected: not in man's ignorance, although there was plenty of that to go around, but in God's wisdom. In the meantime, it stood as a sign of his indifference to a merely worldly reward for entering the mission field which Fee believed God, rather than Cassius Clay, had chosen for him. Even though the work in Madison County might appear trivial and unpromising, Fee extolled its importance to the American Missionary Association [hereafter abbreviated as AMA]: "Brethren, let us be united and step into this wide and effectual door which God is opening. . . . Let us not despise the day of small things," Fee advised, "God can take the weak things of this world and confound the wise."[4]

Actually, neither John G. nor his wife Matilda Fee wanted to go to Berea: before Cassius Clay's invitation came, Fee had considered moving from Lewis County back to Bracken, since he had churches in both places, and relationships in Bracken County were strong, encouraging and familiar. The couple would have been at home, near her supportive family. Nothing stood in the way of their fellowship with Matilda's parents; by 1850, her father Vincent Hamilton had freed his last remaining slave—only nominally his slave, in any case. Nevertheless, Matilda told her husband, "If you feel that it is duty [to go to Madison County], we will go and leave the future with God."[5]

Even after the decision had been made, the Fees were still reluctant and unhappy; Fee confided to Whipple:

> I have made arrangements to move to Madison co. The trial will be great to me but more especially to my wife who dreads much the leaving the churches here—the advantages of some good society, kind friends relatives—also our little home which with years of care & replanting we have rendered comfortable. There we shall be without good schools or good churches and with but few friends who will sympathize [sic] much with us at first—all strange.[6]

Fee insisted on one final preparation for his wife and himself before leaving for Madison County. For a long time he had had been studying the Christian rite of baptism, a subject of deep and engrossing interest to him, because it seemed to Fee baptism was foundational to the rest of one's Christian life—if the first step were wrong, the whole journey might go astray. Through his studies of scripture and of all the theological arguments on the matter that he could find, Fee concluded that the only mode of baptism effectual for a Christian was immersion. He and Matilda had been sprinkled in the Presbyterian Church when they were babies; Fee now called that practice 'rhantizing,' so as not to confuse it with the genuine ordinance. When he told his wife his new convictions he was pleased to learn she had been feeling the same for two years.[7]

When Fee and his wife were 're-baptized' in the waters of Cabin Creek it was a crucial religious experience for them; his baptism was a renewal of his covenant with God, putting on the whole armor for the warfare ahead. Still his removal to Madison County was delayed. In June, Fee explained to Clay that he had not yet started for his new home because of "biliousness arising from anxiety and labor." But Fee duly departed from his old home on August 2.[8]

> I gathered our household goods into a two-horse wagon, with David Gillespie, then a mere lad [a member of Fee's Cabin Creek Church in Lewis County], as driver; and I, wife and two children, in a one-horse carriage, started for the new home, one hundred and forty miles in the interior. . . .
> In the evening of the third day we camped in the new house, then without a chimney, or glass in the windows, or a fence around the yard.
> Believing as we did, that we were exactly where the Lord would have us, we lay down and slept calmly, sweetly.[9]

The Glade: Clay's Community
"The establishment of Berea served a great purpose in my political career."
Cassius Clay.

For many years Clay had worked to build a community for himself in the Glade. He had supported abolitionist preacher Wiley B. Fisk in his ministry, offering to build a church for him; in addition, Clay had sold several lots "at nominal prices to [his] most courageous friends for self-protection." In his eagerness to attract settlers who would support him, Clay even gave some of his land away—and not just to John G. Fee. In 1854, the Glade—or the Big Glade, as it was sometimes known—was populated mostly with citizens sympathetic to emancipationism, non-slaveholders, Free-Soilers, economically and morally indebted to their friend, benefactor and leader, Cassius M. Clay.[10]

John Hamilton Rawlings (known as "Ham") was a leader among Clay's followers in the Glade, and he would become known as "Fee's greatest local supporter." Born 1802 in Garrard County, Kentucky, he was the son of Moses Rawlings and Susannah Cox. Moses was reared in Baltimore, Maryland, "by parents of some wealth and was given the advantage of a fair education." Susannah Cox belonged to a "fiery, proud, and aristocratic southern family"; her sister Jane became the wife of David Kennedy, with whose family the Rawlings traveled to Garrard County. Hamilton Rawlings' father was a small slaveholder, but his Kennedy connections, well-known in Kentucky history, owned many slaves (several hundred, according to one account) in the neighborhood where Rawlings grew up. His parents were Presbyterians, members of the Old Paint Lick Church founded by early abolitionist Rev. David Rice In 1783.[11]

In Madison County Rawlings married Margaret W. Moore, who was "related to many of Madison's most wealthy and influential families," almost all of them slaveholders. Her brother Fergusson ("Fog") Moore was a slaveholder in the Glade. For a time Hamilton Rawlings owned slaves himself; in 1838 he sold a slave woman and her three children for debt. Later, in 1848, he inherited a boy from his father. By 1850, however, he openly declared his opposition to slavery.[12]

After his good friend Cassius Clay gave him a farm in the Glade worth about a thousand dollars, Rawlings began spreading antislavery propaganda among the local residents. As early as 1850 Rawlings "had accumulated a hand-full of militant anti-slavery advocates in his section." Rawlings remained Clay's "staunch friend," and eventually maintained his allegiance to Fee at the same time. (He even did some colportage for Fee, but never devoted full time to the job.)[13]

Twice a delegate to the Free-Soil National Conventions (1848, 1852), Rawlings went as a delegate in 1856 to the first Republican Convention ever held; four years later he was delegate to the Republican National Convention in Chicago where he supported the nomination of Abraham Lincoln and, undoubtedly, the vice-presidency of Cassius Clay.[14]

Clay wanted the Glade to initiate his political success with the mountainous regions of the state, to become his doorway into the Appalachian stronghold; he had a vision of the mountains of Kentucky "where there were but few slaves, and people courageous; so that, if they were once committed to liberation of the slaves, we could have a permanent nucleus of political and physical force. . . . " The establishment of Berea, Clay stated, "served a great purpose in my political career."[15]

Clay referred to the Bereans as his "boys" and imagined himself leading them in guerilla warfare against the slaveholding establishment, and, upon occasion, he did call them to arms in his own defense or in defense of Fee. To him, the Glade was a political power-base, representing votes, and even, as he says, 'physical force': his 'boys,' his people, his potential army.[16]

Nothing could be further from Fee's view of the same people. Since Clay wished to retain control of the Glade and its inhabitants, he made a singular error when he invited Fee to minister there. Fee could never simply be Clay's preacher, shaping sermons to further political ends, because Rev. John G. Fee considered himself God's man; his mission was based on "a covenant, made with God to preach in [his] native state, the gospel of impartial love." For him that gospel implied radical abolitionism; he called for immediate, uncompensated emancipation of all slaves; he demanded that Christians refuse to commune with slaveholders, because slavery itself was sinful: in fact, it was, in John Wesley's words, 'the sum of all villainies.' To John G. Fee, Clay's political base was a mission field, white to the harvest—not votes to be gained, but souls to be won, and, moreover, won to do God's will by freeing slaves.[17]

6

In 1854, anyone looking at the Glade itself would have required a gifted, perhaps fevered, imagination to see prospects for the realization of either Clay or Fee's vision. Clay imagined a constitutional overturning of the slave power from the political base that would begin in the Glade and filter throughout the mountain region of Kentucky; Fee envisioned a religous revival spreading by 'moral suasion' throughout the South. Both men were looking at a sparsely populated wilderness when they conceived these dreams. One basis for their relationship was their shared ability to dream fantastically.

The state of society around Berea was, in the word of one observer: "deplorable." The people were "poor, uneducated, ignorant." Many of them, both men and women, were illiterate. "Their clothing [was] poor, and many [were], even in . . . inhospitable weather, but half covered." Cassius Clay himself spoke of the Glade before Fee's coming:

> I knew the community in and around Berea when I was a boy, and I say that they were of the most vicious people that ever I did know; a drunken, tobacco-chewing, whiskey-drinking people; debauching and fighting could there be seen as plainly as the noon day sun. . . . The inhabitants dwelt in huts without windows and with mud floors; the children [indulged] in idleness and dissipation.[18]

The Glade was known (for the distance of a few miles, that is) for only two things in 1854: its tiny abolitionist church, with fewer than a dozen members in 1853, utterly powerless in its social and geographical context—irritating, no doubt, to slaveholders in the neighborhood, but scarcely more than irritating—and for its racetrack. Although one would hardly expect to find any connection between the race course and the church, it seems that Wiley Fisk, minister of Glade Church, was "a victorious jockey."[19]

A few families were established in the Glade and its immediate neighborhood: many of whom were charter members of the church; some of whom were smallscale slaveholders, owning fewer than ten slaves. The people who were to shape Berea, however, were not located simply in the immediate wilderness. Nearby communities were to become deeply involved in Berea's history and development. South of Berea, in Rockcastle County, but not far away even in those days, was a community, larger and older than the Glade, called Scaffold Cane, where Fee was to pastor another small church. Also in Rockcastle

County were the neighborhoods of Boone's Fork and Cummins (northwest of Mt. Vernon), the latter named after a family most numerous (then and now) in the area; the communities around Silver Creek and Big Hill, east of Berea, were already in place in 1854. West of Berea, the Paint Lick community flourished, straddling the line between Madison and Garrard Counties, one of the oldest towns in the state, eventually to provide many of the citizens of the Berea area.[20]

Most of the communities around the Glade were slaveholding, even the Rockcastle County neighborhoods in the mountainous regions had slaves, while slavery was very common in Paint Lick and Silver Creek and not unknown even in Big Hill. So, on the east, the west and the south there was slavery—not to the extent that it existed in the Bluegrass, but still powerfully entrenched. North of the Glade stretched the Bluegrass, all slavery: Richmond; Lexington, the biggest slave market in Kentucky. By 1849, Fayette was the largest slaveholding county in the state. By the end of 1850 slave dealers were as prevalent in Lexington as mule traders; more than two dozen dealers regularly advertised in Lexington newspapers. By 1850 only eight counties (including Jefferson and Fayette) had more slaves than Madison County: out of a total of 15,727 people Madison County had 5,393 slaves, more than one-third of the population in bondage. Between Berea and the free state of Ohio lay over 100 miles of enemy territory. The Glade was a wonderful place for an abolitionist colony! Nothing could have seemed more ill-advised, more ill-starred than the location of Fee's ministry deep in central Kentucky. Fee's enemies described Berea's position as being "in the heart of as strong a pro-slavery community as can be found in the South."[21]

The Glade was situated at a meeting place, a seam in Kentucky's geography—the place where Bluegrass and mountains meet. But it was more than a geographical juncture; at Berea, slaveholders, slaves and non-slaveholders met, planters and mountaineers, slavery and freedom. The efforts of Clay and Fee would add yet another element to the already volatile brew—namely abolitionists.

Berea was always a place of conflict and potential; at first it was *unsettled* in a double sense. Both Clay and Fee looked at the Glade, in many respects most unpromising, and saw possibilities. Their visions drew them together long enough to give an incredible undertaking its start, an undertaking that would result in a town, churches, schools, a college, and, most importantly, in a daring and unique social, economic, educational, religious experiment.

Fee's Glade Church
"We make no distinction at our Communion, because of the color or condition of members; we know our Saviour would not." John G. Fee.

Glade Church, under the ministry of Wiley Fisk, had been in existence for a relatively brief time before Fee's first visit, and the congregation had been but loosely established; membership had not been confined to non-slaveholders. All the members of Fisk's Reform Baptist Church (the Christian Church at the Glade) did not join Fee's church—part of the congregation, many of them slaveholders, retained the old organization. The church which Fee pulled out from Fisk's original group called itself Glade Church, but apparently the remaining congregation did too. For part of 1854 Fisk and Fee pastored *rival* churches.[22]

Fee organized a free church along the same lines as his earlier churches in northern Kentucky: his was to be a thoroughgoing abolitionist and reforming church, refusing fellowship to slaveholders, recognizing slavery as a sin in itself, anti-caste, anti-sectarian, anti-rum, anti-secret society. (One might add anti-tobacco and anti-papist, which would be true, although these last two features seldom appear on the official lists.) The church was free in the sense that it was under the jurisdiction of none of the recognized denominations, because all the established churches in the South condoned slavery, in one degree or another. It was free in the sense that all pews were accessible to anyone and cost nothing; no ranking by wealth was permitted. It was not free in the sense of having no internal discipline, for Fee's churches were extremely strict and demanding upon their members.

The Glade Church, newly organized in 1853, consisted of 13 baptized believers; Fee's other new churches were probably about the same size. Light is cast on the origins of Glade Church in the records of a rival church: Scaffold Cane Baptist. In the entry for June 3, 1853, we read that a charge was brought "against bro. John Dobbs and Samuel Williford junr for abruptly leaving the church declaring a non-fellowship with all slave holders and joining another society." Both Dobbs and Williford were excluded from the church's meeting on August 3, 1853, and at the same time "a charge was. . . laid in against Bro Elisha Dobbs for the same offence and after a few remarks he was Excluded." These three men probably joined Fee's new Union Church in Rockcastle County rather than the Glade, but, in any case, the pattern is clear. When Fee, or any of his abolitionist cohorts, entered a neighborhood, he was not asked to join the ministerial association, not welcomed by established pastors. Fee's avowed intention was to pull people out of those churches where slavery was not viewed as a sin and he succeeded in doing just that. Fisk claimed the 1853 revival drew converts from Baptists, Methodists and Presbyterians.[23]

Many new members in Fee's congregations represented growing enmity in the surrounding community. All his churches began with external conflict virtually inevitable and internal dissension highly likely. After all, the division of a church was foundational for Fee's ministry. One of the deponents in a divorce case *Burnam v. Burnam* mentions that the Glade Church had been sharply divided, adding specifically that Sarah Burnam had been on one side of the issue and her husband on the other. In any case, the doctrine of non-fellowship with slaveholders was as divisive as anything could be; it meant something very drastic to people in Madison County. For example, Glade Church member John Burnam, Sr.'s wealthy Richmond relatives owned many slaves, and his son Harrison Burnam was a slaveholder and a supporter of the rival church. Other members of Fee's Glade Church had many slaveholding relatives.

Fee's congregations in Madison and Rockcastle Counties consisted of people who had owned slaves themselves and had many connections with the peculiar institution. The reality of the situation was very complicated, and, for the people involved, no doubt, very painful—brother against brother, wife against husband, father against son. The Southern church had systematized a great tolerance for slavery and slaveholders, providing an involved and learned theology to maintain the status quo and soothe away possible doubts about God's will in the matter. Families within the system had more or less docilely accepted what was most comfortable anyway, since slavery was interwoven into every aspect of life in the South, and it was a rare family that did not possess some connection with the peculiar institution. People who did not own slaves were frequently related to people who did. Fee's doctrine, strictly applied as he wanted it to be, had to begin tearing family allegiance apart—in fact, doing for the members of his church, exactly what had been done for him: forcing them to sense a higher calling than family and social solidarity.

The establishment of Glade Church under Fee's leadership was also to have an immediate practical effect upon the region. About this time Cassius Clay was subdividing his previously mentioned 600 acres in the Glade (minus Fee's pitiful ten acres, of course), "and several persons then expressing a desire to be in the new church movement, with its protest against slave-holding and for a gospel with justice and mercy in it, Mr. Clay directed the surveyor to lay off, in the Glade, a village plot." Turning to Fee, Clay said, "Mr. Fee, you name it."

"We were then," Fee says,

> maintaining that the scriptures of the Old and New Testaments taught the doctrine of love to all men; the duty of justice and mercy, and that they were specific against man-stealing, slave-holding— oppression in all of its forms; and what we then asked was that the people imitating the example of the ancient Bereans, "inquire whether these things be so," and, as suggestive of this duty, called the place Berea. But, after a time, finding that the place for the church and co-operation with working friends was not down in the valley, but up on the ridge—the little plateau—we transferred the name, with its purposed work, up to the present site on the ridge; and now, as then, propose to inquire, in the light of God's word, what is truth—in reference to all things—in church and state.

So Berea was on the Ridge, not in the Glade, even Fee's "Glade" church was no longer in the Glade. Fee was not being perfectly candid in claiming only religious motives for moving to the Ridge, for this new location also represented a degree of freedom from Cassius Clay's influence, as he did not own all the land up there. Already Clay and Fee were beginning to differ.[24]

Two slave women joined the congregation between 1854 and 1859, and the importance of these members, slaves in an anti-slavery church, is incalculable, for the congregation had free pews and "one communion." In many Southern churches blacks attended with whites. Whites were determined that their chattel should hear exactly the right doctrines in church, not what they might hear in an unsupervised black church. Many prominent white Kentuckians felt "that separate Negro preachings and ignorant negro preachers should be suppressed by law." But the blacks were segregated, either in a gallery or on the back rows, and not allowed to commune at the same time as white members—during the same service, but not at the same time.[25]

James G. Birney of nearby Danville, Kentucky, writing in 1840, describes the practices of Southern worship:

In the Methodist, Baptist, Presbyterian and Episcopal churches, the colored people, during service, sit in a *negro pew*. They are not permitted to sit in any other, nor would they be permitted to sit, even if invited, in the pews of white persons. This applies to all colored persons, whether to *members* or not, and even to licensed ministers of their respective connections. The "negro pew" is almost as rigidly kept up in the free states as in the slave.

Black witnesses also testify to the same customs. Dan Bogie, a former slave in Garrard County, recalled, "There was no church for slaves, but we went to the white folks' church—we sat in the gallery."[26]

But Fee provides the most striking description of the practices of the Kentucky churches in an account of the Sharon Presbyterian Church, where his parents and other relatives were members:

Here, slaves, though members with their masters, were not allowed to sit in the same part of the church house nor at the same time partake of the Lord's Supper with their white fellow Christians. The slaves at this time sat in a gallery at the end of the church house, and when white Christians had been served, one of the elders would say: "Now you black ones, if you wish to commune, come down." This they did by an outside, uncovered rough stairway, and then around outside the house came on to the doors of entrance, and facing the congregation came to the seats vacated for them, and thus ate the Lord's Supper. Thus did slaves indeed "strive to enter into the kingdom of heaven."[27]

In Fee's new Glade Church blacks and whites communed together. Fee describes a service at the Glade:

The next Sabbath was Communion season. [One of the slave women] was present. When I was preaching, I saw her lips, like Hannah of old, move in prayer whilst tears of love stole down her sable cheeks. We make no distinction at our Communion, because of the color or condition of members: we know our Savior would not: and when the invitation was made for communicants to come to the Lord's table, she came with others, as a sister. At the closing hymn she extended her hand, in token of fellowship, and it was cordially received by brethren and sisters. As I turned, I saw the good brother at whose house she lives (he is not a slaveholder, nor is this woman hired to him) literally bathed in tears.[28]

Matilda Bently, the subject of this description, was about 50 years old at them time—living with the child of her former mistress, where she was treated kindly. But shortly before the service described above, her youngest child had been taken from her. "What," she asked, "but the religion of Christ could have kept me when I wrapped my babe's clothes up for it to be taken away—it was sold from my breast." Her husband had been sold. Of her nine children, two had been sent South, "the others scattered to different masters." This tragic life, permanently wounded by slavery, would define the abolitionist mission in Kentucky.[29]

The coming of John G. Fee to Berea was the beginning of a revolution.

Cassius Clay's Political Career and Ambitions; His Attitudes toward Abolitionists
"I think your prospects for V. President are good." Fee to Clay.

In 1834, Cassius Clay was so impatient to begin his political career that he announced candidacy for the lower house of the Kentucky legislature before he was legally old enough. He had to withdraw from the race because he was only 23, and the state constitution required that he be 25 to take the office. A mere six years later, in 1840, at an age when many politicians might just be beginning, he won the last election he was ever to win.[30]

Cassius Clay wanted to be president of the United States; Kentucky legislator, Kentucky governor, and then. . . . Clay was one of those people whose life is marked (or deformed) by the position he did not achieve: like Daniel Webster, John C. Calhoun, or his own distant cousin, Henry Clay, Cassius yearned for the highest office in the land. Any estimation of Cassius Clay's attitudes during one of the most crucial stages of the history of abolitionism in Kentucky, from December 1859 to March 1860, must take into account the fact that he began his campaign to become the Republican candidate for president in January 1860.[31]

Before the Republican Party came into existence Clay had been an Emancipationist, which is what he named the party he had formed for himself and apparently all by himself. "Although he called a convention to nominate candidates for the Emancipation ticket, it never met," so Clay simply "announced himself as the party's gubernatorial candidate." The only other candidate on the ticket was Dr. George D. Blakey for lieutenant governor, whom Clay invited to run with him. Needless to say, Clay did not win the election, or even come close. But in the course of his campaign there was one undoubted area of achievement.[32]

John G. Fee recorded his impressions of Clay's gubernatorial race in 1851:

He will have discussed the question of slavery in all the large
towns & cities in the state and 80 out of about 100 counties in the
state & expects the candidate for Lieutenant to visit all others save
four thus showing that the question can be discussed all over the
state. What I have believed tis now demonstrated so that the door in
Ky may be considered as open.[33]

Cassius Marcellus Clay's opposition to slavery shaped his entire life. For
the child of Green Clay—"the largest slaveowner in the state," according to his
son—to become an emancipationist was simply unprecedented. Green Clay was
one of the first settlers in Kentucky (Cassius says *the* first), enormously wealthy
and influential, highly connected (Governor James Garrard was his brother-in-
law), owning land from the Ohio to the Mississippi River, thousands of acres. He
too had a political career, serving in the Kentucky legislature in 1793 and 1794.
Cassius Clay describes his father as a "stern man, absorbed in affairs," spending
"but little time with the children." Becoming an antislavery advocate, Clay had to
defy his father and all he represented.[34]

In his autobiography Clay identifies an incident involving injustice to a
female slave as formative in his view of slavery. A beautiful mulatto woman, no
more than 18, was attacked by a drunken overseer and his cohorts; in defending
herself she killed one of the men with a butcher knife. Clay, still a young boy, and
his sister Eliza were tending their own little flower gardens at White Hall when, he
says, "I heard a scream and looking up, what was my horror to see Mary coming
into the yard with a butcher's knife, and her clothes all bloody." As a man of
fortune, Clay's father managed to get his slave acquitted and set free, but after his
death Mary had to be sold South, as was customary in border states in cases of
'criminal' slaves. Clay explains that his eldest brother, Sidney Payne Clay, an
emancipationist himself, was forced by the terms of his father's will and as chief
executor to perform the sale. So the power of the Southern father reached from the
grave.

Clay writes:

Never shall I forget—and through all these years it rests
upon my memory as the stamp upon a bright coin—the scene, when
Mary was tied by the wrists and sent from home and friends, and the
loved features of her native land—the home of her infancy and

girlish days—into Southern banishment forever; and yet held guiltless by a jury of, not her 'peers,' but her oppressors! Never shall I forget those two faces—of my brother and Mary—the oppressor and the oppressed, rigid with equal agony! She cast an imploring look at me, as if in appeal; but meekly went, without a word as a 'sheep to the slaughter.'[35]

However his opposition toward slavery began, in later life Cassius Clay seldom justified his opposition to the system on humanitarian grounds; his crusade for emancipation certainly never depended on the idea that slavery was inhumane to black people. Nevertheless, in his *Memoirs* he narrates still other tales of cruelty and injustice to slaves, incidents which he says "nerved [him] to a more deadly warfare against the 'Lost Cause.'"[36]

In a memorable passage in his *Memoirs* Clay tells of going north to Yale, with his soul full of hatred for slavery. But having never heard an abolitionist, scarcely knowing what an abolitionist was, he had no way to define his own feelings until he heard William Lloyd Garrison reveal "all the horrors of slavery . . . . my parents were slave-holders; all my known kindred in Kentucky were slave-holders; and I regarded it as I did other evils of humanity, as the fixed Law of Nature or of God, and submitted as best I might. But Garrison dragged out the monster from all his citadels, and left him stabbed to the vitals, and dying at the feet of every logical and honest mind." (The image is absolutely characteristic of Clay.) Clay claims he had never been so agitated in public before; his emotions were "tumultuous . . . I then resolved . . . that, when I had the strength, if ever, I would give slavery a death struggle." Garrison's sentiments, Clay says, "aroused my whole soul." Clay may have been converted to antislavery by the speeches of William Lloyd Garrison, but Clay's mature emancipationist thought never reflected the 'higher law' morality of Garrisonian or evangelical abolitionism.[37]

In New England Clay had seen remarkable prosperity based on a non-slaveholding economy, and throughout his life he was to maintain that slavery, far from serving the economic interests of the South, had retarded the development of the whole region. His Kentucky System called for a diversified, balanced economy, farming of many different crops, and manufacturing. He wanted a program of public assistance to encourage such a development. Kentucky, he thought, enjoyed the advantages of the South and the North: vast acres of farmland, like the South, and a mountainous region with minerals and water power, like New England—the manuacturing economy in Clay's plan would be established in the Kentucky mountains, which he called "American Switzerland." The Kentucky System would unite the various regions of Kentucky, and "elevate a party to power," his party, Cassius Clay's party. Beyond his own state, Cassius Clay's free labor argument against slavery appealed to both moderate and conservative Republicans throughout the country. Only one thing prevented Kentucky from becoming one of the most prosperous regions in the history of the world, and that one thing was, of course, slavery.[38]

In Kentucky non-slaveholders always outnumbered slaveowners; Clay's ambition was to convince all those people who never had owned slaves that the slave system was taking money out of their pockets, filling jobs that white workers should have, perpetrating an economy which by its very nature robbed the common workingman of his rightful opportunities. In much of Kentucky, the planting class and their non-slaveholding neighbors were inextricably bound by economic ties. In the mountains, especially deep in the mountain counties, almost no one owned slaves. Clay believed that if he could once gain the commitment of those mountaineers to his Kentucky System his political career would be launched.

Clay knew he had to educate Kentucky's voters to believe that the slavery system harmed them—he would not maintain that slavery was a *sin*, but that it was an *evil*, a big distinction. It was a system which harmed people, but not a wrong for which each individual should feel personally responsible. No one had to repent of it. Even so, the slaveowners failed to appreciate Clay's reasoning and did not want him to reach his audience. Clay charged that in the South free white workers were "barred by despotic intolerance from receiving any light by which they can know their rights, and free themselves from the competition of slave labor, which brings ignorance and beggary to their doors." The "six hundred thousand free white laborers of Kentucky," Clay said, were the people "against whose every vital interest slavery wages an eternal and implacable war!" Slaves, in effect, were taking food out of the mouths of white men.[39]

Clay believed that if he could simply deliver his views to enough Kentuckians, enlightened self-interest would take care of the rest. "In a Republic, the majority had the power to change any law. When he amassed a majority in Kentucky he would liberate the slaves by legal means," through constitutional amendment. Thus, Clay's political program had three planks, ideas from which he apparently never deviated: his Kentucky System, the 'sacredness' of constitutional law, and emancipation. But Clay's emancipationist aim was to create freedom and economic opportunity for whites only. Under his scheme blacks would, indeed, be freed, but not because they had any right to freedom. "If we are for emancipation," Clay said, "it is that Kentucky may be virtuous and prosperous. If we seek liberty for the blacks, it is . . . that the white laborers of the state may be men and build us all up by their power and energy." In fact, he was "activated by a still higher motive—the greater motive of achieving the complete independence and liberty of [his] own, the white Anglo-Saxon race of America."[40]

Clay's plan for the blacks, in some respects, resembled freedom scarcely at all. Many people were curious to know what he intended to do with the former slaves while free Kentucky whites were enjoying their big boom from a diversified government-supported economy. "The emancipation [Clay] advocated would come gradually, after a long preparatory period in which he anticipated that most of the slaves would be sent out of the state." "No more will be left among us," Clay said, "than we shall absolutely need." And few would be needed, for, in Clay's view, "Slaves would not manufacture if they would; and could not if they would!" an observation which he would have applied to freed blacks as well. "I have studied the Negro character," Clay wrote, "They lack self-reliance—we can make nothing out of them. God has made them for the sun and the banana." Clay fought the slave system, "not because he loved the Negro, but because he wanted to assist the white." He always maintained that blacks were inferior.[41]

The slaveowning aristocracy would dissolve, the slaves conveniently disappear, and the sturdy free white laborers of the mountains, now prosperous manufacturers and Clay's permanent constituency, would bear him on their shoulders to the highest office in the land: apparently this was his scenario—one part political theory, one part racial prejudice, and one part pipedream.

And no part religion. Clay, who "despised the religious antislavery movement," saw freeing of slaves as only a means to an end, never as his actual goal. Slavery would have to be swept away, and former slaves along with it simply in order to make room for something better. His agenda was political, economic and legal. The radical abolitionists (Garrisonian or evangelical) were not prepared to accept such limitations, since their program was religious, humanitarian and moral. Clay would have claimed his aims were practical and realistic, while theirs were impractical and unrealistic; they would have claimed their aims were visionary and inspiring, while his were expedient and pedestrian. Maybe they were both right.[42]

In any case, Clay opposed them, describing them as "a horde of fanatical incendiaries . . . springing up in the North." The radicals would free slaves immediately, because property rights must never take precedence over human rights. Many of them, like Fee, taught that no law could deprive any human being of her or his God-given rights; the evangelical camp of the radical abolitionists maintained the authority of the Bible over the Constitution or any man-made law: God's word was supreme, greater than governments. "I am opposed to depriving slave owners of their property by other than constitutional, legal means," Clay wrote, "I have no sympathy with those who would liberate slaves by any other means; and I have no connection with such people. I must, as a citizen, resist their efforts by force, if necessary.'[43]

In 1845, Clay maintained, quite truly, that he was not an abolitionist, and, not quite truly, that he had no connection with the abolition movement; to him identification with them would brand him as a madman or a fanatic; beyond that, radicalism was "revolutionary and insurrectionary." It might lead to rebellion of slaves against their masters, and that was in Clay's view worse than treason. "I am for my own, the white race, against all other races on earth," he wrote, and again: "With regard to servile insurrection I should certainly not desert my own blood for any other—where the destruction of one or the other race seems necessary." In fact, Cassius Clay simply shared the common view of abolitionists and black people that prevailed among white Southerners of his class.[44]

So we come to one of the most mystifying aspects of the life of Cassius Clay: his friendship with a man whom he knew to be a radical abolitionist, his patronage of the *leader* of the religious antislavery movement in Kentucky. What did Cassius Clay want with Reverend John G. Fee?

18

Clay and Fee: A Friendship Begins
"I am a stranger to you in person but I trust not to some of the emotions which move your philanthropic heart." Fee to Clay.

On April 4, 1844, from Bracken County, Kentucky, John G. Fee begins his first letter to Cassius Clay by misspelling Clay's name, addressing "the Hon Cashius M. Clay" [Clay had by this served his time in the Kentucky legislature and earned his Hon.] "Sir," Fee writes,

> I am a stranger to you in person but I trust not to some of the emotions which move your philanthropic heart.
> I have for many months desired to see you in person & converse with you freely on subjects of national policy & interest especially that of slavery.[45]

He introduces himself to Clay as a Presbyterian, "a licensed though unworthy minister of the Gospel of Christ," a native Kentuckian, "the son of a beloved Father who is unfortunately the owner of slaves—have been raised from my infancy in the midst of slavery. I have seen its evil & felt its curse." Here Clay surely saw a parallel to his own experience.

> I desire from you a free expression of your view on [American slavery] & <u>as to what is the duties of American citizens in their respective spheres</u> in life. For whilst it is the duty of every one to investigate & think for himself yet as a statesman, a man of research, observation & foresight beyond anything which I can claim your suggestions would be received with great profit and deference.

Clearly, Fee knew how to adopt a thoroughly flattering tone, but there is no reason to doubt the sincerity of his admiration for the older man. (Clay was 34, Fee 28 when this letter was written.) Even in his first youthful burst of enthusiasm for Clay, however, Fee claims the right to think for himself, a right he was to exercise from this point onward. A few years later he would announce it even more emphatically: " I like to hear your opinions on all things," he wrote to Clay (September 18, 1849), "reserving to myself as every man ought to do the privilege of deciding for myself."[46]

How, Fee asks,

do you suppose the slavery system in our state will be abolished? I say our state because some suppose our state will precede the rest of the south [in freeing slaves].

(Ironically, of course, Kentucky would be the last state where slaves were freed.)

. . .Will [it] be done by some revolution in national or governmental affairs such as rebellion of the slaves aided by England & some from the North[?]
Or by an accumulation of facts proving slave labour to be a wrong pecuniary policy[?] [Clay's own position]
Or 3rdly by force of moral truth—that it is morally wrong to hold our fellow men beyond a certain period of bondage[?] [Fee's position] Or will it be by all of these combined?

These questions pave the way for Fee's major concern: "What is the duty of the ministry of Kentucky?" Should they leave the issue in the hands of statesmen and politicians, minding their own business, so to speak? "Or should they, treating it as a sin against God & man, make it a religious question & raise their voice[s] against it?" Whether slavery would be overthrown by revolution or by other means was crucial to Fee in deciding his own course.

Were I persuaded that the labours of the ministry are not necessary to the accomplishment of the emancipation of the slave & that it will be done by some other means—so much greater is the advantage of doing good in a free state above those in a slave state that I should not stay here one month.
But if slavery will be abolished partly or chiefly by the force of moral truth then it seems as though it is the duty of the ministry to stay & apply the truth to the hearts & consciences of men. [Otherwise,] the minister of the gospel had better go where he can do most in his appropriate sphere—the conversion of the world.

When Cassius Clay read this letter he may have seen it as the expression of a thinker who, while not exactly in agreement with himself, was bent upon very similar goals: understanding the world theoretically, and finding a place for his own peculiar talents in it. Their conclusions were seldom in accord, but both Fee and Clay were intent on intellectually grasping every major issue of their time, especially slavery. Both men also assumed that ideas should lead to social involvement: whether in the form of Christian ministry or political action.

Many of your fellow-citizens look with great solicitude upon your every address or action upon the subject, [Fee continues, obviously including himself]. They feel that God in his providence has raised you up to take a permanent place in the great work of disenthralling your country of its greatest curse, your fellow men from their greatest calamity. I have recently written to twelve or fifteen of the ministers & laymen of our state who take antislavery papers inquiring & proposing. They write in return that they are each doing what they can in their sphere but "expect Cashius M. Clay to do more than a thousand of us." May it be so & may God bless you, preserve your health & life—give you grace still to stand upon the broad platform of truth & to continue to speak with boldness what you believe to be for the good of your country, the welfare of your fellow men & the glory of your God.

Clay was probably unaccustomed to receiving letters which pronounced a benediction over him; he had been cursed so often that he may have welcomed a blessing!

. . . Your fellow citizens who sympathize with you on this subject & very many who do not—admire the freedom & boldness with which you speak your sentiments. And even those who in word & act curse & denounce you yet in their souls—they are bound to reverence the man who speaks & acts upon principle.

And reward him with public office, Fee predicted, although he said he had evidence that Clay would "ask no other reward than the consciousness of rectitude . . . , the welfare of [his] country & happiness of [his] fellow beings." What evidence he had for this rather extraordinary view of Clay's character does not emerge, but Fee was convinced that God had raised Clay up for a great work: he was to recur to this idea over and over, sometimes with prophetic fervor. His idealistic admiration of Clay, without even having met him, was deep and ardent; he believed in Clay's courage, dedication and unselfishness. Clay was a godsend, and Fee received him as a gift to be cherished, a man to be encouraged, aided and set before the people.

Fee closed his letter with apparent humility:

I have no claims upon you for a reply to these questions. I know that the duties of your office requires much of your time & that it cannot be expected that your time should be consumed by writing to every one who would wish to hold correspondence on this subject, yet an answer to this letter would be to me a source of profit at the present time and if you find it convenient to do so you will much oblige your friend and fellow citizen

John G. Fee

Of course, Clay answered. He was impressed by his correspondent's intelligence and insight into his (Clay's) character. Fee saw Clay exactly as he wanted to be seen—philanthropic, courageous, a man of principle, a great benefactor of humanity. In the general hostility gathering around Clay, Fee's first letter provided great refreshment, with its combination of understanding, stimulation, praise, flattery, encouragement, patriotism, concern and prophetic fervor; Fee conveyed a sense of Clay's future unfolding, his life's work blooming. And, to top it all off, the writer revealed a certain humility, suggesting that he wished to serve. Here was a man who recognized Cassius Clay's greatness!

Clay and Fee: A Mutual Relationship
"If were not allowed to speak freely according to our constitutional rights, our whole scheme of emancipation failed." Cassius M. Clay.

John G. Fee was no match for Cassius Clay physically; Clay was over six feet tall, strongly developed, remarkably handsome in his youth. A contemporary said, "There is a more striking combination of manly beauty and strength in his face than in the face of any man whom I ever saw." The portrait of Clay in the Madison County Courthouse in Richmond, Kentucky, supports this appraisal. His voice was as impressive as his appearance, an orator's voice, deep and resonant.[47]

Fee, on the other hand, was very unprepossessing. In his *Memoirs* Clay describes Fee as "rather below medium size, slender with a head large in proportion to a rather delicate body. His features are not remarkable, being rather heavy than classical." To complete this portrait of insignificant personal appearance, Clay adds that Fee's voice "is piping, with but little inflection or compass; so that he is a better writer than speaker."[48]

In other respects, the friends were well-matched; for a decade their relationship was marked by mutuality and growing affection. Each man read, praised, encouraged and distributed the other's writing. Fee's *Anti-Slavery Manual* appeared in separate numbers in Clay's ill-fated antislavery newspaper, the *True American*, and Clay "personally distributed . . . many copies of the Manual . . .

and many copies of [Fee's] tract on 'Nonfellowship'" in Madison County. Fee
had, likewise, worked to distribute Clay's writings; in 1849, he wrote to Clay
requesting copies to sell. Fee had already induced his in-laws to become Clay
supporters; "my Father in Law V. [Vincent] Hamilton," Fee informed Clay, "is
greatly delighted with your books, considers you one of the best writers he ever
read." Fee's sister-in-law, Laura Hamilton, was also becoming a Clay enthusiast;
Fee requested a book for her with Clay's portrait in it, "for all who will read want
to see what sort of a monster C. M. Clay is."[49]

Fee was deeply upset by Clay's giving up the *True American*. "[Clay's
newspaper] was doing more," Fee wrote, "to wake up attention, investigation, and
discussion than had been done here, by all other means, for ten years." Each man
was confident of the other's writing and editorial ability. In 1849, Fee urged Clay
to edit a newspaper for the proposed state antislavery society, and before inviting
Fee to Madison County, Clay had proposed more than once that Fee go to Newport
or Covington, Kentucky, and edit a paper with Clay paying his salary and
expenses. Had Fee accepted, the second *True American* would have been his
work. In any case, the offer indicates Clay's high regard for Fee's abilities.[50]

Their mutual support extended into their respective realms of politics and
religion. Clay publicly approved Fee's ministry, long before it was transferred to
Madison County, and Fee supported Clay's political career for years. Fee was
Clay's preacher and Clay was Fee's politician.

As early as 1846, Fee invited Clay to Lewis County to speak to the people
on slavery and emancipation (actually, Fee had instigated a petition asking Clay to
come, signed by 27 citizens), and Clay accepted, "commending highly the courage
of the men who had made the call." But the war with Mexico prevented his
keeping the appointment. "C. M. Clay approved the movement here [in Cabin
Creek]," Fee wrote, "from the first . . . attending our meeting . . . last fall in
Bracken, Clay said to one of the members, 'if he had a free church in Madison to
go to he should attend church every Sabbath.'" (When he had a free church in
Madison County, Clay did *not* attend it every Sunday!) "In 1849, when Clay
participated in a constituent election on behalf of emancipation candidates, Fee
supported him . . . and he became corresponding secretary of Clay's Republican
Club." Ten years later, Fee reported to Clay from Pittsburgh, Pennsylvania, one of
his stops on a fund-raising trip: "I have repeatedly spoken of you in public and

private. I think the spirit is rising in the Republican ranks and will yet demand a representative man. If you . . . are on the ticket . . . I shall expect to work with the Republicans."[51]

It is obvious from Fee's letters (not a single letter, but from years of them) that he tried to read every word Clay ever wrote and every word he was quoted as saying. John G. Fee probably knew Cassius M. Clay's mind as well as or better than any other contemporary. He frequently disagreed with Clay's position, but he always knew what it was. But then Clay knew where Fee stood, too; he could not avoid knowing.

In most respects the Fee-Clay relationship up to 1854 seems to have been ideally balanced—neither man was actually dominant, in spite of Clay's edge in physique and finances. After Fee accepted Clay's invitation to Madison County, their friendship underwent a great change: it had always been more than a personal relationship because they had been deeply involved in one another's careers already. But the new deal made their bond inescapably a public matter—now Clay was Fee's patron-protector: a role that was to become a two-edged sword.

Fee had suffered persecution before he ever came to central Kentucky; he had been "waylaid, shot at, clubbed, stoned," frequently harassed, but what he was to endure after coming to Berea made his earlier encounters seem tame.[52]

In the spring of 1855, Fee was mobbed at Dripping Springs near Crab Orchard, where he had a regular appointment for preaching. Warned that a hostile crowd was waiting for him in the church, he entered anyway. A spokesman informed Fee that he would have to listen to six resolutions which the group had prepared, and then answer yes or no. Characteristically, Fee expressed his willingness to listen and then answered "without pause" each of the six resolutions with a separate argument. The crowd had expected him to withdraw quietly, without talking all day, and eventually began to threaten him. Fee told them, "You all know I am not a man of violence—I carry no weapons of defence. If any person is hurt, the guilt and responsibility will be on those who do the hurting." So the mob, led by two or three determined ruffians, seized him, "hustled" him from the house, dragged him out of the yard, and asked him to get on his horse. He refused, pointing out that their procedure was illegal. "They then put me on my horse and asked me to ride," Fee wrote, "I declined. They then led and drove and thus escorted me one or two miles on my way home."[53]

Fee's congregations at the Glade in Madison County and at Boone's Fork and Green's Schoolhouse in Rockcastle County adopted and published resolutions in his defense, and Fee appealed to the Garrard Civil Court, which refused to bring any suit against the mob. He always sought legal redress in civil courts, believing it to be "not only wise policy, but religious duty." In central Kentucky, his appeals to magistrates never resulted in anything—local authorities simply would not protect him or see justice done on his behalf.[54]

But Cassius Clay, returning from an antislavery speaking tour of the East, took more direct action. "If we were not allowed to speak freely according to our constitutional rights," he said, "our whole scheme for emancipation failed." Clay was convinced that the attack on Fee had really been directed toward himself. After making an appointment to lecture in Crab Orchard himself, Clay appeared there "surrounded with armed followers," and exercised his freedom of speech. In fact, his army probably consisted of his followers from the Glade, armed "with rifles, shotguns, revolvers and kitchen knives." He followed that up by speaking at Stanford, seat of Lincoln County; his appearance there has become a legend (the details of which he himself disclaimed)—he is supposed to have carried up the aisle a carpetbag containing a Bible, a copy of the Constitution, a bowie knife and two pistols and challenged anyone who did not recognize the authority of the printed words to deny the authority of his weapons.[55]

In May, Clay organized a meeting in Jessamine County, far from the scene of the mobbing—there he spoke for three hours, and encouraged the citizens to adopt resolutions supporting freedom of speech, press, religious opinion and worship. On June 29, Clay spoke at Brush Creek, the next day at Scaffold Cane in Rockcastle, reading the Jessamine Resolutions and asking for support in his proposed return to Dripping Springs with Fee "so that the antislavery clergyman could speak . . . with the backing of force if necessary."

Another mob threatened Fee in Rockcastle County in early summer (1855), but one [Shadrach] Roberts dispelled the crowd without even saying a word—"his known sympathy with liberty and free speech," Fee says, were sufficient. That he was strong and robust and evidently carrying a huge knife may have contributed to the mobs' discouragement as well.[56]

In Clay's friendship and presence also there was safety. At Fee's suggestion Fee and Clay organized a Fourth of July meeting in Rockcastle County (or in the Glade) in 1855 to speak together "in behalf of human freedom." The meeting was a great success. "A large audience gathered was collected of orderly, quiet citizens. C. M. Clay in an address, eloquent and pertinent, enchained the audience for two hours," on the subject of the evils of slavery; this was followed by Fee's short address on "the relation of the church of Christ to the subject of liberty."[57]

Fee's public description of this occasion was characteristically sanguine and misleading, while Clay's personal response to it was vehemently angry; in a letter to Fee written four days after the meeting, Clay took his supposed disciple to task:

> The great cause of [my] anger against you was the allegation that you gave tracts to slaves—there were some in their possession they said, and the slaves said by you—as the story goes. I told them no, that you did not propose to give slaves tracts, and only bibles by the consent of the masters. I call your attention once more to the only safe ground of opposition to slavery in my judgement. That it is the creature of law—and we propose not to violate the law—but to unmake it by law. That it is our constitutional right to create slavery—the same right in the same way to un make it. As to the slaves in the matter we have nothing to do with them in any way. From a religious point of view if you offer the bible and the masters say no: then you have done your duty— the responsibility rests upon them not you. Any other communication with slaves except through the master is not to be thought of by us. There's no obligation upon us—nor is it all expedient. I trust your views coincide with mine in this respect.[58]

Although Fee denied the charge that he was putting antislavery material into the hands of slaves, which would have been insurrectionary in everyone's view, including Fee's, it is doubtful that he agreed with any of the other opinions Clay expressed in this revealing passage.[59]

In the same letter, Clay advised Fee upon what he called nonessentials. "I think we ought to avoid using offensive language," Clay stated,

> as much as is consistent with our duty. For instance in preaching against adultery—we don't denounce all such as atrocious scoundrels! Thus I think the "sum of all villainies" is not an expedient term in times of excitement . . . Now as a friend I will make a criticism on your manner. I think you lose in force by too much excitement in gesticulation. I think in the main you overdo Demosthenes' precept 'action, action & c.' I think all oratory more effective when the attitudes are easy and natural and I may say

usual. For instance, you stood with (on the fourth) with one foot on the table and the other on the bench—you stooped down—and stamped violently with your feet. Now as a friend I tell you I think you lost effect by all that: on this question we are supposed already to be <u>fanatical</u>—which being translated, means to that extent—<u>mad</u>! . . . I think you would be more effective to be more <u>collected</u> and <u>calm</u>. Now I may have as many faults as you. I wish some friend would always tell me of them—thus only can we improve.[60]

This description of Fee's oratorical techniques is a revelation of his character, forceful, unself-conscious, vehement: to Clay the ferocious little preacher, overcome with the excitement of his ideas, waving his arms and stamping his feet, really looked and sounded like a fanatic.

Fee never moderated his preaching style, which had also greatly offended some other "orderly, quiet citizens" at the 4th of July meeting. In reaction a Rockcastle County meeting of antislavery opponents convened at Mount Vernon to forbid antislavery speaking in the county. The demands of the committee were presented to Clay, who refused to abide by them, but immediately began publicizing the issue of free speech in Kentucky throughout the state and the nation. In addition, he announced that he and Fee would both speak at Scaffold Cane later in the month.

Opposition began to organize, with representatives from five counties coordinating resistance to antislavery. "Orators were sent out to incite the slaveholders. . . . Families fled from their houses and Negroes were thrown in jail in Mount Vernon and Crab Orchard." The day before the meeting Clay wrote the *Cincinnati Gazette*: "Tomorrow I go to the field of contest to determine whether liberty of speech and religious freedom is longer possible in a slave state!" On the 21st of July, Clay and Fee kept their appointment and spoke before an attentive audience consisting mostly of sympathizers. Opponents of the meeting "feebly rallied in the neighborhood," but gave up without a fight. "Clay's victory was complete. He had vindicated freedom of speech in a slave state and had given the 'Slave Power' their first check in a slave state." In addition, he had enhanced his political position in the state, and elevated himself to a commanding position in the Republican Party.[61]

This sequence of events had also given Clay heroic stature in John G. Fee's eyes. In Fee's defence Clay had spared neither trouble nor expense, endangering himself and publicly winning for them both the right to speak. For Fee, July 21, 1855, marked the zenith of his relationship to a great patron: the courageous, magnanimous Cassius Clay. But Clay had asked Fee to "always tell" him about his faults, and Fee was more than willing to oblige.

So Fee told Clay that he should not carry weapons, especially concealed ones, even though Clay had carried the weapons in Fee's defense. "There is no principle of morals more clear with me," Clay protested, [note his emphatic underlinings; Fee was not the only person who could become excited!]

> than my right to resist unjust and illegal agression at all times. "When needed" is a simple question of expediency with me—not question of criminal imputations from others. With regard to carrying concealed weapons—it comes within the letter but not the spirit of the law—for I avowed to the whole commonwealth that I would be armed on that day. It was simply a matter of taste to wear my pistols inside instead of outside of my pockets . . . The constitutional right to bear arms is expressly guarranteed for just such a purpose as I bore them there. My conscience is clear on that score. [Very graciously Clay adds], I take it in good part that you freely name anything which you would have reformed in me. I use towards those I esteem only the same liberty.[62]

Taking his friend at his word, Fee fired off another critical letter in April 1856. He had just discovered that Clay intended to sell some of his slaves and thus separate them from their families. Fee was horrified as he wrote:

> I did not know until a few days since that any were to be sold. I had not seen an advertisement then . . . Let me urge that if it be possible avoid the sale of those slaves . . . No forms of law will justify us in withholding from men & women their natural rights. [The tortured grammar of Fee's next sentence seems to reveal the fervent incoherence of his feelings:] You nor I would do so from our wives and our children even if law did. . . . [63]

Even though their relationship was strained, the two men felt that their 4th of July meeting of 1855 and the later assembly had been so successful that they should hold another Independence Day meeting at Slate Lick Springs in Madison County. In fact, they agreed to hold a series of such meetings annually.

Fourth of July at Slate Lick Springs
"The provisions in the baskets were spread, but eaten without exhilaration." John G. Fee.

Neither Clay nor Fee expressed any opinion at Slate Lick Springs to surprise the other. Both men were well aware of their differences—they had passed a decade in close communion with one another's views. Yet their public disagreement on the Fourth of July 1856 brought a painful breach between them, and resulted finally in the dissolution of their partnership.

They had been in public as well as private disagreement already that year. Clay, in proposing a Republican ticket for Kentucky, had said, "The National Government has nothing more to do with slavery than with concubinage in Turkey." Fee had replied, "The National Government is responsible for the strength and perpetuity of slavery, by the enactment of the Fugitive Slave law." This exchange laid still more groundwork for their alienation from one another.[64]

The Republican Association of Madison and Rockcastle Counties had agreed to sponsor the meeting, to which all parties were invited. "At [an] early hour many persons were on the ground [he means they were assembled, not that they were sprawled on the grass]. The people continued to come male and female, from all directions until a large and orderly assembly was convened." Fee later estimated the crowd as "hundreds of people." Officers were appointed—the president, James Sayers, called upon William E. Lincoln for an invocation. Then the Declaration of Independence was read, followed by the platform of the National Republican Association. After this, Rev. James S. Davis of Lewis County spoke. Preliminaries over, the two principle speakers approached the podium.[65]

Fee describes how the debate began:

> Mr. Clay insisted that I should speak first. I delined. He insisted. The people slaveholders and nonslaveholders, were waiting. I decided in my own mind, to meet the issue squarely, and rising, with a copy of the Declaration of Independence in my hand, I repeated the words, All men are created free and equal, and endowed by their Creator with certain inalienable rights. I said, "If inalienable, then such are man's relations to God and to himself and family, that he cannot alienate; society cannot, governments cannot alienate. 'Endowed by their Creator,' if so, then it is impious in us to attempt to take them away."

What is more, he said, "This invasion of human rights [slavery]" is condemned by the word of God. "That which outrages natural right and Divine teaching is mere usurpation, and, correctly speaking, is incapable of legalization." In other words, there can be no law for slavery. He concluded his presentation by saying, "A law confessedly contrary to the Law of God ought not by human courts to be enforced," and, referring to the Fugitive Slave Law, said he would refuse to obey it and then suffer the penalty.[66]

Afterward Cassius Clay spoke, first expressing "high personal regard" for Fee, then saying, "As my political friends, I warn you; Mr. Fee's position is revolutionary, insurrectionary. As long as a law is on the statute book, it is to be respected and obeyed until repealed by the Republican majority." Speaking of the Fugitive Slave Law, he said, "As far as this is concerned, I would not obey it; it is contrary to natural right, and I would not degrade my nature by obeying it."

"I seized the concession," Fee writes, "and in my reply said, 'My friend, Mr. Clay has conceded the whole point at issue—that there is a *Higher Law*.' He, now seated in the midst of the congregation, cried out, 'The Fugitive Slave Law is unconstitutional.'" Significantly, Fee adds, "There was manifest confusion in the crowd."[67]

Fee and Clay did not cause much of a disturbance at Slate Lick Springs; James Scott Davis, a speaker on the platform that day, wrote, "On the 4th the gathering was much larger than last year. Bro. Fee, Clay and I made speeches. Bro. Fee took strong radical ground, Clay replied, before his main speech. Quite an animated discussion followed." That is all Davis had to say, writing only two weeks after the event. Pressed for more details, he wrote a few days later, "I believe that in my last I told you of our meeting on the Fourth. There was not the least sign of disturbance."[68]

There had, indeed, been a disturbance, but perhaps it was not primarily an observable event.

In spite of Fee's entreaties Clay refused to visit his friend for thirteen months after the Slate Lick Springs incident. Their debate was to continue in newspapers in both Ohio and Kentucky for four years.[69]

Why was Clay so incensed? Fee's position was absolutely not new to him. Part of his rage may have had a very simple motivation. He prevailed upon Fee to speak first, intending to present his own views as final. But Fee "seized the concession," spoke a second time and turned Clay's own views against him. In any case, the pair certainly knew how to ruin a Fourth of July picnic. According to Fee, "the provisions in the baskets were spread, but eaten without exhilaration."[70]

It would be unfair to Clay not to present a justification for him at this point. Fee's mode of argumentation, continuing throughout his life—represented in his *Anti-Slavery Manual*, his *Sinfulness of Slaveholding*, in his later works on baptism, in all his published letters to editors, in his six-point rebuttal of the mob statement at Crab Orchard, and so on—was elaborate, frequently tedious, absolutely thorough. In an argument he would draw up every one of his opponent's points, major and minor, and, with a doggedness approaching the bulldog variety, deal with every one of them. He met every issue head on: so in his *Anti-Slavery Manual* he brought up all the passages he could find that had ever been used to show the Bible's support for slavery and laboriously worked through all of them, until he had, to his own satisfaction, demolished them all. He was a great asset to have on the team, and absolutely insufferable as an opponent.

Before he was done, Fee had published virtually every nuance of the Slate Lick Springs argument and systematically refuted Clay's embattled position. What made this all so trying for Clay was not just the stubbornness of the little man who opposed him; Clay had learned to tolerate that, and even perhaps to admire it. But Fee opposed him in public, right down the road from Berea, in front of Clay's 'boys' . . . and it was not simply opposition—on one level at least, it was *winning* opposition. Once Fee began an argument he would not let up. It was his conviction that people, by nature, could be convinced of truth; when Clay did not respond to truth on the 4th of July, Fee's assumption was that his friend would certainly come about if he (Fee) would simply sharpen his argument, make Clay see that Fee was right. The effect was to put Clay into a position of self-defense.

Cornered, Clay always fought. No, not always; how could he fight with a man so much smaller than himself, a minister, a pacifist, a man who would not fight, would not carry weapons, would not be aggressive physically? The situation was impossible; nothing that Clay was accustomed to use would work: to perform his usual ritual in the face of insult would simply make him look ridiculous. He could hardly challenge John G. Fee to a duel! So he withdrew his support.

In 1857, he explained his decision in this way:

In the first place . . . I did not withdraw my influence from [Fee], but he his from me. We acted together, from before 1848, upon the basis of *constitutional* opposition to slavery. On the 4th of July 1856, against my urgent advice and solemn protest, he publicly, from the stump, not in the capacity of a minister of the Gospel, but as a politician, made avowal in substance of the doctrines of the *Radical Abolitionists.* That is, as I understand him, slavery being contrary to the higher law—the law of nature and of God—is "no law," unconstitutional and void.

[The same letter ended with what Clay must have felt was the last word in his relationship with John G. Fee:] With regard to Mr. Fee, personally, I entertain towards him the most friendly feelings. I consider him honest and 'godly'. . . . He is a man of ability and mature mind. In the wide verge of life, destiny separates us; he, and those who act with him, must reap the good and evil of their deeds.

The letter just cited appeared in a newspaper. Clay's abandonment of Fee was public—more than a withdrawal of his presence from the region of Berea for thirteen months, but a tacit withdrawal of protection which Fee's enemies were all too ready to understand.[71]

In his role as patron-protector Clay stressed the patron aspect, with a feudal emphasis on what was due him as the provider of money, land and favor. He did not simply want a yes-man, however; real stupidity would have been required to think Fee would ever fill that slot, and Clay was by no means stupid. But in the political arena he wanted only what he considered as political views to be presented, and certainly he wanted his companion-in-arms to be a political asset. Ironically, Clay seems to have been as eager and willing to suppress Fee's freedom of speech as many other aristocratic Southerners would have been.

In their relationship Fee stressed the idea of the protector: Clay was to insure for Fee his civil liberties. Fee had never promised to agree with Clay or anyone else, but both men had agreed on the importance of freedom of speech— and Clay had taken steps in the past to give Fee a public forum and to defend him.

Both men felt betrayed and deeply wounded. But beyond their personal concerns, the very existence of Berea was now in grave danger and the whole antislavery movement in Kentucky was jeopardized.

Fee Without Clay's Protection
"You refuse protection to one guilty only of an expressed opinion different from your own. . . ." Fee to Clay.

One of Clay's children died in April 1857; in Fee's letter of consolation he said, "Oh how many parents in our land are deprived of their children, not by the hand of death which leaves them free from insult or further injury, but by merciless slave drivers, who not only torture the body but famish and corrupt the soul. You will have more sympathy with such." Clay could hardly miss the unspoken assumption that he had thus far shown too little sympathy.[72]

A month later, Fee wrote to Clay asking him to come and "make us another 4th of July speech," but in June, the new church which Fee's congregation had built in Rockcastle County was burned by arsonists. At the Fourth of July meeting another disaster occurred. A friend of Fee's, John Richardson, made a brief speech warning against enslavement of the Negro, in which "he said, 'There are 40 thousand in Canada training daily and they will come down here & cut your throats.' The remark produced quite a sensation, some slaveholders declared he should be taken down [from the podium] . . . C. M. Clay . . . much regretted that remark." He saw it—quite rightly—as incendiary; it incited the supporters of slavery to even more violence.[73]

About two weeks later, after many threats, Fee was mobbed again; he was preaching in an unoccupied dwelling house, when some forty or fifty local men "entered with threats of death, and with hands on their weapons." "[Jim] Smith presented a pistol near my stomach," Fee wrote to Clay, " [and] ordered Jack Fish & Hiatt to take hold of me—they did so—I scuffled some time with them—another got me by the hair & then they moved me." With most of the mob on horseback they forced Fee to walk about a mile; a woman of the church, Jerusha Preston, an aged widow, walked beside Fee for that distance, apparently feeling that the presence of a woman would protect him.[74]

After the first mile Fee's horse was brought and the mob decided to take him out of the county, demanding that he not enter it again. He refused repeatedly to make them any promises. "They then marched me," Fee writes, "some seven or eight miles, amid jeers, taunts and low vulgarity." As they walked along the road "slaves looked on with mingled expressions of amazement and sorrow, masters with laughs and jeers." One man offered Fee a cup of water. "This I told him I should take in Christ's name; he answered, 'yes.'" All along the road Fee talked "with several of the mob about their treatment of [him] and of the slaves, and concerning their souls' salvation." As they marched a downpour of rain commenced, driving them all "by common consent" to shelter in a nearby farmhouse. Fee, "seeing a large Bible on a small table," asked the "man of the house" if he could "read a portion of Scripture and pray." From the 58th chapter of Isaiah, Fee read to his persecutors: "Is not this the fast I have chosen? to loose the bands of wickedness, to undo the heavy burdens, and to let the oppressed go free, and that ye break every yoke?" Then he knelt down and prayed in front of his captors.[75]

After the rain stopped, seven of Fee's persecutors turned back, but nine men, apparently expecting reinforcements upon their arrival, escorted Fee to Crab Orchard, where he had been mobbed before. Fortunately for Fee, the reception there was no more enthusiastic or violent "than if a stage had driven up." The disappointed mob let him go.[76]

Members of his church met afterwards and voted unanimously to have Fee come back. And he agreed to go. But in his letter to Clay a few days later Fee wrote, "I want council [sic]." His family, he said, were having "no small trial" and he himself was ill.[77]

Although Clay answered this letter on the 29th of July, Fee derived little comfort from it. Fee himself wrote (to Simeon Jocelyn, an AMA official) on the same day describing his situation. "I am enduring a most severe trial. The mob feeling still rages. . . . " His friends in Rockcastle County were much intimidated.

> The friends in Madison who went in search of my person [while I was in the hands of the mob] were much insensed [sic] some were dreadfully furious—had they met the mob lives would have been lost. My wife & a neighbor woman [Martha B. Wright] were along—they knew not for twelve hours where I was supposed the mob yet had me. The excitement is yet very great. The mob were of a most reckless class—their acts were so open and brutal that very many persons who never have been committed are now most outspoken. The friends at the meeting house after I was away voted to have me come back and preach. I have been with them twice since—told them no preventing providence I would come to fill my regular appointment—I told the captain of the mob so, he having asked me if I would. . . . C. M. Clay was sent for by some of my friends and when it was supposed I was yet in the hands of the mob refused to come on grounds that I was a Radical and he

could not identify himself with me . . . he yet stands aloof. This is chilling friends here for he tells them I am in such a position that the courts will treat me as an outlaw. This gives comfort to the enemy. My case is at present perilous. My wife is almost overcome with anxiety about my condition. I am worn down with continual riding—not vigorous in health, pressed with care but have the rest of faith.[78]

On August 3, Fee wrote to Clay again. "I must say you are like the Congressman's wife," he told Clay, "you have your faults but I love you still." There was no response to that letter. Once again Fee wrote:

> I have not read anything from you since my reply to yours of July 29th.
> I think your standing aloof is an injury to the cause here— the enemy construes it in various ways, but all, as much as to say, 'he (Fee) ought not to be protected.' Protection is the duty of man to his fellow—when the officer cannot or will not then the people exercise the right belonging to them. This the friends here are determined to do. They have invited me here and they intend to see me protected [Fee is referring here to Berea, which is the return address of this letter] whilst guilty of no crime—no violation of law. You ought to. It will be an injury to you not to. When you were mobbed in Lexington Henry Clay stood aloof because he could not 'identify himself with your principles.' You are doing the same now. My position is a solemn conviction of my duty to God. I care not for party or names. You refuse protection to one guilty only of an expressed opinion different from your own—but no crime . . . The Quakers say the military law ought not to be enforced—yea even refuse to obey, yet they are protected. I know I ought to be . . . I do not want you to do anything for friendship's [sake] merely, but I suggest what I think is duty and for your good as well as that of the cause of freedom & righteousness. I have been routed again—you will hear from the bearer particulars. John G. Fee.
> P. S. Copernicus when threatened with death and required to say 'the earth does not turn'—still said, 'it does turn'—so Fee still says 'a wicked and impious law ought not be enforced' . . . When Herod said destroy all the men children under two years <u>ought that law to have been enforced</u>?[79]

Clay's withdrawal of support had one result he surely did not foresee. If he would not provide protection, then other people would. In August 1857, two of Fee's churchmembers came to meeting armed. A mob threatened Fee at church, but "one of these friends placed his hands upon his revolvers and stepped between them & [Fee]." And Fee found another mode of protection by organizing a band of men who worked for him as distributors of tracts, colporteurs—leaders of the antslavery friends, one of them a magistrate of some influence (Peter H. West)—to arrange public meetings which would pass resolutions to send to civil authorities, and to distribute Fee's own "Address," an appeal for civil liberties in Madison County. All this Fee accomplished before Clay "had time to pour cold water." With some satisfaction Fee wrote, "almost every anti-slavery man had committed himself and gone through the fire with me."[80]

Now Clay not only refused to protect Fee himself, he urged Fee's friends— some of them Clay's followers—not to do so either, on the grounds that defending Fee would identify them with Fee's cause. And those who defended Fee anyway were liable to Clay's censure. Clay told the people that Fee had been "ungrateful."[81]

However, Fee's friends were willing to go to great lengths. "At one time," Fee wrote, "it was expected that the mob was on their way to my house to take me out. Friends offered to guard my house during the night. I said no—it is not necessary. They insisted. I consented. In space of one hour about 30 armed men were around my house to defend it." Clay's opposition to Fee was now fed by a dawning realization that Clay's 'boys' were no longer simply his followers. A certain defiance of Cassius Clay was growing up in the Glade; the whole region might slip from under his influence and follow John G. Fee. Years later, Clay said that Fee had "felt secure enough to set up for himself, not only in religion, but also in politics." When Clay perceived that the man he had brought to central Kentucky to consolidate his (Clay's) position among the Bereans might become their leader himself, his determination to 'stand aloof' became absolute.[82]

On September 17, Fee wrote to Clay again. "The longer I contemplate the difference of opinion between us the more do I regret it." He goes on, "I wish I could see you. I cannot go to you with asshurance [sic] of finding you at home. . . . Could you come out and we have one more talk?"[83]

Clay did not go.

By this time the rift between Clay and Fee was fostering still another change in allegiances. In December 1857, Fee confided to Lewis Tappan, "C. M. Clay stands off and cries 'Revolution & insurrection.' At such a time words of consolation from those who are known friends are most timely—a cordial to a wearied spirit . . . To know that I have friends even in distant places who sympathize with me & pray for me is a most sustaining thought." More and more it seemed to Fee his friends were in the East and North: Christians, not politicians. The eventual plan for Berea would be shaped by a preference for 'outside' people and ideas, a preference that Clay had virtually forced upon Fee. The Berea that began to spring up in 1859 had little or no resemblance to any plan of Cassius Clay's.[84]

In January 1858, Fee sent Clay this account of being mobbed in Estill County:

> Found a quiet well dressed orderly congregation, men & women. About half done preaching a mob of about 30 men with shotguns & rifles on shoulders rode up—demanded that I stop preaching & come out. I continued preaching—a rough fellow rushed forward with gun in hand (others followed) and jerked me out. Asked a pledge to leave & not come back. I declined any pledge whatever. They drew Bro. Jones out—our colporteur—quite law-abiding—voted with the Republicans—they cared not—put him on a horse—took us about 2 miles down a deep hollow to Ky River—Demanded of me again a pledge—I declined—they order Bro. Jones to strip—Tom Oldham (the name given to me—took up Bro Jones linnen [sic]—with sycamore switch—(you know how heavy they grow in wet botoms [sic]) lashed Jones on the bare back until satisfied—They then demanded of me a pledge saying if I [did] not they would give me five times as much. I threw of [sic] my coat & vest. Told them I would meet my suffering but make no pledges and bent down on my feet—They desisted—struck not—I talked to them some time—I make no compromise in any respect, kept my spirit strong & confidence in God undiminished.[85]

One can only surmise how Cassius Clay received this incredible letter; whatever else may be said, it is clear that Fee possessed a kind of courage that Clay never approached.

Fee wrote to Clay again in April 1858: "Let us avoid personal reflections—These engender bad fruits—we are nearer together than pro-slavery men—nearer one than they & we are one. Let us work on for a great result—tis noble. I am not ungrateful to my brother when I hold up God's truth for his and the world's good." He signed this letter "your friend."[86]

He wrote again in June 1858, asking Clay to make the 4th of July speech. Clay accepted. Years later Fee remembered the occasion, although it was not at all memorable:

Not many people were present and in defense of his conservative position [Clay] was without his former enthusiasm. After the address he walked with me into the woodland, then before my door, as we sat down on a log he remarked, "Fee, things look better than I thought they would. I am in heart as much a higher law man as you are, and if we were in Massachusetts we could carry it out; but here we cannot." I replied, "The utterance of moral truth should not be confined to geographical limits, especially in a national canvass."[87]

Fee's account of the same event written some two weeks afterward has a slightly different emphasis. "C.M. Clay has been out—made two speeches—spent the night at my house—had a long talk—made several favorable concessions not before made—agreeably disappointed at the prospect here—went home different— wants nomination for V. President, I think."[88]

The Clay-Fee project was simply running out of steam, as both men turned to pursue other goals: in Clay's case, political office; in Fee's, a brand new school being taught by abolitionists. In July Fee bragged to his friend about the Berea Exhibition [graduation exercises] of 1858:

Two of the Rockcastle mob were there. Persh Hiatts son— slaveholder—one of them was the first to lay hold of me to drag me out of the house last July. I went to him—invited him to our dinner—he did so—I without seeming effort extended to him & others a plate of well-prepared food—I invited him home with me. He declined for the present. I told him to call some other time & I would treat him well. He looked up as he sat on a log into my face & said, "I believe you would."[89]

Perhaps Fee actually intended to needle Clay by telling this turn-the-other-cheek story; they had disagreed about the use of violent means in the antislavery struggle, and Fee was always ready to score a point in an argument.

Fee continued to write to Clay, detailing the progress of the new school, giving political advice, always angling for reconciliation, but always unwilling to yield on any of his own assumptions. In April 1859, he described his feelings very directly,

I have for weeks been desiring to come and see you in person—I formed an attachment to you years since. It is similar to that of a man's attachment to the wife of his youth—there may be little broils once in a while but after all if any body else interferes the wife will take the broomstick.

But we need not loose [sic] ourselves in figures—I love the principle of righteousness more than [I love] you or any other man—And I expect to love men as they love righteousness. I feel that toward man, God's image, you want righteousness done—I have long felt that God has raised you up to do a good work. I think you will get a chance to do that work. I think your prospects for V. President are good.[90]

On June 1, 1859, Fee wrote asking Clay to speak at the 4th of July celebration in McKee, county seat of newly formed Jackson County. The two men apparently appeared separately; Fee preached on Sunday, Clay lectured on Monday.[91]

But time was running out. 'Irrepressible conflict' was now inevitable: the Clay-Fee alliance was about to be broken forever, Berea to disappear (but not forever), the nation to be plunged into war. In October 1859, John Brown led his raid against Harper's Ferry.

CHAPTER TWO

JOHN GREGG FEE: Life, Thought and Connections

His Early Life: Slavery and Freedom divided by a river:
".. . *Looking through my window across the Ohio river, over into my native state
I entered into a solemn covenant with God."* John G. Fee.

John Gregg Fee was born September 9, 1816, in Bracken County,
Kentucky, son of John Fee and his wife Sarah Gregg. Before the 19th century
began, the Scotch-Irish Fee family was already established in this region of
northern Kentucky. John G. Fee's father had been born in neighboring Mason
County twenty-four years earlier, the year Kentucky became a state. Fee's
grandfather, also John Fee, a native of Maryland, lived in Bourbon County by
1791, and died in Bracken County in November 1822, leaving a will in which he
devised slaves to his heirs. So on his father's side Fee belonged to a family that
had been Kentuckians before Kentucky achieved statehood. Fee's father was a
leader in Bracken County, small-scale slaveholder, large landowner, sufficiently
respected and prosperous to be elected to the Kentucky legislature in 1807. All his
life Fee was concerned for the land of his birth—patriotic about Kentucky,
intensely and especially dedicated to his own people, as he always called them,
seeing them as his particular responsibility. Fee's father, "an industrious, thrifty
farmer," inherited a slave from his own father's estate and concluded that he needed
more slaves for "sufficient and permanent labor." He bought and bred slaves until

he had accumulated some 13, the number that John G. Fee recalls his father owning.[1]

Fee's mother, Sarah (Gregg) Fee, was born October 1792, in Loudoun County, Virginia; both her parents were Greggs—and both had been Quakers before her father's decision to fight in the American Revolution. Fee's affection for his mother was deep; he described her as "industrious and economical. A modest, tender-hearted woman, and a fond mother. I was her first born," he wrote in his old age, "She loved me very much, and I loved her in return." Her opposition to his abolitionism must have been particularly hard for him to endure. Shortly after her death (September 16, 1860) he wrote, "This day have I gone with friends to take [my mother] from our home where she so long dwelt to the narrow mansion of the grave . . . This is to me a sorrowful & trying time . . . My mother was to me a dear friend at my darkest hours though opposed as she was at times to my sentiments and practice yet she was always kind and pleasant."[2]

The part of Kentucky where Fee was born played an important role in his development. Bracken is one of the many counties on Kentucky's northern border, which runs for hundreds of miles with the Ohio River. On one side of the river is Ohio, a free state; on the other Kentucky, slave. Like Berea, Bracken County was located at a peculiar seam in the world—you could stand in Augusta, Kentucky, and look across the river into freedom. Hundreds of slaves along the banks of the Ohio did just that—and Fee came to perceive the river exactly as black people did; as a dramatic boundary line, more than a river: like the Jordan, a great crossing into another life.

From Kentucky, a runaway slave had to cross the Ohio to reach any free state. "If the Kentucky authorities could prevent him from crossing the stream on the northern and western boundary, they could prevent any slave from making a successful escape. Consequently the legislature as early as 1823 attempted to solve the problem by passing a law forbidding masters of vessels and others from employing and removing negroes out of the state." This law was followed by another in 1831, which "provided that no ferryman on the Ohio River should transport slaves across from Kentucky . . . slaves could only cross the river when they had the written consent of their masters." "The Ohio River was a great barrier to fugitive slaves," Levi Coffin wrote; but when the river was frozen, he said, "we always expected a stampede of fugitives from Kentucky." Once he aided 14 who had all crossed on the ice at the same time. Strong patrols were maintained along the Ohio in all the border counties to avoid such wholesale escapes.[3]

Of course, all runaways did not elude capture. Seventy-five armed and desperate slaves escaped from Fayette County August 5, 1848, and headed for the Ohio River. Some of the fugitives were surrounded in a hemp field in northern Bracken County and 20 of the captured slaves were lodged in the jail at Brooksville, county seat of Bracken. The seven who were thought to be ringleaders, plus four others, were tried there. Three were sentenced to death and executed in Fee's home county October 28, 1848.[4]

Even before Fee became an abolitionist he perceived the turmoil that the nearness of the river created in the adult world. Being a slaveholder along the Ohio was risky business; any night a man's profits and labor might find a way to cross the water and disappear forever. Fee's father owned some thirteen slaves when Fee was a child—"not many," Fee remarked, "enough to give sanction to the system and strength to caste." That Fee's father suffered from the common border-anxiety is evidenced by a letter Fee wrote to George Whipple; "My father," he stated,

> an Elder in the Pres. ch. (O. S. [Old Style]) sold one of his slaves last Saturday—a boy about 18 years of age born and raised in his own house, sprightly, with good habits, save that he would ride his master's horses at night (this is common among slaves & he was trying to make money, as I am informed, to pay for an extra coat). My father was (as he told me) afraid the boy would run off—attempted to conquer him by severe whipping, could not—sold the boy (well grown) to a regular negro trader—handcuffed & taken off (I did not see it done) but saw those that knew—have had a talk with my father since—he is hardened—pleads Bible defense. . . . [5]

It was a region where the fears and cruelties of slavery were heightened by the mere proximity of another system. On the other side, Ohioans were looking in to Kentucky, wondering what could be done about that wicked state, and, in some cases, planning a moral invasion.[6]

Fee himself described his decision to minister in Kentucky in a dramatic passage referring to the Ohio River both literally and symbolically: "In my bedroom on bended knee, and looking through my window across the Ohio river, over into my native state I entered into a solemn covenant with God to return and there preach [the] gospel of [impartial] love."[7]

Early Life and Education
"I then entered upon a life of prayer which I have never abandoned." John G. Fee.

During his childhood, Fee was safely held within the system. At the age of 14 he was converted "to God as I saw him then," as he puts it, through the efforts of "a godly school teacher," Joseph Corliss, who boarded with the Fee family. In 1896, Fee recalled, "I then entered upon a life of prayer which I have never abandoned." If anyone remarked that the adolescent boy was especially fervent and pious, no one worried about it; Fee wanted to join the Methodist Episcopal Church (apparently Corliss's denomination), but his father, not yet a Christian himself, opposed that move; two years later in 1832 Fee joined the Augusta Presbyterian Church, along with his parents, and some two years after that, decided to become a gospel minister. (The elder Fee had been "awakened" and asked his son to join the church along with his parents.) On August 27, 1836, a group of 23 of the members of Augusta Church, many of them Fee's relatives—parents, uncles, aunts, brother, sister and cousins among them—with the approval of the Ebenezer Presbytery formed a new church in Bracken County, known as the Sharon Presbyterian Church. Like the mother church, Sharon was Old School, very conservative. Fee's father and his uncle James Fee, also a slaveholder, were elected elders of the new church. So Fee and his family worshiped safely within the bosom of a congregation where slaveholders were not just acceptable, but religious leaders as well. In his *Autobiography* Fee recalled a memorable church service:

> Vivid now is the impression made on my youthful mind on seeing a Presbyterian preacher, who was a guest in my grandfather's house, rise before an immense audience and select for his text, "Cursed be Canaan: a servant of servants shall he be unto his brethren." Of course the drift of the discourse was after the plea of the slaveocracy—"God decreed that the children of Ham should be slaves to the children of Shem and Japheth; that Abraham held slaves, and Moses sanctified such."
> All this was intensified by seing a much-venerated neighbor, and slaveholder, who had represented the people in the State Legislature, mount his horse, then uncovering his gray hairs, cry

out in a loud voice, "The greatest sermon between heaven and earth."[8]

All the influence of family, church and state impressed upon the young man the intrinsic "rightness" of the system of slavery. "In my boyhood," Fee wrote,

> I thought nothing about the inherent sinfulness of slavery. I saw it as a prevalent institution in the family life of my relations on my father's side of the house. These were kind to me and occupied what were considered good social positions. I was often scolded for being so much with the slaves, and threatened with punishment when I would intercede for them.[9]

Fee entered Augusta College about 1836, and remained there for two and a half years. It was his hometown school, part of his family's approved way of life; his grandfather had been a trustee of the institution as early as 1798.[10]

The next step in his education was crucial; he crossed the river and entered Miami University in Oxford, Ohio, where he followed "the regular literary . . . course of study," what we would call a classical curriculum. Fee recorded no mention of his time at Miami U.; whatever happened to him there, what he studied, what he learned, how he changed, apparently never seemed worth writing about. Perhaps Miami differed little from Augusta College; it is on record that an early president of Miami U., Robert H. Bishop, forbade the discussion of slavery at his school in 1834; if the gag rule was still keeping students quiet in 1841, Fee was probably perfectly willing to cooperate; "all [his] education, habits, thoughts and plans" were contrary to abolitionism at that time.[11]

After a year at Miami, Fee transferred back to his original college for last term, receiving a degree from Augusta College in August 1840. He had decided to pursue his life's goal of becoming a minister; he enrolled in Lane Theological Seminary at Cincinnati.

Fee at Lane Theological Seminary
"At last I said, 'Lord, if need be, make me an abolitionist.'" John G. Fee.

Lane Seminary was founded in 1828; Fee became a student there 14 years later. Although Lane was a very young institution, by 1842 it had already become famous, or notorious, all over the nation. In 1834, the students of the seminary, led by Theodore Weld, had conducted a series of debates on two vital issues in the antislavery question: immediatism and colonization. In simplest terms, the debaters concluded that slaves should be freed immediately and that programs of colonization, designed to ship blacks back to Africa, ought not be supported. Settling these questions in the Lane debates was more than an academic exercise, however; as a result of the speeches and discussions virtually all the students at Lane were 'converted' to abolitionism, calling for immediate freedom for slaves and equal rights for them as well. And the students had moved out of the debating hall into the public arena: they had been teaching free blacks in Cincinnati, going to church with blacks, walking on the streets with them, *associating* with them.

Most of the faculty and trustees of Lane were appalled, to put it mildly. When the authorities of the school tried to impose a system of regulations curtailing the students' right to discuss slavery, most of the students of Lane Seminary walked out and never returned. This dramatic exodus, known as the Lane Rebellion, was certainly a milestone in the history of academic freedom, but it proved most significant in its contribution to the abolitionist movement, especially at Oberlin College. Many of the Lane Rebels, as they came to be called, moved in a body to Oberlin, where, at their insistence, blacks were also admitted. In 1835, Oberlin became the first interracial, coeducational institution of higher learning in the country.

Meanwhile, Lane Seminary was left almost empty, denuded of students, a subject of unpleasant controversy in the national press. It was enough to ruin a school! Out of 103 theological students only eight remained when the dust settled on Lane's campus.

But explanations were offered, excuses made, accusations passed around, and new students enrolled, so Lane Seminary continued in operation. The *Cincinnati Journal* reported that "Parents and guardians may now send their sons and wards to Lane Seminary, with perfect confidence, that the proper business of a theological seminary will occupy their minds."[12]

So when John G. Fee entered Lane in 1842 he (and his father) might reasonably have expected it to be 'safe.' It was the seminary that the dangerous element had deserted, leaving only respectable moderation behind. Who knows what governed John G. Fee's choice of this particular school? Probably he went there because it was the nearest Presbyterian seminary available, and Lyman

Beecher, its president, one of the most famous ministers of the century, and Cincinnati, a pro-slavery city in free territory, the metropolis of the Ohio River. Fee did not go there because he wanted to discuss slavery pro and con—that much is certain. Lane Seminary would have been the last place to attract a student who wanted to do that. Was he drawn to what he knew of the Lane Rebels? Surely not, for the place to meet them and learn their views was Oberlin. Even today, Lane is known primarily as the school where the radicals walked out; it seems logical to conclude that Fee chose to go to Lane because the conservative element had remained there.

Fee considered his conversion to abolitionism at Lane Seminary the most crucial experience of his life; 53 years later he would write, "From that time onward. . . I have not doubted my acceptance with God." His conversion was effected by two of his fellow students, John Milton Campbell, who had been a classmate of Fee's at Miami, and James C. White, a New Englander; both were older than Fee, White by a good ten years. Campbell, a native of Fleming County, Kentucky, was to sail for Africa two months after his ordination, and die in his new mission field two months after embarking. Fee had been invited to accompany him, but decided his call was back to Kentucky—to the Dark and Bloody Ground, not to the Dark Continent. Others of Fee's classmates had invited him to work in Indiana, but Kentucky really seemed to him the inevitable place for his life's work.[13]

Fee calls the two men "godly brethren" and speaks of their "gentle and affectionate labor" with him; they directed his attention to the fundamental principle of the Christian religion—supreme love to God and impartial love to all people. Fee writes that he "saw that the practical application of the principle was expressed in the Golden Rule: 'All things whatever ye would that men should do to you, do ye even so to them,'" and he saw also that this practical application would make him an abolitionist.

At first, Fee was most disturbed by that awful name—abolitionist, an epithet 'odious' to both North and South. He feared that to adopt that name would "impair [his] usefulness in society, and also in the gospel ministry." Although he describes the incident in a straightforward, even flat-footed way, his battle with himself must have been intense. "The principle was clear," he writes, "the name appropriate." He saw his unwillingness to "meet the duty disclosed" as evidence that his "selfishness had entrenched itself" in just that area of his life.

"I had a place in the grove . . . to which I went every day for prayer. For days I struggled between newly revealed self and present revealed duty. At last I said, 'Lord, if need be, make me an abolitionist.' Immediately I was conscious of an entire surrender—conscious that I had died to the world, and risen with Christ— ready to do his entire will as far as then known to me." He felt that his old self had been crucified; he had been converted, turned around, set on a path "contrary to all my previous education, habits, thoughts and plans." We must take seriously Fee's estimation of the change in himself; he had been a willing participant in the Southern system, but now the slaveholder's dutiful son had become an abolitionist.[14]

But not the slaveholder. The elder John Fee angrily wrote his son: "Bundle up your books and come home; I have spent the last dollar I mean to spend on you in a free state."[15]

Churches and Missionary Societies: Coming Out
"The church . . . [has] a minister who has a slave. This minister, of course, says nothing. . . ." John G. Fee.

Old School Presbyterian and New School as well were both old by the 1830's. Some division along Old and New lines had occurred as early as the Great Awakening almost a century earlier. The Old School groups "came to admire the church's traditional polity and took very seriously the Reformed tenet that matters of church order were within the divine law." Because "the constitution of the church was not a structural convenience which could be altered to suit the circumstances . . . [but] an article of faith," the Old School could not associate with other churches, even Congregational churches with otherwise very similar theological foundations. In addition, the Old School had great difficulty accepting voluntary missonary associations, which might involve workers from a variety of church groups, and it entertained "grave suspicions about the new kind of revivalism that seemed to be breaking out everywhere in the years after 1800." "The conservative set of mind" of the Old School Presbyterians "was observable even in Kentucky during the great revivals there," when whole congregations defected to new practices and experiences.[16]

Under the influence of New School Presbyterianism churches grew up valuing the work of interdenominational societies and willing to cooperate with fellow evangelicals; the New School movement maintained that the traditional forms of church government were less important than the necessity of converting the frontier; voluntary agencies and revivalism were important, perhaps crucial, evangelistic means in home missions. The inclusion of Congregationalism within the New School framework brought with it New England, for two centuries the stronghold of the Congregational form of Puritanism. So New School Presbyterianism was, in a way, an effort to channel the energies of the East into the West; money, educated men and women, culture and religious sophistication might pour into the frontier mission fields from Massachusetts, Connecticut and New York.

The official schism between Old and New School Presbyterians occurred in 1837, a year after Sharon Church was formed. Exactly when John G. Fee withdrew his affiliation from the Old School to the New is unknown, but it was probably at the time of his conversion to abolitionism, as his later objections to Old School principles are based on the church's support of slavery. Both Fee's father and his slaveholding uncle James were Old School elders; both sold slaves away from their families. In 1851, Fee wrote in great indignation, " . . . Old School Presbyterians of the South are, in the North, represented as not separating families but as treating them quite patriarchal. The church of which these . . . elders are a part [has] a minister who has a slave. This minister, of course, says nothing . . . . "[17]

Lane Seminary was primarily New School in its allegiances, and after graduation Fee was licensed to preach by Cincinnati presbytery and ordained by Harmony presbytery (New School) in Kentucky. One of his first calls to a church was from a New School congregation in Louisville; Fee accepted the invitation, but, he writes, "the New School brethren . . . were disappointed in their expectations for help—did not get a house for worship as expected." So the invitation was withdrawn. At about the same time, he seems to have received an invitation from another Louisville church which wished him to withdraw from his abolition presbytery.[18]

In 1845, after visiting Lewis County, Kentucky, where he preached a few sermons and received another invitation, Fee asked the American Home Missionary Society to sponsor his ministry in Lewis County, and received his commission soon afterward—by the 2nd of April.[19]

The American Home Missionary Society, formed in 1826 in the Burned-Over District of Western New York as a New School agency, was a direct outgrowth of the Congregational-Presbyterian Plan of Union. "Its missionaries were a major force in the development of the West, not only as apostles and revivalists, but as educators civic leaders and exponents of eastern culture." Naturally, the organization was supported by individuals and churches in the East, both with money and volunteers. For example, "graduates of Andover and Yale took up the missionary challenge in large numbers" under the auspices of the Home Missionary Society.[20]

Fee's commission with this society was brief—from 1845 to 1848, when he resigned because he had discovered that the organization sponsored slaveholding ministers. However, the brevity of his tenure is no measure of the impact the Society's principles had upon him. First, the HMS advocated voluntary interdenominational cooperation—a kind of program that would be very important to Fee in much of his later work; second, and most significantly, the HMS brought easterners into the West—preachers and other religious workers from Massachusetts, Connecticut, New Hampshire were recruited and sponsored in their ministries in Kentucky, Tennessee, North Carolina. It is impossible to imagine how different Berea would have been (how different it would be even today) had Fee not learned to regard missionaries from New England as his most important helpers in the cause of abolitionism. He was a Southerner, but he came to rely upon Northerners and sometimes to trust them. The American Home Missionary Society laid some groundwork for Fee's later anti-sectarian stance, but also prepared him to accept the moral and religious invasion of one culture by another as an acceptable mode of evangelism. Dozens of Yankees would come to Kentucky at Fee's request to work among the heathen in southern Madison County and surrounding areas.

In September 1850, William Goodell wrote an enormous letter to his father-in-law, Joshua Cady, narrating his (Goodell's) adventures on a recent trip west to

Cincinnati. He had been attending a Christian Anti-Slavery meeting in the city and there he had met the Rev. John G. Fee.

> On Monday morning, I took steamboat, up the Ohio river, in company with John G. Fee [double underlining], to spend a few days with him in Kentucky. Do you not know something of Mr. Fee? . . . He is a minister, aged about 32, a native of Kentucky. His father & mother, still living are pro slavery, & slaveholders. John G. [d. u.] was preparing for the ministry in Ohio when he became an abolitionist, to the great grief of his parents, who consider their family disgraced and his "usefulness destroyed!"— Returning home he told his Presbytery he was an abolitionist, but they licensed him, hoping it would soon wear off.—But it only grew brighter.—He continually preached abolition, & introduced it into the Presbytery at every meeting, till they told him frankly he had exhausted his testimony without any effect upon them, so long as he continued to hold fellowship with them. There was but one thing more that he could do & that was the testimony of withdrawal, if he believed slavery so great a sin! He took them at their own word, and withdrew. He had been mainly supported in preaching by the American Home Missionary Society. On his leaving Presbytery, somebody made an effort to get the Society to stop supporting him. The Society dared not do this. They derived most of their funds from the north—Some from abolitionists: and they were supporting several slave holding ministers & many slave holding churches. To drop the support of a minister merely because he was an abolitionist, would hardly do. So they took the ground of a dignified impartiality, & continued it was not consistent for him to receive support from them. He notified them accordingly not knowing from whom his support was to come—but our Union Miss. Soc. (now the Amer. Miss. Association) extended aid to him, & he continues his labor.[21]

This highly emphatic, indeed breathless, account of Fee's withdrawals (almost simultaneous) from both the American Home Missionary Society and the New School Presbyterian church is undoubtedly accurate, rendered as Fee himself told it to Goodell. Fee's repudiation of the Presbyterian Church seems to have been forced upon him; he first tried to get a rule passed against slaveholders in the church in 1846 and thereafter introduced the same idea at every Presbytery meeting: his Synod passed resolutions which stated that anyone who adopted an ecclesiastical rule against pro-slavery members of the New School Presbyterian Church "should first retire from the obligations of his association with us." Further, the resolutions dealt with Fee directly by disclaiming responsibilty for any interference he may have made "with the relation of master & slave." Finally, Synod enjoined Fee—or rather "affectionately requested and exhorted [him] to review his course on the matter; and to desist from the exercise of the objectionable principle . . . . " All these resolutions were designed to preserve "the peace of our churches." After Fee refused to be silent, his presbytery suggested that his only recourse was to withdraw, and his decision to do so was probably a great relief to them; his 'taking them at their word' was an action later justified by his anti-sectarian principle. His belief that a Christian should have no fellowship with slaveholders was now supported by his own concrete example.[22]

For a brief time, however, Fee had no religious organization of any kind backing him. His presbytery (Harmony) censured him in June 1848, and he resigned his commission from HMS in the next month. Fee had not received a new commission from any organization when he resigned the old one. But by the 10th of October, George Whipple had written Fee telling him the good news: Lewis Tappan had presented Fee's case to the AMA and Whipple was convinced that the committee had decided to commission, without endorsers, without the call of a church, on the strength of Fee's merits alone. Fee must have been more than relieved. Unsponsored for three months, he was literally penniless by October. He wrote Whipple that he had "not provision for more than one week's subsistence in [his] house . . . and not one dollar with which to buy." Nevertheless, his receiving the commission did not put Fee into a state of abject humility and gratitude. Far from it: he asked Whipple to make his payment retroactive, so that he (Fee) could both eat *and* attend an important emancipation convention in Kentucky in November.[23]

From the time he received his AMA commission Fee would be involved in ministry to free churches only, and his position would become not simply non-denominational (a nebulous category that Fee would have scoffed at), but actively *anti*-sectarian, not just without denomination, but positively against it. His antisectarian principle was never an indication of Fee's willingness to cooperate with *every* church, it was a statement of his basic unwillingness to cooperate fully with *any* of them. His AMA commission enabled him to maintain churches of his own founding along his own lines—which coincided with the pattern of the free church movement.

The first free church was formed in 1830, primarily through the efforts of Lewis Tappan. At this stage the designation 'free' was perfectly literal, indicating that no one would have to pay for a private pew; the selling of pews was an ecclesiastical practice resulting—quite naturally—in discrimination against the poor. Tappan's first free church in Albany, New York, grew so rapidly that a second one was soon planned; in 1831, Tappan wrote Theodore Weld asking him to be its minister, but Weld refused.[24]

By 1850, Fee, on the advice of William Goodell (himself a pastor of a free church in Honeoye, New York), decided on the name "Free Christian Church" for his Cabin Creek congregation, although by that time the word 'free' also emphasized an anti-slavery, anti-sectarian position. In his "Non-Fellowship with Slaveholders" Fee wrote that the "come-outer" churches, like his own, were doing "immense good," forcing the old slave churches "to look about for their members."[25]

Fee's secessions from the slavery-supporting church and mission board signaled his willingness to act on matters of principle forcefully and without regard to consequences. In a sense, however, the AMA rescued Fee from the consequences of his stand, providing money, encouragement, fellow-workers, advice—all these important supports pouring in from the North and East. Fee's ministry might have been over when it had barely begun if the AMA had not commissioned him. On the other hand, the AMA work in Kentucky was nothing without Fee: where he went the organization followed—money, men, encouragement, all focused on John G. Fee. He was like a doorway into the region; through him the doctrines and power of Eastern abolitionism, which had already moved west to Ohio, entered Kentucky.[26]

Union Church at Cabin Creek & Bethesda Church in Bracken County
"One John G. Fee, a resident of Lewis County and who professes to be a Minister of the Gospel frequently intrudes himself into our quiet community and promulgates doctrines upon the the subject of negro slavery which we regard as dangerous to the peace and good order of society. . . ." Grand Jury in Bracken County, Kentucky.

After his graduation from Lane Seminary in 1843, Fee returned to his father's house and tried to convert his parents. John Fee the elder, having "supplied himself, from every possible source, with pro-slavery books and pamphlets," retaliated with "a Bible defence of slavery" and failing in that approach "became irritable and violent in his opposition." Turning to temptation instead, Fee's father offered to pay all his son's bills to go to Princeton Theological Seminary, where Fee might have had his abolitionism subverted. Fee refused and "sought to get the gospel of love in the heart of people around," carrying his message to other relatives and the whole neighborhood. Shortly, he was conducting a protracted meeting, his first, for the interested people in Bracken County. "In that meeting," Fee writes, "I saw the conversion of a young woman to whom I soon afterwards became betrothed." He had been in love with her before, although he had felt he could not marry her until after her conversion. Her name was Matilda Hamilton, Fee's first cousin once removed; her mother, like Fee's, had been a Gregg. She was not the only one of Fee's numerous relatives in Bracken County to be swayed by the fervent young preacher. He was offered the pastorate of two churches in Bracken at that point on condition that he should "go along and preach the Gospel and let the subject of slavery alone." Fee refused. But the abolition church Fee organized there on his own terms a few years later would be filled with his Gregg connections, most of whom probably heard him preach in his first revival in 1844.[27]

John G. Fee and Matilda Hamilton were married September 16, 1844, in Bracken County; he was 28 and she was 20. They had known one another all their lives—and now a remarkable lifetime stretched before them. Fee wrote,

> With my covenant, willingly made, I saw the life I must probably live—one of obliquy, persecution and peril. I had decided I would marry no woman who was not a Christian, and one whose views of Christian duty and life would be in harmony with my own. I had heard the testimony of Matilda Hamilton the day of her conversion to God. I had known her from her childhood, I knew the sterling worth of her mother, her decided opposition to human slavery, and that if we went together we must go out not knowing whither we went.[28]

The first church Fee was offered by the New School Presbyterians was in Cynthiana, Kentucky. Attending a meeting of his presbytery there, Fee found himself faced with the prospect of taking communion with local slaveholders. "I saw there," Fee wrote, "the blight of slavery on everything around me." When the Lord's Supper was being served he "left the church house and went out into an adjoining woodland and sat down on a log and wept . . . . " His ecclesiatical connection with people with whom he could not commune struck him as sinful. He refused the pastorate of that church.[29]

Soon after this incident, Fee set out on horseback looking for a place where he could find a people who would listen to him, who had—as he put it—"an 'ear to hear.'" He rode more than 300 miles on his initial journey. At this time, he was offered the pastorate of a church in Louisville, which asked him to separate from his "abolition presbytery." He refused. But he found his congregation about 25 miles from his father's house in another Ohio River border county named for a famous explorer, Capt. Meriwether Lewis. In 1844, Lewis County had a population between 6 and 7,000, with 300 to 400 slaves; so it was a sparsely populated region with relatively few slaves. (Consider, for example, that Madison County in the the same period had a population of 16,000, one-third of which was slave.) Most of the people in the region of Cabin Creek were descendants of Pennsylvanians, with no habit of slavery.[30]

"In Lewis County," Fee writes, "I found a little band of women, three in number, whose husbands were not slaveholders." These women were willing to listen and they were associated as a church, along with two others who were converted during Fee's initial meeting, having invited Fee to be their minister by January 1845. At the end of that month, Fee wrote to the American Home Missionary Society, the same group he later repudiated as supporters of slaveholding ministers, saying, "I knew the fact that you did not like to comission slaveholders to go & preach the principle of love justice & mercy. I had but one fact to state . . . I am not a slaveholder & God forbid I ever should be." He asked the HMS to commission him for his ministry in Lewis County and by April 1, 1845, the matter was official. He was a commissioned worker for the American Home Missionary Association with a church in Lewis County, Kentucky— members: three women, New School Presbyterians, married to non-slaveholders. And he was newly married himself. The extraordinary thing about the whole situation as Fee set out in life was his cheerful assumption that everything was going along beautifully. He did not find it hard to accept his three members; his work would bring in more, the church would grow, become an example, a light on the hill, a beacon to the slaveholding world.[31]

Before entering permanently on his Lewis County pastorate, Fee returned to Bracken County to give an already scheduled lecture at Brooksville, the county seat. There he met threats of violence, entreaties from his relatives and friends, with the same reply—he refused to give up his appointment. Fee's father was so angry he told his son never to enter his door again. He relented a couple of weeks later after Fee preached a sermon in Sharon Church; evidently his father was not made of such stern stuff as his son was.

On April 1, 1846, Fee proudly wrote his first year's report: Union Church at Cabin Creek has been organized with five members (two having dropped in after his invitation), but during the year 13 have been added by profession of faith and one expelled for immoral conduct. In fact, the person expelled for immoral conduct was one of the original members, kicked out of church for lying (the nature of the lie goes unrecorded). At any rate, the church now has 17 members, but the congregation is bigger than that for Fee has organized a Temperance society with 88 members at the first meeting. No slaveholders in the church, he reports, and he has been experiencing persecution for preaching that the Bible is against slavery.[32]

Fee and his new wife had been boarding with a Methodist family, and at first his congregations had been large. Then he preached a sermon on "the practical application" of the Golden Rule, extending its benefits to whites and blacks alike. "Away went our congregation," he writes, "reduced from 300 to eight to twelve persons." And away go their lodgings; their landlord kicked them out, newlyweds or not. The neighborhood's verdict was clear: "He is an Abolitionist, in favor of 'nigger' equality; his teaching is dangerous to our property, and will breed insurrection and rebellion; he ought to be moved."[33]

But Fee says, "My covenant was upon me to preach the gospel of love in Kentucky." Using money left over from buying the slave woman Juliet Miles, Fee builds himself a little house: "One room, sixteen feet square, . . . plastered with one coat." While he works he and his wife board with Robert and Lydia Boyd, an aging couple, but stalwart [new] members of the brand-new trouble-making church.

Fee was shot at and assaulted, but his little congregation, following wherever he led, "resolved to treat slave-holding as a sin, . . . and refused fellowship to persistent slaveholders." Fee's Synod censured him for "disturbing the peace of Zion" and sent a committee to examine his church. At the next meeting of the Synod, finding his Presbyterian colleagues unwilling to repent—his asking them to do so must have seemed an extraordinary response to their vote of censure—Fee said, "My work with you is done; give me a letter of dismissal." His church at Cabin Creek supported him, came out of the Presbyterian body, and formed an independent church with nine members.[34]

His congregation in Lewis County may have been small, but he had not misjudged them. He had found a people ready to hear and heed his message.

Fee founded Bethesda Church in Bracken County late in 1849, although he had been preaching there off and on for years. Undoubtedly, the church in Fee's home county was of great importance to him for personal, as well as religious, reasons; he attracted many of his own and his wife's relatives into the fold, and also drew some members away from Sharon Presbyterian Church. If Fee experienced any sense of personal triumph over his father, he did not record it. But his planting of a free church in Bracken County must have seemed to his parents the final, irrevocable blow.

Matilda (Hamilton) Fee's mother joined Bethesda Church, as did her grandmother (and Fee's aunt) Mary Gregg and her uncle John D. Gregg. (John D. Gregg was one of Fee's most faithful supporters; for example, Gregg led the Bethesda Church in the movement to become "free"—open equally to black and white members.) By 1851, Samuel Gregg had been added, as well as Greenbury G. Hanson and his son John Gregg Hanson, another of the mutual cousins (first cousin of Matilda Fee, first cousin once removed of her husband).[35]

So in his report for the year ending October 1849, Fee had two churches to describe. Cabin Creek congregation was still growing, with 35 members, 23 of whom had been added by profession and one by letter. (Fee explains that many people had tried to get letters to transfer membership to his church, but only one had succeeded because the other churches refused to honor the requests.) Members had come from Presbyterian, Methodist and Baptist congregations. In addition, he states, Cabin Creek had lost members every year by removal because persecuted members had fled the South altogether. The average attendance for the year was 100, and 31 of the 35 members had pledged total abstinence, the remaining four believing "the church is sufficient." Altogether, 54 people had signed the temperance pledge; 63 scholars were enrolled in Sabbath School, which was in need of a good library.[36]

It is clear from the figures he reports that Fee's churches were filled with mostly non-members. Some in attendance might be slaveholders, even though no member could be: all communicants had to be free of known, persistent sin.

Fee's report for Bethesda, not yet organized as a church, mentions only that the average attendance is 150.

Beyond the not particularly impressive numbers, what did Fee think he was accomplishing? What was the point of going through all the difficulties he encountered in Kentucky when he could have accepted lucrative positions in Ohio or Indiana, as he points out himself? He was invited to many places where his ministry would not have been impeded as it obviously was in Kentucky. A Grand Jury in Bracken County (on September 17, 1850) charged that

> one John G. Fee, a resident of Lewis County and who professes to be a Minister of the Gospel frequently intrudes himself into our quiet community and promulgates doctrines upon the subject of negro slavery which we regard as dangerous to the peace and good order of society, which every good citizen ought, in our opinion, to deprecate as fraught with nothing but evil to the country.[37]

When he applied to the AMA for assistance in his Kentucky ministry, that organization pressed him to justify such a step. For them Fee articulated a rather subtle perception of his advantages in Kentucky; "By living here," he wrote, "my influence is greater here than if I lived in Ohio, and greater in Ohio when I go there than if I lived there." Fee was aware of the interest his career aroused in northern circles, an interest which would continue and grow for many years: ministers in safer places were not entitled to nearly so much attention—or publicity.[38]

Fee later provided a more systematic rationale for his decision to work in his native state; he lists six advantages of his slave-state antislavery ministry: (1) "planting in slave territory a church having no connection or fellowship with slavery;" (2) "establishing the precedent that such can live in a slave state;" (3) "waking up continual agitation in surrounding churches, on the subject of fellowship with slaveholding;" (4) "training here persons who will move abroad in this and into other states to plant similar churches;" (5) "having an organized body here continually, not merely talking, but circulating antislavery documents among their neighbors, relatives and acquaintances;" and (6) "holding correspondence with friends throughout the state, and forwarding to them antislavery documents, thus preparing the way for similar congregations to our own in other counties." Clearly, Fee regards his work as a significant beginning, a precedent, but also as a part of a larger movement—he expects dramatic growth. In addition, every purpose he sets down involves him and his churches in direct confrontation with the slaveholding power: in deliberate agitation, conscious undermining—a little army moving out in various strategic ways to fight.[39]

The foe saw the whole business as a war too.

In September 1851, the Cabin Creek congregation suffered the loss of its church building. As Fee reported it:

> The house in which we regularly worship—near to my house and where we have our sabbath school—a house occupied as a church and school house was burned down night before last. It was the work of an incendiary, an Enemy. The kindling material was seen by Bro. [Robert] Boyd who got to the house soon after the flames commenced, burned up almost everything in it.[40]

This incident was excellent preparation for Berea.

Both Fee's congregations began building new churches about the same time; by August 29, 1851, Fee was taking pledges from Bethesda Church members for a new structure—the land to be purchased from Matilda Fee's parents. From Fee's point of view, his churches were achieving more than permanent meeting houses; "both groups [had] voted to admit blacks on an equal basis with whites." In fact, Fee had asked the Bracken County congregation before they began to build if they were willing to have their church be free—that is, open to all, black or white, free or slave. (The Vinegar family, slaves in Bracken County, were members of Bethesda Church before coming to Berea in the 1860's; two Sunday School classes in that church were comprised of black members. I have been unable to determine if Union Church in Lewis County, where slaves were few, ever actually received a black member.)[41]

In spite of fire, in spite of persecution, in spite of his own immediate family, in spite of everything, Fee's new enterprise was prospering.

An Abolitionist's Families: Hostile Fees and Helpful Greggs
"Old Misses Gregg has set Henry free & pays him for his work. That is the honest way of doing of business." A friend of the Greggs in 1851.

Some writers have denied that John Gregg Fee's father disinherited him, claiming that Fee received a fair share from his father in the form of land, before the old man made a will leaving his eldest son exactly one dollar. Why anyone should want to justify the elder Fee's behavior is a mystery: a letter that Fee wrote to an AMA official on the occasion of his father's funeral sets the matter beyond dispute.[42]

John Fee died September 3, 1859, after a long illness; he had been sick at least since 1857, for in February of that year Fee wrote Simeon Jocelyn, "My Father is very ill—speaks more kindly than he has for 8 years, urges me to come back & see him. Pray for him that he may repent of his slaveholding."[43]

Later, it seemed to Fee that something of a reconciliation had taken place. On one of Fee's visits to Bracken County in the summer of 1858, his father and sister attended his meetings, much to Fee's delight. When he went to Bracken County to attend the last services for his father he took his wife and five children with him. He did not know until he arrived that he had no expectations from his father. On September 16, 1859, he wrote, "My family are here [in Bracken County.] I learn I have no share in my father's estate. I shall be straitened to get them back home." Clearly, he had expected a fair division, but received nothing. By the time of his father's death Fee's sister Adeliza (three years younger than himself) was dead, but she left two children by her marriage to Elijah T. Currans (a cousin of Ulysses S. Grant). Fee's only brother James William Fee (born 1822) had removed to New Orleans by 1848, where he became a wealthy cotton factor; James had been married less than a year when his father died and his wife had a brand new baby, Charles Baldwin Fee, who would grow up to become, like his father, a cotton broker in New Orleans. The youngest of the family was Sarah Ann (known as Sallie), who was over 30 when her father died; she remained single the rest of her life.[44]

Underlying their occasional friendliness was an enmity to Fee's principles that his immediate family never relinquished. 'Cotton broker in New Orleans' tells its own story; Fee's brother established a family that became prominent in New Orleans—a far cry from Berea. Fee mentions his brother only in connection with the Juliet Miles tragedy—his brother had advised John Fee the elder to sell the slave woman in the first place, as "there were more women in the family than were needed." Later, right before the outbreak of war, Fee's brother was the person who proposed to take all the slave children of Juliet Miles to be sold in New Orleans.[45]

Sarah Fee, who inherited the family plantation, included in her will a bequest to Central Kentucky University (now Eastern Kentucky) for a fellowship to be awarded to any deserving young man, but preferably to any of her nephews or other male relations who might apply. The school Fee's sister honored thus was halfway across the state from where she lived, 15 miles north of Berea College and its acknowledged rival. By 1901, when Sarah Fee wrote her will many of her nephews and cousins had already been 'ruined' by attending the pernicious interracial institution her older brother had founded. While she maintained normal family relations with her brother James, Sallie Fee would not recognize John Gregg Fee, "until just before they both died, when she rather reluctantly and formally greeted him in Augusta."[46]

The Fee side of the family was always in opposition to John Gregg Fee, but the Greggs—well, that is a different story. When he was growing up, John G. Fee was always known as Gregg, never called John; John G. Fee was adopted as his public name, but intimates, like his cousin John Gregg Hanson, called him Gregg the rest of his life. In a way, the name suited him better, because Fee's Gregg relatives, including the Hamiltons and the Hansons, received his message gladly, very much unlike the Fees. Greggs, Hansons and Hamiltons joined his church, supported his ministry, even when he moved to another region of Kentucky; they subscribed to the *American Missionary* at his behest. And at his urging many of them freed their slaves and engaged in antislavery activities of their own. In addition, many of Fee's Gregg connections supported Berea College for decades after Fee had left Bracken County. Fee's ministry most emphatically *counted* with his mother's relatives, but not with his father's. Why?[47]

The obvious answer and probably the true one is simple. The Greggs had been Quakers for many generations. Fee's grandparents were Quakers, and, while none of the younger members of the family were Friends, all were aware of the

Quaker connection. (Some of the Greggs used the Quaker familiar forms in correspondence long after they ceased to be members of any Friends' Meeting). Fee himself used his knowledge of Quakers in advancing his argument that those who engage in civil disobedience are still entitled to their basic rights. Fee's pacifism, maintained through a long lifetime of violence, actual and threatened, owed something to his awareness of Quakerism. He was immensely impressed by the pacifist leader, Elihu Burritt, for whom he named one of his sons; in 1854 Fee wrote Gerrit Smith that he agreed that governments should not even prepare for war.[48]

The Quakers had pioneered the antislavery movement, on both sides of the Atlantic; they were famous for their work in the Underground Railroad—and while it was possible in the early 19th century to find racists among the Quakers (as the Grimke sisters learned) and slaveholders who were Friends, the achievements of Quakers in the realm of social justice were outstanding.

The Greggs had been Quakers almost from the beginning; certainly the first known ancestor of the American Greggs was a Friend, a Scotch-Irish emigrant who settled in Chester, Pennsylvania, in 1682. Some of the family have apparently remained in the Quaker fold from that time till the present day—and it was predominantly Quaker for over a century. Fee's maternal grandparents, John Gregg and Sarah Gregg (her maiden name was Gregg), were disowned from the Monthly Meeting in Loudoun County, Virginia, because he fought in the American Revolution. Their daughter Sarah Gregg married John Fee and their son Aaron Gregg married Mary DeMoss and had many children: including John Demoss Gregg (whose branch of the family supported Fee for generations), Elizabeth (who married Vincent Hamilton and became the mother of Matilda Hamilton Fee) and Rebecca (who married Greenbury Griffith Hanson and had John Gregg Hanson, becoming ancestress of still another large group of Gregg descendants who supported Fee's churches and eventually Berea). By the time Fee died, four of his cousins had served as trustees of Berea College, at least four had taught in some branch of the institution and many more had been students.[49]

The conversion of the Greggs began when John G. Fee's mother-in-law, Elizabeth (Gregg) Hamilton, became his very first convert at a protracted meeting in 1848, followed by her brother John D. Gregg, and then her mother, Mary (DeMoss) Gregg, Matilda Fee's grandmother, an old lady almost 70: these people and their families then formed the nucleus of Fee's Bethesda Church. Abolitionism was already familiar to the Greggs for Aaron Gregg (Fee's uncle, Matilda Fee's grandfather) "was very outspoken in his denunciations of slavery," and freed his slaves as they 'earned' it. "This opposition to slavery," Fee remarked, "and his love of liberty passed to [Aaron Gregg's] children and his children's children, almost without exception."[50]

Mary (DeMoss) Gregg did not live long after her conversion, dying in 1853, but Fee called her "one of our best members." He felt that she had died "in the asshurance [sic] of faith." Before her death she had taken care to free the one slave her husband had left her, and "she gave $120 toward the building of the Free Church."[51]

Her daughter Elizabeth (Gregg) Hamilton proved her abolition sentiments in a more dangerous way. Her husband, Vincent Hamilton, had a brother Theodore (first mayor of Augusta, Kentucky), a slaveholder, who "was in transfer business in New Orleans for many years . . . ." He owned a slave, Ed Mofford, who accompanied him on his travels in the U. S. and in Europe. In the 1850's, Theodore Hamilton came back to Bracken County and located in Augusta, where he died, having named his brother Vincent as one of his executors. Theodore's heirs decided to sell Ed Mofford, but no one told him of the decision; Mrs. Theodore Hamilton simply ordered him to go to town with her one day and delivered him to the Sheriff's office, where he was to be sold. But he escaped.

"He ran toward Vincent Hamilton['s house]. Mrs. Hamilton [was] on the porch when Ed came running up. She hid him under the living room floor," and later the same day entertained Mrs. Theodore Hamilton to tea right over him. Mrs. Hamilton and a young Englishman who was visiting [William E. Lincoln?] helped the runaway slave get across the Ohio River.

Later, Vincent Hamilton, who had formed some justifiable suspicions, asked his wife, "'Betsy, do you know what has become of Ed Mofford?' She looked at him inquiringly and said, 'Vincent, ask no questions.'"[52]

Matilda Hamilton Fee: An Abolitionist in the House
"She has been faithful and firm in all my persecutions & privations, has borne them with a cheerful spirit. . . ." John G. Fee, describing his wife.

Matilda Hamilton Fee was a woman worthy of her grandmother and her mother before her. Fee spoke of her as his "cheerful, loving, active" wife; the hardships through which she maintained her good-temper amount *en toto* to a virtual martyrdom; most of what she suffered was, of course, a direct result of marrying John G. Fee. But she knew what she was undertaking; William Goodell describes her as an "excellent, pious woman, . . . as thoroughly abolition as he." She attended the Christian Anti-Slavery Convention of 1850 along with her husband. (Goodell reports her presence with characteristic underlining: "They both attended the Cincinnati Convention.") "If I thought bringing her would hinder me in Christ's work," Fee wrote, "I would not bring her. But she has been faithful and firm in all my persecutions & privations, has borne them with cheerful spirit—believe she will be encouraged and strengthened by seeing something of the anti-slavery world. It will increase her usefulness with her sex, all with whom she shall hereafter mingle."[53]

Throughout their active lives Matilda Fee assumed her share (or more than her share) of the work in the home and in the church. Women in Fee's churches had the then-unusual privilege of praying aloud in meetings with both male and female present, and he had developed a system of having two prayer meetings a month which only women attended; Matilda Fee was in charge of these sessions. Public prayer—even with other women—was so taboo in Madison County that Matilda was at first terribly disappointed to find her accustomed work impossible. "Where we are the sisters will not pray," Fee observed, "Their former training has been all against it."[54]

Much of Matilda Fee's contribution to the chosen work was cooking, cleaning, sewing, washing for an ever-increasing houseful of children and an apparently endless stream of visiting ministers, relatives, colporteurs, teachers, investigators, boarders—and eventually students, foster children and retired veterans of the mission field. It will be impossible to keep track of the comings and goings in the Fee household from the time of their arrival in Berea, but the reader should bear in mind that the Fee's had solemnly decided to do their own work; the effort to imagine what Mrs. Fee's work must have entailed may prove too great. In all subsequent references to the hospitality of the Fee household, one should find an indication of what a commitment to social justice was costing *her*.

"Entertaining strangers fell heavily upon Mr. & Mrs. Fee," Lizzie Rogers reports, "and I hardly see how they could have stood it, only as each new face brought cheer and courage from an outside world. So far from markets it was wonderful how tempting a table Mrs. Fee provided for her guests." The number of guests she entertained might be considered even more wonderful.[55]

Early descriptions of her emphasize Matilda Hamilton Fee's love for the outdoors, her skill as a horsewoman, her adventurous spirit. Rogers writes, "She loved God's out-doors, in which she lived as much as possible, riding her horse as one to the manner born to see the sick, or cultivating her flowers, and always with the free spirit of one who had never been kept in cramped-up quarters." Certainly, she was a brave woman. Once when her husband was threatened with assault if he ventured forth to a preaching engagement, Matilda Fee was the only person courageous enough to accompany him. They rode on horseback to the appointed place where the hoodlums stole their horse, Ben ("the horse her father had given to her") out of the stable, took him into the forest, and tied some pieces of wood to his tail, "thinking he would be greatly frightened and they see some fun." Ben took the matter so gently that they declared he had "religion" and let him go. . . . But Matilda wept when she discovered her much-loved horse was gone. Fee describes another occasion when he was mobbed in her presence. A man on horseback was attempting to hit Fee over the head with a club, but Matilda Fee, also riding, kept interposing herself and her horse between the assailant and his intended victim; she was so skillful and so determined that the ruffian eventually gave up without having struck her husband a single blow.[56]

In Madison County she frequently accompanied Fee to his dangerous assignments, even when she had to carry a babe in arms. On one such trip the Fees were warned that if he returned to Rockcastle County to preach he would be met with a large force and not allowed to speak. Matilda Fee told them that if he was living her husband would come. In another incident, already mentioned, she rode with a group of Bereans in an effort to rescue her husband from still another mob. Fee had been seized in Rockcastle county and taken off. In his *Berea: Its History and Work* Fee related his wife's ordeal:

During the night, a friend, James Waters, came across the country, and came to my house exactly as the clock was striking twelve. My wife recognized his voice and said, "Mr. Fee is taken"; for all night she seemed to have had an apprehension of my condition. Waters, after some minutes of delay, said, with a tremulous voice, "He is in the hands of a violent mob, and where they have gone with him God only knows."

. . . Burritt . . . then a boy eight years old, said, "Mother, we can all pray for Pa." The mother and children, with Miss Tucker, a lady friend from Oberlin, Ohio, all knelt down and offered earnest prayer.

Soon Mrs. W. B. Wright, the wife of our nearest neighbor, was at our house, and promptly offered to go with my wife in search of me; and by dawn of day, twenty-two men were ready with their guns to go with the women.

Waters, who knew the character of the men who had seized me, had expressed the belief that I would not be found alive.

In less than three hours the company was near to the place where I had last been seen in the hands of the mob. Just at this moment a friend rode up and informed them that I had been seen that morning riding quietly toward my home. All quickly retraced their steps and soon found me quite happy with little ones, who had been left in the care of Miss Tucker.[57]

Of her older friend Lizzie Rogers wrote: "Mrs. Fee was a dark pretty brunette, a born Kentuckian as well as her husband, and as brave a woman as ever walked Berea's streets, and worthy to be the wife of a brave man . . . Her example and words were always fearless, and though her black eyes snapped under the injustice of her fellow countrymen, she never flinched in times of danger."[58]

Matilda Fee's good cheer usually remained unshaken, even in most trying times. When Fee returned home after being mobbed with Robert Jones, she was "not apparently surprised nor dismayed." In fact, Fee said, "In these trials my wife was more cheery than I . . . I did not habitually rejoice. . . ."[59]

Matilda Fee was a talented and perceptive person in her own right: mere Mrs. Fee is an injustice to her. Early in the ministry at Berea she had an experience which reveals much of her character and insight. Her own account of the incident presents it best:

Last sabbath evening a very sable slave called at our door, and with that humble politeness which the African appears instinctively to possess, asked me if I could give him a book. I asked him if he was slave; and also if he could read. To each question he replied, "Yes, madam."

I told him for such we have Bibles, and that we are glad to have an opportunity to give them. When I handed him one I asked him to read a verse for me, which he did intelligibly, though his sight was slightly dimmed by age. He turned to Exodus 21:16 and read 'He that stealeth a man and selleth him, or if he be found in his hands, he shall certainly be put to death.' . . . As he repeated his thanks for the Bible, I told him it was not my present but a gift from friends in other states who give money for purchasing bibles for slaves . . .

He said, "Thank them for the Bible."

I asked his name, and that of his master of whom he spoke in terms of kindness, and said he was thankful that his master thought none the less of him because of his knowledge of books. He spoke of his wife and children as he looked for a "Family Record." I was sorry he found none. Slaves, like ourselves, have attachment for their children, and love to have their names to look upon even if they cannot always retain their persons . . .

The slave man stood in a kind of wistful reverie, gazing around at our humble home, then at me and my children around me, asked, "Do you work yourself?" I replied yes. He then asked, "Do you not need help?" I answered sometimes very much. He then spoke of his wife being a good "house-woman," and that she was hired out every year. I told him we believe "the *laborer* is worthy of his hire" and that my husband could not consent to the injustice of paying one person for the services of another. He then exclaimed, "O justice, justice!! What a noble sight is a just man!" And as he raised his toil hardened hands, looking at them said, "I could work almost without tiring if I could receive regular wages as other men do."[60]

Fee urged his wife to write of this meeting for publication and the story duly appeared under the title "Thank Them for the Bible" in the *11th Annual Report of the American Missionary Association* (1857). By nature, Fee wrote, "she has a better talent for writing than I have—much wish she would prepare occasional articles for the press. Such might do good & do her good."[61]

In the life they had chosen there would seldom be time or energy left over for any such project. In a remarkable tribute, Fee said he found in his wife, "affection, sympathy, courage, cheer, activity, frugality and endurance, which few could have combined, and which greatly sustained me in the dark and trying hours that attended most of our pathway. "This much," he added, "is due to truth . . . . "[62]

Fee's Children and Other Abolitionists from the Cradle
"We [children] supposed everyone had mobs." Laura Fee.

Throughout the Fee's pre-Civil War experience at Berea they had three small children to think of—and eventually a new baby as well. In 1854, when Clay issued his invitation to Fee, Laura was 9, Burritt was 5 and Howard 3.

When Lizzie Rogers first met the Fees in 1858, Laura, Burritt, Howard and Tappan (then a baby) "comprised the Fee family, and a bright, happy family it was, planted on that hostile soil. The parents' hearts were kept bright by the noise of happy children's voices, and the children lived on as most children do, feeling secure in their father's home, and I think gave little heed to the dangers, even if they knew of them, that weighed upon older folk."[63]

Lizzie Rogers paints a charming picture of Fee's children, and her estimation of their bright heedlessness is probably true, as far as it goes. Laura Fee herself said, "We children never thought anything more about mobs than about thunderstorms. We supposed everybody had mobs!". But like offspring of many 19th century reformers, Fee's children were duly apprised of the large issues confronting them in the world. Both Fee and his wife took their children everywhere with them, frequently into situations of conflict and danger. When Matilda Fee visited Juliet Miles in prison she informed even her smallest children of the black woman's tragedy. " . . . My infant boy," Matilda wrote, "comes and looking earnestly into my face asks, 'Mama, is poor aunt Juliet in the dark jail yet?'" Significantly, Matilda Fee provided a history of Juliet's unhappy experience for the "Children's Department" in the *American Missionary* magazine, stating that she had not told the children such a story to "sadden [their] joyous and bird-like sympathies, but to further enlist [their] sympathies in the great cause of human freedom."[64]

The "Children's Department" in the *American Missionary* must qualify as one of the most sepulchral, morally earnest columns ever published, full of news from world-fronts of the abolitionist battle. The "Children's Department" avoided none of the issues and none of the troubles of the day—it contained no humor, nothing trivial, and nothing *special* for its young audience, except a slight simplification of language. Children, it constantly reminded the reader, were like everyone else, making eternal choices every day—and they were expected to begin early preparing themselves for service in God's Kingdom. "Every Child Can Do Something" one issue annnounced, rather more cheerfully than usual; other titles appearing for childish consumption in the *American Missionary* included such items as "The Dying Child's Gifts," "The Little Slave Girl," "An Orphan's Faith," " . . . When I'm to Die," and "Children Leading Their Parents to Christ." The AMA was not alone in approaching the young with reforming zeal—books such as *The Slaves' Friend* and *The Child's Antislavery Book* were written especially for youthful abolitionists. In August 1859, the AMA announced an increase of Children's and Young Peoples' Anti-Slavery Associations, extolling this growth as a sign of great promise, when the young . . . are uniting in this holy enterprise." The abolitionists, Fee among them, regarded their children as "potential footsoldiers in the vanguard of righteousness." And, typically, reformers had no intenton of exempting children from adult care, nor from religious duties.[65]

Fee baptized his eldest son Burritt when the boy was seven years old. "At five," this precocious child "would read the Scriptures and pray with the family. He knew what trust in Christ was and the symbolic import of his burial in baptism." Fee baptized all his children on their professions of faith in Christ (except Tappan, who was not yet four years old)—all were baptized between the ages of ten and eleven. "Early in life children may be trained," Fee remarked, "trained to love and serve the lord." "I sought even in their names," he wrote, referring to Burritt, Howard and Tappan, "to give them incentive to righteousness and humanity."[66]

It should come as no surprise that Fee's children began their own missionary labors at extremely early ages: both Laura and Burritt became formally involved in their father's work while they were teenagers—she teaching at Berea before the school's official opening in 1866, he (also teaching) at Camp Nelson before he was 16 (another of Fee's sons, Howard Samuel, became principal of Ariel Academy, the school Fee founded at Camp Nelson, while he was still in his twenties). Nor should it surprise us to realize that Berea students, frequently very young ones, were considered prime targets for conversion and what we might call indoctrination: an abolitionist school, quite simply, was designed to foster abolitionism, even among toddlers. (See Appendix 1: Fee's Children)

The abolitionist attitude toward children was in keeping with the Oberlin complex of ideas: the assumption that the world could be improved by any individual's work and dedication, even a child's. In addition, the family itself had become virtually a "sacred" institution by the mid-19th century: one reform writer of the period stated, "The predicted renovation of the world will be largely secured by [the family]": William Goodell, a great influence on Fee's thinking, agreed with that lofty estimation of the family's potential. Fee himself certainly prepared his own family, wife and children as fellow missionaries, expecting their active support, informing them of his concerns, soliciting their contributions, training them for "usefulness."[67]

Manual Labor and Revivalism
"I have heard slaveholders and professing Christians, too, say 'It would be just as right to enslave white *men as black men, if the law would allow it." John G. Fee.*

Although conversion was his most dramatic experience at Lane Seminary, Fee undoubtedly made some other important discoveries there: for example, manual labor and revivalism. Lane Seminary was chartered as a manual labor school, founded on the principles pioneered by George W. Gale and John Frost at Oneida Manual Labor School in New York; many of the Lane Rebels, including their leader, Theodore Weld, had studied at Oneida before coming to Cincinnati. The principle of manual labor education was adopted not simply to display the dignity of work; it provided an opportunity for students to pay for education by their own efforts, to become self-reliant, healthy and practically knowledgeable about the world, and, for many of its proponents, participation in the manual labor movement also signaled their willingness to do for themselves the work that slaves might be forced to do: an identification with the poor, an elimination of class distinctions.

Manual labor and abolitionism had been connected almost from the beginning at Oneida Institute. The students there organized the first abolitionist society in New York in June 1833. The movement to make manual labor respectable was part of an impulse to make *laborers*, especially black ones, respectable too. In many places in the United States, particularly in the South, manual labor was not considered a proper occupation for a gentleman—among some slaveholders the enjoyment of leisure time had developed to a fine art; in other classes this was called laziness.[68]

Fee's exposure to a manual labor school had practical effects in his own life. In 1845, he wrote to the secretaries of the American Home Missionary Association: "I & my wife will do our own work as a matter of duty & live as economically as possible [so] that we may preach the gospel to the poor. . . ." After the first year of their experiment in economy and self-sufficiency Fee reported, "We have lived upon little, $260 and can yet live upon little. My wife nurses her own child, does her own sewing, cooking, washing and scrubbing. I have hands that laboured along side with my Father's slaves until I was eighteen. With me yet labour is honorable." Fee and his young wife, both children of slaveholders, would never be waited on again; the decision to do their own work, a decision which they lived by as long as they were physically able, would probably cost both of them as much as many more dramatic commitments in their lives.[69]

"We would dignify labor," he wrote, "by the work of our hands." During their first year in Lewis County, the Fees lived in a little cottage consisting of one room, 16 feet square, with a small bookcase on one side, a small cupboard on the other, their firstborn child Laura in a cradle in the middle, their bed behind. On Sunday evenings they extended a plank from one chair to another and made a bench for the congregation who came there for preaching. "Monday [mornings]," Fee wrote, "whilst I made fires, fed the horse and milked the cow, my wife swept out dirt from previous muddy shoes and scrubbed out stains from tobacco spit as far as she could. The one end to be attained, at whatever sacrifice was the lodgement of fundamental truth in the minds of the people." The juxtaposition of "low' work and lofty ideal is characteristic in Fee's thought—he was a practical egalitarian.[70]

Fee's anti-caste formulations were not simply directed against slavery, but against economic and social inequalities in the free white system. In *Colonization* Fee asserts that caste

> makes war upon all man, all men—the same color and all colors. It despises the laboring man of the same color in India; it despises the laboring man of the same color (white) in Europe; it despises the laboring man of different color (black) here; . . . 'bodily labor must be disreputable for the mere influence of association [with slavery]. Hence it is, that white laborers at the South are styled 'mean whites,' and Robert Breckenridge, of Kentucky, calls white laborers, 'white negroes.'

Taking the matter a step further, Fee maintains that slavery for blacks is perilously close to enslavement for whites as well. "I have heard slaveholders,' he says, "and professing Christians, too, say 'It would be just as right to enslave *white* men as black men, if the law would allow it."[71]

American revivalism—as we know it—was virtually an invention of Charles Grandison Finney. In the 1820's and '30's his new measure revival meetings led to the dramatic conversion of thousands of people; the sweeping religious fervor he inspired led to so many local revivals in Western New York that the region came to be known as the Burned Over District, scorched clean by fires of Christian fervor. Finney's theology was widely influential. His "work and the way he understood the gospel 'released a mighty impulse toward social reform' that shook the nation and helped destroy slavery." Finney's views were crucial in forming the program of the Lane Rebels, both in their conclusions and in their actions.[72]

According to Finney, human beings were created by God as free moral agents. By definition, a *free* moral agent could not belong to someone else; on the other hand, a free *moral* agent was responsible for his or her own choices and actions, "responsible and therefore able to stop sinning." It made sense on this view to demand that a sinner repudiate sin immediately, once sin was recognized. For example, once a slaveowner was made to see slaveholding as a sin, he or she ought to take action instantly. "Immediate emancipation was the positive statement of the logical consequence of the idea of the free, responsible individual required to quit sinning immediately."

Another basic aspect of Finney's thought was his emphasis on Christian activism—conversion, on his terms, meant not only immediate abandonment of sin, but also immediate adoption of some useful mode of conduct. Benevolence was moral exercise, the application of the will in God's service *willingly*. If the convert were truly converted he or she would "take right ground on any subject that might be proposed," such as "education of ministers, for missions, for moral reforms, for slaves"—and beyond that, the convert would immediately begin to express "benevolence in action." He would "*aim at being useful in the highest degree possible*." 'Usefulness' was, indeed, the primary virtue extolled by American Protestant thinkers of this era.[73]

It was theoretically possible for dedicated Christians to reach perfection through unlimited exercise of such benevolence—when sufficient numbers had attained this goal the millenial age would be ushered in. So individual men and women, in their own spheres of action, were working for the coming of the kingdom—their energies dedicated, poured out for God's ultimate purpose. "God had given men and women a role in shaping society and . . . nothing had to be accepted as it was."[74]

The direct, forceful application of Finney's revival theology to antislavery principles was made by Theodore Weld, a Finney's convert, and Weld's application emerged most clearly at Lane Seminary, where it shaped John G. Fee's conversion experience a few years later. Fee's remarks about his own "selfishness" are a confirmation that Finney revival techniques were applied to him: Finney taught that the "essence of sin was selfishness," which directly contradicted God's character of benevolence, a character that was to be reflected in the lives of converts, "doing good" and becoming "useful." Fee's language, as well as his practices, was always to reflect this influence on his thought.[75]

Throughout his long career, Fee espoused his own doctrines of free will, freedom, responsibility, immediate rejection of sin, benevolence in action, perfectionism and millenial expectations. He was also a revivalist in action, conducting innumerable "protracted meetings" designed to effect conversions to abolitionism. Finney had popularized the protracted meeting that continued for several days or weeks and employed the "anxious bench," a row of seats in front of the church for those under "conviction" of sin. All Fee's revivalistic techniques were simply Finney's New Measures—the great evangelist's means of conducting protracted meetings, which had flourished first in the 1830's in the Burned-Over District. These measures included impassioned preaching, of course, but usually not from the permanent minister of a given church (visiting evangelists became very popular in this era—intinerant ministers were frequently "played up" to the disadvantage of the settled minister, under the assumption "that special efforts under a person of particular talents could create a keener sympathy than the ordinary course of events could achieve.) Another New Measure was the use of frequent and prolonged prayer meetings, at which women as well as men could participate: during these meetings the spiritual few prayed earnestly for the conversion of everyone else. Pastoral visitation to all people in the neighborhood to inquire after the state of their souls was also among the New Measures—preachers did not call on members of their own congregation only, since the whole thrust of a protracted meeting was to rouse "a community-wide anxiety over the inhabitants' spiritual state." Fee applied all the New Measures in his abolitionist preaching.[76]

Fee's Thinking
"I believe nothing but the gospel of Christ, faithfully preached and applied to all known wrongs, will save from the calamities of general vice and the sure judgements of God." John G. Fee.

His evangelical Christianity formed the basis for all his antislavery activities. "The linking of conversion and Christian commitment to a socially relevant cause is the clue to antislavery careers such as Weld's. . . . John Gregg Fee on coming to Lane Seminary long after the abolitionist exodus discovered this nexus for himself."[77]

He left Lane espousing the ideas of the Rebels, and particularly of their leader, Theodore Weld; many of these, to be sure, were applications of Finney's theology to the slavery question. Weld's career at Lane, although very brief, had been both intense and memorable, but he had left Cincinnati long before Fee arrived, and it is doubtful that the two men ever met; Weld's most active contributions to the antislavery movement were over before Fee's career ever began. In fact, Weld withdrew permanently from public involvement in the movement in 1843, the year Fee's career began.[78]

Still, any serious or even curious student at Weld's former school might want to investigate his thought; certainly Campbell and White had fallen under the influence of his message. Probably Fee read Weld's books, but since Weld's two most important works were published anonymously, Fee may have absorbed Weld without knowing whose doctrines he was following. Maybe Fee's real reaction to his seminary training was a rebellion as deep and thorough-going as the student movement of 1834. After seminary, when Fee emerges as a thinker—writing, lecturing, preaching—his ideas resemble in almost every respect the thought of Theodore Weld, as if Fee himself had become the last and most radical of the Lane Rebels.

In Fee's pamphlet, "Colonization. The Present Scheme of Colonization Wrong, Delusive and Retards Emancipation," he states that "much of this tract is an appeal to conscience and Christian principle," because, for example, the British never made any headway in the abolition of the slave trade or of slavery "till [the cause] was taken up by religious men, prosecuted as a concern of the soul, with reference to eternity, with motives drawn from the cross of Christ." In dozens of letters Fee enunciates his belief that the fight against slavery must be a religious one, designed to rouse the conscience of slaveholder and non-slaveholder alike.[79]

In the AMA 6th Annual Report Fee stated: "The American Missionary Association is doing a great good, not merely to the slave, but also to the slaveholder and non-slaveholder, in calling out and sustaining a class of ministers and churches who will not by sophism, plaster over any sin, nor by silence leave souls in the dark regarding it . . . ." Fee's first trip to Madison County in 1853 confirmed his belief that only Christian principles could be effective in the moral war against slavery. "Never have I been more fully persuaded of the necessity of a whole gospel," he stated,

> than during this tour [to Madison, Rockcastle and Jessamine Counties]. All over this fertile and lovely country, intellectual and *moral* decay are as manifest as the noonday sun. That slavery, by engendering pride, caste, cruelty, oppression, fraud, and licentiousness, is the cause of this decay, is undeniable. And, under God, I believe nothing but the gospel of Christ, faithfully preached and *applied* to all known wrongs, will save from the calamities of general vice and the sure judgements of God; but this will reform this or any other people. The history of the past shows that neither politics nor revolution correct the moral wrongs of society.[80]

Fee's insistence on the religious solution was related to the importance of freedom of speech and press. "The hope of success," he said, "lies with the people. These are showing daily more willingness to hear and read. The continual agitation of the question of slavery in Church and State has awakened in them a desire to hear and read for themselves." This awakening of interest—perhaps political in nature—Fee called "the whitening of the harvest," an image drawn straight from parables of Jesus.[81]

Later (in 1855) Fee wrote descrying the impression made in recent newspapers that freedom of speech in central Kentucky depended on one man:

Cassius Clay. " . . . Free speech," Fee protested, "depends not upon C. M. Clay, John G. Fee, or any other man, but, under God, upon the *virtue yet remaining in the hearts of the people.* As early as 1846 Fee had written: "We want facts—truth burning continually before the minds of the people—the whole people—or we cannot expect them to be aroused to action."[82]

The most radical of Fee's basic religious and political views was his egalitarian attitude toward blacks. His pamphlet on "Colonization' (published 1853) develops a bold argument against plans for colonization—using blacks' equality to whites as a major point. Fee states that blacks have the same potential for development as whites, as much intelligence and capability. He maintains that there is no such thing as "natural aversion" to black skin; prejudice is a sin based on pride, not an unavoidable condition of life. He faces squarely his opponents' view that equality for the blacks will result in intermarriage between races. "Better," Fee says, "that we have black faces than black hearts." He goes on to say that "[amalgamation] will cease to be regarded as a crime" when black people are sufficiently "esteemed" for intermarriage to take place. "The colored man," he wrote, "is none the less a man because he is 'colored.'" In his *Anti-Slavery Manual* Fee also presents a detailed argument for the equality of blacks and whites. His behavior, as we shall see in later chapters, was very similar to Weld's; Fee attended black churches, participated in black festivities, religious and otherwise, made a conscious and effective effort to treat all people as equals.[83]

In a letter to the *True American* as early as 1845, Fee wrote, "The means to be employed [in converting Kentucky to antislavery] are the presentation of truth, the force of moral suasion, and the constitutional right of the ballot box." The emphasis upon free discussion in the Lane Rebel's statement of Reasons is clearly also a central part of Fee's doctrine.[84]

In 1851, Fee published his booklet "The Sinfulness of Slaveholding shown by Appeals to Reason and Scripture," in which he advances arguments against slavery derived from the Bible. The ideas he deduces from the Old Testament are exactly similar to those developed in Weld's *Bible Against Slavery*. Both men contend that the essence of slavery is reducing people to articles of property, treating people like things. "Hog and hominy," Fee writes, "are no compensation for lost manhood." Both also argue that the Hebrew bondservant was not at all analogous to the American slave, so that Jewish regulations have no bearing on the situation in the United States. Both men present the case in detail, with much attention to precise interpretations of Hebrew words and phrases. Fee's works deals with both the Old and New Testaments, unlike Weld's which contains only Old Testament references. (His work was supplemented in 1839 by Beriah Green in a work entitled *The Chattel Principle the Abhorrence of Jesus Christ and the Apostles: or No Refuge for American Slavery in the New Testament,* a work apparently designed to convince by its title alone.)[85]

Echoing the introduction to Theodore Weld's *Slavery as It Is,* Fee maintained that slavery was inherently sinful no matter how humane it might appear. "It is oppression still," he wrote, "a violation of the Law of Love." And he used repeatedly Weld's idea of asking a man to imagine himself threatened with enslavement—or, more commonly, his wife and children in the same danger. Fee had himself personally observed some of the more barbaric cruelties of slavery. He wrote: "I have seen women tied to a tree or a timber and whipped with cow-hides on their bare backs until their shrieks would seem to rend the very heavens. I have seen a man, a father, guilty only of the crime of absenting himself from work for a day and two nights, on his return home whipped with a cow-hide on his bare flesh until his blood ran to his heels." Thousands of slaves, Fee maintained, had endured similar treatment—he cited a case in Pulaski, a county near Madison, of a man who had been whipped to death for going to visit his wife in the middle of the night. "Yet this torture of the body was the least part of the agony of slavery," Fee wrote, "The acme of the crime was on the soul. The crushing of human hearts, sundering the ties of husband and wife, parent and child, shrouding all of manhood in the long night of despair—the crime was on the soul!"[86]

Finally, Fee shared the radical abolitionist view of American churches; speaking of himself and his fellow reformers, Fee stated:

> in every community where [we] raised [our] voices against slavery,
> caste, secretism, rum-selling, any popular vice, immediately
> members of the sects [as he called all denominations] would be
> found shrinking from the proclamation of truth and the utterance of
> their own convictions, lest by so doing they should peril the safety
> of their sects, or denominations. With the semblance of piety they
> would say, "Peace is best," and thus smother truth. [We] also saw
> that everywhere the shelves of libraries and book-stores were
> bending beneath the volumes written on theological dogmas, whilst

"truth (practical truth) was fallen in the streets. . . . Ministers were
spending their energies in zealous debates and fervid, eloquent
pleadings over the shibboleths of party, whilst the slave was
groaning in his bondage, and the masters were deluded with false
hopes and a perverted Bible.[87]

No claim can be made for Fee as an original thinker; but his dedication to
applying radical abolitionist principles in the new context of the South might be
considered as significant as conceiving the ideas in the first place. In addition, Fee
held one very important concept that differentiated his views. Partly because he
was himself a Southerner, the son of slaveholders, but mainly because he was a
devoted Christian, Fee maintained a more charitable attitude toward the people
below the Mason-Dixon line than most of his fellow abolitionists espoused—
including Weld. Fee described what missionaries to the South should be: "We
want ministers who have much of the spirit—tenderness yet faithfulness of Christ."
And what they should not be:

Some men seem to oppose slavery because they love to show how
daring they can be in opposing a terrible and dangerous thing.
Others seem to oppose slavery because they hate slavery and abhor
slaveholders; and with some the sensibilities seem to have been [so]
deeply impressed with the horror of slavery (rather than the love of
Christ) that they have but one topic; at least all others soon terminate
or converge in this one.

Fee believed the Christian abolitionist should promote the end of slavery for *love*
of slaveholders, as well as for slaves. "I tremble," he said,

in view of the ultimate fate of slaveholders. If they shall yet banish
from their midst a gospel of impartial love—the only gospel that can
save them from ruinous vices—the only gospel that can give the
hope of a peaceful termination of existing evils, and prevent the
sundering of the ties that bind our nation together, slavery must go
out in blood. . . . Those who will not hear the truth, but deliberately
rush on in wrong doing, God will cut down. [88]

American Missionary Association
"Endeavor particularly to discountenance slavery. . . ." Directive from the AMA.

The American Missionary Association was founded in 1846 at Albany,
New York, "by the merger of several small societies of Congregational origin who

shared a missionary commitment to nonwhite peoples [including American Indians] and a strong antislavery bent." It might never have come into existence if the American Home Missionary Society had not been under attack for its support of slaveholders.[89]

Promoted by the Tappan brothers, especially Lewis, the AMA united three earlier groups: the Western Evangelical Society (of Oberlin), the Committee for the West Indies, an mission which had been working among the Jamaica freedmen for almost a decade, and the Union Missionary Society, with a mission in Mendi, Africa (home of the *Amistad* slaves). "The new organization supervised the Indian Mission in Minnesota, the Mendi Mission . . . , the Jamaica mission and missionary work among the Negroes in Canada and the United States."[90]

The Constitution of the new association provided for a strictly evangelical organization and set forth a statement of beliefs, affirming

> the guilty and lost condition of all men without a Saviour; the Supreme Deity, incarnation and atoning sacrifice of Jesus Christ, the only Saviour of the world; the necessity of regeneration by the Holy Spirit; repentance, faith and holy obedience, [to achieve] salvation; the immortality of the soul; and the retributions of the judgment in the eternal punishment of the wicked and the salvation of the righteous.

The evangelical foundation of the AMA is not surprising since "Lane rebels had played significant roles in each of the societies which formed the Association." Fifteen of the Rebels were involved in the AMA in one way or another, some of them for many years. Many of them were among the Rebels who had moved to Oberlin; people from that institution eventually controlled the AMA almost completely.[91]

At its inception the AMA's purpose was "to send the Gospel to those portions of our own and other countries which are destitute of it, or which present open and urgent fields of effort." Members were required to profess evangelical Christianity as defined above, and to align themselves against slavery and other immoral practices. They also had to contribute money. In all its practices the AMA was to "endeavor particularly to discountenance slavery . . . . "[92]

Three men exercised much of the power and influence of the AMA in its early years: Lewis Tappan, Simeon S. Jocelyn and George Whipple. Lewis

Tappan, the virtual founder of the AMA, was a Christian businessman, who kept the financial affairs of the complex organization in working order; serving as Treasurer, he raised money, paid bills, organized annual Conventions, arranged hospitality for missionaries on furlough, and gave advice (even to Fee). Upon hearing that Fee had allowed some of his followers to bear arms, Tappan advised Fee to rely on God alone to keep him safe; he also urged Fee not to seek legal redress when he was persecuted.

Tappan's philanthropic work in reform projects had been multitudinous before he ever began his labors with the AMA (he was almost 60 at the time). His influence in the realm of evangelical abolitionism was so all-pervasive that many modern scholars classify the abolitionists who fell under his influence as Tappanites. (Mabee, in *Black Freedom*, refers to John G. Fee repeatedly as a Tappanite abolitionist.) Much of the efficiency and success of the AMA was due to his hard work and powers of organization. His age, dignity and manifold connections in the antislavery world lent a sense of stability and "rightness" to the AMA; Fee admired Lewis Tappan immensely—named a son after him, sought his advice and counsel, paid him the respect befitting an older, more experienced leader from whom he could expect guidance and support.[93]

Simeon S. Jocelyn, who held various offices in the AMA for 30 years, was not business-like as Tappan was, but "sweet-natured to a fault." As Chairman of the *Amistad* Committee he had assisted in organizing the AMA. His reform career had begun when he became pastor of a Negro church in New Haven under the control of the American Board of Home Missions. in 1829, he and Arthur Tappan (Lewis's older brother) had proposed the organization of a black college at New Haven, and he had called a National convention of free Negroes in support of this project. Although the college failed (and very quickly too), Jocelyn's convention has been called the first "organized expression of negro solidarity in the nation." Jocelyn's predisposal to sympathize with Fee's Berea project is clear—to his native sympathy he could add some understanding of the problems involved in a white man's ministry to a black population.[94]

But probably the most important member of the AMA was George Whipple, who became Corresponding Secretary shortly after the organization was founded and stayed in office until his death in 1876. "Besides editing the *American Missionary,* Whipple helped establish policy, selected missionaries, settled disputes, inspected missions, and even sent money out of his own pocket to aid missionaries in financial distress." Throughout his career he "adhered to the idea that antislavery could be implemented best through, and as a part of, evangelicalism." Whipple's life well illustrates the myriad interconnections between people, movements and institutions of evangelical reform. Whipple had been a student at Oneida Institute (1827-31), taught school in Kentucky (1831-33), and at Lane Seminary (1833-4). He had become the Lane Rebels' principle teacher in the interrum after their withdrawal from seminary and before their exodus to Oberlin. Still with many of the Lane men, he had enrolled in Oberlin College himself in 1835 and graduated from the seminary in 1836, working as an antislavery agent (one of Weld's "70") in his vacations from school in 1835-37. By the fall of 1836 he was principal of Oberlin's Preparatory Department; two years later he accepted the professorship of mathematics there, a post he retained until 1847, when he became Secretary of the AMA.[95]

As Corresponding Secretary George Whipple received literally hundreds of letters from Fee and his associates; to Whipple were addressed the reports, complaints, bills, character assassinations, demands, counterdemands, tirades, harangues and excuses which the work in Kentucky entailed. For 30 years, Whipple was at the receiving end of a barrage of letters; anyone who has read through the AMA Archives collection from Kentucky for 1847-76 will agree that George Whipple had one of the hardest jobs in the whole enterprise.

For Fee personally Whipple was a perfect mentor—he had even had experience teaching in Kentucky—his faith was unquestionable, his tact and judgement firm and unshakeable, his generosity beyond measure, and his patience simply unbelievable. But Whipple was much more than a recipient of irritating correspondence. In himself he represented some of the best elements of the reform movements in antislavery, education and evangelicalism—precisely the interests which Fee wished to combine in his own work. The journal he edited for the AMA, the *American Missionary*, served the abolition cause well for many years. Fee's letters, punctuated correctly for the first time and vasted improved stylistically, emerged year after year, and much of his more formal writing also appeared first in the pages of Whipple's magazine. Through the years the *American Missionary* built up a sizable number of readers who were aware of Fee's ministry and especially his work at Berea; in the East and North in abolitionist circles, a tiny village in central Kentucky became a very well-known place.

For Fee, the AMA provided more than financial support, more even than fellow workers in the field. In many respects, practically and spiritually, the AMA held the religious rebel in a wider Christian context, much as a denominational church might have done. His actual congregations were small and scattered; even at the height of his pre-Civil War career, none of his congregations ever averaged much more than 100 people, and they were usually much smaller. These little groups were never simply discrete entities, however, because the AMA had charge of them all; even when its function did not exceed advising and consenting, the larger organization maintained the coherence of otherwise disconnected and relatively ineffective enterprises. As long as he was part of the AMA, Fee was participating in a broader Christian plan to evangelize the world, not conducting a private campaign.

The AMA arranged a number of speaking/fund-raising tours for Fee, giving him exposure to a large number of influential figures in the abolition movement, sending him to abolition centres like Oberlin, Syracuse and Peterboro, New York. He visited all three of those places in the summer of 1855, as well as Hartford, Connecticut; Springfield, Massachusetts; Albany and Buffalo, New York; Erie, Pennsylvania, and Cleveland, Ohio. He did not always inspire people to contribute sustantially to his cause, however. At one church, the minister did not propose taking up a collection after Fee spoke ("Well," Fee wrote resignedly, "it was his own house."), and toward the end of his journey Fee discovered one counterfeit dollar among the donations. In Oberlin, Pres. Finney gave Fee the opportunity to address the whole student body, pressing the claims of the AMA—and there many of Berea's future workers heard him speak for the first time.[96]

In practical terms, the AMA put Fee and his work in contact with the whole realm of evangelical abolitionism. On September 26, 1855, Fee complained to Jocelyn about receiving clothes from North Brookfield, Massachusetts, which "did not fit." Useful or not, those clothes represented the power of the AMA to provide Fee with a network of supporting connections. Money—eventually lots of money—clothes, advice, good will, encouragement and workers would come to Berea from far-distant places, from rather unlikely corners of the United States. Funds for rebuilding a burned schoolhouse in Rockcastle County, Kentucky, might (and did) come from a church in Union City, Michigan, or from the Ladies' Antislavery Society of Dover, New Hampshire.[97]

In addition, Fee's intellectual life was fed by the *American Missionary* magazine, bringing him news of other workers in other realms, developing new ideas and arguments, presenting facts and findings from many corners of the world. It provided him with a forum, after the *True American* was no longer available—a stimulus to write and study, but also a continuing motivation to hold himself accountable to other Christians with the same goals.

Fee's spiritual life must have been enhanced by his relationship to George Whipple, Simeon Jocelyn and Lewis Tappan, to whom he confided problems, prayer requests, anxieties, fears, doubts, hopes and occasional triumphs. Religiously, Fee had taken himself out of the old slaveholding context completely; his spiritual life now was not interconnected with the status quo in the South, but with the lives of hundreds of people with whom he actually shared his convictions—evangelical abolitionists, represented by the AMA.

Not everything Fee received from the AMA was wholly beneficial. In December 1857, living as usual on the edge of penury, the Fees received a missionary barrel, which they had been awaiting eagerly for weeks—it contained some old woman's underwear, a number of patched tablecloths, "nothing for the children, some 12 gentlemen's collars not worth twenty-five cents," a large bundle of rags, and, to top it all off, "one or two undergarments ripped open before and down one arm as when taken off of a very sick or dead body."[98]

Abolitionist Conventions
"Resolved: that the friends of a pure Christianity ought to separate themselves from all slaveholding churches. . . ." Resolution no. 9, Christian Antislavery Committee, 1850.

Although John G. Fee considered his primary ministry to be preaching to specific congregations, he was always interested and involved in the world of public affairs: through writing and publishing, and in local, state and national political activities, he sought to reach wider audiences and to make greater contributions. Fee participated, for example, in a four-day debate on the divine authority for slavery with a preacher-lawyer-county judge in Campbell County, Kentucky, which was conducted with "great decorum and undisturbed interest."[99]

As delegate from Lewis County, Fee met with such eminent Kentuckians as Senator Joseph R. Underwood, Henry Clay (delegate from Bourbon County), Robert J. Breckenridge (Fayette County) and Cassius Clay (Madison) at the State Emancipation Convention held in Frankfort, April 1849, as preparation for the Constitutional Convention in October. After some disagreement about a method of emancipation, the delegates adopted a resolution that slavery ought not to be perpetuated in Kentucky, and recommended that importation of slaves be outlawed and gradual emancipation authorized. The Emancipation Convention had no noticeable effect on the new Kentucky constitution, ratified in May 1850—which stated that no slave could be emancipated in Kentucky without being sent out of the state, while no free Negroes might emigrate into Kentucky at all: the 1850 constitution established the right of property as "before and higher than any other," and clearly identified slaves as property. Thus slavery was much stronger under the new constitution. This early failure in political action did not discourage Fee from later involvement, although his ultimate antislavery goals for Kentucky were even farther away in 1850 than they had been earlier.[100]

Fee's participation in Christian antislavery conventions exemplifies his involvement in a large-scale national movement, with connections beyond the borders of Kentucky. In addition, it is important to discover who his colleagues were, not in the field, but in the upper echelons of abolitionism: the writers, thinkers, theorizers, lecturers, ministers who shaped Fee's brand of antislavery doctrine, because Fee himself was the centre of the whole abolitionist movement in Kentucky. What he thought influenced the thinking and behavior of hundreds of people in the state. It has already been established that Fee's affinities are with a whole intellectual-religious community. Finney's revivalism, the Manual Labor movement, Theodore Weld, the Lane Rebellion, Oberlin and Oberlin College, Jonathan Blanchard, Galesburg and Knox College, the Tappan brothers, the free church movement, the AMA, William Goodell, evangelical abolitionism—all are held together by manifold interconnections in a complex fabric of relationships and influences. Not a single idea, but a system, not a single person, but a community of people, not a single organization, but many—all fed into Fee's experience. Through him and others who were to follow him, Kentucky's antislavery activists received a multifaceted but coherent heritage of ideas and goals.

One of the earliest conventions Fee attended was the "Southwestern Anti-Slavery Convention" in Cincinnati, April 1845. There he met Salmon P. Chase, one of the greatest of political abolitionists, serving with him on the committee of resolutions. There he heard George W. Clark sing, "Be free! O Man, be free!" Fee did not meet Elihu Burritt at this convention, but he was so deeply impressed by hearing a letter from Burritt read aloud that he later named his firstborn son for the leader of the peace movement. From this convention Fee returned to preach his first antislavery sermon in Lewis County.[101]

The Christian Anti-Slavery Convention of 1850 was held in Cincinnati (April 17-20), called by "a committee of fifteen including twelve clergymen of eight different denominations. One hundred and fifty delegates attended from most of the Middle and North-western states." Fee served in several capacities, as one of the vice-presidents, on the committee of resolutions and on the committee appointed to plan another convention for the next year. The latter group included George Whipple, Lewis Tappan, Jonathan Blanchard and William Goodell, among others.[102]

William Goodell, in a personal letter (September 14, 1850) described the meetings of 1850 at some length:

> A more interesting Convention, I have seldom if ever attended. Some from the east had travelled nearly a thousand miles, to get [there]. Others, from the West, more than a thousand (as the route lay). All the Western states were represented there. Many Western subscribers to my paper, whom I had never seen, with some of whom I had corresponded, came up & spoke with me, begun [sic] acquaintance, anew. Among the rest was John G. Fee of Kentucky . . . .

The most interesting incident at the convention in Goodell's estimation was—understandably enough—his own speech, delivered spontaneously and in unique circumstances. As he began to speak at an afternoon session, Goodell noticed Dr. Lyman Beecher and his son-in-law Professor Calvin E. Stowe (husband of Harriet Beecher Stowe) in the audience. The presence of these bulwarks of Lane Seminary—Beecher was president, Stowe on the faculty—well-known for their conservative positions, aroused Goodell to a pitch of denunciatory zeal. Without naming names he referred specifically to Lyman Beecher, mentioning venerable fathers who 25 years earlier had preached the coming Millenium and urged the faithful on. "Thousands in the churches, responding to the summons," Goodell said,

> had attempted to 'prepare the way of the Lord, by removing human chattelhood out of the way & by demanding Bibles & religious liberty for slaves—and then, the pioneers of the army of the Millenium turned back, afraid of "the excitement" (!) complaining that the assailants of Satan's kingdom went "too fast & too far"—& that American Slavery must not be disturbed till the reflex influence of the Colony at Liberia—two hundred years hence, [double underlining] should begin [d. u.], gradually & without any "excitement' to melt the fetters of the slaves!

Thus, Goodell charged, immediatism had been replaced by the most pernicious gradualism, with abolitionists resigned to wait two centuries before seeing the end of slavery, merely in order to maintain "the peace of the church," "the primacy of ecclesiastical bodies," and patronage and endowments for "theological seminaries." Upon hearing these denunciations, Lyman Beecher, who was sitting close enough for the speaker to scrutinize him, "changed his position, sinking back into his pew corner, and covering up his face with both hands, in the sight of scores who took notice of it." At this moment, Calvin Stowe made good his escape, but apparently Beecher remained, as Goodell continued his jeremiad, speaking over an hour.[103]

It would be surprising to find that Lyman Beecher ever attended another Christian Antislavery Convention. But it comes as no surprise to learn that the proceedings of the Convention approved the doctrine of antislavery secession. This proposal, Resolution no. 9, was presented by the Rev. John G. Fee.

> Resolved:—That the friends of a pure Christianity ought to separate themselves from all slaveholding churches, and all churches, ecclesiastical bodies, and Missionary Associations, that are not fully divorced from slaveholding; and we, who may still be in connection with such bodies, pledge ourselves that we will separate ourselves from them, unless they will speedily separate themselves from all support of, or fellowship with slaveholding.

The resolution was passed unanimously.[104]

The Christian Anti-Slavery Convention of 1851 was held in Chicago with 250 men in attendance, described in secular newspapers as "fanatics and enemies of the country." One hundred and thirty were from Illinois; others from all over the Northeast and Middle West, with the largest delegation from outside Illinois coming from Ohio and including Asa Mahan, John Keep, Henry Cowles, and Charles Grandison Finney from Oberlin (and six Oberlin graduates as well). Jonathan Blanchard was elected president of this convention, and "served as chairman of a committee of three [Fee was another member] to inquire into slavery connections of home missionary organizations."[105]

The Christian Anti-Slavery Convention of 1852, held in Cincinnati, elected Fee president, and endorsed a boycott of all slave-produced goods. Among the featured speakers were Samuel J. May, Hon. George W. Julian and black orators Charles Lenox Remond and Frederick Douglass.[106]

Other Abolitionists & Fee
"Solemnly beautiful. God bless the man." John G. Fee reacting to the ideas of Jonathan Blanchard.

A New York abolitionist whose thought had a continuing impact on Fee over a period of years was William Goodell, antislavery author and editor (and, incidentally, grandfather of Berea College's third president, William Goodell Frost). A native of Chenango County, New York, in the Burned Over District, Goodell was an ardent reformer with an interest in many causes: the free church movement, Grahamism, Magdalen societies, abolitionism among them. He was Garrison's successor in the *National Philanthropist*, then edited the *Genius of Temperance,* followed by the *Emancipator* (established by the Tappans in 1833). In 1835 he became editor of an abolitionist paper, *Friend of Man*, in Utica, where he was one of the leading agitators, working with Benjamin Lundy and Gerrit Smith. Early in 1843, he removed from Utica to Honeoye, a country village south of Rochester, where he founded a free church (or union congregation, as it was called) and began publishing the *Christian Investigator*. His church at Honeoye called itself "The Church of God at Honeoye," and made actual Christian Living the exclusive test of membership with provisos on the millenium, teetotalism and abolitionism. He, along with Gerrit Smith and others, was one of the early crusaders for such churches. The slogan of Goodell's "Come-Outerism" was "Proslavery or Apparently Neutral Churches are Anti-Christian." Fee was personally acquainted with Goodell, who a took a decided interest in Fee's career, giving him advice on legal, moral and practical questions. Fee's "Non Fellowship with Slaveholders the Duty of Christians" (1855) was, by his own admission, indebted to a tract on the same subject by William Goodell, "Duty of Secession from a Corrupt Church." As an early immediatist, Goodell guided Fee to adopt many of his own views; as a friend and neighbor of Gerrit Smith, Goodell probably promoted the relationship which Fee and Smith maintained through decades before and after the Civil War. [107]

Another famous abolitionist, Rev. Jonathan Blanchard, later president of both Knox College and Wheaton, was a friend of both Weld and Fee. Among other connections Blanchard had served as one of Weld's "70" antislavery agents, beginning in September 1836. About a decade later (October 1845) Blanchard and Nathan Lewis Rice, an Old School Presbyterian minister of Cincinnati, conducted a public and extremely well-attended debate in that city on the question, "Is slaveholding in itself sinful and the relation between master and slave a sinful relation?" Blanchard argued basically that "no Christian could maintain any ecclesiastical relation that implied approbation of slavery or any church connection in which silence meant assent to slavery."[108]

A copy of the Blanchard-Rice debate, belonging to Jonn G. Fee, and marked and annotated in his handwriting, shows how much he owed to Blanchard's argument. In fact, Fee's annotations reveal not only his acceptance of Blanchard's views, but his fervent delight in them.

Rice, the pro-slavery speaker in the debate, inspires Fee to many marginal objections. Rice writes, for example, that "no man can treat his slaves cruelly in Kentucky, without being scorned by decent men." Fee comments, "There are many instances of cruelty not scorned by men." Rice maintains that the condition of free blacks is "often worse than that of slaves." Fee replies, "Ask those blacks if they are willing to go back into slavery and bro Rice if he would not rather be a poor man than a slave." Fee's reactions to Rice's side of the debate may be summarized in one comment: "Not true as I can prove." The marginalia in response to Rice show Fee identifying wholly with Blanchard, even it seems imagining himself in Blanchard's position—arguing along with him and even going beyond him with his own (Fee's) particular Southern experience.[109]

Fee's notes on Blanchard are frequently sheer enthusiasm. "Morally sublime," he writes in response to this passage:

You may cloud the solemn truth that holding slaves is a sin with prejudice, or darken it by reproach, or dazzle and confound it with ecclesiastical subtleties of trained polemicism and wire-drawn argument; yet there it stands, bold, honest, open, and uncompromising; and its voice will be heard, and obeyed, when the flimsy and carping objections which may be heaped upon it are perished, passes away and forgot. [110]

Referring to a certain class of ministers, theologians and Bible commentators, Blanchard writes,

When slavery is the subject I have never known a man of this class willing to meet and discuss it, as it actually exists, upon the ordinary and well-known principles of right and wrong. Instead of this, they dive into the dusky regions of antiquity, like rats into cellars, and, guided to despotism by an instinct as precise as that which guides that animal to cheese, they pick up all the instances of restriction upon human liberty which belonged to dark and despotic ages, and twist them into a snake-coil of argument to bind down American Christianity to the toleration of slavery. . . .

Fee's comment: "The severest rebuke that I ever heard or read from mortal lips."[111]

Beside another passage Fee scribbles, "Never surpassed in human words," by another, "This is like Elijah mocking the priests of Baal," by another simply, "Solemn admonition." Blanchard writes that he wants to die "having humbly striven in all things to follow his Lord, like Him also [one who] has been faithful to his poor." Beside this passage Fee wrote; "Solemnly beautiful. God bless the man." Fee's reaction to a position which he apparently found not just rationally compelling but immensely stirring is summarized in the quotation he wrote under his own signature on the first page of the book, "Put away the evil of their doing!"[112]

One of the passages in Blanchard's argument which Fee obviously admired most was a citation from another writer, James A. Thome. In *Emancipation in the West Indies* Thome describes the moment of freedom—a large group of slaves were assembled in a church waiting the official word; when it came "They broke forth in prayer, they shouted, they sang, glory, alleluia; they clapped their hands, leaped up, fell down, clasped each other in their free arms, cried, laughed, and to

& fro, tossing their unfettered arms. But high above the whole, there was a mighty sound, which ever and anon swelled—it was the utterings in broken negro dialect of gratitude to God." Beside this paragraph Fee wrote, "May God grant us such a sight."[113]

James A. Thome, a Lane Rebel from Fee's hometown of Augusta, Kentucky, was a man whom Fee certainly knew, and he was major link between Fee and Theodore Weld. Thome had served as one of Weld's "70" agents, and together they "conceived the idea of studying conditions" of emancipated slaves in Antigua, Barbados and Jamaica. They wanted to disprove the widespread "contention of the proslavery press that emancipation had been a failure." Although Thome spent six months in the field, doing all the research, Weld worked with him extensively in the production *Emancipation in the West Indies* (1838). The work advanced a case for immediate emancipation, showing that in Antigua, the only one of the islands where emancipation had been complete and unconditional, the most striking progress had been made by the black population. In fact, Thome's *Emancipation* is supposed to have shifted the abolitionist movement into a real immediatist policy—after its publication antislavery advocates no longer asked for "immediate emancipation, gradually accomplished," but immediate emancipation accomplished at once.[114]

This latter goal became the center of John G. Fee's religious campaign in Berea, the sharp, controversial focus of his mission in the heart of slaveholding Kentucky.

CHAPTER THREE

FEE'S ARMY: COLPORTEURS AND MINOR PREACHERS

What is a colporteur? Oxford's Dictionary defines 'colporteur' as "a hawker of books, newspapers, etc.," especially, in English usage, "one employed by a religious society." The word derives from the French *col,* which means neck; so a colporteur is etymologically one who carries something around his neck (probably a book satchel); the activity is called colportage.

As the word is used by Fee and others (incidentally, Fee always misspells it), a colporteur is a person hired to distribute and sell books, tracts, especially antislavery writings. Generally, colporteurs worked under the supervision of a missionary, moving out from some central location into relatively inaccessible districts. Fee's workers almost always rode horseback, carrying their literature in specially made saddlebags (probably not around their necks). All Fee's colporteurs were commissioned workers of the AMA, charged with some specific tasks, which were considered of great importance to the missionary effort as a whole: they gave Bibles and testaments free to slaves who could read and to white people too poor to buy them; they distributed tracts, sometimes temperance or anti-tobacco tracts, usually antislavery writings; they sold Helper's *Impending Crisis*, Fee's "Nonfellowship" and *Anti-Slavery Manual*, Thome's *Emancipation in the West Indies,* and books by such authors as William Goodell, John Wesley, Horace Mann—books of political theory, sermons, lectures, and even novels (at one point Fee requested a cheap edition of *Uncle Tom's Cabin* for his colporteurs to sell); sometimes the colporteurs were expected to lecture or exhort; always they undertook to ride from house to house and—even if a sale was impossible—engage each household in conversation about slavery. In an area where many people were pro-slavery such activities did not insure a welcome for colporteurs at every home. Sometimes the workers helped to organize churches and conduct protracted meetings, and they also taught Sunday School classes. In the course of their work they also spied out the land—learned who was friendly and who was not, which neighborhoods safe and which dangerous. Fee wrote, "A colporture certainly can do great good in exploring and finding out places & men who sympathize & in scattering documents."[1]

For a long time Fee was the only missionary in Kentucky, so *all* colporteurs were his responsibility. They were generally paid about $20 for 26 full-days work per month. The work was uncomfortable, arduous (in thinly populated regions a colporteur might have to ride ten miles or more between houses), and occasionally dangerous. It is small wonder, therefore, that locating and supervising colporteurs became one of Fee's most overwhelming missionary assignments. Sometimes it was almost impossible to accomplish anything, and occasionally the colporteur situation was entirely counter-productive for everyone and well-nigh unendurable for Fee.[2]

Joseph W. Gillespie, one of Fee's first workers, was a member of the Cabin Creek Church in Lewis County, where his primary work was "to supply the slaves within his reach with the Bible," but he also conducted "conversation [with] almost every family on the sinfulness of slavery, and the duty of separating entirely from it in all Christian organizations." His colportage in northern Kentucky was brief, perhaps less than two years; the first (extant) report for him is dated 1849, and, by January 1851, he had quit the field because his wife was sick; other family problems cropped up when Gillespie's wife and daughter were brought before Magistrate's Court to be charged with theft—"taking clothing during the time of death & burial of a neighbor woman." Fee went their bail, the first of many instances of a hidden cost in colporteur supervision. The importance of Gillespie in the colporteur line is obviously not his exciting contribution. He did little and virtually nothing is known of him. But he was a local man, a Kentuckian—the first of Fee's attempts to use a native in the field.[3]

William Haines: First Northern Colporteur
"No man in this world has given me so much trouble & no one done our cause so much injury." Fee describing William Haines.

William Haines was probably the first of Fee's Northern colporteurs. Born in Pennsylvania and formerly a Quaker, Haines was about 48 years old when he began colporteuring in 1850. He had lived in Ohio, then moved to Indiana, thence to Cincinnati and then to Bracken County, Kentucky, where he met John G. Fee.[4]

From the first Haines was a problem in the field. "He was talking too much about what he had done," Fee complained to Whipple, "Starting as he did with his 'first love' & zeal in the cause, yet meaning no harm." Fee endeavored to correct Haines, who altered his behavior, while apparently developing some resentment. Fee objected to Haines' "habit of saying sharp & in many cases hard things of those doing wrong." As an example, Fee cited the following case: Haines had been talking to a woman who owned five slaves, "one about the size & near the color of his little daughter. He told her . . . that she done [sic] no more for her slaves than a Quaker does for his horses, feed, salt, sleek them well so that they would do much work & sell for good price." Fee's rebuke of Haines' critical statement to the woman is revealing of Fee's own attitudes and methods. "I suggested to him," Fee wrote, "that [the] same end might have been reached after this manner by asking in a meek & mild manner a question—'Madam, or sister, do you—or do we—when we do no more than you say you do do any more than the Quaker does for his horses?'" Don't shrink from telling the truth, he advised Haines, but be "wise as a serpent."[5]

Fee would have trouble locating a colporteur with a modicum of common sense; the wisdom of a serpent was far beyond William Haines.

In April 1850, Haines filed a typical report of his activities; it was enormous. Fee wrote to the AMA: "You said send the whole of Bro. Haines' report in his own language—so in his last one—36 pages & 19 thousand words (his calculation) 'nough said'—you have it." Very few of Fee's workers were ever to provoke him to deliberate humor again.[6]

Haines' big reports were symptomatic: he talked too much; it was part of a colporteur's job to talk, and a more important part to know when to stop talking. After one more gargantuan report, Haines wrote George Whipple with stirring news: "At this agreeable moment of leasure [sic] I drop you this note to inform you that I am now under arrest, charged by the commonwealth of Kentucky with aiding and assisting slaves in making their escape. . . . I am now alone under lock and key in the secondary story of a house on Main Street [in Maysville, Kentucky.]"[7]

Haines' family was under the care of John G. Fee, who had also located a college mate of his own to serve as Haines' lawyer.

Haines maintained that he had not talked to any slaves, but to a free man of color who asked Haines' advice about his enslaved wife and children. Apparently, Haines' counsel had been overheard and reported, since his encounter with the freedman had occurred on the public street, and, as many slaves had run off recently, the case was creating quite a stir. Fee reported: "In a warrant taken out by a member of the Baptist Church (known here as the 'iron sides Baptists') Bro. Haines is charged with feloniously attempting to entice or steal away the slave woman of Hezekiah Jenkins, Hannah and her children."

One of the main witnesses in the trial reported a conversation that his uncle had had with Haines in which Haines told him (the uncle) what Haines had said to the black man. Fee transcribed the whole conversation (3rd or 4th hand, by this time) to send to Whipple:

> It was as follows "On the road to Maysville a free man" (in the highway openly) "asked him for advice how to get his wife and children away saying the master is in debt and they may be sold down the river." To which he says Mr. Haines said he replied, "You say you are a free man. Do you live near the back water?" (Water from the Ohio River) Yes "Can you borrow a skift?" Yes. "Can your wife cook enough to last you a day and a night?" Yes "Can you row across the river?" Yes. "Well, you say you can do all this, I don't tell you to do it—but if you get clear thank your God—not me." Admitting this true, [Fee writes] I suppose Bro. Haines thought he was not violating the letter of the law.[8]

Although this incident appears almost ludicrous, it had serious repercussions. Soon Haines was "running down with diarrhea" in the damp jail. And Fee was suffering even direr consequences; as he was leaving the jail after visiting Haines, he was attacked. One of Fee's neighbors, who had "more children by a slave woman in his kitchen, than by his lawful wife, rushed suddenly upon [Fee], struck [him] across [the] head with a club," hitting so hard he broke the club on Fee's skull. Badly injured, Fee managed to reach his home, "almost blinded and covered with blood." Then, someone burned down the small house where the school and Fee's church were housed. Haines' case cost Fee money and time and energy and almost his life.[9]

In justifiable indignation, Fee complained, "Bro. Haines still talks of riding again if he gets out. I do not believe the people will let him ride. He might have rode on perhaps a lifetime had he not talked so much—and so indiscreetly." Fee procured bail for him and then endured a time of anxiety when Haines left the state and took his family to Indiana, after having promised to stand his trial. Haines returned, however, much to Fee's relief—and apparent surprise.[10]

On August 17, 1850, Fee sent Whipple some happy news for a change; "With feelings of pleasure & thankfulness beyond what I can describe I announce to you that this day by a jury of twelve sworn men our friend Wm Haines was decided not guilty. [Double underlining]" By that time Haines had moved to a free state, and Fee was left with a lawyer's fee of $100. The AMA paid it, eventually.[11]

That was the end of the colportage of William Haines. Fee's final comment on the affair constitutes one of his harshest judgments: "I told Haines in my last letter that he had cost the society & friends enough money & trouble for his indiscretions & for conscience sake to say no more. No man in this world has given me so much trouble & no one done our cause so much injury. For some two or three months whilst those trials were pending . . . I was almost constantly on the go, rallying friends &c. until I was exhausted body & mind." But this was not the final word on the use of Northern workers in a Southern mission field.[12]

Hiram Casteel: Appalachian Abolitionist
"His bitterest enemies could not put their finger on a single blemish in his character & this is his native country." Francis Hawley.

Before John G. Fee settled permanently in Berea, he was already supervising colportage in Madison County and the surrounding regions; as early as 1853, when he was still based in Cabin Creek himself, Fee was trying to find the right men for central Kentucky. It was not difficult to locate people willing simply to distibute tracts on a volunteer basis. In March 1854, 42 men from Madison and Rockcastle counties sent a petition to the AMA enunciating abolitionist sympathies and asking for tracts to distribute. The signatures on that document constituted the list of possible candidates for colporteur work around Berea, and three of the signers actually became colporteurs (Peter H. West, S. M. Shearer and A. G. W. Parker). The first man to sign the petition was Hiram Casteel, and he was also the first man Fee wanted for the work.[13] (See Appendix 2: Colporteurs' Appeal)

Hiram Casteel, a Baptist minister, never accepted an AMA commission. He did several day's labor in traveling and preaching for Fee in 1854, for which he recieved the princely sum of $1.00. However, Casteel's ministry is vital evidence of a neglected area of antislavery activity. When Fee wrote of Casteel in 1855 ("He is believed to be a very honest, faithful man and perhaps will make a good colporture."), the Baptist preacher had been a committed abolitonist "for more than 12 months" already. Elder Francis Hawley, writing of Casteel in 1854, stated that Casteel had "been inclined to favor the cause" for years, "but within the last year he has come out fully & openly committed himself." It is very unlikely that Fee's personal ministry had anything to do with Casteel's position. Apparently, Casteel had formulated it on his own.[14]

For preaching abolitionism openly in a Baptist church of which he was minister and in which the leading member was a slaveholder, Casteel was tried and "abused' by the church, forbidden to preach in it and in three other churches he had pastored. Since much of the preaching in the mountains was done in private homes he was able to go on with his ministry anyway, even though church buildings were closed to him.[15]

Casteel was minister at Clover Bottom, Pond Creek, Big Spring and Indian Spring; a native of Laurel County, where he had been one of the first teachers, Casteel was a purely Appalachian phenomenon, an abolitionist Christian mostly uninfluenced by Northern ideas and mostly unaided by the outside world. Hawley wrote that Casteel "was silenced from speaking because he would speak for the slave. He is a man who stands high as a good man & a man of inflexible integrity & has produced great excitement as he was pastor of the churches." At another time Hawley stated that "a large section of the county is or will soon be open to a pure Christianity through Elder Hiram Casteel."[16]

Wiley Fisk praised Casteel too, saying there was "no cast in him," and that "he could do more in Laurel than any [other] man"; he was, in Fisk's opinion, better suited for an abolitionist ministry in the mountains than anyone," John G.

Fee not excepted." Hawley found in Casteel another feature that exceeded Fee's capacities: "To make appointments for a northern abolitionist [Hawley] & that a full-blooded one & then go with him to those appointments is more than any southern minister has dared to do. Fee has not done it on new ground."[17]

Casteel had a large family, was very poor and comparatively uneducated. Yet he was "a man of native talent & sound common sense—well acquainted with the Bible & very shrewd . . . a man of undoubted piety." "His bitterest enemies," Hawley wrote, could not "put their finger on a single blemish in his character & this is his native country."[18]

Clearly, there were people in the mountains with their own contributions to make to the antislavery cause. No sound interpretation of abolitionism in Kentucky could be advanced without taking into account men like Hiram Casteel, whose ministry was conducted in an obscure place, unreported, almost unmentioned. How many others never found their way into any record at all?

No wonder Fee wanted Casteel for a colporteur; but he could not get him because the Baptist minister had work of his own to do. Fee had to take what he *could* get; his first three central Kentucky colporteurs were far from the calibre of Casteel, in many respects—even so, they too represented the willingness of mountain people to work for the antislavery cause.

Peter H. West: Lazy and Talkative
"I say to you I need [the money] bad." Peter H. West, reporting to the AMA.

Unattractive as $20 for 26 full days of work may sound, some local citizens needed money so badly that they competed for colporteur jobs. No doubt this indicates the poverty level in the mountainous regions of central Kentucky in the 1850's. At any rate, Isaac Lane, who never became a colporteur, only a volunteer tract distributor, raised some commotion in his efforts to attain the post and apparently expressed bitterness and resentment against Fee and others after he (Lane) was turned down (not once, but repeatedly). Fee would never consent to Lane's commission because Lane had been "drunk and swearing" in public. Wiley Fisk, a great friend of Isaac Lane's, went over Fee's head, trying to get the AMA to issue a commission on his (Fisk's) recommendation. Cassius Clay recommended Lane too. But Fee thought him "smart but not a true man," and Fee's objections won the day.[19]

Fee suspected at least one of his three colporteurs (Parker, Peter H. West, Shearer) of taking the job primarily for money, which was not acceptable motivation in Fee's pious eyes. Peter H. West, "a broken down old Virginia trader," was 47 years old when he was commissioned as an AMA colporteur in 1853; he lived on Clear Creek in Rockcastle County with his wife and 10 children. It was never any secret—how could it be?—that he needed money desperately. Fee's first description of him reveals as much; Peter H. West, he states, "was unfortunate some years since in trade to the south . . . now a poor man with considerable family." But he has qualifications besides need: "He was a praying working man, member of the Methodist church, joining in the free church movement whilst [Fee and his co-workers] were up in his county. . . he writes well—can do business well—prays in public and has exhorted a little—He is long & well known in Madison co."[20]

After Fee's initial description of Peter H. West, however, his enthusiasm starts to wane. West's ability to pray in public does not seem to amount to much. He is, Fee writes, "without any natural address & the one prayer I heard was very short & feeble—yet I am told that was not a fair specimen."[21]

At any rate, Peter H. West was commissioned and Fee was to regret it rather extensively. For years he tried to get West's commission taken away, but once West had established his own communications with the AMA he managed to stay on and on and on, in spite of Fee's growing conviction of West's inadequacy for the job. At one point, West applied to the Association for more money than the salary he had agreed upon with Fee; Fee wrote, "It is possible for P. H. West to have forgotten that his commision was for six months at 150 and that next six months [was] $125. But not probable."[22]

More financial difficulties followed. "West told me to write to you for some more money—that he was pressed for want of it. It is perhaps because he has been trading for sometime past in the hog business." The next year West wrote on his own behalf saying, "I say to you I need [the money] bad."[23]

Fee discovered from West's reports that the colporteur was reporting virtually every move he made as work for the cause. West persisted in claiming a day's labor for attending church services (some readers may find themselves sympathizing with this novel approach to worship). Peter H. West, Fee maintained, "charges for all he does." In addition, some of his claimed days were short on both ends. "He loves to sleep too late of mornings—loves to stop too soon of evenings—spend his time going to meetings and then sit & talk with the company rather than to talk to sinners or visit—loves a fine horse to ride and will neglect the cause to save his horse—He loves to get money easy. . . . He talks right and [he] sings well but that is not enough."[24]

In spite of Fee's criticisms and repeated requests that West's commission not be renewed, the AMA kept him on for years; Fee occasionally relented and gave tacit approval to retaining West, always grudgingly. West did have some redeeming features; he knew everyone in southern Madison County and in Rockcastle County, he had relatives by the dozens, and he was a great talker. He himself reported to the AMA literally dozens of his conversations and arguments: talks with non-slaveholders and slaveholders alike, discussions after church, public quarrels in taverns—in report after report he uses the same formula. 'He said, then I replied, and he replied and then I replied'—till his whole life seems a running dialogue. Maybe the people at AMA headquarters thought the information conveyed by this unquenchable source of local color was worth receiving.

An excerpt from P. H. West's report (May 13, 1854):

> Apr. 30—attended ch. at bro Hutson's here bro <u>Casteel</u> really preached a <u>whole</u> Gospel sermond—one man a professor after meeting said that bro Casteel was a fine man but he got of [off] the tract—I replied he was now just come on the right tract—that Christ was no respecter of pursons he replied that slavery was right that god had cursed <u>Cain</u> & therefore slavery was right and that it was a political matter & the church had nothing to do with it I replied that <u>God</u> would certainly ask him if he gave his Vote in the fear of God & for the promotion of his Kingdom and that he appeared to be a man more righteous in his politics than he was in his religion.[25]

Like William Haines before him, Peter H. West caused trouble with his free conversation, in one instance a great deal of trouble. West had sick in bed for 10 days, but finally got up to go to Mt. Vernon for the August Superior court. He went because a lot of people would be in town on court day, not because he himself had to appear there. Right after he arrived some of his friends told him that J. P. Smith, with whom he was well-acquainted, and Bro. Isaac Lane had had "a difficulty." Smith had approached Lane and said, "Some of you damn abolitionists stole 2 of my negroes." They had high words and would have come to blows if friends had not intervened.

Since Lane was "High Strung" West decided to attempt a reconciliation by approaching J. P. Smith, whom he found in a tavern eating his dinner, surrounded by other diners. West waited until Smith was finished eating and then broached the subject with him.

"He turned round faceing me," West reported, "with a countenance of a demon & replyed <u>Sir we intend to put a stop to this question</u>. It shan't be discussed in this county. We intend to get up a meeting and pass resolutions & put a stop to this new preaching of Fisk & Fee in this county." West "replyed" and Smith "replyed" and soon other people in the tavern joined this altercation and it became a public dispute, apparently at the shouting level. Some of the pro-slavery faction present on this occasion (including Smith apparently) took action the same week with a plot to entrap A. G. W. Parker, West's fellow colporteur. West himself reported (almost bragging) that his indiscreet talk led directly to the Parker incident—if so, his tavern conversation caused an incommensurate amount of hardship and pain for many people.[26]

West rode in fear of losing his job. "Don't send in Northern men," he wrote (with a shrewd awareness of which way the wind was blowing) "to pull down what we have through blood & tears built up. I don't mean all Northern Men," he added hastily, remembering—too late—that he was addressing Northerners in the AMA, "But some that we had we want no more."[27]

Eventually, West, whose eyesight was failing, rode around less and worked more effectively with his "flourishing sabbath school at Union Meeting house," which was on his land in Rockcastle County. He still wanted more than $20 a month. "That will not sustain no man here at the present high prices of Everything." By February 1857, he had become well-informed of Fee's opinion of him and he wrote a letter of self-defense to the AMA:

> They [for 'they' read Fee] say they will pay all necessary Expenses Such as Lodging, now I supose I must not Eat nor my horse nor cross Bridges & Tolegates &c. if this is Just I dont know Justice— next They Say I must rise Early and talk about nothing but personal Salvation is this not Slavery if it is not I dont know what Slavery is. to come & go rise & Talk at <u>Master's</u> biding. I do think I have bin

well enough tried in this cause to prove to all concerned my
faithfulness it may be I am not Energetic as some would it believed
but [paper torn] but I have my Way of gitting at Men to get them to
think of the great question of Salvation of the Soul . . . I have
Explained I have done all that god requires me to do—and still I am
found guilty of not doing enough . . . You know that $20 will not
Sustain me if I comence riding I want to do it for god and not for
man alone but we have to live while we do live.

This report, like most of the official reports, had to pass through the hands of John
G. Fee. He commented that West "manifests an unnecessarily querulous spirit."[28]

West was elected Magistrate for Rockcastle County, which eased his
financial situation somewhat. He continued as colporteur, but his function was
changed. Now that "he is a magistrate," Fee wrote, "he can do us important
services in many respects."[29]

Occasionally, West writes with a kind of untutored perception and
sympathy that does him credit. No doubt he needed money; certainly he talked too
much; probably he was lazy, but he wrote in one of his reports:

Then there is here who profess to be followers of the meek
and lowly savior and preachers not a few who will sell & buy Christ
in person of his poor and say they can not love a negro as well as a
white man because they stink so—this I heard a preacher of the
baptist faith say not 3 weeks ago in a public congregation—may
God have mercy on all such ministers and Teach them the common
brotherhood of all men.

S. M. Shearer: Weapon-Carrier
*"He had too long indulged the southern spirit of fight." Fee, describing S.M.
Shearer.*

S. M. Shearer, a younger man than West, but like him a resident of
Rockcastle County (they were neighbors on Clear Creek), was commissioned at
about the same time in 1853. Fee liked Shearer much better than he liked West,
and expressed his preference every time he reported on the pair. If anyone were to
be dismissed it should be West, and Shearer (or Sharer, as Fee always writes it)
should be retained. Fee believed that Shearer would be "faithful and industrious,"
had the "best intellect" of his colporteurs and was "naturally a sensible man."[30]

Fee saw one flaw in the young man immediately, however. He had a "sanguine temperament . . . has too long indulged the southern spirit of fight." Fee thought this could be corrected, although he confessed again, "He has a great deal of the Ky fighting spirit, has carried Bowie knife since he has been a colporteur—don't manifest much of the spirit of Christ." A year later Shearer had been "returned by [the] grand jury for carrying concealed weapons"; and he had told a friend of his he would continue doing so, although he later promised George Candee he would not. Still Fee did not lose hope; he wrote, "Sharer has been much benefited by our last meeting—made a public acknowledgement that he trusted too much in carnal weapons—grieved the spirit of God. I think he will not carry [weapons] again."[31]

Unlike West, Shearer did not charge for everything and this generosity of spirit endeared him to Fee. Some suggestion of what a colporteur's life must have been like emerges from Shearer's report of his first month's labor (October 28, 1853). He had spent his first day (September 26) invoicing books, then for five days he had ridden about visiting 46 families only one of which was 'oposed' to his message. On October 2 through 5, he visited five families and found two of them opposed, and he also made appointments for preaching. From the 6th to the 11th he visited four families and attended Glade Church for two days. From the 11th of October to the 21st, he visited 47 families, 38 of whom were "unfriendly," which must have been remarkably encouraging. This 10-day period of bad luck was capped off on the 21st when it "Rained all day." In the meantime he had also organized a church at Horse Lick. On the 26th and 27th of October, he attended church at Union in Rockcastle County and on the 28th (his last day of the month) he visited seven families and found them all unfriendly.

During the month's work he sold $15.50 worth of book (a large number given the prices at that time); had expenses amounting to $1.85; gave away five Bibles and six New Testaments to the poor, having found not a single slave who could read. At the end of this report he wrote: "You will recollect that our county is Hilly & thin settled some times I have rode as far as 13 miles before I could find a house."[32]

It sounds like a remarkable piece of work, but in a few months, Fee was writing, "Our colportures are doing but little, I expect Bro. Sharer to take hold in good earnest in about one week. He will purchase another horse and hire a hand to work in his stead. He will then give himself wholy [sic] to the work."[33]

Shearer was to continue, but was probably never really reliable. West reported on his fellow worker, "bro Shearer is doing nothing for the cause he still says he intends to commence riding again but does not so far nor do I think he will do much more." (Of course, West wanted Shearer replaced by West's friend "bro. Kinkade.")[34]

Not surprisingly, Fee was upset with both his workers: Shearer and West, his colportage team. He wrote,

> We need documents and the right kind of men. Our colportures are doing nothing at prest.—they are busy in their hogs & corn. It would be better if we had men who would give their whole attention to the work and men capable of holding meetings and men who not only want freedom for selfish purposes but who had sympathy also with the poor slave.
> Yet I do not see that you can do anything better at present than to let them ride until you find better men. I still hope for Sharer when he shall get his domestic affairs . . . arranged.[35]
> [And again he wrote:] I am afflicted over our colportures in the interior. They are not doing what they ought yet I can do no better. There is the laziness of the slave system. Just as natural to southerners as lying [is] to Spartans.[36]

One may sense Fee's embarrassment at trying to explain the habits of his Southern compatriots to men in distant New York City.

If Fee was embarrassed by his native-born colporteurs, Francis Hawley, New Englander, self-described 'full-blooded abolitionist,' was absolutely appalled by them. He complained to the AMA: "Neither P. West or Shearer are fit for the place [as colporteurs] though they may be as good as can be found. They are lazy, they want to be among friends near home they should have gone over double perhaps three times the ground." His criticisms go on and on. They are handing out tracts the contents of which they do not understand, they like to visit, they have no "deep piety," and finally "they are not intelligent. They think they must spend much time talking with the families they visit when for the want of understanding the subject their talk does but little good." He goes on to say that "Bro Fee is one of the best men living, his whole heart is given to the work, but this much I will say, I do not think he is a good judge of character & can easily be imposed upon."[37]

Stung by Hawley's imputation (reported to him by the AMA), Fee leaped to Shearer's defense, pointing out that he had not traveled much because he had few documents to carry (books and tracts were very slow to arrive from New York: sometimes Fee's workers simply ran out of material for days or weeks), had family duties keeping him at home, and had no encouragement from Fisk to travel with him. (By this time Fisk was moving into active opposition to Fee's ministry). Shearer, Fee stated, had probably not charged the society for one hour not spent in the actual service. And finally, he added, "Bro Shearer like many other southern men, needs _instruction_ & patient labor. I believe he will be very useful . . . In Peter H. West I have not the same measure of confidence."

Still the situation was urgent; Fee wrote in the same letter, "As to colportures from the North laboring here, I say send them on. I suppose that they can labor here as certainly as Northern preachers [like Hawley, he might have added]. They cannot labor without more opposition than southern men."[38]

A. G. W. Parker: A Most Unfortunate Colporteur
"Reporte for the first month Jan the 3th visited a family 1 prayer 4 day Jan 4 familys 1 prayer 4 also 5 Christains on Indian creek. . . ." A.G.W. Parker's report to the AMA, errors intact.

West and Shearer managed years of colporteur work without landing themselves in serious difficulties; perhaps their laziness helped. Another Southerner, commissioned at approximately the same time, did not fare so well. In fact, A. G. W. Parker was one of the unluckiest workers connected with the Berea mission. Parker, a native of South Carolina, born 1815 or '16, had lived in Virginia and then Tennessee before settling in Rockcastle County around 1850. It was probably a misfortune for him that, unlike West and Shearer, he was not a native of central Kentucky.

Fee was most enthusiastic about using A. G. W. Parker as a colporteur. Parker, a Methodist, expected to be licensed to preach: he was a married man with a couple of small children. Agreeing with Fee on the caste question, Parker was willing to withdraw from all slaveholding connection. He had intended to begin some kind of ministry in any case so the offer of a colportage position was welcome to him. Fee formed a high estimation of Parker's character almost immediately, finding him "calm, sober, & yet tender hearted." Fee was also impressed by Parker's "eagerness to take notes," but was horrified a little later to discover that the note-taking was misleading and Parker a very poor writer and speller. "He could not make to you a suitable report," Fee confessed ruefully to the AMA.[39]

Four months after Fee recommended him as colporteur, A. G. W. Parker was imprisoned in Rockcastle County, charged with having tried to induce a slave to escape. Fee had been in the midst of his protracted meetings at the Glade when Parker was arrested, leading Cassius Clay and others to assume that the Parker affair was initiated solely to break up Fee's revival. Clay insisted that Fee continue and went himself to Rockcastle County where "at great hazard & [with] much difficulty [he] bailed out Bro. Parker." Since Parker was entitled to only $20 salary at the time of his arrest it may be safely assumed that he had ridden as colporteur for only a month before his arrest. The incident had, however, been very well-timed. August Court of 1853, the same court day West had gone to Mt. Vernon to observe, was just over and it would be six months before Parker could be tried.

All of Parker's friends, including Fee and Clay, believed that he had been framed. Peter H. West reported what was undoubtedly the accepted local gossip on the matter: "[The] pro slavery [party] took advantage of Brother Parker by taking a negro to his house one nite and eave dropping till he said something that they could get hold of and took him and put him in jail." Apparently the slave had been prompted to ask Parker questions about how to escape until Parker should actually give the black man advice or offer assistance. The men who planned the entrapment—"drunks," according to West—had been among West's audience the day of his public argument in Mt. Vernon.[40]

The arrest of Parker was followed by a meeting at Mt. Vernon composed of 10 proslaveholding men who passed resolutions that Cassius Clay was not to visit their county anymore, that Fisk and Fee were not to preach there, that Parker was to leave the state in 20 days and that Peter H. West should not distribute any more books and tracts in the county.[41]

Parker's career was endangered by more than arrest; helpful sources reported to John G. Fee that Parker had been drunk the winter before and "wanted to hug a mulatto woman." Parker himself confessed that he had drunk alcohol, but "promised that whiskey should not again go down his throat." Fee remained supportive. "If Parker should prove innocent of these things I should be glad for him to travel as a colporture because the enemy ought not to be allowed to thwart good plans by lies." Parker prays very well and expresses the right views; he is humble and trusting, familiar with the Bible, candid and not covetous. He is "a little too careless in dress, but he "seemed to want no pay until he should get into actual service. If he has not told me a falsehood in denying that he was drunk and attempted to hug that woman I shall like him better in spirit than any other colporture I have here in Kentucky."[42]

Since it was impossible for Parker to ride until his case was settled, Fee hired Shearer to replace him. Cassius Clay employed a lawyer for Parker, attended two courts in Mt. Vernon, paid the tavern bills of a number of friends who went to the trial to defend Parker; Clay himself made one or two speeches, later published, in the defense. Parker was acquitted April 1855, a year and a half after his arrest.

His troubles were just beginning.

In March 1856, he was being tried in Mt. Vernon again (or still)—Clay and many abolitionists were in court defending him.[43]

Fee suggested to the AMA that Parker might go to Africa with missionary George Thompson; Parker was willing and his skill as a carpenter might have been useful, but apparently the Association was not interested.[44]

Parker stayed in Rockcastle County until his house was burned down by arsonists in the summer of 1857, when he moved into Madison County. Fee had been hesitant to rehire him as a colporteur because of his near illiteracy and his lack of energy (proverbial Southern laziness again, or perhaps hunger), but when Parker arrived in Berea homeless and destitute he was recommissioned. By September 10, 1857, he was being paid as a colporteur and he continued successfully for several months, but by November 1858 Fee was recommending a new colporteur, saying that "Bro Parker [had] been away for some two weeks. The friends say," Fee reported ruefully, "he is neglecting his family & will not work." By December Fee said he "felt constrained to help Bro. Parker . . . who is very poor."[45]

In February 1859, Parker was on trial again for an unspecified offense, but also functioning once more as a colporteur. He filed a report in April for his work since January—it is written in his own hand, childish and unformed, with lines mixed, straggling and running into one another, almost indecipherable. Here is the first week's data: "Reporte for the first month Jan the 3th visited a family 1 prayer 4 day Jan 4 familys 1 prayer 4 also 5 Christains on indian creek Jacson co Ky 5 day Jan 4 family 1 prayr 6 day 5 familys 1 prayr 7 day 2 familys 1 prayr 1 abc * Jan 8 Returned home"[46]

Another colporteur, Robert Jones, described one of A. G. W. Parker's meetings—which must have been a fairly typical one for Parker and the other colporteurs as well. The congregation gathered and Parker (or someone) read aloud from John G. Fee's tract (or "track," as Jones spells it), "The Sinfulness of Slaveholding." "One man said he would not believe that and throwing it at an Antislavery man Standing near told him to take his testament and it was picked up and held back at him and they told him that [he] had better read the work. Yet the meeting past off nice."[47]

All that spring Parker worked, but by that time Fee saw more and more deficiencies in him. "Bro. Parker persists in tobacco chewing," Fee wrote—he "is not persevering, is passionate." Fee recommends him no longer, even though he is antislavery.[48]

Parker filed his last colportage report in June 1859. Rev. John A. R. Rogers copied the report out in his graceful handwriting, probably rewording it as well:

> A. G. W. Parker to the Am. Miss. Assoc. for Services in Distributing Bibles to Slaves. I have spent eleven days in visiting slaveholding families for the purpose of giving Bibles to such slaves as could read. In 52 of such families I found 507 slaves and of that number 21 read a little. To 18 of the 21 slaves I have give Bibles. Twelve of these were men & 6 women. All of the men but one were professed Christians & most of them preachers & I think good men. One of the 6 women who received Bibles was a professor [of Christianity].
>
> In prosecuting my work I receive many looks from the slaveholders who not infrequently put on very long faces when I announce to them my errand.
>
> The number of slaves in the families visited range from 2 to 83. In two of these families there are two slaves in each who can

read, in none of the others but one who can read at all and in many
of them not a slave who can spell out a word of the story of Jesus.
June 11, 1859   A. G. W. Parker[49]

Parker remained in Berea, probably doing carpentry work, until he and his
family were driven out among the first exiles in December 1859. He returned
briefly in 1860, when he figured in an incident that will be related in a subsequent
chapter. Apparently his connection with Berea was permanently broken; after 1860
his name is never mentioned again in any contemporary account.

Robert Jones: Brave, Faithful and Arthritic
"Every blow left its mark." Otis B. Waters.

Fee's last important colporteur before the Civil War was also by far the
most faithful and certainly the most effective. By the time Robert Jones began to
work for him, however, Fee had become so generally disillusioned with
colporteurs that Jones' work never satisfied him.

Jones was born in Madison County around 1810, and it seems likely that
many of his Jones relatives were slaveholders, some of them prominently
connected slaveholders. When Jackson County was formed Jones' home fell
within that territory; he apparently lived near Clover Bottom Creek. Shearer said
Jones and his family were nearer to heaven than any other folks he ever knew
because they lived on the highest peak in Jackson County.[50]

Robert Jones and his wife Mary Clemmons were related to numerous
families in that region of the mountains. By the time Jones was invited to be a
colporteur in 1857, he and his wife had 13 children, all living, and she was
expecting no. 14, who was named Fee G. Jones.[51]

Jones had been a member of the Methodist convention, but he was one of
the first men in central Kentucky to "come out" as a Christian abolitionist, and by
1857 he had been leading church meetings for two years. Fee thought Jones was
"as desirable a man as can be found here now for this work."[52]

His first assignment as colporteur involved travelling for a trial period of
one month with Fee, by this time mistrustful of colporteurs beginning work on
their own. Fee hesitated to use him, because Jones was "quite illiterate." Fee was
also afraid that Jones might "lack energy and [the] ability to make reports in good

style." But Fee stated in September that Jones "our probationary colporteur is doing very well. He is delighted with his work."[53]

Jones filed his first report in October 1857, but the document shows signs of another hand and mind (clearly Fee's).

> The region of the country I have traveled over is one which is broken and not many slaveholders in that region. Free labor alone can subsist upon a thin soil.
> Most of the slaveholders I visited were willing to talk on the subject of slavery but hold on against their better judgement. One slave owner and some three nonslaveowners were the only ones in a month's labor unwilling to read. This shows an important fact; to wit the people—the great majority are accessible. There is certainly a much greater willingness now to read and hear in many portions of this state than four or five years since. Many fields are open to colportures. In what are known as Mountain and border counties with suitable laborers an entire revolution could be effected in the public mind on the subject of slavery. This is the great and all absorbing topic.[54]

In January 1858, Fee and Jones were seized near Lewis Chapel by a mob which threatened to drown them in the Kentucky River. One of the mob made Jones ride behind him and they took them to

> the river and descended into a dark, lonely ravine upon its banks. Fee was talking to the men, but at length one of them said they had not come to hear a sermon; they must attend to their business. They then proceeded a little way farther to a thicket on the bank of the river. They here ordered Bro. Jones to strip; he pulled off his coat and vest and stopped. They jeered him and told him to "strip his linen." They removed all his clothing except his shirt. Then bending him over they turned that up and one of the leaders of the gang proceeded to whip him upon the naked back with a sycamore switch or switches—these grow large & heavy. Every blow left its mark. His wounds . . . are of no slight character . . . Bro Jones suffered greatly under his cruel whipping. Next morning the blood had settled upon his back in a place as large as a person's two hands.[55]

The terror of this incident emerges clearly in this retelling (authored by Otis B. Waters)—the lonely spot by the river, the threat of death, the brutal, sadistic men, not just opposed to abolitionists, but actively seeking out the pleasure of inflicting pain. Immediately after his whipping Jones was so disabled he could not walk, but when he recovered he continued as colporteur, in spite of his dreadful experience with the local perverts. In fact, his beating seems to have won him friends. In May 1858, he reported (in his own words, his own handwriting this time):

> I Traveled threw the fourth month with out any dificulty that was serious. The people all seam to Receive the Antislavery pamphlets to Read more freer, and our Discourses was more about Me being Mobed than any other one subject and more People have Come out and said they was Abolitionist in this month than any month before and the people in this new Jackson County thinks thare is a majority of Abolitionist in it.[56]

However, when Jones called upon a slaveholding family, "both master and mistress spared no words of reprobation of him and his work." They refused to hear any of his preaching or read of any his tracts. "But they finally quieted down, and he introduced the expediency argument against slavery, and read to them from the tract entitled,*"Is it expedient to introduce Slavery into Kansas?"*[57]

A typical itinerary for a month of Jones' work reports his travels in Madison County, Rockcastle County, Jackson County, Clay County, and Owsley County, with visits to Clover Creek, Laurel Fork, McKee, Indian Creek, Bro. Fee's house, Pond Creek, Spivy Branch, Sexton, Williford Fork, Burning Springs, Cornelius Fork, Station Camp Creek and Redlick Creek.[58]

It is with some amazement that we read Fee's statement that "Bro. Jones is slow & afflicted with rheumatism in his nees [sic]—" and that he has "no horse." Jones walked to all his assignments. Fee was troubled by Jones' "inefficiency."[59]

Once again Jones found himself in trouble, when he traveled with George Candee and William Kendrick to a meeting in Laurel County in December 1859. A mob intercepted them on the way to the meeting house, took them five or six miles farther and "shared[sheared]" their hair and beards, daubed tar on their heads and faces, and, without moving on to the feathers, left them.[60]

Robert Jones did not give up his job, however, or his loyalty. During and after the Civil War he remained faithful to the cause which he had adopted. Although Fee was never satisfied, Jones seems to have made a vital contribution: his primary work was in Jackson County, which through the years would provide the Berea project with many of its most tenaciously loyal supporters. That loyalty was first revealed in Robert Jones, abused, threatened, beaten, tarred (but not feathered), humiliated and under-appreciated, plodding on through the mountains, undeterred, book bag around his neck, stubborn, tough and resilient.

Problems with Colportage
"I believe success under God in this state depends upon a speedy occupancy of the ground by Godly & efficient laborers." John G. Fee.

These accounts of Fee's colporteurs do not include some people who simply distributed tracts on a day-to-day basis but were not commissioned (like J. Hamilton Rawlings, Albert Cornelison and other local citizens), nor do they include—naturally enough—all the numerous people whom Fee tried to get to work for him. Fee considered many men for colporteur positions, invited many who refused and some who accepted and then failed to show up. Some of the young men who functioned as preachers and teachers also did colportage, but except for them Fee succeeded in attracting only local men to the task in central Kentucky. From the first, keeping colporteurs in the field was a great burden. The problems Fee encountered in this relatively small assignment exemplify the difficulties, minor and major, that would arise over and over again in the Berea experiment.

Some of the trouble was always simply natural: acts of God, people dying, getting sick, getting old; weather conditions, crop failure, a rainy season, mountains. Other difficulties arose from purely personal sources: finding those who could devote all their time to a low-paying, arduous job was hard—men had to stop riding out and get their crops in or butcher their hogs; on another level, Fee found his workers lacking in common sense, too outspoken, indiscreet, full of rivalries and jealousies, contentious, belligerent, greedy, and, most of all, lazy. These problems were simply those that existed when a person kept working, and many colporteurs did not; faithfulness to the cause was rare.

Some of the problems were social: the enmity of the community as a whole was always pressing, so pressing in some instances that a few Kentucky colporteurs pulled up stakes and fled to the free states. Legal problems also beset Fee and his workers, not just those who were prosecuted. At one point, Kentucky passed a law against peddlers which was applied to some of Fee's workers.[61]

But the biggest problem of all was prejudice: not just white prejudice against black, or slaveholder against non-slaveholder, but more subtle varieties. Obviously, Southerners were prejudiced against Northerners, but the reverse was also true; Fee himself seems to have regarded every specifically Southern trait as an outgrowth of the evil of slavery: the slow-moving, slow-speaking, hospitality-conscious workers who loved to "visit" come under his condemnation, even though he was Southern himself: his Northern friends were frequently simply aghast at typical characteristics of native Kentuckians, even Kentuckians who were not mountaineers. And the latter group, with its almost universal deficiency in formal education, was usually treated—if not officially regarded—as inferior, the educated finding it just as difficult to comprehend the ignorant as the other way round. There were economically determined attitudes too, of course, with the familiar categories of rich and poor, ambitious and lazy, clean and dirty.

The development of Fee's idea that education would necessarily be central to the overcoming of slavery in Kentucky owed a great deal to his experiences with colporteurs during the period from 1846 to 1859. The colporteur trouble also predisposed him to look North and East for help—what he needed was enterprising, efficient, go-getting New England Puritans in the field. And he was soon to get them; along with the surprise of discovering that the problems of an antislavery mission in Kentucky could not be solved by Yankees either.

From the time Fee settled in Berea until the exiles his experience consisted primarily of problems and difficulties, frustrations and anxieties. One result of this barrage of trouble was a change in his own attitude. He was so hopeful at first, about the situation, about individuals—for example, look at his continuing faith in S. M. Shearer and A. G. W. Parker. For months he kept renewing his confidence in these men, in spite of their poor performances. A little later, after repeated betrayals and disappointments, Fee began to sour: a certain naive generosity and enthusiasm in his spirit was spoiled, perhaps forever; people in general became very hard for Fee to trust, and Fee himself became increasingly difficult to please, much less satisfy.

A measure of intolerance crept into Fee's judgements, a humorless inflexibility that frequently seems unkind and occasionally approaches injustice. No one measured up to his standards—no one was as faithful and devoted, as self-sacrificing, as ardent and hardworking as he was himself. True, and probably no one else involved in the work came as close to spiritual tyranny as Fee did.

For the most part, Fee overcame the temptations implicit in his position, but occasionally one glimpses an aspect of Fee's character that is frightening, even repellent. He had all the makings and opportunities of a religious dictator; he was too genuinely humble for this side of his personality to emerge victorious, but he was also too single-minded about his calling to recognize his own ruthlessness. Part of the problem with the colporteurs was John G. Fee; his character shaped and warped the abolitionist mission from the first. He would always be part of the problem, as well as part of its solution. As he began his work in central Kentucky he encountered so many difficulties himself that he can scarcely be blamed for not realizing the drawbacks in his own attitudes.

Fee's first letter to the AMA after he had actually settled in Berea (dated October 1854) vividly presents some of his initial hardships: "I am here in Madison. I have $1.25 cts. I need many things. However small the due me If I can get it it will be of great aid to me. I shall find it difficult to borrow from strangers. My privations & those of my family are great."

"Not so great as those of the slave."[62]

In November he wrote:

I have during this time [two months] had no protracted meetings. I have been meeting different points in order to survey the ruins and encourage the faithful. The backsliding of Bro Fisk and the little service done in the latter part of his term of labors occasioned the backsliding of many & falling away of several at almost every point. It will take much labor to regain what has been lost in the public mind. . . . The field here is larger than the one I left but the churches are far more feeble & the house of worship very poor.

In that context he goes on to write of the need for colporteurs and other workers.[63]

By March 1855, the situation had worsened: defecting colporteurs, people who said they would come and then did not. "These failures and many changes press me greatly," Fee wrote,

I lament them—they discourage the people—give appearance of instability—I cannot help it. Many are going back. Poor weak creatures. They have had not former discipline—not taught to <u>live</u> [double underlining] and <u>endure</u> [d. u.] for Christ.

> I am almost worn down with labor, care and anxiety. . . .
> My family much discouraged in view of the state of society, schools,
> churches, privations, etc. Oh, the curse of slavery and the
> excellence of the gospel. . . ![64]

Fee saw all the work that had been done ready to slip away, fall back as if it had not been. He wrote in desperation, "I believe success under God in this state depends upon a speedy occupancy of the ground by Godly & efficient laborers." By November the church at Scaffold Cane had folded, many of its members moving out of the state; Boone's Fork now had only three members, but a few had been added to Union and Brush Creek. Clover Bottom had 9 and the Glade 30.[65]

Earlier he had written: "The churches in the interior are suffering for help. The awakening mind must be fed or it will go back or go wrong. God opens now—let us step in. He calls by his providence—Let us obey now! [double underlining] NOW! [d. u.][66]

The problem was urgent, even desperate; Fee had left his relatively successful ministry in northern Kentucky and come to a place where it appeared that total failure was eminent.

Ruefully and with some resignation he wrote, "Yet we cannot always have perfect men."[67]

FEE'S ARMY: THE MINOR PREACHERS
"This field seems to try men from the North as well as our colportures from the South." John G. Fee.

Unlike colporteurs, the abolitionist preachers who worked in the Kentucky mission field before the Civil War were virtually *all* Northerners, most of them Oberlin students or graduates.

The first six ministers are designated minor preachers on account of their relatively brief tenures in the region. None of them resided in any one place in Kentucky permanently; those who were married did not bring their wives and families (Hawley and Emerick, for example)—all of them preached in several different churches while traveling through the Commonwealth, mostly confining themselves to areas where Fee had congregations (in Lewis and Bracken Counties). Although his supervision of visiting ministers was not as thoroughgoing and authoritative as with colporteurs, Fee did have the task of coordinating all their efforts, providing hospitality for them, reporting to the AMA, and trying to induce men to come to Kentucky. Occasionally, he also attempted to induce a visitor to stay—unfortunately, it was also necessary at times to make a special effort to get rid of one.

The Northern men who were willing to work in Kentucky were an extremely diverse group. Most of them were reasonably well-educated and efficient; for that reason, among others, the experiences of the preachers were not the same as those of the colporteurs. But the ministers had, and created, problems of their own.

Rev. Francis Hawley: Critic from the East
"I take great pains to demonstrate the most unpopular anti-slavery truthes so as to secure the conscience of all & I think . . . I have generally succeeded in my object."
Francis Hawley.

Francis Hawley first appeared in Kentucky in 1853, when he was 51 years old, expressly invited on the recommendation of William Goodell. Also on Goodell's recommendation, Fee invited Hawley to Cabin Creek to perform the baptism of John and Matilda Fee. Rev. Hawley, a native of Connecticut, would seem an odd choice for this service, but, in a way, he was uniquely qualified. When he was in his twenties he had moved to South Carolina, where he set up a business, then became an agent of the Bible and Tract Societies, and eventually a Baptist minister in North Carolina. "His dislike for slavery" drove him back to Connecticut, and eventually he removed his antislavery ministry to western New York, joined the free church movement, retaining the Baptist doctrine of immersion. Incidentally, his "dislike" for slavery was so intense that he contributed a major narrative account of that institution to Weld's *Slavery as It Is.* [68]

Fee approved of Hawley's "principles and views" and found him "smart and industrious." Fee reported:

> I have just returned from a fourth visit to Madison Co.—90 miles—again we have had an encouraging meeting, good attention, quiet, orderly congregations—four additions—Bro Hawley went with me. The people here [in Bracken County] and there heard him gladly; thus again demonstrating the fact that the South is open to Eastern and Northern men—men who will preach a whole gospel. Those

> who know Bro Hawley know he never "prophesies smooth things"—he speaks the truth without compromise.

Thus, it seemed, the region was right for missionary efforts from abroad. But almost from the very beginning Fee perceived that Hawley was all wrong for the region. In March 1855, Fee wrote, Hawley "is not fitted for this field, though he thinks he is. He loves to do what he told a friend he loved to do—'harpoon the people'. He loves to laugh how he makes them squirm."[69]

It appears that Hawley did not confine his harpooning tactics to pointing out the peoples' sins—which is, of course, a standard method of making congregations squirm. He was also fond of specifying their other deficiencies. Sixty years later George Candee still recalled Francis Hawley who "could not endure the primitive [sic] ways of the mountain people of Kentucky. He told these people that they lived in houses that his people would not degrade a horse or cow by stabling them in." Fee described the same practice: "At most places the people complain of his severe remarks in his preaching—hard unfeeling air—also severe remarks about their poor houses—dress—habits &c." According to Fee, Hawley had "no tenderness"; he was "pugnacious," delivering his sermons with "fists clenched—voice not soft—air sometimes taunting." Citing an example of Hawley's provoking behavior, Fee relayed the followed anecdote:

> Sometime [his] repartees are sharp. For instance, a brother the other day was objecting to Emancipation on the soil [that is, freeing slaves without sending them away] by saying he had no daughters but he had a handsome wife and if Negroes were free some one might get her for a wife. ["]Well,["] said Bro Hawley, "She might be better off than she now is"—i.e. a negro would or might be better than the white husband—However true it be it reddened the husband—I expect disaffection.[70]

After Hawley left Kentucky the first time, Fee stated, "His [Bro. Hawley's] congregations have run down. He preferred to go alone—made no efforts to make organizations nor solicit persons to confess Christ—a sermon at a place generally—then gone." So it was Hawley's practice to strike once, insult everyone within the sound of his voice, and then move on. The usefulness of this ministry may not be obvious, but Fee was so pressed for laborers that he accepted Hawley's offer to return in the spring and go into new territory with Wiley Fisk.[71]

In June 1854, Fee desperately urged Hawley's return (the letter ending, "Let us obey Now! NOW!" which has already been quoted), and added that Hawley "need not fear biliousness, the county is healthy."[72]

Hawley appeared right on schedule, but his performance was exactly what Fee had every reason to expect:

> Bro. Hawley is often cutting & severe with no tenderness—The matter of his sermons is generally good. They were made however for a congregation of New England members that need sever [sic] gouging to rouse them.
> He intends to stay here no longer than Spring, will not remove his family. Has given the people to understand that his family could not bear the privations of society here—against this I warned him. [Fee added that Hawley always] makes sure his expenses are met.[73]

In addition, Hawley would talk to no one, "sinners or anyone else unless it is about slavery," a method which led people to believe that Fee's free churches were only a "political scheme." Fee stated: "He seems to be satisfied when he has said something against slavery—more concerned for this than for conversions of souls in all respects." Peter H. West, reporting on Hawley, wrote rather mildly, "His preaching is Tolerably well recd. Some object & say he is Two hard." Some persecution had begun because Hawley was a Northern man.[74]

In the same month Hawley also reported, his own account simply attesting the accuracy with which he had been presented by others. "I take great pains to demonstrate the most *unpopular* [my own italics] anti-slavery truthes so as to secure the conscience of all & I think that I have the best evidence that I have generally succeeded in my object." He fails to mention the nature of the evidence; apparently, it was own his enjoyable awareness that he was making everyone damned uncomfortable.[75]

As has been pointed out, Hawley found the colporteurs Fee had enlisted totally inadequate. He refused to permit Peter H. West to travel with him, something that Wiley Fisk amiably allowed. To make matters worse, Hawley himself announced that he had written to the AMA denouncing the colporteurs; West's friends were very upset, and there was "considerable feeling against Bro. Hawley in consequence of it." Then to make matters even worse, Hawley became fast friends with Wiley Fisk and Isaac Lane—a scheming alliance which disturbed Fee very much.[76]

Fee tried to be fair in reporting about Hawley, while becoming more and more disillusioned with him. In October 1854, he wrote, "In reference to Bro. Hawley let me say first that I like his principles or views better perhaps than any man who has labored with me here. He is also industrious." However, Fee was not impressed with Hawley's piety:

> He studies his bible but little [d. u.]—reads newspapers as his apparent chief delight—talks but little about personal piety or experience. Appears to pray but little—was untruthful to one poor slave in our travels telling him as we left him after feeding and saddling our horses 'I have no small money,' when I knew he had and had given him some not 5 minutes before. About this I talked to him. He answered . . . that he had thought about it since—but he said he had been without small money so long that he thought he had none. I know that he had not—one hour previous he paid small money to the ferryman. [Perhaps, Fee said, Hawley's apparent stinginess might be attributed to] a habit of close dealing during life.

Recalling another incident Fee remarked that Hawley had complained that his pantaloons were thin and he could not afford to buy others, although Fee had recently given him $10 from Cassius Clay. Hawley, Fee said, seemed "anxious about his support—says he cannot labor for less than $400." Fee asked to be paid no more than $300 annually himself to set a good example. Finally, Fee concluded "Bro. Hawley loves money."[77]

Hawley believed his own ministry was the best sort for Kentucky. He advised the AMA about the necessity of having Northern colporteurs in the field, and provided a long list of attributes such men should have, describing individuals roughly corresponding to himself. For example—"In one sense [the effective colporteur] should be prudent in another he should have [no prudence] at all."[78]

In spite of their agreement on principles (including free church ideas, abolitionism and temperance) Hawley and Fee were not working closely with one another by the time Hawley's mission was drawing to an end. "As for Bro Hawley," Fee wrote,

> I do not see him usually more than once in each month. He works off in the mountains by himself touching at a point & then going to another. He is thick with Isaac Lane a backslidden man, one who

has since his profession been drunk & swearing. He is now doing some better, but is yet striving to ensnare most of the members who are most efficient.

Fee concluded, "When Bro. Hawley gets back to New York I wish he may be kept there," and advised that Hawley be employed as a collecting agent, to lecture rather than preach. (Fee had also urged George Candee to write to the AMA describing Hawley's methods.)[79]

Hawley was so tight with money that he had never rented a room for himself, but lived with his horse, as Fee put it, relying upon others (apparently Matilda Fee) to do his "washing & mending," while talking "of justice & against covetousness." Hawley cut his intended stay in Kentucky short, not waiting till spring, but going home in the winter of 1854. Fee explained that Hawley had been meeting in schoolhouses and "not one in twenty schoolhouses have means to warm them." (School was usually in session in summer and fall.) On his way back to New York Hawley visited Fisk in December 1854, writing his last report from Fisk's house.[80]

Hawley's ministry in Kentucky was surely a failure: in fact, it was still producing criticism more than fifty years later. However, on January 14, 1876, Francis Hawley, by then a longtime resident of Westfield, Massachusetts, and an old man, wrote to John G. Fee, whose life's work had resulted in the the founding of Berea College, to reminisce fondly about good old days in Kentucky. By that time Fee may also have forgotten exactly how trying the days with Francis Hawley had been.[81]

John Wesley White: Pious but Sickly

John Wesley White, son of a Methodist minister near Cincinnati, was enrolled at Oberlin when he accepted Fee's invitation (March 1855) to come to Berea; he had been married, but his wife had died in August 1854, and he was himself in rather poor health. He was not experienced, but had "preached with much acceptance." By October 1855, White was laboring in the field, working in tandem with George Candee; and Fee was very pleased: he wrote, "[Bro. White] is pious, preaches well, and is well received by all." This happy state of affairs lasted only a few weeks and then White became very seriously ill. By the end of

November, White had been sick for six weeks out of the two months he had been in Berea, but he was recovering, and Fee expected him to apply for an AMA commission.[82]

In February 1856, Fee observed that White had been confined to his room for seven weeks with chills "which he brought from Ohio," a point insisted upon because Fee was engaged at that time in writing letters to convince the world at large that Berea was a "very healthful" spot. Bro. White, Fee reported, was "a man of feeble constitution." Even so when he recovered from his near-fatal illness, he was in better health than he had been for years. Fee had paid the doctor, and insisted on receiving no reimbursement for White's washing, boarding and nursing at his house.[83]

White stayed five months in all, preaching at the Glade, Union and Cummins in Rockcastle County; in his report to the AMA, White stated that he had regular appointments at Green's Schoolhouse in the cold winter and "the openness of the house" had held attendance down to an average of 20. He does not state what the drafty, unheated school building accomplished for his health. "Moral condition of things in Ky," he wrote, "I find to be truly deplorable."[84]

Rev. George Clark: Out of Season

Rev. George Clark, born Brooklyn, Connecticut, August 14, 1805, was a graduate of Yale (1833), a student at Lane Seminary in 1834 and one of the Lane Rebels. After his graduation from Oberlin Seminary in 1836, Clark became an evangelist, with a busy career in revivalism.[85]

Fee invited Clark to come to Kentucky in September and October 1855, but apparently communications broke down between them for when Clark arrived at the end of October or beginning of November, he was not expected. No preparations had been made, and Fee was disturbed by the relative failure of Clark's revival. Clark preached not only in and around Berea but also at Cabin Creek and in Bracken County, substituting for James Scott Davis, who was on a preaching trip in his native Virginia. It was an incredible mix-up, for Clark arrived in Berea while Fee was in Bracken; White was apparently dying at Fee's house, and Matilda Fee was ill as well; Clark himself was feeble and used to comforts. But the weather was rainy, the nights dark, the roads muddy; and no one had circulated news of the meeting, because they were all sick in bed. Then Clark went to Lewis County and found Davis gone to Woodstock, Virginia.[86]

After preaching in central Kentucky, Clark wrote; "I never before so fully realized the obstacles to the work of publishing a pure gospel in the midst of slavery." His opinion, coming from a minister with almost twenty years of experience in various fields, must bear no little weight. Berea was an incredibly difficult mission, even for people who arrived on time.[87]

Rev. Jacob Emerick: Pious and Wealthy

Rev. Jacob Emerick (of German descent, as his name suggests) was a United Brethren minister from Middletown, Ohio, where he was born around 1807. He owned a large and prosperous farm near Middletown, but periodically he left the management of his business in the hands of others and went out preaching. His first connection with the AMA work in Kentucky seems to have been through James Scott Davis; Emerick preached in Bracken and Lewis Counties at Davis's invitation in December 1855, and was very well received.[88]

Then he went home to Ohio, promising to return to northern Kentucky the next December. For years he alternated his missionary labors in Ohio and Kentucky. His work in Ohio had resulted in the formation of three churches by 1859, one in Jacksonburg and two on the Ohio-Kentucky border. Eventually, he met Fee and consented to visit Madison County. Fee was enthusiastic about him: "Bro. Emerick," Fee wrote, "is a man of little education—true he has read systems of theology—especially Finney's—has had a good memory, has had many years experience in the ministry . . . preaches with much popular effect—no man has ever been so well received from a free state. A man of age will command the confidence of the people better than young men."[89]

As usual, Fee perceived some weaknesses, but Emerick's strengths outweighed them:

> Bro Emerick knows nothing about English Grammar—writes very badly. Yet he is quite an energetic business man—started a poor boy—has received but little whilst in the ministry. Has quite a talent for making money, did not get much by his wife yet he has a farm of 505 acres . . . has recently put up a house worth 5 thousand. He's worth perhaps fifty thousand dollars—maybe more—He has

two or three children—single—grown. He thinks he will put his
farm into other hands and give himself to the ministry.[90]

Fee thought Emerick would be very useful as an evangelist to travel from
point to point. Of course, Emerick wanted to be paid for his work (Fee stated that
were he in Emerick's position, he would not). Still Emerick was obviously not
pursuing the ministry for any financial considerations, and the people wanted
Emerick back; "he [had] a very popular talent with the common people." Otis
Waters described Emerick more briskly—"an illiterate old fashioned Methodist
preacher transformed into an ultra Christian Unionist."[91]

Emerick was commissioned by the AMA in 1857; the same year he donated
$500 to John G. Fee's Land-school plan; he also returned $150 to the AMA,
writing that money was not his object. He wanted to help build churches, but, he
wrote, "It is not my intention to lay by money, it is my intention to do what I think
is right with the money." In any case, he had been paying his own expenses for
the past three years of his ministry, unemployed by any society, so he was
accustomed to laboring for virtually nothing. He was an extraordinary mixture of
piety and wealth, both sorely needed in Berea.[92]

In 1858, Emerick became a member of Berea College's first board of
trustees.

John Milton McLain: Fleeing from Trouble

John Milton McLain of Ironton, Ohio, brought more than his fair share of
problems with him when he arrived in Berea in March 1857. His coming must
have been somewhat surprising since no one—apparently—had invited him and he
was not a commissioned worker of the AMA. He had been a student in Oberlin
Seminary 1854-6 and he styled himself Rev. McLain.[93]

McLain, according to his own account, was almost overwhelmed with his
first experiences in a slaveholding state.

> I came on the stage from Lexington to Madison a few days
> since. In the stage was a colored woman & her child. After riding
> some miles her master, who sat next her, leaned forward & in an
> undertone—as if conscious of his guilt—inquired if Court met in
> Richmond the next day. Then can I sell this woman & her child

> tomorrow? Oh yes. On hearing this I became sick. I tremled [sic] and well nigh fainted. Why I was in the oppressor's land. Here was a living victim before my eyes. I thought Oh if that were my sister or my Mother.

It is hard to believe the matter came as such a shock: what did McLain expect? In any case, he found himself experiencing "almost deathly sensations," from which he was roused by "a man formerly from the <u>North</u>! He commenced discussion to me on the <u>kindness, hospitality</u> &c. of Kentuckians. How <u>kind</u> to their slaves &c. Of course with this living ostensible proof of their humanity before my eyes I was <u>convinced</u>."

McLain was even more shocked by his traveling companion's informing him that many farmers bought slave women "just to <u>Breed</u>" and that it was "counted no scandal for a man to have a lot of women beside his wife & have children by them."

Later, he was shocked even more deeply still by having a slaveholder in the coach confirm all these matters and boast about his own (apparently sexual) experiences.

McLain was surprised to discover that opposition in Kentucky was not "solely nor chiefly on account of anti-slavery preaching" because "anti-liquor drinking [speeches were] more disliked."

McLain reported that three slaves had attended the last sabbath meeting. "One of them, I am told," he wrote, "is a second Uncle Tom." (Uncle Tom in abolitionist circles was the central black hero, pious, self-sacrificing and naturally noble: not exactly the title's present connotation.) Then he observed the most shocking matter of all: "You would be amazed," he wrote, "to see how ignorant the youth of this country are." They do not know their catechism—"many can't tell <u>who made them</u>."[94]

McLain's trip to Kentucky seems to have been a total revelation to him: he had no inkling that slaveowners sold slaves, bred them for sale and had sexual relations with them. And some Northerners approved of this system! When McLain evinces surprise at discovering an Appalachian child ignorant of the catechism his whole account begins to seem ingenuous at best. Isn't he *posing* as a wide-eyed innocent from the happy North?

Perhaps John Milton McLain's naivete was a function of his youth and inexperience, although he cannot have been extremely young in 1857, for he had spent four years at Marietta College (in Ohio) and two at Oberlin Seminary and had been married. And, unfortunately, McLain had had many other experiences as well. He liked Kentucky so much he told Fee he wanted a commission from the AMA. Innocently, Fee recommended the young man. McLain had been commissioned by the AMA before, working in Iowa; so Fee assumed the organization knew all about him. Just to be sure he wrote what he had learned about the visitor from Ohio: McLain was in some trouble with his presbytery on a "pecuniary matter," and Oberlin Seminary had refused to graduate him. "I have heard," Fee stated, "that Pres. Finney [of Oberlin] says he thinks the Lord intends to make a useful man of Bro. McLain but that bro. McLain has such a temper that the Lord will almost have to kill him before he makes him useful."[95]

Meanwhile, McLain was finding his ministry less enjoyable but more adventurous than ever with a mob of 14 or 15 men pursuing him through Pulaski County "like a wild beast" with the intention of killing him; he got away.[96]

But he could not get away from his past. McLain himself wrote to the AMA to clarify his experiences. He had given up the ministry at one point (when he was a senior in Marietta College) because his fiancee begged him to; after he abandoned his ambition, he married the young woman and went into business. Everything went wrong for him; his business failed, and, he confessed, he had done wrong "in process of trying to save some of his property."

"I was distressed more & more for a long time," he wrote, "I repeatedly conversed with my wife about being a minister. Her reply, 'You be a minister! You'd make a pretty minister' so discouraged me that I bore in silence my reproaches of conscience." Eventually he had decided to resume his theological studies; "in a few days my wife also announced to me for the first time that she would not live with me & assigning as her only reason 'I do not love you well enough.'"He had been suspended from his church, which had censured him for using the title Reverend improperly, and he had been suspended from Seminary.[97]

McLain had come to Kentucky not because he was attracted to the work, but because he was fleeing an unpleasant situation in Ohio. The AMA refused the request for McLain's new commission; he was not in good standing with them either.

McLain and Richardson (another traveling abolitionist preacher) had been present the day Fee was mobbed at Crab Orchard. They were not threatened themselves, but accompanied Fee on his forced march. Without Fee's knowledge, McLain published a highly inaccurate account of this incident in the *Kentucky Gazette*, maintaining, for one thing, that the attack had taken place because of Otis Waters' attempts to start a school in Rockcastle County. Fee countered that claim with the following rather mysterious assertion, "I do not suppose the immediate cause of this outbreak was the attempt to establish a school there. . . . I suppose it was the work chiefly of one man whose wife joined the church. He is reported by one who has gone to Kansas as aiding in burning the church. The situation Bro. McLain sustains to his wife is a continual barrier in a field like this." Bro. McLain had been talking to Fee and Richardson about taking another wife, even though he had no expectations of a divorce.[98]

The juxtaposition of the man whose wife joined the church and McLain's situation with his own wife is equivocal. Was McLain having an affair with a parishioner's wife? Was the church burned by an irate, cuckolded husband? Did McLain write his report in order to *conceal* what had really happened? Fee's suspicion, whatever it was, indicates that people who opposed him might not have been motivated simply by pure hatred of antislavery principles; at least, he did not think they were.

At any rate, McLain was finished. Fee found his case "a most trying one," because Fee perceived that McLain wanted to have a ministry, wanted to do right, wanted to work in the mission field—and he was industrious and pious. But he was strangely irresponsible. "He has lawsuits still to manage," Fee said, "has not he says been out for ten years. Yet this does not seem to engage his mind."[99]

McLain humbly accepted the AMA's refusal to commission him, but he wrote a confidential letter to the organization saying that Fee was out of money and in debt; he implored the AMA to send Fee more financial assistance. McLain wanted to be helpful, but he was too feckless and irresponsible to be anything but a handicap in Fee's work. In September 1857, Fee reported that McLain had gone back to Ohio, and from there to Illinois; Fee was greatly relieved.[100]

The people described above (colporteurs and minor preachers) did not necessarily operate successively; many of them worked in Kentucky simultaneously—one would go, another stay until another arrived, someone else would arrive, then someone would leave, and so on. Sometimes no one would be working with Fee at all. For example, in April 1856, White and Candee, who had been working together, were both gone and Fee was "alone again." In August of the same year: "Again I find myself almost alone, so far as preachers are concerned, in the interior." But at another point, Hawley and Candee were in Berea at the same time; and when Rev. George Clark arrived unexpectedly, Fee, Candee, White and Clark were all living at the Fee house; the timing was uncontrollable and often totally counter-productive.[101]

"None of the brethren," Fee complained, "like to stop anywhere else but with me. They will scatter out soon. Tis best—general good demands it." Fee refused to take any money for the hospitality he and his wife offered. The visiting preachers, the resident teachers and others boarded for free. Naturally, it was harder to feed and care for a whole houseful of people at once than one visitor at a time; not infrequently Fee's household in this period would number 9 or 10 people.[102]

But Fee *needed* help. In his report for the year ending September 1857, he wrote that he had preached every sabbath of the year save two or three, and then he was at a protracted meeting with a helper preaching. "I have seen no place where I thought I could take rest." During the year he had preached regularly at Berea, at Union, at Roundstone, at Cummins, occasionally at Cavender and Clover Bottom and frequently in surrounding counties: more than six congregations, many miles apart. In another report he complained that his labors were "scattered over five counties trying to keep them alive until some one would come as a pastor."[103]

A passing remark in one of Fee's letters sums up the whole matter very well: "This field seems to try men from the North as well as our colportures from the South."[104]

CHAPTER FOUR

THREE MISSIONARIES FROM OBERLIN:
JAMES SCOTT DAVIS, GEORGE CANDEE
AND WILLIAM E. LINCOLN

Oberlin: Programs of Reform
*"Lamenting the degeneracy of the church and the deplorable condition of our
perishing world. . . ." Covenant of Oberlin Colony.*

Missionaries from Oberlin, Ohio, poured into Kentucky in the late 1850's;
they came to preach, to teach, to settle. Why did they come? What did they think
they were doing?

It is important to explore the connections between Oberlin and Berea in
terms of common goals, principles and activities. Eventually Berea would be called
"Oberlin in the South"—a very apt title in many respects, but also quite misleading.
Berea was patently *not* Oberlin, as many were to discover to their horror. It is true,
however, that Berea from its inception imitated Oberlin in idealogy and method and
depended almost entirely on Oberlin for workers. Practically speaking, Berea
could not have existed without the men and women Oberlin trained; Fee believed
(for good reasons) that Berea had to have 'imported' laborers from the North—
and, for the most part, they simply would not come from anywhere but Oberlin.[1]

Oberlin was built by people who believed they could improve the world.
Their assumption may be considered the foundation stone for all the diverse
manifestations of reforming zeal in Oberlin's early history. The 19th century was

the century of the Christian reform movement, and Oberlin, according to its historian Robert S. Fletcher, was "the embodiment of the movement."[2]

One of the founders of Oberlin—college and colony—John J. Shipherd wrote, in a letter to his parents dated August 6, 1832: "I propose through God's assistance to plant a colony . . .whose chief aim shall be to glorify God and do good to men, to the utmost extent of their ability." Schools would be maintained in the colony "to educate school teachers for our desolate valley and many ministers for our dying world." Manual Labor for students was a part of his plan, which required the settlement of approximately 28 Christian families.[3]

With his friend Philo P. Stewart, Shipherd negotiated with the owners of a large (500 acre), very flat tract of land in Russia township, Lorain County, in northern Ohio, and located Oberlin near the settlements of Elyria and Brownhelm. Like these villages, Oberlin was settled almost wholly from western Massachusetts and Connecticut—with Stockbridge, Massachusetts, supplying some of the most well-known families. In 1819, Col. Henry Brown of Stockbridge led a band of his neighbors to northern Ohio where they settled Brownhelm, near the later site of Oberlin. These Stockbridge families included Pease, Barnum, Patten, Fairchild, Curtis, Shepherd, Peck and Baldwin and others who became intimately involved in Oberlin's work in the years to follow.[4]

The Covenant of Oberlin Colony, while it was in effect only a few years, provides ample evidence of the original impulse behind the whole project. Its preamble begins,

> Lamenting the degeneracy of the church and the deplorable condition of our perishing world, and ardently desirous of bringing both under the entire influence of the blessed gospel of peace; and viewing with peculiar interest the influence which the valley of the Mississippi must assert over our nation and the nations of the earth; and having, as we trust, in answer to devout supplication, been guided by the counsel of the Lord: The undersigned covenant together under the name of the Oberlin Colony. . . .

The signers agreed to move to Oberlin as soon as possible, to maintain "a community of interest," to hold no more property than necessary, and to donate as much of their resources as possible to "the spread of the Gospel." Moving beyond economic considerations the signers agreed to "eat only plain and wholesome food, renouncing all bad habits," including use of tobacco in any form and "strong and unnecessary drinks," namely tea and coffee [alcohol was too obvious to be mentioned]. They also renounced everything expensive, "that is simply calculated to gratify the palate." In matters of dress they agreed to "renounce all the world's expensive and unwholesome fashions of dress, particularly tight dressing and ornamental attire." Their houses, furniture, and so on, had to be plain and durable.

They promised to act "as the body of Christ" caring for widows, orphans and the sick and needy.

The ninth resolution dealt with the prospective school: "We take special pains to educate *all* [my own italics] our children thoroughly, and train them up in body, intellect and heart, for the service of the Lord." The 10th resolution involved a promise to identify the interests of Oberlin Institute as their own and to "do what we can to extend its influence to our fallen race."

Finally, the covenanters agreed to "sustain the institution of the Gospel at home" and among neighbors, striving also "to maintain deep-toned and elevated personal piety, 'to provoke each other to love and good works,' to live together in all things as brethren, and to glorify God in our bodies and spirits, which are His."[5]

The founders of Oberlin aimed for universal reform, nothing less. Although only physiological reform and the health movement figure in Oberlin's Covenant, temperance, manual labor, antislavery, the peace movement, moral reform and experimental education (maybe implied in the Covenant) were soon part of Oberlin's program. From the beginning the Oberlin doctrine included the goal of spreading itself all over the world, beginning in the valley of the Mississippi; Christian missions had been promulgating some form of the Christian message for centuries. But the Oberlin portfolio of reform was probably the most radical version of the gospel the United States had yet seen.

In a way, Oberlin enjoyed a second founding in 1835, when many of the Lane Rebels, along with their teacher Asa Mahan, pledged to migrate as a group to the school in northern Ohio, if Charles G. Finney would also agree to come and if Oberlin would admit black students as well. This influx of mature young men, ardent Christian abolitionists, saved the then-faltering college and transformed the whole pattern of belief and action of Oberlin for years to come. From the arrival of the Lane Rebels, Oberlin dated its uniqueness as the first interracial, coeducational institution of higher learning in the country. (It was not the first interracial school, nor the first coeducational one, but the first to combine the two). And from their arrival Oberlin also dated its deserved reputation as the most radical school in the whole United States—the educational wing of the "Church of Abolition."

Behind Oberlin's reforming zeal lay the revival preaching of Charles Grandison Finney, who would become Oberlin's president in 1851. Finney's doctrine of perfectionism, or 'holiness,' leant itself to support of a wide variety of sanctifying activities. Individuals could make themselves better and help other individuals to improve themselves, and since individuals make up the world, the world could therefore be reformed. As president of Oberlin College Finney had a direct, powerful impact on faculty and students. His revivals continued on campus; his teaching and preaching and his ideas touched everyone at Oberlin before the war. Under his leadership Oberlin College was as emphatically religious as any institution of higher learning could ever become. Worship services, prayer meetings, Bible studies, societies and clubs all more or less marked by pious purposes—every form of Protestant influence that could be applied was applied. Christian students were urged to loftier and loftier spiritual goals; unconverted students were labored over, exhorted, prayed for, and treated to visits from faculty members or the president himself for personal counsel. Oberlin was for all intents and purposes "God's college." Any student who entered Oberlin College could reasonably expect years of intense Christian indoctrination, almost total submersion in religious concerns.

Small wonder that many Oberlin students became missionaries: men and women were encouraged to spend their vacations (which were in the wintertime) in the field. After all, it was not necessary to wait for graduation to become "useful." Many Oberlin missionaries, such as William E. Lincoln and Otis B. Waters, worked in Kentucky during the winter break. Every year hundreds of students went out into teaching positions, many of them temporary. Others became intinerant preachers for a season. Alumni, of course, were expected to choose a life's work dedicated to God's service; ministers and missionaries abounded. Seldom has any country seen such a taskforce as this small army of Yankees, zealots for personal piety and universal reform, men and women who were willing—as they would demonstrate—to risk life itself in the cause.[6]

Why did they come to Kentucky? Because it was a mission field.

What did they think they were doing? Reforming the world.

What was it like to attend Oberlin? Some students found the piety displayed there a bit much. William E. Lincoln, arriving from England, found it exactly to his taste. "When I got to Oberlin," he wrote, "I was struck with wonder, at the manifest presence of God, everywhere." But one girl he met had a different reaction. In "angry disgust, [she] said, 'I have to attend 21 different prayers in the course of the day.' Before recitation, prayer; before eating, prayer, once a day at chapel, prayer & so on." Lincoln claimed that "she exaggerated; but rightly characterized the spirit of Oberlin in those days."[7]

Robert S. Fletcher writes, "The serious mindedness of early Oberlin is appalling. The consciousness of a wicked world and an approaching day of atonement clouded the spirits of students and teachers. Life was a serious business and death was momentarily awaited. Anything which diverted the attention from religion was sinful." Finney himself believed that "glee, fun, hilarious mirth, games, charades and pleasure seeking grieve the Holy Spirit. . . ." William E. Lincoln remembered that a friend of his, Arabella Phillips, the young lady who objected to praying so much, made a joke by exploiting the common Oberlin practice of addressing everyone as "Brother," "Sister," or, in cases where great respect was due: "Father." Finney himself met Miss Phillips on campus and "he looking at her said 'Good morning, Daughter of the Devil' She extending her hand said 'I'm glad to see you, Father'." A funny story? No, not according to either Finney or Lincoln, who reported, "He [Finney] in tears at the witty answer plead[ed] with her to give her heart to God, & I think made a deep impression. I think he succeeded."[8]

Edward Henry Fairchild, writing to reassure Finney himself in 1860, boasted of Oberlin,

> . . . from many dissipating things we are free. We have no balls, no cotillion parties, no kissing parties, no late parties, no midnight parades of Sons of Malta, no secret societies of any kind, no horse racing, no circuses, no gambling establishments, no drinking saloons, no brothels, no Sabbath excursions, no street fights, or street drunkards, no military parades, no county fairs, very little swearing, very little smoking, almost no cases of discipline, very little mischief among the students, almost perfect friendship between Faculty and students, no rebellions, no outbursts, &c. Indeed, with all our faults, I know of no place that compares with this for the general prevalence of good order and religious principle.[9]

Given this framework, it is scarcely surprising that Oberlin students found themselves hemmed in by rules and regulations governing virtually every aspect of life. They were expected to be useful during a day stretching from 4 or 5 o'clock in the morning till 10 at night, although some found it necessary to rise earlier. Time was very fully occupied in the waking hours, with private prayer, chapel (both before breakfast in early days), breakfast, classes, dinner, work, chapel, supper, Bible reading, prayer and study forming a typical male student's schedule.[10]

Part of the rationale for filling up student time was probably a certain anxiety about allowing too much freedom in an institution with men and women, black and white, all working together. Regulations about socal contact and sexual relationships were the strictest of all, rigid and repressive to a degree. As might be expected, students were forbidden to visit members of the opposite sex in their rooms, and marriage automatically led to a student's dismissal, as William E. Lincoln was to learn from practical experience. Women were allowed very little liberty, with special restrictions on when and where they could walk—any excursion with a gentleman could be undertaken only with special permission. No young lady was permitted to "leave her boarding place for any *length of time,* excepting for her regular exercises in the institution, without previous consultation with the matron of the family." Students discovered in infraction of rules were required to make public confession in chapel.[11]

Exactly how repressive the system was emerges clearly in the story of the "Oberlin Lynching", an incident publicized throughout the country. An 18-year-old male student, Horace Norton from Ripley, Ohio, wrote some 'obscene letters' to female students, including one inviting a young woman to a secret rendezvous in the woods on the outskirts of the village. These letters were intercepted and a committee of 15 male students—including some advanced members of the Theological department, among them the future president of Berea College— agreed to send Norton an acceptance note in a female handwriting and then meet him themselves. Norton was duly caught in the woods; the men tried to bring him to repentence, but when their efforts met with no success, they bared Norton's back, "laid him across a log and gave him twenty-five lashes." Edward Henry Fairchild, who had the honor of whipping Norton, recalled the "Lynchers" prayed for guidance before the punishment was administered and "wept like little children while the tragedy was performed." The next morning Norton was expelled for immoral conduct. Norton's father, "a professor of religion,"understandably upset, appeared on campus "armed with pistols [and a] bowie knife" to demand justice and sued the men who confessed to their part in the affair, Fairchild among them; the case was eventually appealed to the Ohio Supreme Court and the Lynchers were fined $550. Oberlin College inflicted no punishment on them at all. "There were some in Oberlin," Fletcher writes, "quite evidently who looked upon them as heroes." James H. Fairchild, brother of the leading "Lyncher" noted, "One singular fact is that the female part of the community exculpates [the "Lynchers"] from all blame . . . and some parents have sent their daughters to Oberlin for education who hesitated to do it before." Describing the trial, Fairchild called it "a strange sight. [The "Lynchers"] are in the pulpit one day and in the criminal box the next." Religious papers in the East published some "very bitter" accounts of the affair, pointing to it as "the natural result of the doctrines held at Oberlin."[12]

Some of Berea's workers, arriving fresh from Oberlin, acted a little as if they just broken out of prison; all carried with them an urge to repress others, even when they could not suppress themselves. Ardent piety, tender-hearted kindness and cruel inhibition frequently existed side by side: Oberlin workers often viewed central Kentucky as the most immoral place in the world, a heightened and probably inaccurate view, which years at Oberlin had predisposed them to make. Kentuckians were not necessarily the wickedest people on earth, although the Oberlinites may well have been the most judgmental. Still their piety was almost always genuine, their devotion to God deep, their dedication, in many cases, utterly amazing.

In 1858, shortly before Berea College's abortive first founding, Berea was primarily the center of a mission field. From the tiny village on the Ridge, Fee supervised a small band of colporteurs, teachers and fellow preachers: three of whom, besides himself, were considered to be "missionaries," ministers with relatively permanent assignments to found new free churches and maintain established ones. They were the leaders of the abolitionist movement in Kentucky.

On April 8, 1858, the four missionaries (John G. Fee, John A. R. Rogers, James Scott Davis and George Candee) addressed a joint letter to the AMA, defining their work so that prayer might be undertaken for them "more intelligently." They stated that they were in Kentucky not merely to wage antislavery war, but to "plant and train spiritual churches which shall honor Christ and be a power for the salvation of the world. To connive at sin," they continued, "however popular, would be to give up our object. . . . Consequently we treat slavery as we do any other manifest sin." Pointing out the success of the mission, the ministers mentioned their free churches, maintained in five Kentucky counties (Lewis, Bracken, Madison, Rockcastle and Jackson); enumerating their dangers, they reminded their readers of mob violence and continued threats. "[We] wish our friends," they wrote, "to clearly understand that we need God's protecting care as truly as did the primitive Christians or the Protestants of Luther's day."[13]

James Scott Davis
"Let the righteous smite me, it shall be a kindness." James Scott Davis to the AMA.

James Scott Davis was born in Winchester, Virginia, July 2, 1828, son of a printer and newspaperman, Samuel Davis, and his remarkable wife, Mary (Brown) Davis. Samuel Davis edited the *Winchester Republican*; by about 1832 he was editor of the *Wheeling Gazette* in what is now West Virginia. With his eldest son, Henry Kirk White Davis, the father set out for the West, and, after an abortive attempt to establish a newspaper in Cassville, Wisconsin, settled in Peoria, Illinois, where he edited the *Peoria Register & North Western Gazette* from 1837 until his retirement in 1842.[14]

James Scott Davis, although he chose the ministry for a career, was, like his father and brothers, a knowledgeable printer and skillful writer. Throughout his life he engaged in some form of journalism, functioning, for example, as the Kentucky correspondent for the *Congregational Herald*.[15]

The most remarkable member of this family of journalists was Mary Brown Davis, abolitionist, feminist and temperance reformer; she had been born into an affluent Southern family, long-established in Alexandria, Virginia. She sprang from generations of professional men, doctors and lawyers, comfortable slaveholding people. Her father William Brown had studied law under Bushrod Washington with Henry Clay, but at the age of 25 he abandoned his profession and retired to his estate in Fauquier County, removing in 1824 to Winchester; at one time he owned as many as 50 slaves, one of whom was his daughter's mammy.

Mary Brown Davis began publishing antislavery pieces in 1839 in Benjamin Lundy's *Genius of Universal Emancipation.* Her work appeared for years in the *Western Citizen*, an abolitionist newspaper in Chicago. Signing only her initials, "M.B.D.," she wrote of her experiences with slavery in her childhood, applying her direct knowledge to formulate attacks upon the 'peculiar institution.' In 1843, she organized the Peoria Anti-Slavery Society and campaigned in favor of dress reforms when Mrs. Bloomer was becoming notorious for wearing a garment of the same name. In her widowhood, Mrs. Davis became a regular contributor to a pioneer periodical, the Oquawka *Spectator*, and she also wrote for the *Galesburg Free Democrat* when her son edited it in 1854.[16]

From his mother James Scott Davis and his brothers learned the sentiments of abolitionism very early; his father, owner of two slaves in Virginia while he was resident in Illinois, became an abolitionist several years after hs wife had already begun her campaign. In 1842 "the notorious abolitionist" Rev. William T. Allan (a Lane Rebel), tried to establish a local antislavey society in Peoria, but was prevented by a mob. "The riot made an abolitionist out of Samuel Davis."[17]

Four years later another proslavery attack was directed against Samuel Davis himself. A fellow citizen "beat him . . . pushed him against a window and tried to gouge out his eyes." Although Davis was an old man by this time a crowd simply looked on, while a magistrate who tried to interfere was restrained "by a confederate of Davis's attacker, and when [James Scott Davis] came to rescue his father he was hit on the head with a cane." Finally two men did come to Davis's assistance, but only after he and his son had been "badly and bloodily battered."[18]

His parents' ideas and experiences were certainly formative for James Scott Davis. After the father's death in 1849, the Davis family, mother and three of her sons, moved to Galesburg, Illinois, a church-colony-college community with roots in Finney evangelism, Oneida Manual Labor Institute, the Lane Rebellion and (obviously) relationships and affinities with Oberlin. James Scott Davis attended Knox College, the institution at Galesburg, graduating in 1851. At his commencement exercises John G. Fee, the visiting speaker, described his "work of establishing anti-slavery churches in Kentucky." After graduation Davis traveled to Chicago to the Christian Anti-Slavery convention there, probably accompanying Blanchard and Fee, who also left from Galesburg. Davis received his first impression of Fee at this time. It must have been a very favorable one.[19]

From Galesburg, Davis went to Oberlin to attend seminary. Naturally, he performed his manual labor assignment in the Oberlin printing office. At school he met John A. R. Rogers, and the two earnest young men soon became fast friends; they had a great deal in common—Davis was as mission-minded as his new friend. He also met Rogers' younger sister Amelia, who was to become Mrs. James Scott Davis. In his diary Rogers records many references to Davis during the Oberlin years—noting visits, conversations, trips they took together to conventions and church meetings, lectures, sometimes 'double-dating,' James and Amelia, Rogers and one of his girlfriends.[20]

In August 1854, Rogers jotted down a couple of typically reticent entries: "9th Wed. Stormy debate in Lit. Society. J. S. Davis ends." and "Aug 11th Friday. Meeting of the The. Soc. about conduct of J. S. Davis." Apparently, Davis had contributed some thunder to the stormy meeting, the topic of which goes unrecorded.

Before his graduation from seminary, Davis had announced that after commencement he would be "ready to go preach where Providence directs." He had written to Fee about going to Kentucky, although he had also considered Kansas or Illinois, where antislavery ministers were needed, and where his widowed mother lived. But as a Southerner himself he had long regarded the South as his future field: and Fee definitely wanted him in northern Kentucky. Davis worried that he would not have time to further his studies; some missionaries to the West he considered to be mentally ill-equipped, and he feared becoming intellectually stagnant himself. He wanted to understand Finney's Theology, Hamilton's Philosophy, Hebrew and Greek exegesis. Another consideration he expressed by noting, "I shall probably before I have been long in the ministry find that . . . 'it is not good to be alone.'"[21]

After his graduation from Oberlin Seminary (1854) Davis, 26 years old, went immediately to Lewis County, Kentucky, as replacement in the northern Kentucky churches of John G. Fee, having accepted Fee's invitation by September 1. He was acceptable to Fee's congregations who had refused to consider any Yankee candidates. Commissioned by the AMA, he asked the Association to pay his travel expenses to Kentucky, so he could take his books—"the number of which," he wrote, "is really quite small."[22]

Davis reported to the AMA, writing from Germantown in Bracken County, October 3:

> Last Sabbath, I preached at Glenville (Cabin Creek) Lewis co., and thus entered upon my labors as supply of the church at that place and the church here. I feel that a great responsibility rests upon me, but knowing that God never calls his children to a station without giving them grace to discharge its duties, I begin to occupy this post without fear, for I think Providence has pointed me towards it.

He entered his new mission field with a thorough and appropriate education and in typical financial straits. Although planning to buy Fee's house in Lewis County, Davis had "just three dollar bills on the State Bank of Ohio, and one of these [was] worn & torn." He was already engaged to Amelia Rogers, and her financial situation equalled his own: "[She] is about as poor as I am," he reported, "and I am glad of it." J. S. D. and Amelia Rogers planned to marry in October the next year, but the wedding would not take place until June 16, 1856, when Rev. John Morgan of Oberlin married the young couple at her parents' home in Pittsfield, Ohio, a few miles from Oberlin. (Davis announced his wedding to the AMA in June, but he was evidently thinking ahead for he asked that the Association send him and his bride a box of bedclothes by the next winter.) In the meantime, Davis's initial financial difficulties were complicated by his unhappy discovery that the congregations in northern Kentucky had been paying Fee only in product, so that getting them to pay cash was a problem.[23]

At first Fee was happy with the young colleague whose attitude toward money was so similar to his own. He wrote, when Davis was barely established, "With Bro. Davis I am greatly pleased. He is faithful yet kind—I hope much from him. Bro. Hawley will offend ten men to Davises one & yet not be more faithful nor more successful."[24]

In spite of his poverty Davis was also pleased with his new work. "The congregations are very orderly and quite respectable as to numbers," he stated, "Most of the members are young, but their consciences seem to be alive and a good degree developed. I of course notice a difference between this people and congregations of New England parentage; yet I think half a score of years will make a change here. Bro. Fee has left his mark. It is very easy to follow in his footsteps."[25]

Still the work was demanding: in one quarter Davis reported preaching 10 times in Bracken County (eight times at Bethesda, once at Camp Creek, once at Mr. Robinson's), 14 times in Lewis County (nine at Glenville, two at Crooked Creek, three at private houses), and three times in Fleming County at Bro. James M. West's. A young lady, he noted, had been expelled from church for dancing. On a happier note, both Fee and Jonathan Blanchard, then president of Knox College, went to Bracken County and preached in the Summer of 1855.[26]

Three years before, Davis had inquired about establishing a free church in Woodstock, Virginia. In the fall of 1855 he was invited to "come & see" and he planned to go "with great diffidence. I am young," he wrote, "and look younger than I am."[27]

So, late in 1855, Davis visited churches in Woodstock, the region where he had really wanted to settle in the first place. Woodstock was quite near Davis's birthplace, and he liked what he saw there. Very few slaves were owned in the neighborhood; the inhabitants, mostly Germans from Pennsylvania, had never heard an antislavery sermon before Davis preached to them, but had developed a distaste for the slavery system on their own. Davis found in Woodstock a confirmed abolitionist, George Rye, who had been "endeavoring to place himself in circumstances such as will enable him to give his time and interest to the slavery movement" since the late 1830's. Other prominent men also expressed interest in antislavery and Rye proposed that Davis go to Woodstock as an acknowledged abolitionist preacher. Rye wrote (in a letter published in the *Galesburg Democrat*), "There is no minister of the Gospel in all Virginia, that I am aware of, that preaches against the sin of slaveholding, and . . . it is of the very first importance that every place in the South should be supplied where there is any probability of success with an antislavery minister. This is one of those places if a proper man can be found; and I think the finger of providence has pointed to the man—Rev. James Scott Davis."[28]

Davis wanted to go very badly; his Kentucky congregations revealed themselves as tiresomely quarrelsome (at one point the Bracken County congregation had a big altercation because someone had distributed an anti-tobacco tract in the church), but he was stuck—as an honorable man he could not leave the position he had promised to fill and no one (perhaps understandably) wanted to take his place. He wrote to Simeon Jocelyn at the AMA in January 1856 asking for prayers that he (Davis) would be a faithful pastor. "I feel very deficient," he said, "Naturally, I lack many requisites and have many proclivities which tend to hinder my usefulness. I should at once withdraw from the service had I not faith that God can and will, in this earthen vessel, manifest the excellency of his power. . . ." When a young Englishman from Oberlin, William E. Lincoln, came to visit unexpectedly in March, Davis was hoping against hope that Providence had sent a replacement so he could escape to Woodstock. No such luck. Lincoln had other irons in the fire, as we shall see. He helped Davis for a short time and then moved on. Davis enjoyed a "liberty" in the Spring 1856, when he not only preached 23 times in northern Kentucky, but also took a trip, lectured in Boston, preached in Blue Hill, lectured again "on our position in Ky." at Searsport and Bangor, Maine, West Medway, Hinsdale and Peru, Massachusetts. He was married in June, probably on his way back to Kentucky from his eastern tour.[29]

In February 1857 Davis and Fee held a protracted meeting at Bethesda Church in Bracken County, resulting in more than a dozen new members. "The subject of slavery," Davis stated, "threw no damper upon the revival" because the congregation was accustomed "to hear this abomination treated as a heinous sin." Altogether hopeful at this point, Davis urged upon "anti-slavery Christian men [their] duty of emigrating with their families" to Kentucky. In a long letter published in the *American Missionary*, Davis described the regions around his churches in Lewis and Bracken Counties, informing prospective settlers of Kentucky's "salubrious" climate and "beautiful clear water." He had already heard from a man with a large· family living in Minnesota Territory, and from a Vermonter, who was debating whether his Christian duty required that he "lend [his] feeble aid in planting free institutions" in Kansas, "that fair and beautiful land," or that he "settle and diffuse carefully, yet boldly, the principles of truth, freedom and benevolence" in Kentucky. For the moment, Davis was "greatly cheered" by these prospects—none of which would come to fruition under his leadership.[30]

Soon Davis was supervising at least one colporteur of his own, Oliver P. Grigson. Fee and Davis had bought a horse for Grigson, but the county judge of Bracken had refused the new worker a license to sell books. Davis was eager to get his new brother-in-law, John Rogers, into the Kentucky field. In August, he suggested Rogers as a possible helper for Fee himself, and applied to the AMA on Rogers' behalf without even telling him beforehand.[31]

The congregation at Cabin Creek was quarreling again, but Davis stayed on, and rather sadly reported in October 1857,

> The church here voted unanimously to retain me another year, but of course this might be expected; for there was no one else to choose.
> I have been much cast down for some weeks past, and have felt that some one else could accomplish more here than I have done. Yesterday, however, somewhat revived me and today I feel like thanking God and taking courage.[32]

Beginning in the same month, Davis published at least two open letters to Cassius M. Clay in which he (Davis) defended John G. Fee's position at Slate Lick Springs and called upon Clay to restore his support to Fee. He said, "I fear that friends in Northern States will misapprehend your withdrawal of aid from Brother Fee, and infer that your zeal is slackening in the cause of universal liberty." In a personal letter dated November 5, 1857, Davis (apparently answering a question from Fee) wrote to Fee, stating as far as he could remember, what Fee had actually said at Slate Lick Springs; his account, incidentally, agrees with Fee's own claims about what he argued that day.[33]

Rogers arrived in Lewis County November 1857, and for some months, with his brother-in-law's help, Davis was happy in his ministry again. He and Rogers preached together, conducted meetings, prayed together. Davis must have been ecstatic when Fee wrote (probably in January 1858) telling Rogers *not* to come to Berea; this was at a time when the whole abolitionist community at Madison County seemed to be in jeopardy. Davis fired off a letter to the AMA at the end of February, suggesting that Rogers take over the Glenville Church while Davis would retain the Bracken County ministry only—for awhile at least. On February 4, he "asked at prayer meeting for dismission from the pastorship of the church at Cabin Creek." His freedom from his burdensome Kentucky ministry was almost in sight.[34]

In the meantime, George Candee, now located in Jackson County, Kentucky, was proposing a plan of his own—he was living in a newly formed county, which had just elected public officials favorable to abolitionism. It was a perfect place for an antislavery newspaper to be established, and the perfect editor would be James Scott Davis, experienced printer and newspaper writer. Neither of these plans came to fruition, for Fee suddenly changed his mind and summoned Rogers to work in Berea. By the end of March 1858, Rogers and his family had left Cabin Creek, and Davis was caught again with no prospect of release, preaching in Pendleton County in spite of death threats, visiting Jackson County in April to fill some appointments for Candee and stopping in Berea on the way back home.[35]

When Davis arrived in Berea he found Fee still in "a state of great depression" because of the defection of Cassius Clay the summer before. The people of Berea had considered Clay the "great champion of liberty" and his aloofness alarmed and discouraged them. Davis wrote, "The vacillation and weakness of some of the brethren was to Bro Fee a source of anxiety far more wearing than that occasioned by violence from without; and from these causes, his bodily strength was giving away." While Davis was in Berea, Fee's health improved a great deal; Davis preached for him every Sabbath, and occasionally through the week as well. "Meetings were attended," Davis stated, "and Bro. Fee was encouraged by seeing the friends resuming their former calm and undisturbed appearance."[36]

After that visit Fee wrote that Davis was a "Brother I love, much love." Davis was faithful to his post and to his leader—however distasteful he found it, however frustrating it became to have his own independent ministry in Virginia offered but continually denied him.[37]

When the first board of trustees for the school in Berea met September 1858, James Scott Davis was a charter member. He had just turned 30; the position honored so young a man, but it also obviously tied him in place. And it was a dangerous place: in May 1859, Davis was prevented from speaking in Mason County by an armed mob of about twenty men. A week or two before this incident, "a negro had killed his master, about six miles from [the church], and the excitement was very great."[38]

Like John G. Fee before him, Davis found that he could defy mobs and continue his ministry. But two unforeseen incidents tore him loose from his Kentucky ministry, both of which no doubt seemed cataclysmic to him: the first, personal disgrace; the second, official exile from the Commonwealth.

Less than a year after Davis's appointment as trustee, Fee received a letter from J. B. Mallett (then teaching in Bracken County) begging him to come to the trial of James Scott Davis at Bethesda Church (July 20, 1859). He was accused of sexual misconduct (perhaps adultery). Mallett stated, "I never felt so bad about any thing in my life. . . . Almost all the . . . people consider him guilty. . . . Mr. Gregg's people do not." Rogers, then in Berea, did not learn of Davis's trouble until August 1, when Rogers wrote in his diary: "Learned of Bro. Davis' trials in Bracken. O Lord comfort him."[39]

On the 4th of October, the elders of Bethesda Church, John D. Gregg and John Humlong, reported Davis's dismissal to the AMA. They stated that they (as a church) had been through "a severe and fiery trial," then they detailed Davis's own admissions:

> During [Davis's] visit to this place to fill his regular appointment he was invited by one of the neighbors to spend the night. He complied. There was a lady there, also a visitor, an acquaintance of Mr. Davis, as she has formerly lived in his family.
> The man and woman of the house were called out to attend to some of their domestic affairs leaving Brother Davis & this lady in the house. Brother Davis states that the lady left the room where he was and passed into another. In a short time he went into the same room; while there he caressed her once or twice. They then returned not staying there more than two or three moments. The next morning he was reading while she was attending to some housework; uninvited or unasked she came and sat on his knee a moment, then resumed her work.

Although Davis had been charged with "more flagrant" crimes, the elders stated that they believed his confession to be true; while the church at Bethesda granted him formal forgiveness, the decision had been that "he could not occupy this field any extent in building up Christ's kingdom. . . ."[40]

Davis's own letter to Simeon Jocelyn, composed on the same day as the elders' report, was totally, abjectly contrite. Quoting a psalm, he wrote, "Let the righteous smite me, it shall be a kindness." Some of the righteous had already smitten. Lewis Tappan had told Davis the seriousness of what he had done in no uncertain terms, with a number of "considerations increasing [Davis's] guilt."[41]

Davis humbly acknowledged all the guilt laid upon him and more. Even though what he had done may seem trivial to us, we must recall that Davis bore a full-fledged Oberlin-trained conscience, stricter than ordinary, in an age when the slightest sexual misbehavior was *ordinarily* considered horrendous. In addition, he had endangered the whole Kentucky mission by his carelessness—Fee's work as well as his own. For a man who wanted to be helpful as badly as Davis did, his sin must have seemed greater than he could bear. "My labors in Bracken are probably done," he said and added, "Mother resides in Chicago—a widow—and I sincerely hope and pray that nothing of this may come to her ears."[42]

At the end of October, Humphrey Marshall wrote from Lewis County to inform the AMA that the congregation of the church at Glenville had invited Davis back. They at least retained their respect for him—perhaps.

Fee's opinion of Davis's misconduct is clearly expressed in a letter to Jocelyn in which he says, "You ask is there something against Bro. Davis? Yes! Much." Fee intimated to the AMA that Davis had never made "a frank confession to the Cabin Creek Church of what he did do," and spoke of general dissatisfaction. Davis had apparently rushed through the church meeting to get himself re-called to Lewis County. As 1859 was drawing to a close all the workers involved in the Kentucky mission were too engrossed in events threatening their homes, their work and their very lives to worry much about Davis's disgrace. He and his family were expelled from Kentucky along with the Bereans, and it comes as no surprise that he was the only one of the four missionaries who never returned.[43]

Rev. George Candee
"If ever a wanderer was made happy, I was the boy." George Candee, describing his arrival at Berea.

George Candee was the youngest of the AMA missionaries in Kentucky before the Civil War, the youngest of Fee's preachers, the youngest among those men who are called Berea's founders. He was born in Volney, Oswego County, New York, in the Burned Over District March 5, 1831, but by 1834 his parents had moved to Michigan, where his father was the keeper of an "Underground railroad station." In his old age Candee described himself as "a born abolitionist. . . . I took to Oberlin as a duck to water." Candee entered Oberlin Prep. in 1851, and he was still an academy student when he paid his first visit to Berea in the fall of 1854, aged 23.[44]

Candee lived to be 93 years old, surviving all his Berea contemporaries. His reminiscences, mostly composed in his old age, occur in several forms; some written as early as 1901 (in a long letter to Berea president William G. Frost). Other Candee recollections, heavily edited by Frost, appeared serially in the *Berea Citizen* in 1913; still other stories were recounted by Candee's children, while he was alive but relatively feeble and unable to write extensively for himself. In some cases, he appears to have dictated anecdotes that his children copied down. Where it has not been possible to narrate an event by using his contemporary letters—of which there are a great many—I have relied most heavily on Candee's unedited story composed in 1901, merely supplementing from the later sources.

Candee recalled that before he ever met John G. Fee, the abolitionist missionary was "[his] ideal of a man." When Fee attended a conference at Oberlin with George Whipple, Simeon Jocelyn and others, Candee was there as a student. "I fell in love with the young preacher," Candee wrote, "and was 'bound' to join him in his humane work.' The young man's letters support this assertion written in his extreme old age. Candee loved John G. Fee and determined, without invitation or direct encouragement, to follow him into the wilderness.[45]

In the fall of 1854, two of Candee's fellow students at Oberlin, Obid Marshall of Lewis County, Kentucky (a member of Cabin Creek Church) and Otis B. Waters, were going to Kentucky to teach, Marshall in his native county, and Waters in Bracken County in conjunction with Bethesda Church. They persuaded Candee to go with them and "find whatever work might come to hand," teaching or preaching. The young men knew that Fee had been invited to Madison County, and even some of the circumstances of Clay's offer, but they supposed that Fee was still living in Lewis County, and Candee thought, of course, that he would be able to accompany his school "chums" all the way to his destination. They had already boarded the train from Ohio when Obid Marshall opened a letter he had picked up at the post office on the way to the station, a letter which revealed that Fee was already in Berea. Marshall knew that Berea was in Madison County and that the county seat was Richmond, and that Richmond might be reached from Lexington, but that was the extent of his information. "So," Candee wrote,

> I must part with these brethren and go on my hunt for Bro. Fee. I found when I paid my fare to Lexington I had just 23 cts. left. Yet on I went, praying the Lord to provide for me. When I got to

Lexington I found I was 25 miles from Richmond, but that there were two stages running there. I hastened to one of the stage offices and inquired the fare to Richmond, was answered "25 cts., cheap enough." I told the agent I had only 23 cts. "That will do," he said and gave me a ticket. I rode on hungry and lonesome enough.

Arriving at Richmond almost overcome by anxiety, he took supper and lodgings at the Francis House, where he had to leave his overcoat and satchel for security until he could find Fee and "then send and pay the bill and get my things." By this time he had only the clothes on his back. And when he asked at his hotel where Berea was, no one had ever heard of it.

At the post office he had better luck, being informed that there was a post office called Berea "somewhere" in the neighborhood of Big Hill. He started toward Big Hill, asking for more directions along the way. He was told that "Cash Clay had started a town out at 'the Glade' and had named it Berea. It was somewhere at the right from Gay's store [present Bobtown]." On he went, found Gay's store, asked directions again—on the final leg of his journey he "met an old man [Francis Hawley] on an old horse," who told Candee to his great relief that Berea did indeed exist, that he [Hawley] had just come from Fee's house, and Fee was at home. "If ever a wanderer was made happy," Candee wrote, "I was the boy."

Although it must have been something of a surprise when the young man arrived without coat or bag or money—or prior notice for that matter—the Fees made him welcome. "As welcome," he said, "as mortals could be in this life. I hope they will welcome me again ere many years!"[46]

During Candee's first stay at Berea, Fee sent the AMA an appraisal of him:

> There is now at my house a Bro. George Candee from Oberlin. He is a young man of more than ordinary piety— prayerful, humble, patient, kind, discrete and yet faithful. I saw him at Oberlin twelve months since. He has been preaching about 12 months but is not a regular graduate. He has preached for us some four times—preaches well. Will do more good than half a dozen like Bro. Hawley. He is without a dollar—was when he came here. I gave him a little. He asks not as Rev. Hawley, Will the society give me four hundred dollars? If they don't I can't work. He asks first where does the interests of Christ's kingdom require that I should work. He has decided to work here this winter—I believe God will provide a way for me to get along if I help those who have need.

Fee requested that the AMA send Candee "something."[47]

Candee's later report that Fee had taken him "under his wing" certainly seems to have been true. He preached with Fee for three or four months during the winter of 1854-55, receiving $20 from the AMA, although he had no contract at the time. As Candee was preparing to return to school at Oberlin at the end of his first months in Berea, Fee wrote, "He expects to return. He has labored here faithfully . . . at different places and almost everywhere his labors have been well received. He has had no expenses. I have boarded him & furnished him all needed money." Boone's Fork had raised $5 for Candee, and the Glade might come up with something.[48]

It may be seen as symbolic that when George Candee arrived at Berea, he met Francis Hawley leaving, "an old man on an old horse"—for Candee's ministry to mountain people was to prove as great a success as Hawley's was a failure. The old critic of all Appalachian habits of life was being replaced by a young man who would live with the people as they lived themselves.[49]

Candee left Berea in February 1855, promising to return the next fall; before his return Fee pointed out to the AMA that Bro. Candee at Oberlin was "pressed" for money. Candee planned to come to Madison County as a colporteur, an idea that pleased Fee, although he believed Candee "would be better if he were older. . . . " Fee's report of Candee's character had grown somewhat less enthusiastic on closer acquaintance. He described the younger man as "constitutionally . . . obstinate." Candee had confessed to once being prone to anger and painfully stubborn—but now he was more apt to be contentious and manifestly worried in spirit." He often grieved at these latter weaknesses, although Fee perceived him as "one of the most consecrated man . . . of his years—24. . . ." Candee was "not," Fee stated, ". . . bland nor very social," and he made "no special efforts to conciliate the feelings of those whom he [opposed]."[50]

In the fall of 1855, Candee and Fee were chopping wood together and began discussing a school, perhaps a college, "in which to educate youth of the land—educate not merely to a knowledge of the sciences, so called, but also to the principle of love in religion, and liberty and justice in government." Neither Fee nor Candee mentioned this conversation in letters written at the time; later on neither man could remember the exact date of the dialogue, nor could they recall who had introduced the subject of the school. Candee believed he had done it, since he was fresh from Oberlin and full of "schoolism," as he put it. Later (in 1885) Fee was to place the woodpile conversation vaguely in the wrong year, during Candee's first visit (1854) rather than the second (1855). Evidence in contemporary letters points to the latter, since arrangements for the proposed school began in January 1856, and the preliminary structure was built in Rockcastle County and opened with Otis B. Waters as teacher later that year. (Waters filed his first report in November 1856.) Candee did remember that he and Fee had discussed a possible school "at different times" during their early work together and had been envisioning a high school, in any case. But one of Fee's first letters on the subject of the proposed school (written November 1855) mentions the college idea, although Fee concedes that even a good high school would be desirable.[51]

Candee's second visit to Berea ended in March of 1856. The following winter he did not go back to Kentucky but remained North and preached a year at Brighton, Ohio, where he was married August 27, 1857. His bride Eliza Ann Ogden was, like her husband, a native of New York and an Oberlin student. When Candee received his degree from Oberlin Seminary in 1857, the young couple decided to go to Kentucky for permanent work. While he was finishing his education Candee never doubted that he would ultimately work in Kentucky: "I as much Expect to Labor South after I complete my studies here," he wrote, "as I Expect to preach the gospel."[52]

Fee expected that Candee would "do good service and endure hardness as a soldier." There would be a great deal to endure.[53]

Candee's new assignment was preaching and teaching from a base in Pulaski County; on the way there he left his wife at the Fees'; about 14 miles north of Somerset, Candee found lodging with the Widow Miranda (Dean) McQuary, matriarch of a well-to-do and prominent local family; her son William was a magistrate in his precinct. Candee planned to stay at the Widow's house during the winter while preaching in her neighborhood and looking for a permanent place to settle.[54]

When he went to Berea to fetch his wife, he remained there for awhile. He and his wife, John Clark Richardson and his wife, and Otis B. Waters were all staying at Fee's at the same time. Fee remarked that "they do not find it convenient to go elsewhere—accustomed to places of retirement & study—I do not blame them." He said it was a lot of work for his wife, however "who [was] without help and not well." But it was good "to have at last wives of ministers who sympathize with us." The Fees were especially pleased with Eliza Candee, whose piety and humility matched her husband's.[55]

Soon after Candee returned, prospects in Pulaski County darkened. "The people in this neighborhood are very much opposed and timid," Candee wrote, "But few come to meeting." Some efforts were being made to arrange a school for him to teach, but he had expected to be able to preach in Union about 10 miles away, where he had preached before. Now great opposition was being expressed there, and he would not be permitted in the Cummins region either.

"Some of my former, yes and present, warm friends have sent word to have me not come to their houses. Though some others are not yet afraid. I have staid several nights at Widow [Jerusha] Preston's house . . . and have preached there once . . . when my life was threatened. All our friends are very timid." He went on to say that he was very glad that Cassius Clay had withdrawn his support, "for," he said, "I think that the danger of war and bloodshed has done more to frighten friends and enrage enemies than anything else."[56]

However, Candee did not feel that he personally was doing much good.

On January 25, 1858, he wrote to the AMA, "more unsettled than ever." He had started teaching school on the fourth of January in Mrs. McQuary's neighborhood, "but the enemies of Christ" had burned the schoolhouse down a mere twenty days later. Before he had begun teaching, the mob had tried to scare him away by firing guns around the house. Candee announced that he was returning to Madison County to decide what to do next. "For my part," he wrote,

> I must say that ever since I came here last fall I have had no faith to expect much to be done here by such mere missionary efforts, more than to benefit the few who are already prepared to receive us. My conviction is that these slaveholding states are doomed to as sure destruction as the Jewish nation was when Christ appeared.

He compared his present experience in Kentucky with what he had seen three years earlier, stating that those who were friendly then had remained so, while those in opposition had grown more violent, especially where it was thought that freedom might prevail.[57]

Then Candee presented his own analysis of the situation in Berea:

> I don't think that Bro Fee could live where he is for a single week, if
> Madison County felt his influence as much, or even one fourth part
> as much as Rockcastle. Madison is one of the most influential
> counties in the state, and the wealthy planters regard Bro. Fee and
> his operations as harmless. And I believe that whenever they regard
> him as dangerous they will drive him off. This is my honest belief.

Events would prove his beliefs accurate, as well as honest.

He was nearly hopeless, but he admitted "there may be localities where we could labor for the good of a few, but if the influence should be felt far I should expect to be routed." So Candee saw Kentucky abolitionists in a no-win situation: either safe in a very small, insignificant ministry, or destroyed for noticeable success. When he got back to Madison County he found that Fee had been mobbed again, and his opinion seemed to be confirmed. Candee and his wife stayed on at Fee's, and the younger minister was "very much discouraged." During this period Fee advised John Rogers not to come to Berea, and Candee began to consider leaving the state.[58]

Less than a month later (March 2, 1858), Candee had found a region which restored his hope and set him dreaming once more of new possibilities. He had acquired a horse and ridden to an appointment forty miles away: the place was Jackson County, newly formed from Madison, Estill, Rockcastle, Laurel, Clay and Owsley Counties, in 1858; it was "rough and wild," with population very sparse and the people ignorant. Candee described the state of the citizens:

> Very many cannot read (I mean adults) and but comparatively few
> can read well enough to understand their own reading. Those who
> can read well seem to consume the tracts which the colporteurs
> circulate with great greediness. The mountain people are very strong
> and healthy, naturally quick witted and sensible. If they had the
> advantages of education they would make intellectual giants. But
> Oh! the present poverty and wretchedness cannot be described. . . .
> Most people live in little log cabins, having their kitchens, parlors &
> bed rooms all in one room. Their rooms are lighted at night by pine
> knots or other fuel, and in the day time by open doors and cracks
> through the log walls. Not one dwelling house in ten, where I
> visited has a single pane of glass about it. I don't know of a school
> house or meeting house in that county that has any windows in it
> more than mere openings through the walls.

Their poverty was not necessary, Candee believed, for the area was suitable for manufacturing with five or six large creeks for power. He was sure that Yankees could manage it. "It is thought," he wrote, beginning to warm to his subject, "that there is antislavery force enough in this country to elect every officer if it is rightly directed. The friends talk of runing [sic] a Radical abolitionist for county judge. If they succeed in securing the chief offices it will render that county as favorable a field of operation as I know of. we shall then be secure in our lawful operations and can be driven off, or interupted [sic], only by legislation and force." He envisioned a paper published at the county seat, James S. Davis for editor. Renewed in hope, Candee decided to labor in different parts of Jackson County until he found a place to locate, or else leave Kentucky altogether.[59]

A couple of weeks later he reported that the Radical abolitionist candidate had refused to run, but one Isaac Faubus would. "He's not an abolitionist," Candee said, "But some of his fam.[ily] are." For example, his brother Morgan Faubus, member of a Campbellite church, the congregation of which wanted Candee to remain in Jackson County as their minister. Candee was surprised that members of that sect should want him, but they were not alone. "Nearly or quite all of the friends in Jackson co. wish me to move there and preach for them."[60]

The election went favorably, with four or five magistrates of the new county abolitionists; one of these, magistrate in the Cavender district, a stronghold of radicalism, was named Elisha Harrison. Candee was overjoyed. "We are expecting to move to the county seat next week," he wrote, "Shall have to rent a room until we can build a shanty. There are but two or three houses within 1/2 a mile of the location for town." He had been on a trip North trying to get money and men to secure the town to abolitionist influences. He had found many people willing to come if they could sell out.

McKee, newly formed seat of Jackson County, a town as yet unbuilt, was located on land of Solomon Stephens, who had been opposed to Candee, but now wanted him to come. Many former members of a Baptist church, which had almost disappeared when their minister Hiram Casteel had declared for abolitionism, were now ready to join an antislavery church themselves. Candee expected to have four or five appointments each Sabbath, enough work for two missionaries. Officially he asked the AMA for commission to preach at Blanton's, Robertson's, Faubus's, probably at Clover Bottom and probably at McKee.[61]

By August 12, Candee, very much encouraged, was pastoring five churches averaging 50 each, including one organized at McKee, where he and his wife had also been engaged by the local trustees to teach the public school, although there was as yet no schoolhouse in town. Candee asked the AMA to send someone to help.

He was still pleased with Judge Isaac Faubus (County Judge of Jackson, 1858-62), who, although he had been threatened before the election if he did not stop Candee's preaching, had flatly refused to do so. After assuming office Faubus had been accused by his friends of entertaining "the abolitionist preacher" and being an abolitionist himself. At a gathering with his proslavery supporters Faubus told them that he did entertain Candee and that Candee had just as good a right to be an abolitionist as Faubus did to be a democrat. " . . . You see," Candee exulted, "the men in the mountains have never worn the yoke, and it is hard for them to bow the neck to the oppressor. Nor will they suffer the rights of other civil citizens to be trampled upon by the slave power."[62]

All was not totally blissful, however; by the middle of October, Candee and his wife were trying to build a log cabin to ease their miserable living situation. They were renting one room with no fire in it, and their cookstove was outdoors. They had no money, no house, no home, but he was intent on the salvation of people in and about McKee. Opposition had begun to stir. ". . . A few young men who call themselves the Town Dogs . . . try to disturb night meetings by barking and howling at a good distance off in time of worship."[63]

More trouble developed. Candee was relying on being paid for teaching the public school, but some pro-slavery men notified Frankfort that Candee's school had some colored children in it, mulattoes who had been counted "in the number of children to receive the public fund." Candee protested that the children were white, that their father had been allowed to vote. (But it seems likely that Candee was mistaken. The father of the children was probably mulatto, their mother white—no doubt the children appeared wholly Causcasian.) He was troubled also by a class of Baptists who taught people that it was a sin for a minister to be paid.[64]

In the midst of these financial difficulties, which put the Candees in dire straits, George Candee wrote to Jocelyn confessing that he felt distant from God. "My heart clustered round the things I have left behind," he wrote, "I have indulged in many ungrateful wishes that the Lord would let us return. He has given me a loving comforting companion and when I have had trouble I have sought and found comfort in her instead of seeking it in the Lord."[65]

By January 1859, Candee and his wife, both suffering from pneumonia, were confined to bed night and day; in spite of illness he conducted a prayer meeting in their house every other night with the people coming to them, apparently praying around their bedside. In the meantime, two men had killed one another in a drunken fray in McKee—one had been shot and died in a few minutes, the other was beaten with stones, and lay unconscious for three days before dying. The latter had been Candee's worst enemy, the man who had sent to the state capital to have the school money stopped and who had threatened the people attending Candee's prayer meeting.

The State Auditor had written to McKee complaining about the school admitting "Niggers"; Candee found the feeling against him increasing. By the end of January the church in McKee was reduced to Candee and wife and Robert Jones and wife. Soon "five members of colored families united with the Church," but their presence deterred many from attending, according to Candee. "We are called," he said, "the 'Nigger Church' [and] we *rejoice* in our persecution." [66]

In February 1859, he received a letter threatening his life, because Candee had had a free black *and* John G. Fee present at a prayer meeting. The letter writer, one Taylor, wrote,

> I intend accomplishing my object with regard to such things at all hazards, if Jackson co will not assist in the right, Madison, Rockcastle, Laurel &c will. I have all assurance, if you want a negro church let it be out of white, honest & respectable white people society. You may depend on this, life may be Sacrificed, but it must be stoped & Soon too.[67]

William E. Lincoln: the Eccentric Englishman
"I do not know how [Lincoln] will wear. The people here are subjected to continual experiment with young men. Old men, cautious as experienced rats, will not venture." John G. Fee.

A foreigner is always liable to appear eccentric; although he was born and bred in London, England, William E. Lincoln spent most of his life in the United States. No doubt the perfectly normal behavior of a 19th century Englishman seemed odd in Ohio, and even odder in Kentucky. Nevertheless, the number and variety of witnesses who agree on the subject, and the all-pervasive evidence in his own writing (as a young man and as an old man) support the belief that William E. Lincoln was very odd indeed, perhaps unbalanced, not simply a pleasant sort of crank. Something about him does not ring true: his tendency to exaggerate (or is he lying?), his eagerness to take credit for all sorts of achievements and special insights or relationships, his evident self-pity, his attempts to mar the reputations of others—the list could go on and on. His contemporaries found him—almost from the first recorded impression to the last—difficult to deal with, unpredictable, mercurial, unstable.

Yet his exhuberance and enthusiasm, his physical courage and his appetite for experience make him a fascinating character. Even in his old age some of the vitality of youth clings to his accounts of early Berea.

With Lincoln, as with Candee, the historian must choose among various versions of events—for Lincoln, like Candee, lived to be quite old, old enough that President William G. Frost prompted him to record his impressions of Berea for posterity. Much of Lincoln's story is told, therefore, from the perspective of 50 or 55 years later; in spite of the brevity of his stay in Kentucky before the Civil War, Lincoln is anxious to be considered a central figure in the history of Berea.

In 1904, when Berea College was involved in trying to decide whether to become an all-white or all-black school in response to Kentucky's Day Law, William E. Lincoln wrote an essay, "As to the Right of the Colored Race to Berea, Ky.," intended to influence the general decision. In it, he argues that Berea College should send away its white students, because the blacks—historically speaking—have clearer claim to the institution. (My purpose in presenting Lincoln's "As to the Right. . . ." is not to debunk this conclusion, for an excellent case could be made from available evidence [which is not what Lincoln used] that Berea before 1904 belonged to black students in a unique way.) Lincoln's essay reveals not only his opinion of Berea's past, but his own character.

He emphasizes his intimacy with Fee: "Outside of his family, perhaps, no man had the confidence of John G. Fee, the founder of Berea College, more than I from 1854 to 1867." Fee and Lincoln seem to have met in 1856, but Lincoln characteristically deals in large claims with small inaccuracies so that details need not trouble us. In John G. Fee's *History of Berea* William E. Lincoln's name is not mentioned. Lincoln was so far from having Fee's confidence, as we shall see, that Fee's plans for a school in central Kentucky had to be delayed while he looked for a teacher more suitable than the young Englishman.[68]

Lincoln accounted for Fee's great confidence in him by the following story: Fee, it seems, had been shot at by a passing horseman only a few days before. Lincoln and Fee were walking together at night, Lincoln carrying a lantern. They heard

> a loud half drunken cry . . . in front of Fee's house demanding help and a light. Bro. Fee said to me, "It may be a trap to kill us." In an instant I started on ahead with the lantern. He said, "Wait for me, Bro. Lincoln." My reply was, "I can be better spared than you." This with the dangers shared and the studies month on Baptism, the Constitution in reference to slavery and other questions brought us very close together. I speak with authority and certainty and without the possibility of mistake on this whole subject up to 1867.[69]

In the thirteen years from 1854 to 1867 Lincoln was actually in Berea a little over a year. In any case, he makes no attempt to cover "the whole subject." What he basically has to relate is a story of a "wondrous prayer," which he and Fee shared at some early but unspecified time. After supper one night "Fee said, 'I feel troubled. Let us go and have a season of prayer.' Under a young oak tree we read a little from the Bible by moonlight and then he prayed. The sweet faith of that prayer was a revelation to me." Lincoln states that he intends to reproduce the prayer "roughly." Fee first uttered a lamentation about the deadness of the church, "then a cry for the slave." So much Lincoln had expected, but "then," he writes, "came the amazement to me: He prayed that he might be an instrument to found a school in which the blacks should have full opportunity to develope and grow and learn, and to this end he asked God to move the hearts of his children to give the money. . . . In this prayer the consideration of the poor white was not excluded; but the whole burden of J. G. Fee's cry was for the slave. After both praying we both arose in tears." This, Lincoln states, was the "grain of mustard seed prayer" that began the whole thing. "The materialization of this wondrous prayer came some time after in the following way." John Burnam (whom Lincoln describes as a slaveholder—Burnam was *not* a slaveholder, as censuses of 1850 and 1860 and the tax list of 1855 clearly show) offered to build a schoolhouse if Lincoln would teach in it for six months without pay. Lincoln agreed "and from that school by slow accretions has grown Berea College. I was the first teacher and also joint preacher with Bro. Fee." In the final paragraph of "As to the Right. . . ." Lincoln writes, "Berea College and ground was consecrated by Bro. Fee and myself to the slave."[70]

In other writings of his old age Lincoln not only elevates himself to the position of co-founder, but takes care to minimize the very real achievements of George Candee and John A. R. Rogers, among others.

Did Fee actually pray such a prayer of consecration in Lincoln's hearing? Fee never wrote about it, perhaps for good reason. Is it likely that Fee would pray *in 1856* to be the founder of a school for *slaves*? *The slave as college student*: Slaveowners, of course, would send their chattel off to school quite willingly, eager for blacks to drop their work in order to study at a Radical Abolitionist institution. Lincoln's account emphasizes that the incident took place *before* he began teaching in 1856, his whole point apparently being that Berea College was *for* slaves from the beginning. Lincoln is, no doubt, eager to defend the rights of blacks to Berea College, but he seems even more determined to put himself in a position of historical credit ("Berea College was consecrated by Bro. Fee and *myself*"); he craved the distinction of being one of Berea's founders, so the "grain of mustard seed prayer" had to be placed in 1856, at the beginning. . . . The most reasonable conclusion is so simple and obvious it need not be stated.

William Elleby Lincoln, born September 8, 1831, was the son of London physician John C. Lincoln, and grandson of a surgeon of the same name. The first event Lincoln records in his *Memoirs* is his introduction to *Uncle Tom's Cabin*. A friend urged Lincoln to read it, but he was reluctant to spend time in novel reading, until his friend "urged the moral idea of the book." "The effect on me was life enduring," Lincoln wrote, "With weeping I kneeled & promised God, that I would never cease struggling until the last slave was free."[71]

In 1849 or '50, Lincoln met Charles Grandison Finney, on tour of Great Britain to raise money for Oberlin College. If Harriet Beecher Stowe brought Lincoln to his knees, Finney knocked him flat. Lincoln heard the great revivalist preach first in Borough Road Baptist Chapel in London, the church where Lincoln was a member. He was so impressed that when Finney moved on to a spot eight miles away, Lincoln walked to the church and back home twice every Sunday: a total of 32 miles, as he proudly points out. Not only that—finding that Finney's attendance was small at first, Lincoln had tickets printed "headed 'Life, Death, Heaven & Hell,'" engaged three friends to help him distribute them and "personally urged attendance" until the crowds rose to 5000.

At the time of Finney's visit, Lincoln remembers, 1000 people a day were dying of cholera in London; Finney preached on the text, "Because sentence against an evil work is not executed speedily; therefore the heart of the children of men is fully set in them to do evil," and concluded, "Who can wonder that God shall drive His chariot, axle deep in the blood of the bodies of men." At this point, Lincoln states," The whole congregation groaned as one & men fell from their seats to the floor, as if struck by bullets. . . . President [Finney] ordered their cravats to be loosened, & their friends to quietly care for them & not to remove them." At the end of this sermon 600 people were converted, including Lincoln's mother, who had walked the eight miles too.

On the basis of his experience with Finney in England, Lincoln decided to come to the United States, specifically to attend Oberlin. He arrived in the summer of 1853 and enrolled in the Preparatory Department; in 1855 he entered the college. At that time he found Oberlin, like its president, very inspiring. He writes, "At commencements even we students saw to it that every visitor was warned to flee from the wrath to come; or comforted, by our mutual faith. It was really a time for work for Christ."[72]

When Lincoln became ill at Oberlin, he was cared for by Prof. Henry E. Peck, who invited the invalid to move into Peck's house and charged him nothing. After Lincoln had recovered somewhat, Peck suggested that Lincoln should go to Kentucky and help "a Bro. Fee, who preached abolitionism. . . ." Lincoln set out, "determined," he says, "if I had to die, to die preaching."

The details of his trip are many and variegated. On a boat from Cincinnati to Maysville he saved the life of a Roman Catholic priest who was being threatened with drowning by a mob. In gratitude the priest asked Lincoln to share his cabin, where Lincoln proposed that they should pray "a prayer of thanks to god for [their] preservation." The priest excused himself first on the basis that he had to read his offices, then with the claim that he had "a very severe headache." Lincoln perceived that "the poor man under his Romish darkness tho't it wrong to pray with a Protestant."

Adding insult to injury the priest invited Lincoln to a tavern after they docked; here the priest became drunk, sang a song about "a girl's pretty shape," and generally drew Lincoln's disgust. Lincoln concluded that "Romanism had quenched all nobility out of him." That night Lincoln had to sleep with a drunken Irishman, and the next day, walking on his way to Cabin Creek, he stopped a fight between some Catholic laborers, who mistook him for a priest because he was dressed in standard English garb.[73]

He arrived in Cabin Creek about March 20, 1856; Fee was not there, although Lincoln may have thought he would be; James S. Davis received Lincoln cordially, having known him at Oberlin. Davis described him by saying, "He appears to be devotedly pious, and much interested in Kentucky," writing also of Lincoln's "earnest efforts in the preparing of himself for more extensive usefulness" and his excellence as a Latin scholar. Lincoln had found the winds off the lake in northern Ohio "hurtful to his lungs," and he hoped that the Kentucky climate would prove more beneficial. He wanted to work as a colporteur under the auspices of the AMA.[74]

Davis was rather apprehensive about such a project, because Lincoln's being an Englishman might "subject him to ill-treatment." Davis decided that the risk should be set before Lincoln and the choice left up to him. By April, Lincoln was on his way to the interior to work for Fee, who had written "a pressing invitation" for him to come. Fee was in the midst of one of his colporteur crises. And Lincoln was eager to get started because he had decided to quit school and proceed with his ministry.[75]

Lincoln describes Fee as "the meekest, bravest, noblest man I have met in this world . . . a hero of God. . . a man of heavy intellect with a purpose to do all the will of God. . . ." Fee's reaction to Lincoln was less enthusiastic; Lincoln's scholarship was "sufficient," his experience as a preacher "limited." "He seems to be pious," but "not as devoted as Bro Candee nor [of] equal ability." Lincoln was a bit sickly with "tender lungs." He "has been raised," Fee complained, "without any particular trade or pursuit—expects to have everything done for him." Still Lincoln was not covetous. "I do not know how he will wear," Fee wrote, "the people here are subjected to continual experiment with young men. Old men, cautious as experienced rats, will not venture."[76]

Soon after his arrival in Berea, Lincoln asked the AMA for $100 to buy a horse, stating that he was exhausted and unable to study because he had to walk an average of five miles to each appointment. The organization sent $30, upon which he decided not to be a colporteur. "My reasons," he explained, "are that after prayer & consultation with Bro. Fee I have determined to undertake the school work here; the project [prospect?] for doing good seems so unbounded, the wisdom of the movement so clear, that on the whole I presume the Lord would have me teach." He had preached 19 times, distributed about 200 tracts, visited "somewhat," and spoken to Sunday School some three times. He told the AMA he would cash his $30 and give the money to Fee.[77]

Lincoln was present at Slate Lick Springs on the famous 4th of July in 1856, and apparently made a speech himself, although it is doubtful if anyone noted it.

On the 1st of August 1856, Fee wrote: "Bro. Lincoln has thought it duty to take a school in this county. He has not taken this for gain; or less labor. He is making [a] sacrifice. He is performing more labor for less compensation than if he were preaching. . . . He is certainly doing a most excellent work." But Matilda Fee wrote to Jocelyn in December praising the work of Otis B. Waters, who was then in the field, and saying that she thought Bro. Lincoln would fail. "It appears almost impossible," she said, "to get suitable men here. . . . If there are any martyr spirits in the North O that the Lord will direct such here."[78]

Fee reported that Lincoln was "in many respects a most excellent teacher." But he had virtually given up preaching; he had asked Fee not to make any more appointments for him, and he had deliberately "delayed going to two or three appointments of his own making until the people should go away. He has run down here as a preacher and has from several patrons much opposition as a teacher."

Fee found the new teacher "very impulsive, easily offended," and quick to show it; but Lincoln had "his seasons of deep anguish over his sins." Even as Fee was writing, Lincoln was "in darkness, doubt & resentment," but Fee was hopeful that the young man would "come in a better state" soon. Already Fee was beginning to incline toward another teacher from Oberlin named Otis Bird Waters. When Fee wrote two weeks later Lincoln was doing better, but the new teacher who had been working in Rockcastle County, Otis Waters, "persevering and kind," was doing well.[79]

Lincoln himself seems to have felt oppressed by his setting; in February 1857, he pleaded with the contributors to the AMA not to let John G. Fee and his family "be swallowed up in the ignorance, prejudice & filth of slavery that abounds here." He asked for a free subscription to the *American Missionary* magazine for two of his students, Mary J. Moore and Francis Thompson, those being among the few of his students who were God's servants. "Missionaries shall yet come out of this land of darkness," he wrote, and added, in defense of his request for free subscriptions, "I am poor not because I am careless or lazy; but because I preach and teach here. [double underlining]" He begged for settlers to join them in Kentucky and asked for $20,000 to be given to 20 families of God whose presence in Kentucky would "lighten & gladden [Fee's] weary darksome way. . . . Why I have written above, I know not," Lincoln stated, "I am moved by impulsiveness [or impressions]."[80]

In the early spring Lincoln and colporteur McLain took a preaching tour lasting about a month. McLain wrote that he was pleased with the field "tho one of much trial & real hardship." He and Lincoln "walked 113 miles all through the mountains." Their food, McLain said, was "usually dodgers & bacon. Once venison once wild turkey once a squirrel. Bro. Lincoln . . . is a good brother but peculiar in his manners."[81]

Lincoln wrote the story of his & McLain's adventures when he was an old man, but he still conveys their various, extraordinary experience vividly [paragraphing and punctuation have been supplied for clarity; no other changes have been made in the text, all one paragraph in the original]:

> The state of the mountaineers off the roads was pitiable. Two of us, after traveling 20 miles from early dawn, on coming to 2 hog-backs, not seeing man nor house at all all the 20 miles we took the wrong hogback: & being very weary weary [sic] we looked all around for some sign of habitation. At last we saw smoke afar off.
> To reach it, we had to descend the hogback; & for one of us torn clothing, caused by sliding down the steep descent, caused laughter & need of repair by string & a pin or two to the seat of pants. While the bro. was repairing damage, I looked up the valley in wh. we had gotten after descending the brambly, bushey [sic] steep hillside; & saw a deer come onto a rock a mile or more off on the other side of the valley, seen agst. the sun, wh. was hidden

behind him he stood out distinct & clear; & the horned animal after looking up & down the precipitous sides of his hog back stamped his foot & shaking his head turned back into the forest.

Soon we went on; & following a brawling brook, came to a loghouse. A woman with breast exposed & shrivled [sic], gazed at us, without tho't of shame; soon the man came out, we being wearied & a little footsore, asked for dinner.

"Come in" & seats gave us very welcome rest.

Soon "Sall, these fellows want dinner, can they get it?"

"I reckon."

Then a yell to be heard a mile; after being repeated bro't a faint reply, "Yes, Pa."

"Bring some corn." Then our host wanted to know "Who be ye, anyhow?"

"Preachers"

"Ah I know, you be Fee men."

"No: God Almighty men."

"Ah well, that's the same."

Then we gave him news from the outside world. He listened eagerly & put question after question.

Soon, Mose, his son, a strong lad, bro't the basket full of corn. Now for the preparation for dinner. The mother screamed for her daughter of 13 to find hen eggs; after searching she brot 12 duck eggs; saying she could find no hen eggs. A keen hunting knife, long & sharp as a razor cut slice after slice from something black hanging on the door. To my amazement it was bacon, black as soot on the outside & yellow to the core of 1/2 in. which was white. First she broke the duck eggs into an iron pot, & then chipped pieces of bacon into it & stirred bacon & eggs together. The odor was in truth nauseating, while being cooked. Now for bread; the father ordered girl & boy to shell the corn: when it was put into a hand grinder, i. e. a stone below & one above, into the middle of which upper stone the corn was dropped & the upper stone turned swiftly by hand; a stick from a hole made in its outer rim, to the ceiling, gave the means of turning. The corn being green somewhat, was very hard to grind, & stick & upper stone & corn ground & partially broken, would be scattered over table & floor. All was carefully swept up with a coarse home made hickory broom. Then in the hands of the mother, after being moistened, the mass was patted & slapped into shape, & being covered with glowing coals to bake. Many kernels of corn were unbroken, only hardened.

My companion was dyspeptic, & whispered to me "You must do the eating." I noticed he made friends with the dogs & while I was talking at dinner, I saw why. When all were looking at me, he cleared his plate to the dogs.

Our host soon after said to me, "Your friend eats heartily— why don't you pitch in?"

After dinner & prayer I inquired price. Then my friend bridled & let me know Kentuckians were truly hospitable.

At the meeting, every man was armed for the slaveholders had threatened to stop the preaching. The mode of advertiseing was truly from the Highlands of Scotland. . . I would get to the preaching place: sat at 4 oclock. Then I would have to write as many notices as there were children capable of running swiftly. Each would take a notice, learn the words, & running to the ordered house, cry out the appointment. The boy of that house would take the papers & run to the next house, & bawl out the appointment, & so on till all neighbors for 6 miles round knew of it. The hour was usually 7 p. m. As the hour came near, we heard distant fireing [sic]; then more frequent, & the animals & birds by the firing were driven to the meeting house as a center. The first time I went to the door, mine host, said dryly, "Preacher, the dogs are a good protection, & I generally close the door." Then I understood, & a pattering of stray shots & the spit of a bullet as the people neared the house showed the wisdom of his warning.[82]

This story reveals an attraction of the Kentucky mission field that has not been mentioned; it was an adventure. Even a boy's adventure—McLain and Lincoln scrambling down the steep hillside, McLain ripping his pants and Lincoln laughing at him, the deer appearing silhouetted against the sun; the good-humored sneakiness the men share over the unpalatable food; the meeting, with its running children and the shots in the woods—for all the world reminiscent of Tom Sawyer and Huck Finn. The young preachers are frisky and eager, and, in a sense, free of responsibility (but not condescension) as they charge through the mountains: not the usual conception of abolitionist ministers at work!

In spite of these rather strenuous effort on Lincoln's part (or maybe because of them), Fee was dissatisfied with him. He told the AMA that he would be ready to start his proposed school in Rockcastle County immediately, "if I were satisfied with Bro. Lincoln." Fee thought Lincoln had many good qualities: he was self-sacrificing, open, frank, willing to work "when called out." Lincoln had changed his mind about quitting school and now expressed a wish to prepare as a teacher of classical languages. He "wants a place in our school," Fee wrote, "if we succeed—were he stable he would be just the man."[83]

A month later Fee was still saying, "If we had the right kind of teacher, I should at once, or soon, commence the proposed school." Fee was concerned because Lincoln had told Mrs. Fee of returning a check for $30 to the AMA, but Fee could not account for it. "I expect he will return to Oberlin & finish Greek, study Hebrew," Fee wrote, "If he were not so impulsive & uncertain I shold [sic] like to retain him for our school."[84]

In May 1857, Lincoln reported to the AMA concerning his five months in Kentucky: he had been preaching "going from place to place," and teaching, for which activity he presumably stayed in one place. He said he had preached nearly every Sabbath while he was in Kentucky, although he had missed 15 to 20 Sundays during the time from "circumstances." Passing over this discrepancy, he stated he had taught some Sunday School, but because of his inexperience in preaching he felt "the effect in that wicked place was not much visible." The next month he applied for an AMA commission as an itinerant preacher in Kentucky during the fall and winter (apparently, he had forgotten his own admissions of inadequacy). "Let salary be liberal," he wrote, "as I am in debt"; he needed money for his studies. "Who can wonder at so few staying for ministry," he mused, "It is hard killing work, but who would forsake it?"[85]

By mid-July Lincoln was complaining to Jocelyn that he could not move from Ohio for want of money. If Fee invited him down to Kentucky (Lincoln continued hopeful), he would have to borrow money to go. "Bro Fee is wise & good," Lincoln wrote, "& the secret of the Lord is with him. We can on both sides be content with his judgement of my fitness for labor in slave states for is he not a prince in Israel?" Still, if Fee did not want him, Lincoln said he was willing to go anywhere the AMA would send him.

Fee did not want him. "Bro Fee seems to have a slight unwillingness for me to go to Ky wh. may be on a/c [account] of the danger & my impetuousity. I cannot clearly see the will of God." But Lincoln still wanted to go to Kentucky and wrote that he thought he would start for Berea anyway—no matter what Fee said. (Fee had been quickly demoted from his royal status in Israel!) *But* Lincoln also expressed his willingness to go to Indiana or Africa. He waxed eloquent over the latter possibility: "It will be hard & honorable; sad & joy; but 'thy will not mine be done.'"[86]

A little later (August 1857), still uncommissioned, Lincoln wrote virtually demanding that the AMA take him on. "Circumstances," he wrote, "make it wise for me to leave Oberlin at once. I am in debt & have not wherewith to pay; & so must go, earn." He wanted to labor in Kentucky, where he thought John G. Fee needed him. "Of course if Bro Fee should think it unwise for me come down," he added, "I shall consider the commission null & void so far as Ky is concerned." Lincoln asked for $25 a month plus travel expenses and cautioned that his health would not permit him to teach; he would need open air and would expect to preach, walk and visit.

Lincoln returned to Oberlin for the term 1857-58, but he was prepared to leave school again when the AMA invited him [at least, so he assumed] to take a commission in Indiana in October 1857. In apparent elation he wrote to George Whipple, "Your call I recognize as the call of God—I am ready—Do let me be quiet; till I start & furnish me with books & facilities of learning & speaking Arabic; also of breaking ground in Hebrew—Bless God that I am so highly honored—I should have been very glad of 1 years more study but 'not my will but Thine be done—'" The American Missionary appointment seems to have been, in reality, very tentative. On October 21, Lincoln wrote asking for a definite appointment. "I would suffer this uncertainty at no hands but yours. It implies doubt of something & so all regard it." At least, he said, the AMA might send him $5 for laundry, since he had not a cent.[87]

On the 2nd of November, Lincoln, ill and in the depths of despair, wrote to Fee:

> At Night—The Faculty here [at Oberlin] refuses to ordain me or to participate in my ordination. This will settle things in New York [with the AMA]; so that I shall not go. Do you want me in Ky? If not—well; if so I am ready. "Tho' he slay me; yet will I trust him." It is bitter—I am publicly disgraced—but hear—I'll be the first scholar in my class. I'll leap one year in college. I'll be a paragon of a student God helping me & smiling his consent. Oh my head tonight. It is swimming God preserve my health. [As a postscript, in handwriting violently out of control, almost unreadable, he scrawled,] Faculty say self-sacrificing, Force, etc. but Jerky. They say He's a Xtian.[88]

The same day he had written wildly to the AMA; his great idol, Charles G. Finney had apparently repudiated him, and threatened to write the Association concerning him. Lincoln said he knew what Finney would write and, lest Finney should forget Lincoln proposed to supply the information himself—among other things: that Lincoln's statements were "not to be relied on," that Lincoln "knew very very little of theology," that Lincoln was "not the man to go, if we could get

162

anybody else." Lincoln ascribed Finney's attitude toward him to the fact that Lincoln had once disagreed with Finney publicly in a class Finney was teaching; Lincoln had found one mistake in Finney's theology book, but the whole class laughed at Lincoln and Finney said, "Pshaw." Once again Lincoln's handwriting indicates virtual breakdown as he concludes, "I am wholly careless."[89]

A couple of days later he wrote the AMA again, rather more calmly, giving up the idea of going to Africa, asking for a commission to Kentucky or Indiana. "I am in debt. Do decide quick," he begged, but added, "Waters will teach better in Ky than I. He is by the parents better liked; I by the children." He resolved to study Mendi in preparation for going to Africa, a possibility he had just renounced in an earlier paragraph, and to redeem his character, "which is easy," he said, too hopefully. He wrote, "Am not troubled, feel my disgrace; am conscious of God's smile."[90]

Lincoln had apparently given up the commission in Indiana and Otis Waters was to go there instead. As it worked out, Lincoln went to Indiana after all because Waters returned to Berea. In March 1858, Fee reported that Bro. Lincoln had left his work in Indiana and come to Berea where he spent three weeks. "I advised him by letter not to come," Fee wrote, "there were friends who did not like him & one bitterly opposed & had threatened him because of what he said about this friends children. He came, much feeling existed during his stay. Mr. L. went with me to Jackson co. & did quite well—under the care of one whom he respects he may do well. He has strong impulses."[91]

A month later Lincoln was begging the AMA for a commission to join Fee in Kentucky. And again in June, although Lincoln confessed at that time that Whipple's assertion "as to [Lincoln's] overestimating [his] powers [was] right."[92]

Back to Oberlin for the 1858-59 term, only to be arrested (January 14, 1859) for his heroic part in the Wellington Rescue.[93]

Lincoln's Travels in Kentucky
"You think you are god A'mighty, don't you?". . . I told him plainly he was on the road to Hell. Dialogue between a Kentucky minister and William E. Lincoln.

Some of the incidents in Lincoln's *Memoirs* deserve attention. At the very least, they show what impressions the region and the work made on a young traveler from another country. Once Lincoln went to Breathitt County to fill an appointment for Fee; there the visiting preacher was entertained by a member of the congregation who challenged him to identify people as to race when they entered the church. If you think a man is white, touch my right knee, if colored, my left. Lincoln made 11 mistakes, he said, in 15 minutes. One cannot help wondering what the churchgoers thought about Lincoln's apparent attraction to the other man's knees![94]

In this confusing situation, Lincoln preached a sturdy antislavery sermon, only to find himself faced by two men who rose in the congregation and pointed their pistols at him while he stood in the pulpit. "Ye seek to kill me," Lincoln said, "a man that hath told you the truth." "Then a strange thing occurred. They turned deathly pale, their pistols fell from their hands & clattered on the floor & they themselves fell helpless upon the seat & I thot they were about to fall to the floor." Shades of Finney![95]

After this moving service five or six young slaveholders came up to Lincoln, "tears streaming down their faces," to plead with him to get out of the valley to safety. He replied, "The servant of the Lord must not flee, I shall walk out of the valley." So, although he had a horse, he walked, leading it to demonstrate his courage. Here is Lincoln's description of what followed, quoted without deletions or changes:

> When they had gained the shelter of the rock, 3 bullets hissed by me; I turned my horse, to remonstrate with them; when the 2d volley hit my horse; & she turned so swiftly that he threw me out of the saddle. I caught on the pommel of the saddle by my heel and just saved myself from being dragged to death; & at the same instant the 3d volley hissed just where I shd. have been had I not been nearly unhorsed. This saved my life; for I distinctly hear the bullets pass directly over the saddle. My horse took fright; & galloped up the mountain, leaving even her colt. The cowards galloped off; & I heard their clatter & I know they tho't they had killed me and that I had fallen dead or wounded from horseback.[96]

On another appointment Lincoln was approached by a slaveholder who had seen the young preacher praying by a rail fence. The man told Lincoln he had "16 fine does all young" and invited Lincoln to his farm to pick out the one he wanted, since the slaveholder did not keep "bucks." How many men are chosen for stud service while at prayer? Lincoln denounced the man, who fell in a towering rage and threatened Lincoln with death. "Finding he had left his pistols in the house he picked up a stone & drew back his arm to hurl it." Lincoln closed his eyes and waited for the blow, praying, but the man went back into his house without throwing the stone.[97]

Passing by the same farm later, Lincoln heard a woman screaming. But he approached the sound slowly, since he was afraid it might be a trap set for him. He was oppressed by the thought "that no slave girl had any safety from the lust of men." Finally he came to a field where "a beautiful black slave girl, [was] sobbing as if her heart was broken & also hoeing hysterically." He went up to her and asked if he could do anything for her, but she replied, "I know who you is, the abolition preacher; you go 'long, you can't help me; you'll on'y get you'self in trouble; you go 'long; you can't help me." Lincoln "cast a look of stern reproach upon the violator" (not mentioned in the narrative until that point) and then went down to an old mill where he stopped and prayed that God would swiftly destroy slavery. He discovered later that two slaveholders were hidden in the mill listening to his prayer and they said, "Old Massa [God] would surely hear the prayers of the Feeites & end Slavery."[98]

A striking episode should be rendered in Lincoln's own version for full effect:

> I was preaching in one place, where a Campbellite minister had 2 families, his parlor family, from a white wife & a kitchen family by a black woman. The whites were educated in a Ky. college; the expenses were met by selling his black family one by one, as, by age, they became valuable. You may imagine my sermon. The preacher (Baker) was enraged & gave way to low blackguardisms. He spat tobacco juice with remarkable accuracy, thro' the holes of the andirons of the fireplace for a time; & then a huge dog came, & putting his head between his paws, looked at & enjoyed the fire; for the snow was on the ground. I saw him draw the attention of the boys to the dog & wink & then he sent a strong decoction from a fresh chew of tobacco, as spittle right into the eye of the dog. With a horrible cry, the dog ran amongst the women, who shrieking jumped upon the forms on wh. they were sitting. Several of these were overturned & the scene of confusion, of sprawling women & girls, stopped the sermon. After quiet was restored by opening the door for the howling dog; who fled still howling I resumed & if the former part of the sermon was fiery, the latter part was a blaze. The poor wretch, after the close, thus spoke,

"You think you are god A'mighty, don't you?". . . I told him plainly
he was on the road to Hell.[99]

One night after Lincoln's preaching a steady rain storm came up. The men
in the congregation all went home but the women slept on the floor, some 25 of
them. Lincoln writes,

> I tried to give up the bed, but was compelled to take it. The
> undressing & nightgown taxed my ingenuity & drew the laughing
> commendation of the host who then told the girls to go to sleep
> causing hearty laughter. During the night the dogs & some sheep or
> goats fought under the bed. The hurts I got were not a few. . . . [100]
> Another night, after preaching, I woke up in a drench of
> perspiration. During the night, the snow had covered the bed &
> room with 6 inches of snow. The broom to clear the place was
> needed first. My host had covered my clothes with sheep skins &
> laughed at my asking, "Why he had put so heavy a blanket over me
> during the night."[101]

True stories? If Lincoln was a liar, he practiced his art in a respectable
literary tradition—the master of it being Mark Twain. Perhaps the real mystery is
how an Englishman's fantasies could resemble an American's sense of humor.
Lincoln's anecdotes are almost all an old man's stories; the core of truth in them
may be adorned with details developed through years of retelling. Most of his life
he lived outside Kentucky, so that tales of that wild region could be rendered
legendary without fear. But he not only embroidered the incidents of his own life,
he took them very seriously. It is very clear, most of the time, that he had no sense
of humor at all.

Some of his anecdotes strike a profoundly disturbing note. In a diatribe
against Henry Clay, whom he misidentifies as Cassius' uncle, Lincoln maintains
that Henry loved beautiful slave girls and that he (Lincoln) taught Henry Clay's
mulatto children in the Berea School; any children of Henry Clay, who was long
since deceased, would have been far too old to be among the student body at
Berea.[102]

At another point in his memoirs, Lincoln confesses that he had given Fee's
book on slavery to a slave. "I was liable to 20 years in the Ky. Penitentiary had it
been known. The slave could read & in the evenings would read . . . to fellow
slaves."[103]

Lincoln writes that John Brown tried to recruit him to join in the raid on Harper's Ferry; John Kagi, Brown's associate, also urged Lincoln to participate since he was, Kagi said, "the calmest man in danger, of all the men I have ever known." Lincoln refused to go with John Brown, not because he objected to violence and terrorism, but because he wanted Brown to adopt a better military plan—one that might have some hope of success; Brown should fight from the swamps where retreat would be possible, rather than in the hills, among railroads and good roads.   When Lincoln discovered that only 22 men were participating, he said, "Brother Brown 22 are enough for death; I shall reserve myself for better & wiser plans." Brown confessed that Lincoln was right, but stubbornly adhered to his own course. "We parted," Lincoln states, and "Brown said, 'God bless you, my brother.'" If Lincoln is telling the truth about being associated with John Brown (and he almost certainly is), even if he is telling the truth about giving abolitionist literature to slaves, his testimony gives some credence to the charge which Madison County slaveholders leveled against Fee and his workers: that they were incendiaries and dangerous fanatics. If Lincoln contributed to that local view of Fee and his cohorts—and there is little doubt that he did—then Lincoln's 'contribution' was a very destructive one indeed! In any case, Lincoln was the kind of man who would confirm any Southerner's worst suspicions about the nature of abolitionism: he actually *was* a dangerous fanatic, half-mad, frequently deluded, a monomaniac in thought, word and deed.[104]

At the conclusion of his Kentucky experiences, Lincoln writes once more of John G. Fee. "Bro. Fee was a perfect stranger to fear. God's will was his standard. I must say, I loved & admired him above all men, for his loving, tender, gentleness." And Lincoln adds a summary of his own reactions: "As to myself, while naturally very sensitive to danger, I never knew or dreamed of fear all thro' my Kentucky experience; so sweetly did the Holy Spirit fill me with Peace & Joy. I dreaded pain, but Death. Never."[105]

CHAPTER FIVE

SCHOOL: TEACHERS, A PLAN AND A CONSTITUTION

Otis Bird Waters: An Abolitionist Where He Wasn't Wanted
"Arduous as a thorough missionary work in that field is—and I intended to devote myself faithfully to it—it can hardly be supposed that it would leave a man with no leisure. . . ." Otis B. Waters.

Otis Bird Waters' first missionary assignment was in Bracken County, Kentucky, where he taught in 1854 and 1855, during winter breaks while he was an Oberlin student. Then he was assigned to the Berea mission, but since Lincoln was teaching in Berea itself, Waters' position was in Rockcastle County. He arrived, virtually penniless like everyone else connected to Berea, in November 1856, having been forced to borrow travel money from his Oberlin landlady. Waters' stints in Rockcastle and Madison Counties were brief, but not for financial reasons—he had no desire to be a teacher; he was much more interested in preaching. His letters indicate that he would have remained in Berea if others, particularly John G. Fee, had not regarded his *teaching* as so successful that he might be stuck with that job forever.[1]

The task Waters had to undertake when he first arrived in Rockcastle was demanding. Before he could begin to teach he had to build the schoolhouse (doubling as a church on Sundays). In December, he reported: "I have been laboring upon the meeting and school house at Cummins in Rockcastle co. It is not done yet but I trust will be in a week or two." He had been preaching as well, but intended to teach only a short term of two months and a half, the books for which had been ordered from Lexington.[2]

When Waters reported that the schoolhouse was finished he added proudly, "It is very comfortable and pleasant except in extremely cold weather." By March 1857, he had already been teaching in it for several weeks, and the people were so pleased with him that they were anxious for him to return. He refused to give them an answer. "It was not my desire," he wrote,

> to devote so much attention to this house and school. I wanted to preach and labor directly for the spiritual good of the people, more than has been possible with this work on my hands. The extent to which this occupied my attention and kept me from the work I desired to do, together with the disappointments and delays attending it was sometimes quite a trial to me. What good am I doing? was the desponding query in my mind.[3]

When Waters' winter term ended, he resumed his studies at Oberlin, but he found himself hard-pressed financially. The people in Kentucky, even though they were anxious for him to return, had given him nothing but a pair of stockings worth perhaps 40 cents—and he had been engaged in "double work." As he pointed out to the AMA he had not contracted to do two jobs for one salary. "Arduous as a thorough missionary work in that field is," he wrote,

> and I intended to devote myself faithfully to it—it can hardly be supposed that it would leave a man with no leisure—no time for reading or study aside from the indispensable preparation for preaching. Yet this was the case with me during the whole of the time, both in which I was working upon the house and in which I was teaching. I do not think men ought to be expected to preach, visit and teach . . . pay their board, and run the risk of procuring books . . . for the same compensation that they would receive for performing missionary work alone.

He had taught at the rate of $2.50 per scholar for a term of three months, with an average number of about 13 students, but he had not received all the payments due him, and he had been forced to pay out money himself for lumber for the schoolhouse, in addition to buying the textbooks. But his work did not seem to him a loss—he had noticed some change in the people since the house was completed: supporters were encouraged and those who were prejudiced against the project seemed less excited; his congregations were increasing. "And so I have been thinking lately that if my winter's labor should serve to 'prepare the way of the Lord' it might be as needful and as acceptable a work as that which I covetted." What he had done was pioneering in more than one way.[4]

When Waters began teaching in Rockcastle County, even though his short term there was to be his last in that county, it was an historic occasion. A local family of free blacks sent two of their children to Waters' new school, expressing their intention of sending two or three more. So Waters taught what was probably the first integrated school in central Kentucky.[5]

Shortly after Waters left the region the schoolhouse he had built was burned to the ground "by the enemy" in Rockcastle County, after standing less than six months. Ironically, Waters had been collecting money in Lorain County, Ohio (at Candee's church) to finish the Rockcastle church-schoolhouse—and planning to take up collections for the same purpose in Union City, Michigan, when he visited his parents there, but he did not think people in Michigan would be willing "to give money to pay for a burnt house." His own reaction to the loss of his labors was simple: "I confess," he said, "I was disappointed. I did not think it would be done, although it was so freely threatened." He believed the arson had been committed because Fee and Emerick had been enjoying remarkable success with their protracted meeting at the time. Wicked men "could not endure to see so many attending their meetings, affected by their preaching and uniting with that church." Waters was distressed because Fee, ill able to afford it, had purchased seats for the building at a cost of $16—a total loss.[6]

Other problems, threats, mobs, defections of supposed friends, made it impossible for school or church to open again in Rockcastle County. On his next school vacation, beginning in the winter of 1857, Waters would teach at Berea; he arrived by November, took up residence with the Fees and assumed his duties in "the first 'shake' or 'board' covered school house" that had been built for William Lincoln the year before; the structure cannot have amounted to much. Waters later called it "an old shell." In addition to the children in the Glade District he taught some six or eight young men from other districts, men who were already antislavery, some of them members of free churches; these men were being trained to go out as teachers in other districts and, as Fee put it, "impress the minds of those who shall come under their care."[7]

Waters clarified Fee's vision of what a school could accomplish. His experiment in interracial education, abortive as it was, initiated ideas that grew and eventually prospered, and his training program to equip young people to return to their own districts was seminal. His school at Berea promised much good, according to Fee: in December 1857, Fee wrote to Lewis Tappan saying, "The school is the thing. I am shure [sic] this is needed now. The time has come." When Waters left Berea at the end of his four seasons of teaching in Kentucky, the entire missionary effort took a new turn, with a whole new emphasis on Christian education.[8]

The Plan: Education for "All Colors, Classes, Cheap and Thorough"
"We ought to have a good school here in central Kentucky, which would be to Kentucky what Oberlin is to Ohio." John G. Fee.
"We have . . . been talking about starting an academy and eventually look to a college—giving an education to all colors, classes, cheap and thorough." John G. Fee to Gerrit Smith.

When the Glade called John G. Fee as its minister for a second year (beginning July 15, 1855) the members were unanimous. The church requested the AMA to subsidize Fee, since the church itself could only provide him $25 for the year. Characteristically, although his congregation was small, the remuneration poor and prospects more foreboding than promising, Fee immediately laid plans to consolidate the support of the region. Perhaps a recent conversation with George Candee at a wood pile contributed to this new plan.

The *American Missionary* printed Fee's first sketch for a school in Kentucky:

> We ought to have a good school here in central Kentucky, which would be to Kentucky what Oberlin is to Ohio, Anti-slavery, Anti-caste, Anti-rum, Anti-secret societies, Anti-sin. We have here a very healthful country, far more than Oberlin ever was. Why can we not have such a school here?
> Could we have even a good Academy, and offer facilities for an education to the young men and women, in the mountainous and non-Slaveholding districts, we could do much, and that too most effectively for the overthrow of slavery.[9]

How was this proposal to be realized? Fee asked directly for the financial support of Yankees. Writing to one of his own particular friends, the famous New York abolitionist Gerrit Smith, Fee articulated a succinct, emphatic version of his plan: "We have for months been talking about starting an academy and eventually look to a college—giving an education to all colors, classes, cheap and thorough." Now that Kansas was to be admitted as a free state he thought the aid societies would turn their "attention and means" to Kentucky. They could, he said "by a constant influx of teachers, preachers and emigrants, in a legal, peaceful, and yet most effective manner, make this fertile and healthful State the 'home of the free and the land of the brave.'"[10]

Fee regarded slavery as an integral part of the whole nation, "incorporated into the organic law of the land." Non-slaveholders and slaveholders alike were implicated in the guilt of the system, and every aspect of life was tainted by the one great sin. For these reasons Fee proposed an organic solution. At its inception Berea College was conceived as a school linked to a church and sustained within an intentional community. Its ambitious mission was the overthrow of slavery and the achievement of social justice for all people.[11]

Northern funds were needed for the Kentucky project because the poverty-stricken mountain counties were least corrupted by slavery; so they formed an important part of the mission field in the state. "For this reason," Fee said, "for years to come, much of the work of reform in Kentucky must be sustained from abroad, because it must be sustained in the midst of those who have not much of this world's goods, and who especially have not been taught to give for the support of the Gospel." A solution in the South itself was not sufficient. Morally, the whole United States bore the burden of slavery; practically, Northern support, financial and otherwise, was essential for the success of the Berea project.[12]

When Fee wrote the plan just cited he concluded by soliciting money for a church building and an Academy at Berea; very soon (November 1855), he was mentioning the possibility of a church at Boone's Fork in Rockcastle County, 18 miles away from his house. For some time he vacilated about which county should become his central headquarters; which county should get the school?[13]

Rockcastle was "not so level, sightly or fertile" as Madison, "nor so favorable for roads." But Fee thought Rockcastle could be brought under a righteous influence sooner because it had fewer slaveholders, only about 72, whereas Madison in the fertile portions was solid slavery. Postal routes were about equal in either place; Rockcastle had cheaper land—"good location, soil, timber, water, altitude."[14]

Fee focused on the Cummins neighborhood, "a point of more promise" than any other place in Rockcastle County. It seemed likely that a meeting house/school house could be established there; a man had already offered funds if Fee could "put a school in it right off." "There is a colored family in that neighborhood," Fee wrote,

> esteemed by the neighbors, and of good prosperity as county farmers, their children are of good habits, but by law they are crowded out of the district school, and by teachers and some subscribers, out of the subscription schools. I made the proposition to let this family and all colored persons into the school and church with equal priveleges with all others, and was careful to get trustees willing—two members of the church are among them and they are heartily willing.

So Cummins in Rockcastle had a very important attraction, even though it was so far away: the school there could be integrated. "It is all important," Fee pointed out, "that we be able to demonstrate to the world that true Abolitionists can gather and teach successfully, schools at the south and schools in which caste shall be lived down."[15]

Many people wrote Fee letters of inquiry about colonizing, and even more about the proposed college. Delia A. Webster, an abolitionist from Vermont, who had achieved immense notoriety in Kentucky by being imprisoned in Lexington for helping a runaway slave, offered Fee grounds for a college on her farm across the river from Madison, Indiana, on the Kentucky side, just below the mouth of the Kentucky River. This prospect tempted Fee—the site was extremely pleasant, with easy access to East, West and North. Fee believe that a flourishing college could be built up there very rapidly. Webster was promising $2000 in addition to the land.

But there were drawbacks, chiefly her reputation, which would, Fee wrote, "make our college buildings obnoxious to the mob." (In reality, his own reputation was almost as bad as hers, but that seems not to have occurred to him!) In addition, he thought the location wrong—the greatest good could be done by educating poor people who would then return home or into surrounding counties to teach during the long vacations. "By this means thousands of children & parents will be impressed with the principles of the institution." This being so, he believed the interior location would be most beneficial for Kentucky—a location on the border would encourage students to seek employment in the free states instead.

Fee argued with himself: river land was more fertile; a larger institution could be built on Delia Webster's farm. "Our object however," Fee answered himself, "is not so much to make a 'paying institution,' but one that will do the most good for the state & cause of freedom every where." Still no one had given more than ten acres in central Kentucky, and Cassius Clay was not in a frame of mind to offer anything more. But Fee was hopeful that he would be able to find men who would advance five thousand dollars and take a mortgage on the land; he wanted to purchase400 acres, then parcel it off in lots for a handsome profit, enough to pay the original mortgage and begin college operations too.[16]

On the other hand, some friends of Fee's in Newport, Kentucky, asked him to come there. And he found Campbell County most attractive. He thought it was "the most inviting [field] in the state," and said, "it would be much in accordance with my feelings [d.u.] to go there." For his family's sake also, Campbell County was the best possibility.[17]

In May 1857, the *American Missionary* published Otis Waters' "A Christian Colony in Kentucky," clarifying Fee's new scheme. Waters called "attention to the project of a Christian anti-slavery colony in [Kentucky]. The plan is to have Christian families emigrate from the North, and settle together in some suitable locality, for the purpose of forming a church and sustaining a school, which shall adopt and carry out the highest standards of piety and Christian reform." Waters maintained that some indigenous anti-slavery sentiment existed in Madison, Rockcastle and Estill Counties, so that "a respectable portion of the inhabitants" would welcome such a colony. Finally, as proof of the practicability of the plan, he pointed to his own school in Rockcastle County, "a school, in a house built with the express condition in the bond, that no person shall be debarred from church or school privileges on account of color."[18]

In the same issue John G. Fee published another appeal, ending, "Come on, then, let us be Abolitionists together."[19]

But, of course, Waters was leaving, and Fee was not satisfied with Lincoln. If he had been, the new school would have started in Rockcastle County in April 1857. In May, Fee, still without a satisfactory teacher, was considering moving to Rockcastle County himself, a prospect he dreaded; but he feared the proslavery influence was so much greater in Madison County that the work could never progress there.

Then the recently completed meeting house in Rockcastle County was burned down, just as "the prospects for a good church were daily increasing." Then Fee was mobbed in Rockcastle County. A. G. W. Parker's house was burned down—also in Rockcastle County. "During his absence from home—hour of night—the family (wife & four small children) escaped narrowly saving but little. The friends at Cummins are much depressed," Fee wrote, "alarmed for fear of their property & persons. Quite a number of men last week at court swore publickly that they would take my life." Not only local people were involved. "The flame is fed in Rockcastle," Fee stated, "by a clan of <u>southern</u> South Carolina boarders—gamblers & Ruffians who come up every season—these encourage and treat to whiskey a reckless class who are cats paws for others." One of Fee's primary supporters in Rockcastle County, Stephen G. Cummins, rode 18 miles to Fee's house to warn him that Candee could not preach there. The prospects for a school in Rockcastle were cut off.[20]

Fee felt this was "the darkest hour he ever saw in Ky." But there was encouragement in the midst of all the trouble. At Fee's instigation, the people of the Glade met and passed a resolution against mob law and in favor of liberty of speech and press. Fee thought "most of the friends [at the Glade] would stand firm" and that they would avoid violence themselves.[21]

In the meantime, his appeals in the *American Missionary* continued. The September issue (1857) quoted Fee as saying, "A few Christian families from the free States settling here, would soon put things on a right basis." In a letter he asked, "Why will not colonies from the free states come over and help us[?] Their children can be educated. . . . Men and women must come and do this work. They must do it in the midst of the people as *living* examples."[22]

The mob spirit—as Fee always called it—continued; threats of violence multiplied. But the work continued also: Waters was teaching, colporteurs riding out, Oberlin graduate John Rogers arrived to assess the prospect of coming to

Berea himself. The plan for Berea was articulated in the most adverse circumstances; as the Bereans moved forward with their schemes, external conditions worsened almost daily. Fee's congregation, for awhile, was composed almost entirely of women because the men were afraid to go in the building. "Some men who were friends stood around in the forest, some with guns near by."[23]

"I am here a sojourner, a stranger, a pilgrim," Fee wrote in December 1857, "The endearments of relatives & scenes of youth I crucified to come here. In time of mob violence & popular fury even friends here look upon me with suspicion or distrust." But in the same letter Fee once again puts forward the plan. "Raise ten thousand dollars by shares of $400 or $500 each. With this sum by a tract of land, lay off a town, with lots for the school—sell the remainder in small tracts to good men—refund, thus, the principle with six percent—sell all townlots for benefit of the institution—all premiums on chosen tracts also for the school. . . ." Emerick had promised to give $500; Rogers thought he could get the money, while Fee, in his usual state of dire poverty, only claimed, "I would if I could." Nevertheless, the plan had become Fee's ultimate goal: "If I can see a good school started in Ky I shall feel that I have accomplished the greatest work of my feeble life. I intend to struggle on for this object."[24]

And struggle he did. During this entire period, while local violence increased, Fee was advertising healthful benefits for Northern abolitionists who settled in Kentucky. Never does he point out that such settlers might be placing their lives in jeopardy. As the mobs increased, his appeals for settlers grew more vehement. Without Clay's protection Fee felt himself and his mission terribly vulnerable. If new settlers would hurry, arrive in numbers, the work might be saved. In January 1858, Fee and Jones were captured together, the latter whipped, and both threatened with death. "For weeks there was a reign of terror." People were so terrified that no men but Otis Waters and Hamilton Rawlings would enter Fee's house, for fear of being identified as abolitionist sympathizers. Candee was driven out of Pulaski County, his schoolhouse burned. Cassius Clay remained aloof. "We may be crushed out," Fee wrote.[25]

Then the little community suffered an even more severe trial. One of the men (Fee does not name him) "was used by the mob party to carry threats of our extermination. He alarmed several friends—Several of the leading Republicans got together—concluded to withdraw their influence from me—made it known to the slave power—fears were entertained for my safety. . . ." The men of Fee's church entreated him to leave. "Your friends cannot protect you," they said, "the mob will kill you. . . ." Fee replied, "I came here to do my duty, and the mob shall come they will find me at my post." He called for a day of fasting and prayer—and his friends at the Glade met and resolved to stand by him.[26]

"The threat," he wrote,

> is sooner or later the slave power will come and haul me off & that they will not regard numbers. These things wear on my wife—disturb quietude of the church—press my own spirit. You have seen mob violence, know something of its horror.

He knew it would be safer on the border, for Oberlin teachers had survived in Bracken County, but the region was not so influential, not central. "I feel depressed," Fee said,

> because Friends North are so slow to come here & help—they write & rewrite but come not—we think of trying to concentrate the friends in the state.
> I live not knowing what a day will bring forth. I feel in my brain & spleen the effect of <u>constant multiplied cares</u>—anxiety which is constitutional. My wife is feeling the pressure more than ever. I would be glad could I have a rest for one month—This I have not known for twelve years—My habits of study are almost entirely broken—hundreds of things to see to.[27]

Meanwhile, Waters' school, now in Berea, was succeeding very well. Fee claimed, "The pupils speak and write freely upon the subjects of slavery and freedom." An encouraging new facet had been added to the educational scheme, for three slaveholders were sending their children to the school. "Great good can be done," Fee wrote, "by sustaining good schools." No one had begun to explore the possibility of an abolitionist institution with both slaveholders and non-slaveholders studying in it. When John Rogers and his wife Elizabeth became teachers later in 1858 that was exactly the situation in their school—the distinctive feature of the pre-Civil War institution.[28]

John A. R. Rogers: Berea's Yankee Martyr
"Vincit qui patitur." (He who suffers, conquers). *Berea College motto, proposed by John Rogers.*
Elizabeth Embree Rogers: A Quaker from Philadelphia
"The wife of a military officer shared gladly his inconveniences, his trials, his want of comforts. . . . We Bereans were all soldiers in the army of the Lord." *Elizabeth Rogers.*

Everything in his background supported his ministry; generations of New England congregationalists stood behind his faith. An extended family supported his work: his father and mother heartily endorsed his ministry, with financial aid as well as approval; his uncles and aunts and cousins did likewise; his wife demonstrated her willingness to follow him anywhere. A multitude of friends, fellow students, professors, ministers and parishioners expressed their interest in his work and their support of his goals.

John Almanza Rowley Rogers—known as Almanza to his family—was born November 12, 1828, in Cornwall, Connecticut, where a famous school of missions was established during his childhood. He prepared for college (Yale was his goal) at Williams Academy in Stockbridge, Massachusetts. The whole region on the western borders of Massachusetts and Connecticut, tied together by the Housatonic River running through the Berkshires, constituted a seedbed for the missionary movement in the United States. In 1846, Rogers became a member of the Congregational Church.[29]

His father John Cornwall Rogers, himself an abolitionist, aided his son's ministry materially for many years. Lizzie Rogers described her father-in-law as "a singularly simple-hearted, God-fearing man . . . valued in his church and his community as a pillar of strength." Through him John A. R. Rogers was descended from many of the Puritan founding families of Connecticut. His mother Elizabeth ("Betsy") Hamlin, according to Lizzie Rogers, "was one of the most loving [of] mothers. Her wonderful energy, her keen sense of humor, her high Christian character, made her a noble woman. There was in her religious fervor much of the poetic, and sometimes she seemed almost to rise into the realm of prophecy." Through his mother John Rogers was descended from many founding families of Massachusetts, including many pilgrims of Plymouth

Colony. Rogers had only one sibling, his sister Amelia Elizabeth, some seven years younger than he.[30]

The family moved to Pittsfield, Ohio, before Rogers began college. So Oberlin not Yale became his alma mater. Of course, studying there did nothing to alter his desire to become a missionary: his entire education was designed to foster in him a dedication to exactly the kind of life he chose. He was graduated from Oberlin College in 1851, from the seminary in 1855. There he formed some of the most significant relationships of his life, including a deep friendship with James H. Fairchild, which began in 1858 and lasted until Fairchild's death. While he was a student Rogers lived in Fairchild's home and enjoyed sessions of special study under the professor's tutelage. During his time at Oberlin, Rogers also taught in the Preparatory Department and in the college itself, and spent his vacations teaching in New York City, an experience that roused his desire to minister to the poor. He also frequented the office of the AMA where he became interested in missionary work in the South. Even as an undergraduate he was becoming more and more interested in Kentucky as a mission field—especially Eastern Kentucky—believing that a school like Oberlin should be planted there. When his brother-in-law James Scott Davis moved to Kentucky, Rogers longed to settle there himself.[31]

Mrs. Fee had written of the need for a martyr spirit from the North to come to Kentucky. In the person of John A. R. Rogers, Berea would discover its Yankee martyr.

Rogers claimed descent from John Rogers the Martyr, English Protestant burned at the stake at Smithfield during the reign of Bloody Mary in 1555. The fact that his claim was mistaken is scarcely as revealing as the constant references that Rogers made to this supposed progenitor. Virtually every published account of Rogers' life, in books, articles and newspapers, sets forth his wholly imaginary descent from the martyr, a man whose name he bore and whose fate he apparently wanted to emulate. The supposed family motto of Rogers the Martyr, "*Vincit qui patitur*," (He who suffers, conquers) appears on the seal of Berea College at John A. R. Rogers' instigation. "If we would do much for Christ," he wrote, "we must first be willing to suffer for Him."[32]

He was absolutely attuned to Oberlin, an extension of western Connecticut and Massachusetts into the West, incarnation of the reform spirit, the most

missionary-minded school anyone could ask for. At Oberlin Rogers did not
acquire simply training, an education, a set of opinions, two degrees and
teaching/preaching experience; he acquired a total personality—he made Oberlin a
part of his character, he internalized it all. He was—or he made himself—the
Oberlin ideal: earnest, benevolent, self-sacrificing, utterly humorless, zealous for
learning, ardent to serve. All the characteristic Oberlin concerns became his;
naturally, missionary ambitions were first among them, and there is little doubt
that he had developed these before he ever saw Oberlin. But he picked up
everything else as well. Throughout his life he was preoccupied with questions of
diet and health ("4th Fri [September 1857] I here record three times in which I
have drank coffee and six times in which I have drunk tea unnecessarily."); trivial
employments of any sort were suspect; work had to take precedence over play—
always; rising or going to bed late struck him as heinous sins, for each day had to
be improved. He sought 'perfection' in every aspect of his daily life, from the
moment of rising to the moment of promptly going to sleep. He developed or
suffered a conscience grown to such mammoth proportions that it sometimes
threatened to overwhelm him; occasionally his scruples, his frantic self-scrutiny
and his intense self-condemnation reach the pitch of hysteria. Over and over again
in years of mental agony, he sought perfection, failed to reach it, lacerated himself
for the failure and began the cycle again. He had a fully developed Oberlin
conscience.

The influences upon Rogers' thought appear to have been solidly Oberlin.
Having spent his college and seminary years dutifully absorbing the ideas of
Finney, Fairchild, Peck, Morgan and other Oberlin professors, he continued to
read their books, articles and sermons constantly throughout his later time in
Kentucky. In his journal he notes his reading faithfully—he took Oberlin with
him wherever he went in the form of books he had studied at Oberlin, books
written by former professors and students of Oberlin, and books recommended by
these same professors. The cumulative Oberlinization of John Rogers may not be
unique, but few students have been so influenced, so pervaded by the spirit of a
school. For years, for example, Rogers recorded in his journal the topic of every
sermon and many of the lectures he heard at college. Virtually every one of these
entries also included a brief note of his agreement with what he had heard. For
good or ill, he soaked it all in—the perfect student.

At the same time, Rogers emerges from his own writing as self-conscious to an incredible degree. How could it be otherwise? His life was spent in intense self-scrutiny; his efforts to be self-forgetful and Christ-like and his struggles to keep himself in view at all times sometimes cancelled one another out, leaving Rogers in a state of physical and spiritual exhaustion. Oberlin ideals were high and noble (most of them—some of them were absurd and inhuman); a life lived according to them was a strenuous matter, perhaps an impossible goal.

From his youth Rogers was sickly, his ill-health taking the form of frequent indigestion, headaches and regular bad colds, usually as a result of his conscientiously exposing himself to adverse weather. His early teaching days in New York City came about because he needed to get away from Oberlin to regain his health. Throughout his career his physical well-being remained precarious, almost as precarious as his spiritual well-being. According to Rogers' own diagnosis the latter could be jeopardized in the simplest ways:

> Dec 7th [1853] I laughed too much and did not preserve sufficient dignity.
> Dec 17th [1853] I do not have enough personal dignity or live near enough to Christ.

In an effort to overcome his own levity Rogers offended Professor James H. Fairchild by presiding over the Oberlin Literary Society with too much sternness. (Jan. 18, 1854)

Some characteristic entries in Rogers' journal illustrate the workings of his scrupulous conscience:

> Mar 28th [1854] I am not living as I ought. I fall far below my Ideal of duty.
> Mar 29th Did not live as I ought. Am heedless about getting up at proper time.
> Mar 30th Thurs. Have been altogether too rude. Have associated too much with the ladies.
> Aug 1st Made up my mind fully to live free from care. Felt willing to leave myself entirely in the hands of God.
> Sept 4 Mon. I see that I am not that pure guileless holy Christian that I should be. I will be much more careful to present everything precisely as it is without coloring it in the least. In my devotions felt so grateful to my Heavenly Father for Lizzie's love. May she ever be as now or rather in an increased degree possess the spirit of her Savior. God guide us in his own way. I feel happy to

retire and feel that I have improved this day and I hope done some good. Two things I will try to do tomorrow. First to have more of that peace-giving, inspiring, heart-strengthening and heart-soothing confidence & trust in Jesus. Economize in a better way my time.
Sept 6 Was not wise in morning. Sat up till after midnight.
Sept 26th Tues Must have more confidence—will not allow myself to be so easily disturbed. Will set myself to make L.[Lizzie] happy.

In October 1854, Rogers left Oberlin for an interneship ministry in Cornwall, Connecticut. Elizabeth ("Lizzie") Embree, not yet his wife, had to be left behind, but even his visits with old friends and relatives, and his fairly constant preaching and conducting of prayer meetings, could not distract him from thoughts of her. His own emotions upset him and the ups and downs of his spiritual life increased. He became slightly ill and decided to watch his health with an eagle eye, but his conscience gave him no rest.

Nov 29th Wed. [1854] . . . Great struggles in my heart.
Nov 30th Thurs. Thanksgiving. Not many out to church. Took myself seriously to task for my homesickness. Made up my mind not to yield to such feelings in the slightest. Will not be moved by my feelings but in a noble manly way stand to my post without flinching the least.
Dec 5th Are my thoughts enough upon my work here. Is my heart as full of love as it should be? I will try and always be in bed when the clock strikes 9.
Dec 7th. . . . Hope that I am growing better each day. Greatly desire to have my beloved L. with me that I may impart to her of my feelings and aspirations.
Dec 9th Sat. A happy peaceful day. I have accomplished considerable. the Lord make me so to number my days that I may apply my heart to wisdom. If I endure hardness as a good soldier I always find a rich reward, if not in one day or one week yet always in due season. Am I wiser and better than last Sat. night? Have I improved my time as I should . . . ?
Dec 11th Mon. Have I kept my heart pure today? Have I learned all that I could so that I am both wiser & better than when I rose. How can I make the most of what I have learned today. How can I learn to learn the most possible each day. Let me ask these questions daily.

The next day he was so sick he went to bed, but eventually got up anyway and made his parish calls.

On March 4, 1856, Rogers was ordained in the Congregational Church at Roseville, Illinois; Rev. Edward Beecher, son of Lyman Beecher, pastor of the

First Congregational Church in nearby Galesburg, delivered the sermon. The *Galesburg Free Democrat*, under the editorship of James S. Davis's brother, reported this solemn occasion, emphasizing the particular affection of the new church for the new minister. "Bro Rodgers [sic]," the writer asserted, "enters upon his labors in the West under favorable auspices."[33]

Rogers' journal contains a large gap between December 1855 and May 1856. In that period he was both married and ordained. The two ceremonies receive this notice: "1856 May 24th Sat. I am a married man. I have promised before God to be a faithful and loving husband. I am a minister of Christ set apart by the laying on of hands. Lord help me to examine myself to see what kind of a husband and minister I am." So marriage and ordination gave him, in effect, two more aspects of self-examination.

They were married January 24, 1856, in the home of Elizabeth Embree's wealthy aunt on Arch Street in Philadelphia. "We plighted our troth, using the same words my ancestors had done for generations," Lizzie stated, "the simple words of the Friends." John Rogers required more than a Quaker ceremony, however, and insisted on having an ordained minister add a prayer and pronounce "the solemn words which made [them] man and wife." In later years, they regarded themselves jokingly as doubly married. "Our simple, chaste wedding was as unpretentious as the life we hoped to lead," Lizzie wrote, "Dressed in sober brown, I remember how hard I tried to put the womanly touch to my heavy brown hair, and to put new lines of dignity into my girlish face." She was not yet 17; her husband 26.[34]

The couple went on what Lizzie Rogers was charitable enough to call "a novel wedding trip." In New York, Rogers had worked with the Home for the Friendless in the slums, and he had become an active member of the Female Guardian Society, one of many organizations established in this era for aiding and reforming prostitutes and other 'fallen' women. Since John and Lizzie were going to Illinois where he was to begin a pastorate in Roseville, he thought it would be a good idea to do something useful with the trip. He volunteered the services of his bride and himself in escorting 60 slum children from New York City to Illinois where they might be settled into foster homes. And so they set out, 1000 miles on slow trains—with adolescents and babies, fighting, singing, traveling night and day, packed on hard narrow seats. The coach-load of orphans attracted attention as the journey progressed.

One night the car was visited by a distinguished looking old gentleman who sat down by Lizzie and began kindly questioning her and talking of his wife and beautiful home. He had mistaken her for one of the "Home children"! She led the old man on till finally he asked her if she should like to go home with him and be his little girl. Lizzie replied shyly, "If Mr. Rogers is willing." It would seem that Rogers' new wife was something of a wag. She did remark many years later, "[My husband] converted our wedding trip into a philanthropic enterprise, burying romance fathoms deep under the higher work of doing good to others."[35]

The newlyweds reached Roseville, close to Lizzie's 17th birthday; their home was a little plank house without plastering, inadequate in all seasons. In the first summer Lizzie suffered from typhoid, an illness that dragged on and on, so that she was barely recovered from it when her first child, John Raphael, was born on December 11, 1856. She describes the time as "passing from one stage of suffering and weakness to another."[36]

They were barely settled when John asked Lizzie how she should like to go to Kentucky to start a school for the poor. Her reply was: "Not at all." A few months later at the Congregational Conference in Galesburg, Rogers met an acquaintance from New York City, one Mr. Coffin, who had gone to Kentucky and 'chickened' out because the field was too difficult. (Coffin went to Syria instead!) Rogers intimated that Coffin felt he was too great a man to waste his time in Kentucky. In high dudgeon, Coffin told Rogers "in plain terms, that if he thought it was an easy thing to establish a school in Kentucky, he should do it himself, as he had every qualification. This came as a challenge and Rogers had no sleep that night." The idea of a field that was dangerous, difficult and unrewarding was terribly attractive to him. He asked his wife again if she was "willing to go and help him reach the poor in Kentucky with the Gospel and school," and, according to him, "with wifely devotion and unflinching courage—a courage which through years of struggle and peril to her husband and family never failed—[she] consented to go." The wife of John A. R. Rogers apparently learned very early to keep her anxieties to herself. Years later she remembered her fear more distinctly than her answer, which she supposed had been 'Yes.' So they left

Roseville, which had become comfortable for them, left a salary of $1000 to settle in what seemed to them—and was—enemy territory at a salary of $400.[37]

Rogers in Kentucky 1858-59
"The easiest way to live is to do at once the hardest work one has to do." John Rogers.

Before Rogers' final decision to enter the Kentucky mission field he consulted with his father, with Professor Jonathan Blanchard at Galesburg, who urged him to go, with Dr. Edward Beecher, Bros. Flavel Bascom and Lucius H. Parker and others, who urged him to go, and with Professors Henry Cowles, John Morgan and James H. Fairchild of Oberlin, who urged him to go. Thus a distinguished committee approved his future.[38]

October 11, 1857, Rogers wrote in his journal: "I am to go to Ky. Lord do thou thoroughly prepare me for my work." Having obtained his release from the Roseville congregation and applied to George Whipple for financial support from the AMA, he visited his parents in Pittsfield, Ohio, took another trip east to Connecticut, talked to some of his former teachers at Oberlin—all as if to review his former life before beginning the new one.

On November 23, John and Lizzie, with their infant son Raphael, 11 months old, left Ohio for Kentucky. Rogers was suffering from toothache during the journey, an ailment which prompted him to promise "to lead a more holy life & not to forget the agony." Presumably, he referred to the sufferings of Christ, rather than those of his own mouth.

Once across the Mason and Dixon Line the young couple felt themselves in a foreign country. Lizzie wrote:

> The careless, easy going ways of the white folks, the half servile, half impudent black people filled us with amazement. I remember when stopping at the hotel my awe in seeing the first slave. My awe and sympathy gave way to disgust, as I afterwards found how surlily she gave me the service which I had a right to expect, and I found in the untidy, down-at-the-heels black woman little of the smart, attractive slave that I had expected.[39]

On the 24th they reached Maysville, Kentucky, where Lizzie saw her first, disappointing slave, and the next day walked to Cabin Creek where they celebrated Thanksgiving with the Davises.

From that point on, Rogers plunged into the work alongside his brother-in-law, paying pastoral visits and dividing the preaching load with him. Rogers was scrutinizing northern Kentucky, trying to decide if he should locate there. But on December 14, traveling alone, Rogers began his first journey to Berea. He and Fee had never met, nor had Rogers written or consulted with Fee in any way before this trip.[40]

> 14th Mon. Walked to Blue Lick on road to Bro. Fee's.
> 15th Rose at 4 & walked to Parkersburg thence by R. R. & stage to Richmond.
> 16th Reached Bro Fee's in safety.
> 17th Rained.
> 18th Fri. Preached at school-house. Bro. Emerick preached in the evg.
> 19th Sat. Remained at Bro. Fee's.
> 20th Sun. Preached but not as a Ch. min. should.
> 21st Mon. Started home on foot.
> 22nd Tues. Suffered greatly from sickness. The hand of the Lord is upon me. Ar. at Cin.
> 23rd Wed. Left Cin. for Cab. Cr. Arrived after midnight. Was foolish to walk thus. I promised the Lord if he brought me safe to my family to be a better husband and minister.
> 24th Sick.
> 25th " [in original]
> 26th ". Able to be about the house.

During this initial visit Fee did not encourage Rogers to locate in Berea, but suggested that Estill County might prove a useful field. Although he liked Rogers immediately, Fee did not reveal the college plan to his visitor. Rogers heard "some talk of a church or schoolhouse or both combined in Rockcastle County," but that was all; his report gives the impression he merely overheard the "talk." Fee had never laid eyes on the young man from Ohio. Why should he confide in Rogers at that point? Or volunteer to share the Berea work with him, for that matter? In any case, the location of the proposed college was still unsettled, because recent events in Rockcastle County had been so discouraging. Otis Waters was living at the Fees' when Rogers paid his first visit to Madison County. On December 17, Fee wrote to Tappan saying that he thought the time had come for *the school*, a conviction that may have had something to do with Rogers' presence. But it is more likely that Fee was inspired by Waters' success as a teacher and believed he could induce that ambitious young man to stay on. If so, he doubtless would have preferred to employ Waters, already tested and proven, rather than an unknown quantity named Rogers.[41]

Years later Rogers was still somewhat mystified because Fee had not asked him to come to Berea when they first met. Surely, Rogers had expected it, for his brother-in-law had suggested to the AMA as early as August 1857 that Rogers would be a good man to help Fee. Apparently, Rogers felt that Fee did not "take to [his] personality" at first. Disappointed by Fee's reception, Rogers returned to Cabin Creek, where he passed the winter months reading, studying, preaching, conducting prayer meetings and meditating on the martyrdom of Polycarp. In the middle of February, James S. Davis left Cabin Creek for Pendleton County. "We prayed together," Rogers wrote, emphasizing how much the two men were sharing. For a time the northern Kentucky churches were all Rogers' responsibility. In fact, when Davis returned from Pendleton County, he asked for his dismission from Cabin Creek Church on the assumption that Rogers would take his place.[42]

Less than a week later, on February 10, 1858, Rogers received a letter from Fee asking him to come to Berea to *preach* [my italics]. Fee's invitation to Rogers coincides exactly with his letter to the AMA about the success of Waters' school; it was his growing conviction that "the school is the thing" which led Fee to beg Rogers to come to Berea in April. Rogers accepted, blissfully unaware of Fee's hidden agenda.[43]

On March 29, 1858, the young couple and their infant child left Cabin Creek and arrived in Berea, Kentucky, two days later. The journey took them by stagecoach through the Blue Grass, past "the great homes, with their slave quarters close by, the beautiful pasture lands, the thrift of wealth and the shiftlessness of poverty. . . . " But, as Lizzie remarked, "Nothing could have been much drearier than Berea was." She felt wholly unprepared for the last six miles before reaching Berea, on a road so terrible that it was hard to see how any carriage could make the trip without breaking down. "I must have held on to my baby with a clutch like grim death," she wrote, "and my husband with that never-say-die look on his face, no doubt stiffened my backbone."[44]

And what did they discover when they arrived? "The smallest imaginable speck on the map of Kentucky would have been out of all proportion to mark the town, and to a traveler in search of it, it was a place hard to find. A crooked, narrow dirt road that wound up and down the ridge bordered on either side by tall trees and underbrush." And a few houses, some homes in the lowlands round about, many more out toward the Blue Grass, and even on the ridge a few cabins at either end, but all too far off at that period to be called part of Berea. Like the schoolhouse they were to see the next day, Berea was almost nothing: Fee's house, three cabins and the district schoolhouse. Later, Lizzie wrote that Berea "was all in the brush & full of possibilities."[45]

Even though the school duly opened on April12, with both John and Lizzie teaching, he was quite reluctant to be involved in it. Only necessity pushed him into the schoolhouse, where his wife had too many students for one person to cope with. Rogers' first few months in Berea were exceedingly trying, quite aside from teaching duties which he did not wish to assume, and preaching assignments which he had to fulfill anyway. Living quarters at William Stapp's house consisted of one sparsely furnished room, and, in some respects, Stapp and his family did not make life easier. At one point, Rogers found himself being insulted at William B. Wright's, and Stapp said "some things" to Rogers one Sabbath morning that "greatly tried" him.

Rogers got sick again early in April, but an excellent prayer meeting convinced him that there was hope for Kentucky, if not for himself. Distracted by work, he lost his first check from New York, and followed that up three days later by losing his purse. Still the school improved, although quarrels among the male students irritated Rogers. He tended to grow wearier and wearier.

It did not help matters that he and Fee conducted many late night discussions. Over and over again, Rogers recorded that he had stayed too late at "Bro. Fee's." What were they discussing? Among other things, baptism, a topic which Rogers notes for June 14. Fee was very pleased with his new man this time, delighted with Rogers' teaching and probably equally delighted in finding a theological sparring partner; they could discuss baptism night after night. In a burst of enthusiasm, he wrote to Cassius Clay , "Bro Rogers is not only a scholar and a Christian, but in possession of that good sense that makes him a discreet gentlemen—with social kind manners."[46]

After first term the Rogers family moved out of William Stapp's inadequate room to Teman Thompson's house, where they had "one room tacked on somehow to the back of a larger cabin." Thompson became Rogers' particular friend; so personal associations improved when the Rogers switched quarters, even though the accomodation was no better. On the day of moving Rogers philosophized, "The easiest way to live is to do at once the hardest work one has to do." The next day he wrote, "Went for blackberries. Very weary. Read chemistry."[47]

Toward the end of July, Fee and Rogers traveled into Rockcastle, Pulaski and Whitley Counties to lecture, preach, and "persuade the boys and girls of the hill country to come to the Berea school the following autumn." Their trip was brief, only a week, but for Rogers it was one of his most important and memorable experiences of Appalachian Kentucky. The ministers visited the Burdetts, the Cummins, Jerusha Preston and her family, stayed at Mrs. Miranda McQuary's where Candee's school had been burned, rode to Somerset and Cumberland Falls, where they saw Thomas J. Renfro, who had left Berea, and John Clark Richardson, another AMA worker. In Pulaski County, both Fee and Rogers lectured on slavery and each man preached once.

Rogers described this trip for the *New York Independent* in 1858. He was deeply impressed by the wild, beautiful mountain scenery—magnificent country, full of poverty and deprivation. He was struck "more deeply than ever before with the lack of industry and enterprise." He saw nothing but log cabins, most of them without glass in the windows. He observed the unbalanced diet of the people: "Corn bread, coffee and bacon . . . many people taste rarely little of anything else, except vegetables in the summer time." But the people seemed to him naturally noble in appearance. "One of the mountain men I saw was in form and feature and bearing a perfect facsimile of a Spanish cavalier of the olden time. The degree of admiration I felt for him was lessened when I visited his cheerless cabin, occupied by a numerous family, alike destitute of knowlege and comforts." In a mountain valley Rogers met an old man "of royal mien," a slaveholder about 60 years old, who lived in a solitary mansion surrounded by slave huts, the only white person on the place. He was shocked by an old woman smoking her pipe in church, but he enjoyed the sweet, wild singing of the mountain congregations.[48]

One day Fee lectured on *emancipation in the West Indies* [my own italics]; the next day people listened attentively to two sermons back-to-back and at the end of the service offered the right hand of fellowship to the strange preachers, whose lecture and sermon topics can have done nothing to alleviate their strangeness. Fee and Rogers must have been a true odd couple in mountain communities, each with his own pecularities: Fee with an abolitionist agenda and Rogers with a New England accent. Their Appalachian congregations made them welcome anyway, demonstrating their own courtesy and patience.[49]

Immediately after Fee and Rogers returned from their mountain tour, Jacob Emerick commenced a protracted meeting (two weeks) at Silver Creek Church, three miles east of Berea. At the opening session Rogers publicly confessed his shortcomings, but in his journal did not detail which ones he had mentioned; the list could have been quite long, given the nature of the man's conscience. On August 12, halfway through Emerick's meeting, Rogers joined the Berea Church. Lizzie followed suit on the 18th.

Meanwhile, Rogers was studying hard, commencing Greek in earnest and pondering the subject of baptism. On August 23, he finished *Ripley's Review of Stuart* on baptism and began *Campbell on Baptism*. His scholarship was compulsive, enjoyable and exhausting. He arranged his books, sat up too late, visited Richmond. There on August 30, he saw a "Slave separated from his wife." His only comment: "Was astonished at my own selfishness." He does not explain what form his selfishness had taken: had the poignant scene failed to move him? Was he relieved to be in a superior position himself? Lizzie Rogers described the black man being taken away on the Lexington stage with his wife, groaning and entreating, running behind the vehicle trying to say goodbye or reach him before he disappeared forever. "Far up the street the woman pursued her hopeless journey, and not one hand was lifted to help . . . . One of the men at my side remarked carelessly, 'She takes it hard, don't she?'"[50]

The next day John Rogers "spoke pettishly to Bro. Fee," with whom he was still discussing baptism and staying up too late. But, of course, he left no record of what he said. Evidently, Fee's doctrinal treadmill was trying Rogers' patience to the breaking point.

He continued working too hard and suffered illness periodically; on another trip to Richmond he lost his pocketbook and papers and $3.00. His absentmindedness was chronic, symptomatic of how easily any pressure swayed him. He also mislaid his horse at one point and lost himself in the woods. Life was not all frustration and work, however; the Bereans enjoyed a singing party at Fee's house on Christmas Eve.

Pregnant again, Lizzie did not teach winter term. When her labor began no doctor could be procured; an unskilled neighbor helped and William Norris, the Rogers' second son, was born January 6, 1859. "How little of skill or comfort came to us in the hard places," Lizzie Rogers remarked.[51]

When 1859 began, Rogers was still studying baptism, making progress, he said, without designating toward what end. In the middle of February he discussed baptism with Fee, again or still. In May, he recorded that he had "sinned in talking about baptism," but did not specify in what way. References to the "topic" continue for months. Only gradually—by reading between the lines in Rogers journal, where nothing too unpleasant is allowed—does one deduce that Fee and Rogers' discussions about baptism were arguments, sometimes quite heated arguments. Fee may have found these confrontations challenging and stimulating, even fun, because he loved to argue, point by point, every jot and tittle: Rogers' reaction was quite different; for him the encounters were a strain, inducing tension and anxiety. As Mrs. Rogers remarked, "Sometimes these discussion [on the subject of baptism] in those early days were very heated, and sometimes the differences in opinion . . . heart burnings."[52]

In spring she began teaching again. In the gloomy, threatening times in 1859, Lizzie found herself growing nervous, "brave and timid by turns"; the slightest unusual noises startled her. Helping her husband with a chemical experiment one day she got a little acid in her eye. While she was suffering from this affliction she conceived the idea of using the same substance for protection. She kept a syringe of acid beside her bed to squirt at the eyes of attackers should they ever come.[53]

"It required great courage in those days," she wrote to her children,

to send your father off on his Sunday trips. After teaching all the week he would mount his horse, ride miles into the mountain recesses to preach, and then come back again Sunday evening, or Monday morning, to enter the school room again. There were rumors of attack and mob violence, and I sent him off more than once wondering if my goodby kiss was for the trip, or for the last time.[54]

Writing some fifty years later of her youthful experiences, Lizzie Rogers warns against anyone's thinking of her as "broken down or dispirited." She was twenty years old and she had all the resiliency of youth. "The wife of a military officer shared gladly his inconveniences, his trials, his want of comforts . . . . We Bereans were all soldiers in the army of the Lord, and though we stumbled sometimes, yet our eyes were ever aloft and we were happy in our service."[55]

Rev. John Rogers' service, in spite of his wife's claims, did not always make him happy. From April 1858 through December 1859, he preached almost every Sunday, although his ministerial schedule was interspersed with teaching and trustee duties, family concerns and constantly recurring illnesses. He and Fee frequently alternated assignments—with one man taking morning service while the other conducted a service in the evening. Occasionally, Rogers preached twice on a Sabbath. Throughout 1858 Rogers preached in Berea and at Silver Creek, but he also spoke in Jackson, Pulaski and Rockcastle Counties. To distant engagements he rode a "little one-eyed pony."[56]

Most of his sermons were based on single scriptural texts and themes ("My grace shall be sufficient for thee"; "Cross-bearing"; "Be strong & of good courage"; "Lovest thou me?"). In 1858 he preached an antislavery sermon for a large, interested audience at Silver Creek. In addition to church services Rogers shared responsibility for prayer meetings, sometimes as many as two or three per week, always at least one—and occasionally addressed the Young Peoples' Meeting.

Early in February he traveled to Rockcastle County through snow four inches deep. The next day he developed a bad cold which soon became influenza, but by the following Sunday he considered himself well enough to preach at both Berea and Silver Creek. Another illness followed his ride to a night meeting at Silver Creek in March. Several times he preached in Jackson County at various private homes, trading off with George Candee, who occasionally relieved Rogers and Fee in Madison County churches. Rogers added to his own duties by founding a Temperance organization in May (18 signed the pledge) and starting a Sunday School in October (37 pupils, 7 teachers and 36 spectators, who must have been desperate for entertainment!). In addition, he preached a couple of funeral sermons (April 3 the infant child of A. G. W. Parker was buried with Rogers officiating) and married two couples, including new settlers, Charles E. Griffin and Mrs. Desda Anna Shailer on October 6.

Often his labors were purely frustrating. Once he preached a sermon on prayer to only three people. His congregations—those groups which were large enough to be so designated—behaved very differently from what Rogers was accustomed to: the men came in and went out while he was preaching; "mothers led restless children time and again to the water bucket to appease imaginary thirst." He continued preaching, whether anyone was listening or not, no matter how small the gathering might be.[57]

Fee had found his perfect worker. John G. Fee made inordinate demands of his associates as a matter of course, even though he asked no one to do more or less than he would do himself. John A.R. Rogers, who, unfortunately for his own health and strength, never said no until his body said it for him, undertook to do everything Fee asked and more. He passed the test; Fee's monumental project would hinge on the young would-be martyr from Oberlin. And his even younger wife.

The Rogers' School: 1st Term (April 12, 1858-July 9, 1858)[58]
"On Monday morning [April 12, 1858] we found ourselves duly installed over the beginning of Berea College." Elizabeth Rogers.

John and Elizabeth Rogers were primarily responsible for the Berea school in 1858 and 1859, although for a short time others assisted in teaching. As with previous schools, this one was simply the district school taught in a building provided by the local citizens and under the trusteeship of three local men. It differed from most schools in Kentucky by hiring acknowledged abolitionists as teachers, by enrolling students from neighboring districts, and, eventually, by having an anti-caste rule which made it theoretically possible for black students to attend. The relationship of the AMA missionaries to local education was basically a planned infiltration, abolitionists entering the Kentucky school system at the lowest level and in the simplest way, as gradeschool teachers.[59]

Mrs. Rogers vividly recalled her first view of Berea's schoolhouse: the building was hidden among the trees, with only a little cleared space about it for a playground, and certainly was poorly fitted even for a stable. It was a low, unplastered building of vertical boards, well lighted for a school in that country, but devoid of almost everything but the barest necessities.

In the one room there were a few "rude seats and desks," a teacher's table, rather beautiful, of strong cherry wood, and "possibly a blackboard." The structure had never been painted inside or out and was made of such crude material that painting would not have been effective anyway. It was raining that day, and the windows were broken.

The reaction of John and Lizzie Rogers to this sight is conveyed in her "Personal History": "I do remember," she writes,

> that we scarcely spoke to each other as we stood there. We acted more as though we were standing by the corpse of a dear friend, and indeed I think we buried that day a great deal of romance and prepared ourselves for the real work at hand . . . . It was a dark outlook, and hardly the place for my scholarly husband: and judging as I had to then, only by the present . . . it seemed a waste of his talents. . . .

The advantage of there being "so nearly nothing to commence upon," it seemed to her, was that the spot gave her husband an opportunity to begin his work building on "no man's foundation." [60]

Somehow both the Rogers maintained their enthusiasm and their optimism; "we were too weary to be particular," Lizzie wrote, "too brave, let me say it after all these years, to complain. We were both in a way optimistic, and we endured what could not be cured. . . . " That she endured their trials better than her husband did may never have occurred to her.[61]

On April 12, 1858, John Rogers recorded in his journal, "Commenced teaching. All favorable," a view that would be subject to constant revision. Fee had "drummed up fifteen pupils, his three children among the number. . . . " (These numbers would also change with every report.) Later Lizzie Rogers viewed opening day as an historic occasion: "On Monday morning we found ourselves duly installed over the beginning of Berea College." Briefly, she was totally in charge of the school, her husband presiding only at opening and closing exercises each day. "I was monarch of all I surveyed in that room," she boasted. Soon, however, increasing numbers of student necessitated both John and Lizzie teaching fulltime. "Before long," she stated, "we had all we both could accomplish, and the plannings for the future had to be crowded into the evening hours or wherever leisure might come." When the Rogers began, they found their pupils not advanced beyond the very rudiments. "At once," Rogers wrote, "the best known methods of teaching were adopted and the best educational appliances were secured."[62]

But Rogers did not consider the new educational experiment altogether successful, not by any means. At the beginning of the second week he wrote, "School not yet what I would have it." The next day (April 19) he confessed, "[I] speak as if I was impatient." His mode of speaking was a continuing problem. On the 23rd: "Spoke in singing-school somewhat harshly"; on the 26th: "Spoke too loud in school." Periodically, throughout his records of his teaching experience, Rogers would recur to his sometimes uncontrollably impatient or angry mode of speech; occasionally, his students irritated him a great deal. On the 27th of April, he wrote, "Was somewhat disheartened," but the next day was "a better day in school than any previous." The Monday following: "A wearisome day in school. Not perfect," and the next day his entry was simply, "Work, Work, Work." By the 8th of May, which was a Saturday, he wrote, "Weary as a matter of course." School had been in session a little less than a month. On June 2, Rogers wrote, "Our school is not what it should be." On the 7th, more sanguine, he recorded, "The Lord cheered me & showed me how to teach." And on the 10th, the only corporal punishment Rogers ever mentioned: "Whipped Wm. Burdett. Did so with regret & heart of love."

The school increased rapidly in the first term till fifty names were on the roll. The younger students fell to Lizzie Rogers' care, but she had some students among the older pupils, and moved in and out among them, as she said, "helping them if, or when I could." She found her students endearing from the first. "A few young men who came . . . clothed in rustic garments" convinced her that "clothes did not make a man . . . . For deference of manner to teacher or their girl companions," she wrote, they "might well have passed for pupils of Chesterfield."[63]

Teachers and students visited during noon times and the teachers were not too dignified to play, practicing gymnastics right along with their pupils. John Rogers "encouraged the boys to aid in clearing the under-bush so closely touching the playground," and this task "was turned into a jolly good time. . . . Teacher and pupils did valiant work while the fairer sex aided by their approving words and smiles."[64]

Lizzie Rogers thought that a little song book, the "Oriole," which she and her husband used with the children was one of the best parts of their teaching, "splendidly adapted" to their needs. "Those songs," she said, "set the countryside afire . . . they sang them not only in school but on the hillsides and in the valleys. They entered every home." Even slaves learned the melodies; the whole neighborhood was enchanted with the music.[65]

Each Friday afternoon the school gave show performances—what John Rogers called "literary exercises." The audiences, consisting of parents and friends unaccustomed to public entertainment of any sort, were uncritical of the students' efforts. The younger children recited little poems, while the older ones might present public debates or longer memory pieces. Berea children had never participated in such activities before; it was "a new and fiery ordeal," which every individual had to participate in, no matter how shy or reluctant. In addition, Rogers himself delivered practical lectures in astronomy or geography or some other subject for the benefit of older students and visitors.[66]

And visitors came from miles around to the Friday exercises. New pupils were added every week; the one-room facility was overflowing by the end of the first term. The whole community was full of enthusiasm—here were teachers of skill, imagination, sympathy, charm, talent, themselves overflowing with youth and high-spirits. After a few weeks the young couple could hardly spend a night at their boarding house, "so constant and urgent were the invitations to visit the homes of their pupils."[67]

As the first term came to its successful conclusion, the teachers planned their final show performance for the term: it was to be a big occasion, requiring much preparation. Rogers' journal entries summarize the last ten days of the term:

> 31st [June] Worked on an arbor for holding our Exhibition.
> July 1st Bro Fee thought one thing & I another about the arbor.

2nd Col Clay made an address on Education.

3rd A long talk with C. M. Clay & Bro Fee. Regret I did not more fully push the claims of God to perfect obedience regardless of consequences. C. M. C. made a political speech at the Glade.

4th Preached at the arbor in the morning. Had not made a sufficient preparation.

5th A quiet & pleasant day. Greatly interested in Botany.

6th Spoke to the school about their souls as kindly as possible. Bro [John] Hansel here from Oberlin.

7th Wed. Commenced preparing a stage in the arbor.

8th Thurs. Prepared for the morrow.

The exhibition of July 9, 1858, Berea's first "graduation exercise," was encouraging and memorable; on the whole, it was the most heartening occasion Fee had enjoyed since his arrival in Madison County, and for the young teachers it was simply wonderful. The whole community, not just parents and scholars, prepared for the occasion. "A leafy bower, with towering oaks for pillars, was prepared to seat a larger number than had ever come into the vicinity. . . . Stirring music had been prepared and the community arranged for a free dinner spread on long tables in an adjoining grove."[68]

Fee wrote up the occasion (on July 9, 1858, the day of the Exhibition) for the *American Missionary* magazine, using it as evidence that the time was ripe for a new kind of school: the Berea College of his plan, anti-caste, anti-sectarian, open to the poor, encouraging manual labor. Known and committed abolitionists could teach in Kentucky; Rogers and his wife had demonstrated "how prosperous and efficient" such a school could be, following up the previous work of Lincoln and Waters. Fee saw the successful exhibition as the opening of the final door in central Kentucky. Some five or six hundred people attended. The weather was perfect; "unveiled by a single cloud," the sun shone "in great beauty and glory. All around was quiet and lovely."[69]

Rogers extolled the occasion: "If the school had been successful and enthusiastic, the closing exercises were captivating. At one time the people made the grove ring with their cheers, at another they were bathed in tears."[70]

"Our first term of school finished," Elizabeth Rogers stated, "with a great blaze of trumpets. . . . " People had come from miles around, from adjoining countries; everyone was there; even former mobs were in attendance, attracted by excitement and free food. "The school became at once popular, the flags were flying and banners waving . . . and the Yankee teachers were apparently not so bad after all."[71]

The valedictory was delivered by Green Renfro, who moved his audience to tears, but the sentimental triumph of the student program was the goodbye speech spoken by Minerva Denham. "This young girl," Lizzie said, "starting out with great ease and gusto, suddenly as the goodbye words were to be uttered, broke down in tears and left the stage."[72]

After an interlude of social chat to recover from this lachrymose production, the audience returned to the arbor for six short addresses. The first speaker, Dr. Chase (a relative of Salmon P. Chase, later Secretary of the U. S. Treasury), native of New Hampshire, then practicing medicine in Madison County, was interrupted by "Old Bill Wood," who insisted on being allowed to speak immediately on grounds that he could not tarry until the exercises were over. (William Woods, of Garrard county, was an ex-member of the State Legislature.) Fee described Woods' impromptu utterance for the amusement of Cassius Clay: "The old fellow stormed away about God's designs in our improving our talents and man making living by the sweat of his [double underlining] brow—then to morality and men doing as they would be done by—Liberty our country &c. He expressed his surprise at the large & respectful audience and interesting school instead of a little handful in the brush." Woods had thought of his own days as a teacher in Virginia when he was a youth and his heart was touched by the "manifest sympathy between teachers and pupils." As he was leaving the platform Woods confided to James Blackburn, "Jimmy, the Niggers will be free yet but damn it I intend to hold on to mine as long as I can."[73]

Chase spoke again, or rather resumed. Then Fee addressed the assembled multitude; his topic—classes which should be educated. In his letter to Clay, Fee sketched his categories in very few words: "Females & mountain boys—poor . . . . "

Finally, the speeches were over and everyone ate. "What a delicious array of good things!" Lizzie Rogers wrote some 50 years later. Those who were too poor to bring anything to eat were fed with the best to be had. Members of the Rockcastle mob, perfectly willing to eat food at the school they threatened to burn down, received special attention from John G. Fee himself.

"If there are any who think of [this exhibition day] as an ordinary closing day to an ordinary school," Lizzie Rogers protested, "I think they miss its touch of glory."[74]

On the day itself in his journal John Rogers recorded the following entry: "9th Fri. The Lord helped greatly in all respects. A touching scene when Minerva Denham arose to give her farewell exercise. School is over. Lord I thank thee for thy help."

Fee summed it up: "The outlook on that day, was good for Berea."[75]

Three More Terms, a Board of Trustees and a Constitution
"7th Tues. [September 1858]. Signed the Constitution of Berea College thereby becoming a trustee of the same." Entry in John A.R. Rogers' journal.
"The anti-caste question carried in our school district 23 to 7." John G. Fee's Report on the Glade's Schoolboard election, 1858

During the last few days of July and the first of August, Fee and Rogers toured in the mountains to lecture, preach, visit and recruit possible students. Rogers observed an Appalachian school—what he saw did not please him: " . . . the pupils went out and came in as they pleased. The teacher sat with his heels on a desk. Before I left, he commanded his scholars to study; thereupon the members of the school set their lungs as well as their eyes to work. Spelling, which with reading and writing not unusually comprises the whole course of study, was the order of the house. A roar ensued not unlike that of a park of artillery."[76]

On August 19, John G. Fee suggested to Simeon Jocelyn that Bro. Rogers' wife be paid because "her services were valuable to the school." In the same letter he enclosed a new leaflet that had been printed up to advertise the second term of the school, which would be taught by John and Elizabeth Rogers and John and Ellen Hanson.[77]

Second term opened on September 6, 1858, "under circumstances of great cheer." The next day the preliminary organizational meeting of the first board of trustees for Berea College was held; John G. Fee was called to the chair, and John G. Hanson appointed secretary, a position he was to hold for many years. A committee consisting of John A. R. Rogers, John Smith and William Stapp, was appointed to draft a preamble and resolutions for a constitution, duly signed the same day by John G. Fee, John A. R. Rogers, John Smith, John G. Hanson, John Burnam, Sr., and William Stapp. Three trustees signed later: James S. Davis, Jacob Emerick and George Candee, all of whom were ministering in other places on September 7. The enormously successful first term of the Rogers school had led to this decisive step, the final go-ahead.[78]

When John and Lizzie had begun teaching in 1858, they had had 15 pupils, but the school had increased rapidly to 50. The next year attendance doubled; the number rose to 100 before the term closed. The 100 students in 1859 probably included virtually all the original 15 and those 35 who had swelled the ranks to 50 during the school's first year. Many of the students who studied under William E. Lincoln and Otis B. Waters were still attending the school when the Rogers couple began to teach.[79]

Almost one-fifth of the original students were children or grandchildren of staff members: offspring of trustees, colporteurs and Fee himself. But children came from all directions; even though it was a district school, it engaged the interest of people outside the Glade. Many families from Fee's Rockcastle and Jackson County churches sent their children to Berea. Of course, families from the Glade Church provided most of the students, but many other neighborhood families sent their children to the new school.[80]

Among them, to the Bereans' great surprise, were the slaveholders. "We had in that school," Lizzie Rogers wrote, "planter's daughters, pretty Southern girls, and little maidens who wore most bewitching little print dresses, and white aprons, while close by them sat children clothed in plainest garb, children gathered from the neighboring hillsides." Ann Eliza (Best) Moore recalled that she and her sister Mary were escorted to school every morning by a slave boy named Lige (he called himself Elijah Best after the war), who had to wait for the girls to finish school so he could escort them home. While he waited Lizzie Rogers taught him to read. [81]

One-third of the students belonged to slaveholding families; some 38 students out of 104 had parents who owned one or more slaves; many more students had uncles, aunts, grandparents or cousins who were slaveholders—if such connections were taken into account more than half of the original students at Berea would be included. Some of the students were allied to largescale slaveholders with a great deal of power and money. Ballards, Maupins, Moores,

Todds, Bests, Cornelisons, Denhams—to name a few—were closely akin to Madison County citizens owning 15 slaves or over in 1860; some of the Berea students were nearly related to the few families who owned *most* of the slaves in the whole county. The two Best girls, Ann Eliza and Mary were related through their mother, Nancy Harris, to four families of Harrises in Madison County whose slaves totaled 118 in 1860, and through their grandmother, Sarah Kennedy, they were kin to the famous family which purportedly served as model for the slaveholders in *Uncle Tom's Cabin*. The Denham students had an uncle George Dejarnett, who owned 24 slaves; the Maupin children were related to George W. Maupin (15 slaves) and Leland D. Maupin (23 slaves).[82]

Fee bragged to the AMA: "There is not a slaveholder near us but sends to our school."[78]

At the same time, the school attracted many of the poverty-stricken mountain students who had been expected; some of them were, indeed, grindingly poor, some far too poor to pay the tuition, although Lizzie says no one was turned away on that account.[83]

One Appalachian family, the Prestons, probably represented many of the problems and attitudes of their class. Jerusha Preston, a widow with several children, lived in northern Rockcastle County before the Civil War. Candee found the Prestons willing to shelter him when most of his Rockcastle friends refused to associate with him because of the danger. Fee described Jerusha as being very poor, but "with one of the most interesting families." (Incidentally, in the religious parlance of the mid-19th century the word 'interesting' meant 'spiritually promising.') When Fee and Rogers traveled into the mountains, Jerusha Preston, destitute as she was, gave them hospitality. Rogers described her as "rich in faith and [with] noble children, but destitute of worldly good." The children all wanted to attend the Berea school, including the eldest, David, "the mainstay of the family." While Fee and Rogers were visiting, the little family tried to decide if it might be possible for them to move to Berea, and discussed ways and means for the "widow to secure her children the advantages of education." It was decided that John should go to school for six months in any case; then he could teach—the older girls would harvest the corn (they volunteered to do so) and so on. In December Fee helped the Widow Preston with some financial aid, probably in the form of tuition for her children, most of whom did attend Berea.[84]

John A. R. Rogers' account book 1857-1868 provides many details concerning the financial and labor arrangements of pre-Civil War Berea. Some students worked for the school or for their teachers; William Hughlett, for example, is credited with two weeks work in October 1859. However, at this period Rogers' accounts detail little student labor; parents of students worked for the school more frequently than their children did, trading labor for books and tuition. Mary Jane Moore's tuition for July 1858 was paid by her father Fergusson Moore pasturing, salting and providing corn for Rogers' horse. The barter system was used extensively, with books being traded for a turkey (from Hamilton Rawlings) and tuition being paid with meat (by James Maupin). Mrs. Elder obtained books for her children by sewing a pair of pants for the teacher.[85]

The school and the new settlement at Berea provided small jobs for many people in the region; many students, such as David Preston and Valentine Williams, worked for Fee, Rogers or Hanson for cash—which they may have had to hand right back for fees (in the time-honored system of student labor). The entire neighborhood became financially involved with the Berea project, as hundreds of individual entries in Rogers's account book attest. Most of the people who traded with the Bereans or who worked for them were parents or siblings of students at the school. They did hauling and horseshoeing; they chopped wood, built the daily fire in the schoolhouse during the winter months, repaired the building, cleared forestland, sewed clothing, babysat, ran errands, and were duly paid by Rogers for their work. They provided soap, eggs, hay, wheat, molasses and other staples.

Some students received their tuition free, and John G. Fee personally paid the school expenses of a few, including Elizabeth Rawlings (daughter of Hamilton), who had ambitions to be a schoolteacher. John and Lizzie Rogers paid for some poor students' books.[86]

A successful school in the neighborhood added many new elements to the whole Berea situation, not just educationally. Lizzie Rogers stated, "I am quite sure we owed . . . much of our safety in all our Berea dangers, to a love in the hearts of those scholars, that never died out." In a sense, the students became the guardians of their radical teachers—whereas the adults in the community were sometimes ready to abandon them—or attack them.[87]

As teachers Lizzie and John Rogers received a flood of invitations to visit the families of their pupils; usually they were asked to spend the night and always they were entertained with the best each household could offer. "What a variety of homes we entered," Lizzie said, "now at the home of the planter, and again in lowlier cabins." The Rogers were entertained by "the Bests, the Burnams, the Moores, the Ruckers, the Denhams, the Todds, the Prestons, the Williams, the Wrights, the Elders, the Thompsons" and many others. "I remember so well in some of the homes we entered," Rogers wrote, "we were waited on by obsequious slaves, and in others the mothers prepared our bounteous meals," sometimes in a log cabin with a single room where the frying of the chicken was directly before the guests' eyes.[88]

During second term, the Young Men's Literary Society discussed (or argued) the question: "If a colored person should apply for admission to the school . . . should [he/she] be rejected?" The question had already been settled among the trustees, but the students conducted the first public debate on the issue, and Lizzie Rogers remembered "heated discussion on the questions of the day" in the school during that time. The matter "became a topic of general interest," and more than interest—for the discussion "greatly diminished the number of pupils."[89]

In November 1858, the Berea project received an endorsement from world-famous novelist, Harriet Beecher Stowe, who praised John G. Fee's achievements in Kentucky. Suppose the missionaries of the regular mission societies had gone into the slave states as Fee went into Kentucky, she wrote,

> founding churches on principles of strict anti-slavery communion. They would have been driven out, say you? How do we know? Fee is not driven out of Kentucky. Fee is fighting the battle in Kentucky which we should fight in every slave territory. He is fighting it successfully—necessities, afflictions, distress, only make him stronger. Antislavery churches are rising around him, feeble indeed, in their beginning, but mighty in moral force; and every inch which Christianity seems to gain under such auspices she really does gain.[90]

On December 1st, the second term came to an end. "Exhibition took place," Rogers noted, "The Lord helped. Thanks to him." However, the

Exhibition ending term two was nothing compared to the earlier one. It was winter—and the school, while it seemed likely to be permanent, was now under a cloud. "The Closing Exhibition," Lizzie wrote, "on account of the cold weather must perforce be within the building, and while there was not quite the enthusiasm from outside, nor the great crowds, still everything was done on a wider, deeper scale . . . with more show of real school work."[91]

On the same day, the proposed constitution, with slight modification, was ratified as a whole during a meeting which adjourned at midnight. Naturally, Rogers wrote about it in his journal on the 2nd, "A meeting of the trustees to consult. Bro. Emerick thought the policy of Bro. Fee & others unwise. The Lord's spirit manifestly present at prayer meeting." Work was progressing well, but already opposition to the Berea College plan was emerging. Emerick was not alone in his estimation of Fee's policy, although he may have been the only vocal opponent at this time. Rogers, typically, does not spell out Emerick's objections, but later events point to interracial education as the issue. Prayer settled the trustees' differences this time; later gatherings would be less amenable to godly restraint.

In December 1858, something happened in Berea which changed the whole picture and finally decided the question of a permanent location for Fee's abolitionist community and school. Whenever the opportunity presented itself, Fee invited black people home to eat with his family. Right before Fee was scheduled to leave for Worcester, Massachuesetts, on a fund-raising trip, "a colored man regarded in the community as a good man & who held religious meetings in different places" attended the sabbath afternoon prayer meetings at Glade Church. Fee twice asked him to pray, and then invited him home—and, Fee wrote, "sat him down to my table with my family and other friends." John G. Hanson and John A. R. Rogers likewise entertained the black man in their own homes. "Against this many of the people & some of the church members rebelled," Fee stated. "The question arose about colored persons coming into the school. Some [black people] had attended the school Bro. Waters taught in Rockcastle & I had commended that."[92]

The trustees of the prospective school met, although a full board was not present, and decided it was unwise to purchase land at Berea "until the people should test or settle the point—Shall we have school upon gospel principles[?]—

treat man as man—if not we go hence." A schoolboard election was scheduled with two sets of trustees in the running: Fee's anti-caste group v. supporters of the slaveholders.

"I think nothing short of the power of the Holy Ghost will give the victory," Fee said, "We are now holding daily prayer meetings & shall probably pray ten days longer." To intepret Fee's prognosis as hopeless because he literally sees no earthly way his side can win would be to misconstrue his religious faith completely. He *expected* 'nothing short of the Holy Ghost.' Others were far less hopeful. At this point, Rogers was preparing to leave, to unite with Marshall and Hansel in missionary efforts in northern Kentucky. He was informally asked to go on with his school, but he deferred his answer. Apparently, he doubted that anything worthwhile could be achieved at Berea.[93]

In fact, the whole abolitionist movement seemed doomed to failure in the region. Even at the meeting of the trustees some were 'tenderfooted' on the subject of race. Some members of Fee's own congregation, after six years of exposure to his views, still objected to the smallest hint of social equality between the races outside the church itself. Fee noted the inconsistency: "In church we have two colored members—one communion—This the people seemed to expect—but in school; that a new test & trial to their pride. And against me no small measure of the opposition is hurled." Of course, Davis, Candee, Rogers and Fee agreed that an anti-caste school was right, but after all they were simply the original four AMA missionaries, who had arrived in Berea with their principles already formed; the point had been to convert *others* to their views.[94]

The board of trustees met again, assembling even before school closed. On December 6, Rogers told the people that he had resolved to "teach a Christian school in which all black & white were to be admitted." Two of the district school trustees assented to Rogers' use of the building, but on the 15th a meeting of the district was held to determine if he could be permitted to go on teaching. "Previous to the meeting," Rogers wrote, "I knew not what course to take but felt clear in mind to please the Lord perfectly without reference to men." He was allowed to continue.

On February 26, Fee wrote Clay: "We are lying still [keeping quiet] about our school. We think it wise to let the principle of anti-caste lie before the minds of the people until they shall become familiar with it, not frightened—then start the school."[95]

On April 8, 1859, Fee composed an historic report to the AMA. The Glade district had held its election. "The anti-caste question carried in our school district," Fee exulted, "23 to 7."[96]

The church, the colony, the school would be at Berea.

In a way, the people of the Glade District chose Berea, by inviting Fee, by supporting him and his church (not always with great enthusiasm), by voting to maintain a district school with no racial discrimination, by sending their children to that school. A few leaders of the Glade District formed a small, but very important group of "Fee-ites." Two local men became known as sturdy supporters of Fee's ministry in church and school: John Hamilton Rawlings and Teman Thompson. In addition, three prominent citizens of the Glade District became charter members of Glade Church and later trustees of Berea College: William Stapp, Thomas Jefferson Renfro and John Burnam, Sr. These five were pillars of their community, the nucleus of the indigenous antislavery "movement" in Madison County. All of them had been influenced first by Cassius Clay, and all had lived in the Glade long before Fee arrived.[97]

The spring term of 1859 began on April 18, ten days after the school board election that settled the anti-caste question for the time being. Rogers had been threatened, and the community was full of unrest. Only twenty-four students reported to school on the first day; numbers had plummeted drastically. Lizzie returned to teaching with Anna Shailer caring for Raphael and the new baby William Norris. The young mother would run down the hill at recess to breastfeed her child. In a way, these juxtapositions form an archetypal image of the work at Berea before the Civil War: Lizzie Rogers, young, hopeful, willing and eager, but caught in a social context of tension and foreboding, in a world ready to explode.[98]

On April 22, 1859, Fee reported to the AMA: "the school . . . [is] known all over the land as avowedly anti-caste—about 30 people—we expect 15 or 20 more." The anti-caste announcement, directly espousing abolitionist doctrines, had halted the expansion of the school. Years of growth disappeared virtually overnight, as the school lost almost three-fourths of its students. Fee saw this as merely a temporary setback. Having the work identified as anti-caste was more important to him than any other consideration anyway.[99]

Support for Fee's plan was not immediately in evidence, however. The first trustee meeting of 1859, held on May 12 right after the anti-caste election victory, had no quorum. The minutes record only a prayer by George Candee and Rogers' motion that the board meet again. At the next meeting, apparently later the same day after more members had been pulled in, still another draft of the constitution was presented—this one the work of a committee consisting of Rogers, Davis and Thomas J. Renfro. Another committee, consisting of Fee and Rogers, was appointed to rewrite this draft "altering language not sense." Officers were elected (Fee, president; Rogers, vice-president; Hanson, secretary; Renfro, treasurer) and the Prudential Committee (Fee, Smith, Renfro, Rogers and Hanson) instructed to obtain legal counsel and if possible purchase a tract of land from a local man named John G. Woolwine.[100]

At this meeting the board expressed its confidence "in the fidelity of Rev. J. A. R. Rogers in conducting the Berea School." On May 13, Rogers wrote [in his journal]: "At the adjourned meeting of the trustees there was not a quorum. Seven present proceeded to organize an Inst. called Berea College. Organization completed & self appointed teacher." Did he compose this entry with a sense of enthusiasm or foreboding? Did he feel trapped or relieved? Naturally, he does not reveal such information.

On the 20th of May, John G. Fee visited Cassius Clay at White Hall to ask him to join the board of trustees. Clay declined because the proposed school's "opposition to caste looked plainly to the co-education of the . . . races," a possibility which Clay did not consider "expedient." He "did not believe such a school could be a numerical, nor a financial success. Also he feared evil results to virtue" from educating men and women, black and white in the same school. After five years the Berea project had become totally independent of Clay's guidance, assistance—and protection. The final business of the official Clay-Fee alliance was thus, ironically, a complete turnabout: Fee's invitation to Clay to join a project of Fee's design under Fee's leadership. Probably, Fee issued his invitation without a sense of its irony, but surely the moment was bitter for Clay.[101]

When the board met again the constitution was read aloud for the benefit of William Stapp, unable to read it for himself, who had been absent at the last meeting. His "hearty co-operation" was solicited. The board decided it was possible to get a charter, but realized that the constitution would have to be altered to be legal. No one specified what changes would have to be made. At preliminary meeting no. 5 held at the Berea schoolhouse July 14, the committee on the constitution, Rogers, Hanson and Stapp, presented the document to the seven trustees assembled; on the 15th the board met at six o'clock in the morning. After a three-day discussion the constitution was adopted and articles of agreement signed on July 16, by Fee, Stapp, Renfro, Candee, Rogers and John G. Hanson.[102]

By the night of the 18th, all by-laws had been ratified. The board resolved to inform John Hansel, Edmund B. Fairfield, Elisha Harrison and Humphrey Marshall, Jr., of their meeting, these four men having already been invited to become trustees. (Only one of them ever served: Elisha Harrison; apparently he accepted the position before the war, but his signature as the 10th man for incorporation was not obtained until 1866; perhaps his trusteeship began too late to "count" in 1859.) Rogers, Candee and Hanson were appointed a committee "to draft an address for publication setting forth the purposes and claims of the proposed college."[103]

John G. Fee was empowered to act as general agent for the college "with power to secure such other help as he [might] deem necessary," and 27 local agents were authorized: including David F. Newton, of New York City, a former student at Lane Seminary, who would provide some degree of financial security for Berea for years to come; Simeon S. Jocelyn and Lewis Tappan of the AMA; Freeman Walker of North Brookfield, Massachusetts; Henry E. Peck, professor at Oberlin; Jonathan Blanchard, President of Knox College; Elnathan Davis, of Fitchburg, Massachusetts; President E. B. Fairfield, of Hillsdale, Michigan; James A. Thome, former Lane Rebel; Edgar Needham, of Louisville, Kentucky; Candee, Davis and Rogers; Levi Coffin, the Underground Railroad agent of Richmond, Indiana; James Allen, of Bangor, Maine; and Cassius M. Clay of White Hall. Most of the 27 agents were from the North or East; only six resided in the South, and three of those were AMA missionaries.[104]

Fee, Rogers, Renfro and Hanson were instructed to purchase the Woolwine tract, and, finally, the board resolved to notify Rev. Henry Ward Beecher, George B. Cheever and Harriet Beecher Stowe of the founding of the institution and invite their cooperation.[105]

The board members were, of course, unaware that their particular group would never be assembled again; certainly they did not suspect that board meetings were over for seven long years.

Rogers, as usual, commented only briefly on these actions, although from his account something seems to have been going on besides business:

> 14th. Convention met to frame college. I sinned.
> 15th. Trustees discussed Resolution to the purport that in electing Pres. & Profs. the Trustees wd [would] use no sectarian tests.
> 16th. Disd [discussed] the same 17th Sab. Bros Emerick & Davis preached.
> 18th. Board finished work & adjourned. I was weak & wicked.

In her "Personal History" Lizzie Rogers recorded part of the trustees' agenda that never made it to minutes of the meetings. "During the summer," she wrote,

> a board of trustees was chosen, and long meetings in which matters affecting the school for the future as well as the present were discussed. Undenominational as all the good men tried to be, and eager as they were to have the school stand on broader platforms than those of any sect, there were two great distinct parties among these to-be Trustees, viz: the immersionists and those who held the larger truth that all baptism by water by any form was scriptural. As I think of it now, this more than any question was discussed.

Since Rogers now belonged to the party favoring baptism in any mode, his occasions for sinning and being weak and wicked may have arisen in opposition to Fee, leader of the immersionists, who apparently wanted to use mode of baptism as a test for future workers.[106]

Theoretically, a charter for the college was easy to obtain, "as under a general Law of the State when a proper constitution and by-laws were recorded in the County Clerk's office, and signed by ten citizens of the State as trustees, a charter was thereby secured." At least, getting the charter *would* have been easy if the Bereans could have found ten men willing to sign it. In the fall of 1859 "the Trustees visited Richmond to sign the college papers and make the paper [sic] a legal document, [but] it was . . . impossible to find the full number of Kentucky men willing to subscribe themselves as Trustees." (Some of the trustees were not

Kentuckians, so their support was ineffectual for incorporation.) Lizzie Rogers remarked that if the charter signed in 1859 had become legal it would have been a strange looking one. Some of the original trustees could not write their names and had to sign with X's. "Yet it was to be a college for the poor," she mused, "and I'm not sure but that there would have been a fitness about it." The signing was delayed until the school was broken up in December 1859. After that the charter had to wait until 1866, when it was signed by a newly constituted board with a different membership.[107]

Local opposition had continued to grow—and the little band of Berea workers was frightened. "We felt as it were, the ground rocking beneath our feet," Lizzie Rogers said. The excitement was not simply local; now the whole country was in a turmoil; Northerners living in the South were more and more feared and hated. "The spirit of war and bloodshed was in the air." The tension told on everyone. During this school term one of John Rogers' most positive comments was on July 1st: "Not a very bad day." The same week he confessed that he had been "too grim in the evening with [his] wife."[108]

When the spring term came to an end, the teachers decided it was best not to make much demonstration. "The term closed so quietly," Lizzie said, "I cannot recall anything about it." In his journal Rogers wrote, "[July] 8th Closed school. Lord I do thank thee for thy wonderful mercies which have been toward me."[109]

At the beginning of the fall term of 1859 all connection with the district school was severed—or at least no Berea missionary ever taught there again. Rogers gave up all claim on the schoolroom. Humphrey Marshall, Jr., Fee's protege, arrived from Cabin Creek to become the new teacher, and some former pupils remained to study under him. The AMA missionaries had decided to turn all their attention to the founding of Berea College, which would involve their establishing a new gradeschool of their own. From July to December 1859 none of the Berea colonists taught at all, instead devoting their energies to establishing their colony, maintaining their churches, and readying a new school to open. The board of trustees kept trying to find ten Kentucky citizens to sign a college charter, but that proved impossible. Nevertheless, the elite slaveholders of Richmond, Kentucky, and thereabouts, began to watch Berea with growing apprehension.[110]

CHAPTER SIX

A COLONY IN READINESS; EXILE

The Colonists

By July 1859, the stage was set for collecting funds, purchasing land, welcoming colonists, building town and college. After teaching one term John G. Hanson had erected a sawmill near Berea "for the benefit of the cause of Christ." He was ready to provide the actual building materials of a new community. Oberlin colonists some 25 years earlier had not been so lucky: the trustees of that institution had disagreed about the size of the steam engine needed and so failed to provide a sawmill to cut lumber for the construction work of Oberlin's first year, much to the disappointment of the colonists. No such frustration lay ahead for those planning Berea. The abundant forest and Hanson's enterprise would provide amply.[1]

By September, virtually everything was in readiness. John G. Fee's father died on the 3rd of that month and Fee and his family traveled to Bracken County for the funeral. His fund-raising trip to the East had already been planned as part of his journey to Worcester, Massachusetts, to the annual meeting of the AMA, so he decided to leave for Pennsylvania from Bracken County, while his wife and children returned to Berea. The death of Fee's father marked a kind of symbolic beginning; from his father's grave Fee commenced a most important journey: the first official fund-raising tour for the institution that Fee wanted for his life's work, a journey that would begin in triumph and end in terror.[2]

212

John Smith: 1st Colonist
"I am here in this land of darkness trying to stay up the hands of these dear brethren." John Smith.

The first Northern colonist to arrive in Berea in 1858 was in many ways the most unsuitable: an old man, John Smith, native of New Hampshire, soon to be one of Berea's first trustees. He was about 72 when he arrived; he had left an aged wife and several grown children near Columbus, Ohio, and set out on his own. A rather wealthy farmer, he planned to invest in the Berea scheme; he had proven his reforming zeal by his work with the Ojibway Indians in Minnesota under the auspices of the AMA. Berea was so much better than what he was used to that Smith found prospects there very encouraging. While he looked about him he was living at Fee's. Smith provided the money when Fee, Rogers and he purchased a tract of land near Berea which was about to fall into the hands of slaveholders; the tract was to be Smith's contribution to the colony.[3]

In July 1858, Smith felt impelled to report to the AMA concerning his new venture. "In addressing you," he wrote,

> I go at the work in former stile at the age of 70 [slightly underestimated]. I felt my duty in the early age of missions to give myself to the work. . . . When the cause of the bondsman came up I felt he of all men was most miserable but the door was shut against slave & master. In the summer of 50 the cause of the poor Indian came up abused by government & white settlers. I will go to do what I can to redress his wrongs while I live.

He spent four years among the Indians, then had to return home to settle some property question among his children. He had intended at that time to look for a way of ministering to slaves, but hesitated for four years before venturing to Berea in April 1858. His move was in opposition to his own household, kinsmen and neighbors, "except one[,] a man of God who greatly strengthened [his] faith."

"I am here in this land of darkness," Smith stated, "trying to stay up the hands of these dear brethren." Fee, he described as "this Moses who has taken his life in his hand & so long stood in the gap." Since he was writing to the AMA, Smith indulged the usual appeal, for "Farmers, Mechanics, Implements of husbandry . . . to constitute a mission in a Heathen land."

At the end of his first report Smith described his own activities: "I labor some visit some Read pray leave tracts where they can read. Yea, need only to be among them to see the low estate of this people." He said if he asked them about their soul's interests, they did not know how to answer. "What church do you belong to?" "I never joined any church." "Have you thought about the immortality of the soul, Heaven & Hell." "Yes, I have thought right smart about it." Smith concluded his letter with the formulaic, but apparently heartfelt, "Lord how long[?]"[4]

And Smith stayed on. He continued to negotiate to buy land, but not, Fee discovered, in order to live on it. Smith was satisfied to live with Fee. "He expects to pay his way," Fee complained,

> by work at little chores—do what he can at meetings—by attending
> & praying. He is not disposed to go out and labor among the
> people, as I expected. He is like most old men, he loves to be quiet
> at home—His wife is old—not in her right mind—provided for in
> home of one of their children—Tis a little singular that he should be
> away from his family so much. I think he is a praying good man.
> He increased the labor of my wife who is without help. Our house
> has to be the stopping & staying place for all—there is no public
> house near.[5]

Still if Smith stayed he would take charge of supervising the colporteurs, and that would be a relief for Fee.

Smith produced one more report for the AMA in August 1858. He had been on a tour in Jackson County where he had found "the inhabitants among the mountains poor generally with regard to this world's good & low in the cultivation of the mind." He read to families without Bibles, prayed with them, and talked to them about new birth. Some he found could read a little, others quite well. The women of the community walked six miles to a social meeting where a sabbath school without a preacher was organized. Smith thought the prospects good for church and school in Jackson County.[6]

While Fee was gone from Berea to see his sick father in November 1858, Smith went back to Ohio and brought his senile wife to live with the Fees too. When Fee returned he could scarcely conceal his irritation with the two old people added to his household. Now, at any rate, Smith did announce that he might build a little house on the tract of land he had bought. His wife was only deranged part of the time anyway.[7]

More Colonists Arrive

"For several weeks past there has been an almost constant stream of Northern immigrants passing through this place for that point. Besides this, numerous heavy boxes have been forwarded to Berea through this place, and each party going there have been heavily loaded with baggage, even the ladies' trunks being so heavy as to require the united strength of several men to transfer them from place to place." Arrival of Berea Colonists, reported in the Richmond Democrat.

Among the first colonists were Charles E. Griffin and Anna Shailer who had arrived as early as September 1858. Rogers mentioned "Charles and Anna" as a couple many times in his journal before they ever appeared on the Berea scene, so presumably they had been engaged for some time. Griffin, a native of Michigan, was about 21 years old in 1858; the son of one of Rogers' parishioners in Roseville, Illinois, Charles Griffin was a protege of Rogers', or more than a protege, for Griffin's parents had placed the young man directly under Rogers' care and authority. Rogers was instrumental in getting Griffin accepted into Oberlin Prep. 1857-8 (Rogers' account book records his paying Griffin's expenses from Galesburg, Illinois, to Oberlin, and providing his boots, tick, room rent, incidentals, books and cash.)[8]

Desda Anne Shailer (usually called Anna) was born in London, England, and somehow made her way to Ohio where she became a close friend of the Rogers family. Born in 1827, she was a widow, some years older than Charles E. Griffin. They were married October 6, 1859, by John Rogers.[9]

Soon other colonists began arriving; early in September 1859 came Rev. John F. Boughton with his wife Sally Etta and daughter Libbie, a twelve-year-old with consumption. The Boughtons, all natives of New York, had come from Oberlin where he was a student in seminary; he had worked as a colporteur in New York and had been licensed as a Congregational minister before beginning formal theological training. John F. Boughton, who had expressed interest in Berea as early as September 1858, had been urged to emigrate by Waters, Rogers and Fayette Shipherd. Boughton applied to the AMA for a commission, and entered immediately into his labors, preaching at the Glade and Silver Creek, and purchasing building supplies for a new house in October and November. As a man of some means, Boughton added to the new sense of prosperity at Berea. The people of the region liked his preaching, and his wife also endeared herself to the Bereans.[10]

Another colonist may have settled in Berea by September: W. H. Torry, an Irishman from Tennessee. Virtually nothing is known of him, save that he had a family with four members besides himself (a wife and probably three children); Torry and his family, however it was constituted, were driven from Kentucky at the time of the Exile; contemporary documents mention him only in connection with that event, giving no information about when he came to Berea, or why, or anything else. A later account identifies him as a day laborer and small farmer who lived in the Glade.[11]

Another (probably) young man, apparently single, may have been living in Berea by September. His last name was Shoals (or Sholes). Only one reference to him appears in any contemporary account (he is named on Clay's List of Exiles); we can only speculate concerning him: perhaps he was a younger brother of Ellen (Shoals) Hanson and a member of the Hanson household.[12]

The single men from Oberlin who arrived at Berea in the fall and early winter of 1859 had probably been influenced by John A. R. Rogers, who had, in September, addressed the church in Pittsfield, Ohio, about the wants of Kentucky as a mission field. On that occasion several students conferred with him about going to Kentucky. Rogers told them that "the work was one of abundant trials & required more than ordinary energy & tact."[13]

Two men arrived from Ohio on November 6, 1859: Swinglehurst A. Life and Rev. J. D. ("Jack") Reed. Life, with his extraordinary first name, was a native of England, about 25 when he came to Berea, a carpenter and cabinetmaker from Oberlin. Reed (frequently misidentified as I. D. Reed—an error that appears in earliest references because John Rogers made capital I's and J's exactly alike) had a family (wife, son and daughter) which he left in Hamilton County, Ohio, when he came to Berea. By December 1859, he had decided to stay and was probably preparing to send for his family. Reed, born 1817 or '18 in Pennsylvania, was a Free Will Baptist minister, very poor, whom Rogers had met before, perhaps near Oberlin. Reed and Life immediately began working on Rogers' house in November.[14]

Another carpenter-settler, E. T. Hayes (Ezekiel Timothy) probably arrived in late November or early December. A student at Oberlin Prep., 1858-60, Hayes was a native of Ottawa, Illinois, born August 13, 1835. He was a Congregationalist. By December 1859, Hayes was working with Life on the Rogers house and perhaps other constructions.[15]

Charles E. and Anna Griffin, W. H. Torry and family, a man named Shoals, Rev. and Mrs. John F. Boughton and daughter Libbie, Swinglehurst Life, Rev. J. D. Reed, E. T. Hayes; these 14 people, along with the few workers already established at Berea, constituted the Berea Colony.The colonists, including two new ministers and three carpenters, were not numerous, but they had practical and spiritual qualifications. However, of the men who settled at Berea as colonists by the fall of 1859 only three were family men and one of them never had time to bring his family; the four remaining were single (although one of them married after he arrived). All but two of the seven hailed from the North or East (Torry from Tennessee and Shoals, perhaps from Kentucky, were the exceptions); three of the seven came from Oberlin. Only Charles and Anna Griffin would have the opportunity to live in Berea as long as a year. The others stayed in Madison County less than four months. Nothing they built would remain.

This tiny group of emigrants motivated the slaveowners of Madison County to strike at last. Their coming marked the beginning of the end. Fee had been roughly tolerated for five years; with the arrival of Yankees in an appreciable number all toleration ceased. Now the fire touched the fuse.

Small as the colonizing movement was, it struck slaveholders as exactly analogous to the settlement of Kansas by abolitionists and other Northerners determined to have the state enter the Union free. A civil war had already been fought in "Bleeding Kansas," which provided also the terrifying example of John Brown, antislavery fanatic, who, with a little band of followers, mostly his own sons, had massacred five pro-slavery colonists in Kansas in 1856. On October 16 through 18, 1859, John Brown, financially supported by a number of New England and New York abolitionists (including Fee's friend, Gerrit Smith), led a raid against Harper's Ferry, Virginia, a raid designed to foment a slave uprising and establish a free state in the southern Appalachians. Brown's raid, even as it failed, spread alarm, even terror, throughout the South, which blamed the abolitionists and the Black Republicans for the event. To some abolitionists Brown was a hero, of course, and eventually a martyr. For some of the citizens of Madison County, John Brown was frighteningly similar to their own local abolitionist "fanatic" John G. Fee. What was Fee preparing in the Glade? Why were the Northerners settling there? When would he strike and how?[16]

The terror of a slave uprising, which had haunted the South since Nat Turner's rebellion, aggravated now by national events of undeniable ferocity, was roused to a fever pitch. Berea, in all innocence, was suddenly more important to everyone in Kentucky than it had ever been before. For years the place had been too insignificant to notice, almost too small to find! For a little while it had achieved some success and notoriety, but now it became a region of nightmares, a hot-bed of wild-eyed murderers, aiming to wake all those blacks, thousands of them, to violence. In this apocalyptic vision the slaves who had not been allowed to escape became themselves the inescapable danger; they were everywhere, in white homes and backyards, living around each mansion, in every city, on the farms and plantations: thousands of them.

If the slaveholders of Kentucky feared and hated people who wanted slaves to be freed through peaceful means, imagine their reaction to people who they thought were encouraging slaves to take their freedom violently. Unjustified as it was, that is exactly what white Kentuckians came to believe the Bereans were doing. The pro-slavery Kentucky press, under the control of the wealthiest slaveholders, made sure that its readership was fully misinformed about the Berea project. On some level, a few people must have known that they were printing exaggerations, distortions and outright lies; a very few probably knew there was nothing to fear. Most, however, simply believed what they read and feared accordingly. Eventually, only the obliteration of Berea from the map of Kentucky could ease the fears which grew in the fall of 1859.

Fee's Fund-raising: in the Spirit of John Brown
"We need more John Browns—not in the manner of his action, but in *his spirit of consecration. . . ." John G. Fee 's sermon in Plymouth Congregational Church.*

On September 15, 1859, in a letter to the editor of the *National Era*, Fee expressed his concern lest the Republican Party compromise its antislavery position; he advised against the formation of a mere "white man's party" and called for "a well-tried standard bearer," one who would not protect slavery. Finally, he urged action at a grass-roots level—county organizations to appoint lecturers, raise funds, distribute documents; he appealed to every concerned individual to exercise his duties and rights as a citizen. "How shall we pray for God's kingdom to come," he asked, "when we perpetuate the devil's kingdom?. . . Tis a false religion. . . that cannot live in the convention and at the ballot-box, as well as in the closet [traditional room for prayer]."[17]

The next day Fee wrote to Jocelyn saying that he expected to stay one more week in Germantown (Bracken County) and then start in time to be in Philadelphia over the first Sabbath of October (October 2).[18]

While he was still in Philadelphia, Fee completed an article (dated October 5) for the *American Missionary* magazine under the heading "Distribution of Bibles to Slaves—The Colored Preacher." He wrote about two slave men who called at his house for Bibles a few days before he left Kentucky. From them he "learned that many more slaves than formerly [were] learning to read," being taught by other slaves and children of their masters. He also narrated an experience he had in Frankfort, the capital of Kentucky, on an occasion when he traveled to that city to visit Juliet Miles in prison. In the evening Fee and his daughter Laura attended "one of the places of worship of the colored people (Baptists). Almost all were slaves; they were well dressed, [an] orderly and attentive congregation." The black minister who spoke impressed Fee very favorably: "Never have I seen any person that appeared to be more fully and more sweetly baptized into the spirit of his work. His congregation rose with him in quiet, happy feeling, and I found myself overcome and literally weeping like a child."[19]

This church service renewed Fee's faith in his own mission. "If those who deny the brotherhood of man and the equal capacity of the colored race," he wrote, "could have listened to that *black* man, their skepticism would have been found dissipated." In talking to the preacher after the service, Fee discovered that he had been a slave only eighteen months before when he had bought himself.[20]

These writings of Fee's, coinciding with his fund-raising trip, demonstrate that he had not lost sight of the primary goals of the enterprise for which he was trying to raise money—first and foremost, antislavery and equality of the races. The effort to raise money aroused in John G. Fee a heightened desire to present all the truth as he saw it; so a time of fund-raising was precisely the right moment to speak out most forcefully. Asking for money, an activity which renders some people diplomatic to the point of evasion, made John G. Fee more direct and open than ever. Donors should have his full counsel, so to speak.

After several weeks of encouraging success in New England (in Brookfield, Litchburg, Worcester (where he attended the annual meeting of the AMA) and Boston, in Massachusetts, Providence, Rhode Island, and New Haven, Connecticut), Fee, at the suggestion of Lewis Tappan, arrived at the church of Henry Ward Beecher, Plymouth Congregational Church in Brooklyn, wealthy, influential, widely famed. Beecher himself was one of "the princes of the pulpit," son of Lyman Beecher, brother of Harriet Beecher Stowe, an enormously successful minister who preached on most of the current issues of the day, including slavery, and edited two journals which were widely read. His name was a household word—he was a religious 'star' of the first magnitude, the Billy Graham of his day. For a relatively obscure country preacher from Kentucky the opportunity to address Beecher's congregation was the chance of a lifetime.[21]

Fee's address was delivered in the evening on Sunday November 13. Beecher introduced him, saying that Fee might be better known to him and a few others than to the congregation at large. He described Fee as a man who had suffered persecution for his belief "that slave-holding disqualified a man for church-membership." Fee was a Kentuckian, willing to work in a slave state and "suffer for the poor and ignorant." Beecher hailed him as a forerunner of other men whose willingness to endure martyrdom for the cause of freedom would lead to the overthrow of slavery. "I am glad, therefore," Beecher said, "to give way tonight to a better man than I am; and at the close of his discourse, I shall ask you to contribute toward the maintenance of the cause for which he is laboring."[22]

Fee spoke for an hour and a half to a large, attentive audience. He began by laying down general principles: a people reflect, he said, what their religion is; if their religion is one of form or abstraction, or mere reverence, it "will have only a form of godliness"; the power of religion is "supreme love to God and impartial love to [one's] fellow men." He described the condition of the religious community in Kentucky, where, he said, popular religion was not the Gospel of Christ, for impartial love to all people was omitted from it. Then Fee spoke of his own experience, how he had gone to a free state for his education, how Christian abolitionists had worked with him and eventually converted him to that cause. He had found that he had to have "a religion of principle," not just an emotive religion.

Called to be a preacher, he felt constrained to go home to Kentucky and preach to master and slave. "He felt a sympathy for the slave" amidst all his wrongs, Fee said, "but he felt a sympathy for his master also. . . . "

He told of his experiences with the New School Presbyterian Church, his breaking away, the founding of free churches. He described the mob violence he had endured. Then he told his audience about the counties in Kentucky where antislavery preachers could preach, where radical, antislavery tracts could be distributed safely and successfully. The workers in Kentucky needed more men, more means. And they wanted a central school where both male and female could be educated, "not only in science, but in heart-religion." He told the crowd what had been done and what had been planned "and made a strong appeal for the necessary means. He said they wanted men like John Brown—of his boldness and honesty—of his self-sacrificing spirit—not to carry the sword, but the Gospel of Love."[23]

Beecher followed Fee's sermon with a few remarks. "We have the right," he said, "to bombard the South with a gospel of love—we have the right to tell them of their sins—put education there—labor for their conversion—although we have no right to carry war and destruction." Beecher then held up a draft for $15 that he had received from Switzerland, "with a request that he would give it where it would do the most good in the cause of Emancipation"; the first donation in the offering: to American Switzerland. Beecher made a contribution of his own, and the congregation responded too, giving a total of $217.50 on the spot.

Fee had certainly told Beecher's church the whole story, and the meeting was a definite success. John Brown was a name in every newspaper in the United States at this time; he had been tried, but not yet convicted; it would have been most surprising if Fee had not mentioned him. No abolitionist could speak at this period of America's history and say *nothing* about John Brown.[24]

The *New York Tribune* printed what were purported to be Fee's exact words in the sermon:

> We need more John Browns—not in the *manner of his action, but in* his spirit of consecration—men who would go not to entice away a few slaves, for that would not remove the difficulty—men who would go out, not with carnal weapons, but with the "Sword of the Spirit,' the Bible: and who in love, would appeal to

slaveholders and non-slaveholders, if needs be, to give up property and life.

Fee's notes for this sermon, scribbled in pencil, provide evidence that the *Tribune*'s version of his words was perfectly accurate.[25]

The *New York Times* for November 15, 1859, reported a "Prayer Meeting for the Insurgents" held on the behalf of John Brown and Gerrit Smith in the Lyceum of Dr. Cheever's Church in Union Square. John G. Fee "delivered a brief address on the question of Slavery, arguing that it was above all things, a question involving the principles of Christian religion." At the conclusion, he "invoked the Divine blessing on the Church—especially on its Anti-Slavery work. He prayed that the 'conflict' now come between justice and despotism would be directed by the Divine Power; that Jonas might be sent to the South, and to all the people in the land, to call them to repentance."[26]

Furor in Kentucky: Propaganda Victory for the Southern Press
"Well, let brother Beecher and brother Fee come along to Kentucky with their John Browns. The mountaineers know how to welcome such traitors with bloody hands to hospitable graves." Kentucky Statesman.

In Lexington, Kentucky, the story about Fee's sermon in Beecher's church looked like this: the headline—JOHN BROWNS FOR KENTUCKY. (*Kentucky Statesman*, November 18, 1859)

> The Louisville Courier of yesterday says, "Rev. John G. Fee, a fanatical abolitionist, who is a native of this State, and a resident of some one of the mountain counties, is now in the east collecting founds [sic] for his nefarious work. Last Sunday night he preached in Henry Ward Beecher's church in Brooklyn and said that more John Brown's were wanted, especially for Kentucky. He also gave a detailed account of his operations here, which partakes somewhat of the Munchausen style of story-telling [fairy tales].
> Mr. Fee says that while working in the cause, he was shot at, struck with clubs and otherwise maltreated; but his assailants were fearfully punished and he fully revenged. One of the men was drowned, another had his bowels ripped out in a fight, and a third was killed in a quarrel. In the interior of our State, he says he was subjected to even greater violence, having been taken from his pulpit, and dragged along the road. Forty men, with guns, had surrounded the church, and took himself and Brother Jones some distance and demanded of them to leave the neighborhood. They tied Mr. Jones to a tree and dealt him one hundred lashed, but finally

concluded not to molest him (the preacher) for fear of "injuring the party." God came out among these men and three of them were killed in fights with each other.

These are mere samples of Mr. Fee's art of "drawing the long bow" [telling false stories].

To carry on the work Mr. F. desires to distribute a million tracts in Kentucky—He thinks it would do no good to circulate them in such counties as Woodford and Bourbon, but that much can be accomplished in the mountains.

The Rev. Fee concluded his harangue by calling on the congregation for $3,900 to revolutionize Kentucky. Of course Henry Ward Beecher seconded the appeal, and presented a check for $15, which he had received from a young Swiss, whose father was a clergyman in Rucken, Switzerland. This money had been collected by the young persons of the congregation and sent to him to be appropriated in such a manner as to accomplish the greatest good for the slave. He could do no better that to contribute it on the part of the mountaineers of Switzerland to the mountaineers of Kentucky.

Well, let brother Beecher and brother Fee come along to Kentucky with their John Browns. The mountaineers know how to welcome such traitors with bloody hands to hospitable graves.[27]

One fact emerges clearly from the *Louisville Courier*'s account; whoever wrote the story had an accurate and substantial version in front of him, from which he deleted all details which might clarify Fee's real position.

Ironically, a speech of Cassius Clay's, also touching on John Brown, was unfavorably reported in the same issue of the *Kentucky Statesman* (November18, 1859).

C. M. CLAY AT COVINGTON—Col. C. M. Clay addressed the people of Covington on Wednesday last. Subject (of course) *antislavery*. We have seen no report of his speech, claiming to be all complete, but the comments of the press indicate that his principles have undergone no change for the better. He is reported to have frequently referred to the Harper's ferry affair, and although he admitted that Brown and his confederates had committed a fearful crime, he warned "some of his Fellow Kentuckians, that if they did not mend their they would make a few more Ossawattomies." He charged that the democratic party of Kansas "drove Old Brown from his plantation, and were responsible for the whole outbreak." It is but justice to the citizens of Covington to state, however, that the Colonel received no countenance from his auditory. His speech was only applauded by the colored "element" of the opposition.[28]

At a prayer meeting Rogers spoke about "the privilege of self-denial and not shrinking from death." The next day (November 21) he read the newspaper. "Did not feel very happy in so doing," he wrote. On the 22nd he went to Richmond; found there "much excitement against Bro. Fee." He recorded a prayer in his journal, "Lord, dwell in me so richly as to deliver from fear of sinning & dying."

A Richmond, Kentucky, newspaper, the *Kentucky Messenger,* carried the following story at about this time; this article was probably among those which Rogers read and found disturbing:

> The headline: JOHN G. FEE
> This man has been at Brooklyn, New York, and addressing the people in the church of Beecher, on the subject of slavery in the South generally, and in Kentucky particularly. . . . The only thing that induces us to notice him is the fact that he lives in the county and is surrounded by a gang of his followers, at a little village called Berea, some sixteen miles south of this town. That he is a fanatic we have no doubt; that he is a bad man, we doubt still less. He is only another exemplification of a class of men [who may be described as] 'wearing the livery of heaven, to serve the devil in.' As to his opinions, and those of his followers, they amount to nothing, but if ever he is found interfering with the slaves of his neighbors, teaching them disobedience, or in any overt act stimulating them to revolt, we hope he will on a proper case made out, he brought to trial, and we do not doubt that a Madison jury will send him to the penitentiary.
> The Louisville *Courier* contains an epitome of his remarks at Brooklyn, has been very mysteriously taken from our office, and we therefore cannot publish them; but they are *inflammatory* and *incendiary* in character, and the people of the county owe it to themselves to hold a meeting, at least by next County court day, to consider whether or not the carrying out of the principles of Fee, requires THAT THEY SHALL BE MURDERED IN COLD BLOOD![29]

The threats against Fee, still absent in the East, and against the whole Berea settlement were becoming more and more frequent, more and more frightening. A few members of the Berea community reacted with a martial spirit. A. G. W. Parker, for example, "was loud in his denunciations against slaveholders & declared they should never interfere with him." He was, it seems, "one of the ball & rifle men."[30]

On November 29, Matilda Fee wrote to Simeon Jocelyn, conveying the state of affairs at Berea very directly and poignantly. "The religious part of our community who stand as our friends," she wrote,

> are comeing [sic] to me daily and almost hourly to tell me to warn my husband not to attempt to return to Ky now so much excitement prevails at Lexington & Richmond. I was urged two weeks since to go to meet him at Cin.[cinnati] & warn him of his danger. Since that time the excitement is much greater, owing to many false statements in the southern newspapers. What the result of this great commotion will be & how it may affect the efforts put forth here time only will reveal. For months past the cause here has been prospering beyond our most sanguine expectations & we are by no means cast down in spirit. All appear calm & full of hope & trust in God. If you know of my Dear husband's whereabouts please forward this to him. If the Lord has work for him in the north he will retain him if not his arm will be sufficient to protect him. If Mr Fee thinks it best I will meet him in Richmond, Lexington or Cin. My anxiety is sometimes so great that one would think my faith small. I often think the purest & best will be the most fit sacrifice to offer on the altar of liberty. May the Lord direct us all.[31]

Matilda Fee did go to Cincinnati to meet her husband, leaving her children behind in Berea. Before her departure she and the other Bereans feared that Fee might attempt to return unexpectedly, as he would not have heard the rumors that men were watching for him in Lexington in order to kill him.

Burritt Fee, the eldest of Fee's sons, then only 11, told his mother: "Well, if they kill father I feel that he will be at rest; all will be well with him. Now, mother, if they should kill you, could I feel[,] left alone[,] that you too were ready to die?" Mrs. Fee reassured him that "she was willing that the will of God be done." J. B. Mallett, reporting this remarkable exchange, wrote, "She [Matilda Fee] is an host in herself. A thousand such women would renovate Kentucky. Ten thousand Matilda Fees . . . would abolish slavery in the United States."[32]

The *Kentucky Statesman,* a Lexington paper, of November 29 (the same day Mrs. Fee wrote her letter to Jocelyn), quoted a long story from the *Richmond Democrat* of the week before. Under the headline 'Excitement in Madison County' the article commented first upon the fact that "the two leading men of the Black Republican party" in Madison, that is, Clay and Fee, had both made public addresses within the last two weeks alluding "in almost similar terms to the inhumane outrage at Harper's Ferry." The connection Clay wanted to erase was still present in the minds of central Kentuckians, it seems.

The *Richmond Democrat* continued:

> The Glade precinct of this county is the head-quarters of Black Republicanism in this section. The village of Berea, the home of this man Fee, is in that precinct, and is situated about fifteen miles south-east of Richmond. [Note that Richmond papers continually identify Berea's location for those in the county would might be able to find it!] For several weeks past there has been an almost constant stream of Northern immigrants passing through this place for that point. Besides this, numerous heavy boxes have been forwarded to Berea through this place, and each party going there have been heavily loaded with baggage, even the ladies' trunks being so heavy to require the united strength of several men to transfer them from place to place.

The writer of the article, aiming for subtlety at this point, never quite comes out and says the Bereans are importing guns to give to slaves for an armed insurrection. But that is clearly enough the conclusion meant to be drawn.

> In addition, the leading men of this faction openly boast that they intend to revolutionize the sentiment of this portion of the State, and to hereafter hold the controlling influence in political affairs.
>
> Much excitement has been created in this county by these facts, and it seems constantly on the increase.

While the Bereans were a very insignificant portion of Madison County's population, their intention seemed to be to augment their numbers and importance and thus draw the support of Black Republicans of the North.

> Their position, in the heart of as strong a pro-slavery community as can be found in the South, is being urged by this man Fee as an inducement to collect money from his political brethren of the North, with the implied and expressed purpose of making converts among his neighbors; when he well knows, and any honest Northern man who will spend a few weeks with us will be convinced that so far from this little faction gaining recruits from their neighbors, their numbers are insignificant, and their principles looked upon with loathing and utter contempt by almost every citizen of our glorious country. Madison will never be revolutionized by such patriots as these, and the sooner they are convinced of this fact, the better it will be for their well-being and happiness.[33]

The *Richmond Democrat's* approach to Fee and Berea is tellingly ambiguous. The abolitionists are presented as both trivial and a threat; they have imported what the *Democrat* wishes to imply are boxes of arms and ammunition, but they remain nevertheless beneath notice and "insignificant." Fear them, the newspaper urged, don't fear them! Be terrified, but don't get upset. A particularly Southern schizophrenia is revealed in the Richmond editor's attitude toward Berea—like Cassius Clay, Madison County at large could not admit to fear, even as terror began to motivate more and more of the citizenry to unreasoning and unwarranted attacks upon innocent men and women. No, cowardice must be called courage; as repression must be called liberty, as tyranny must be called democracy in action. As the slaveholders of Madison County approached one of their most shameful hours, their protests of innocence, high-minded morality and religious fervor grew loud and shrill. Words could not express how deeply the Bereans had wronged the powerful elite of Madison County by their religious and educational activities!

According to John Rogers, many

> Kentucky women told their husbands that they could not sleep at night for fear of the impending raid from Berea hill, when the slaves would rise and their homes be burned. It was also pointed out that the school at Berea might be a ruse to hide the plan of establishing a military stronghold for the support of the rebellion of the slaves. It was shown how perfectly situated it was on its long ridge with its semicircle of mountains in the rear and its outlook upon the bluegrass region for all the strategic purposes of war.[34]

People who believe absurdities commit atrocities. The citizens of Madison County were being given the right propaganda to motivate them to perform a vile injustice without compunction. Of course, they thought they were right—of course, they thought slavery was right; perhaps no one could expect a very lofty moral achievement from them. But the Bereans had not taken the measure of how low their enemies would go.

The Committee v. the Colonists
"The association of J. G. Fee and others is a combination of an incendiary character, not only at war with the best interest of this community, but destructive of all organized society." *Resolution of the Madison County Committee.*

Rogers was still reporting hopefully on December 3, 1859. In a letter to the AMA he stated,

> Rev. Mr. Boughton & family have moved to this place & materially added to its prosperity. The labors of Bro Boughton in this region will not fail to accomplish much for the honor of Christ and the edification of his people. Bro. Hays & Life have also selected Berea for their home and at this time Rev. M. Reed of Ohio, a brother beloved, is here . . . & will probably make his residence in this portion of the state.[35]

On December 5, the citizens of Madison County met at the Court House in Richmond to appoint a committee "to consider and report [sic] a subsequent meeting what is the proper course to be pursued with regard to the proceedings that the citizens should take in reference to the Black Republicans in their midst." John D. Harris called the meeting to order; Col. Reuben J. Munday was elected chairman, John C. Terril appointed secretary. A committee was named to report to the next meeting "on the proper course to be pursued in the matter."

> WHEREAS. The present attitude of the Abolition party, and their open and avowed assaults upon the constitutional rights of the South; and the strong reasons which we have to believe that they have sent their agents and emissaries into our midst, whose sole and only purpose and design is to propagate their political heresies, and thereby to disturb our vested constitutional rights and our public peace and quiet, therefore.

Five resolutions follow: the first enunciates the committee's opposition to and repudiation of abolitionism and announces the pledge "to put a stop to it by all fair and proper means and measures." The second resolution states that the committee will circulate a copy of its resolutions for their fellow citizens to sign. The other resolutions deal with revising the resolutions themselves, call for Richmond's two newspapers to announce another public meeting on the 17th of December and direct the same papers to publish the proceedings of the meeting.

> Resolved, in the opinion of this meeting, the association of
> J. G. Fee and others is a combination of an incendiary character, not
> only at war with the best interest of this community, but destructive
> of all organized society.[36]

The movement against abolitionists in Kentucky was state-wide (no doubt it stretched over the whole South, but in much of the South, unlike Kentucky, no abolitionists were to be found). On October 28 and 29, a mob had destroyed the office of an abolitionist newspaper, "The True South," published by William Shreve Bailey at Newport, Kentucky. Candee had been threatened in Jackson County. James S. Davis was also in danger. In Bracken County it was rumored that abolitionists were going to set fire to Germantown and a military company had been organized to patrol at night. Rev. G. H. Damon, a worker in Bracken County, had already fled to Ohio by December 9; there was, he wrote, "so much excitement which I had not been accustomed to and then the nature of it was such as to make it very unpleasant for me to remain longer. . . . " On the 10th, Davis arrived in Berea with his wife and mother-in-law (John Rogers' mother), who had been visiting at Cabin Creek. "The coming of our brother Mr. Davis and family," Lizzie wrote, "escaping from danger [in Cabin Creek] did not particularly add to our feeling of safety." The night before the Davises arrived Bro. Baxter Todd had brought a message to John Rogers that 36 men were coming to tell the Bereans to leave or take the consequences.[37]

Mrs. Fee, left alone with her children, was a tower of strength to the Bereans. Lizzie Rogers thought later that Matilda Fee had been John Rogers' greatest help during the crisis. "Men and women grew braver if more silent," Lizzie Rogers wrote, "and daily we watched for what was to come, and we grew to fear the worst; the tension was terrible, and I believe I grew to wish the mob would come, do their worst and have it over."[38]

The slaveholders around Berea said little. "While they with their Richmond neighbors disliked Berea's sentiments," Lizzie said, "they loved us." But they were mostly too cowed to speak up; one old man did plead for the Bereans, but he was silenced at a public meeting and told that only his age prevented him from sharing the fate of the Fee-ites. Hamilton Rawlings remained loyal; "our traveling newspaper," Lizzie called him, "[bringing] us news that we could not get outside.

His advent in our home was a signal of hope or despair, and in those days he brought no cheerful news."[39]

Still the Bereans intended to stay. The Rogers had their first butchering and put away meat and lard for the winter's use. James S. Davis wrote to the AMA, which had renewed his commission in spite of the scandal he had caused in Bracken County, saying that friends in Berea wished him to stay there. His own preference would be, he said, to return to Cabin Creek, but if the Association desired him to stay in Madison he would do so. "There is great excitement in this county," he wrote, "and unless God overrules the wrath of man there will be great trouble. The Lord defend his own." On the 11th of December Davis preached upon the freedom of grace and the fulness of God's favor. On the 12th, with 15 scholars in attendance, Rogers opened the Berea School with Davis and Rev. Boughton assisting him. This session of the school lasted such a short time that it has not been counted among the terms; nevertheless its opening reveals the determination of the Bereans to remain and continue in the face of mounting opposition.[40]

On the 13th of December, William Kendrick reported to the AMA that the slave power intended "to kill Mr. Fee, if he comes to Kentucky." The next day John G. Fee, then in Pennsylvania, completed a pamphlet "To the citizens of Madison co., Ky." in which he attempted to explain his position; it was already too late, but communication was so slow that Fee wrote another installment "Circular NO. 2" on December 27, 1859, also addressed to the Citizens of Madison County, who by that time had already taken decisive, indeed irreversible, action. Prophetically Fee wrote:

> Freedom will come to the slave. God and humanity are against slavery. The world is moving for its overthrow. If moral means can be used, it will pass away peaceably, as in the West Indies. . . . If not then God will let loose his judgments. I feel at this time that I would be willing to bleed at every pore if by so doing I could induce Southern men to come to a fair investigation of the truth. . . . [41]

On December 16, as Richmond seethed with preparations for the public meeting to be held the next day, Rogers rode to the county seat to attempt to drum up some support there. "In many things greatly failed," he wrote, "Assume an apologetic attitude too much. Was too anxious to be thought well of. Looked to Bro. Davis for counsel when I ought to have turned to God. Coming home looked death in the face & was at peace."

On the 17th of December, while the Bereans kept a day of fasting and prayer, the people of Madison County held their public meeting as scheduled. The Bereans prayed that God might "so move those in authority that we might lead quiet lives." Their prayer was not answered—at least, not with the answer they sought.

In Richmond the courthouse was filled, "although it was a cold, wet, disagreeable day . . . the oldest, most respectable, and law-abiding citizens were in attendance. The tone of the meeting was firm and dignified, the whole county being united. . . . The meeting. . . proved that the *whole* people are in favor of first principles—self-preservation."[42]

Chairman Reuben J. Munday called the public meeting to order. The resolutions of the previous meeting had received 773 signatures, none of which were obtained from the slaveholders in the immediate vicinity of Berea, but during the meeting on the 17th a great many other Madison County citizens signed. R. R. Stone reported the following Address and resolutions which were adopted:

> We, the citizens of Madison County, believing that there exists in communities, as in individuals a right of self-preservation, of which no law can deprive them, and justly amenable to God and enlightened public opinion for all our acts—having in our own bosoms a living reason for what we do—make this our justification.
> That notwithstanding every plan of emancipation which ingenuity could devise, was fully discussed during the canvass which preceded the formation of our present Constitution, and all rejected by almost universal consent, as working injury to both the black race and the white, and the future policy of the State settled for long time to come, if not forever, there has been a continual agitation for the question of slavery, and particularly by very small numbers of factious men, abolitionist, and others getting together, and calling themselves a meeting or convention of the Republican party, when it is perfectly notorious that no such political party has any existence here, or even in the State, so far as we know, and that such agitation does and must excite in our slaves a spirit of rebellious insubordination, causing large numbers to be sold into a sever bondage than any amongst us, to the disruption of family ties, laceration of feelings, of both white and black, without any accompanying good; that such agitation, when followed by such effects is a crime, *which is not, but should be suppressed by law*

[my own italics]. More especially when following upon, and in consequence of this there has come amongst us a set of men, not citizens of this county, and with the exception of one, not of the State, agents and emissaries of Northern Abolition societies, from which they receive remittances, derive their support—That these societies are our enemies, if indeed they are not the enemies of all mankind, teaching a new religion, to be propogated by the pike, with a baptism of fire and blood, worshiping a new God—not the God of our revolutionary fathers, from whom we derive all our blessings and whose wise and beneficent will is the peace and happiness of the whole family of man. Having a higher law than any known to the Constitution under which we live, justifying plunder, treason, and survile [sic] insurrection.[43]

So Higher Law was now meeting Higher Law. Since, by the Committee's own admission, the enemies of slavery could not be suppressed legally, a higher law than the Constitution had to be invoked. In direct and deliberate imitation of their abolitionist foes, the slaveholders held up their own superior deity: the God of the American Revolution, the God of the South, the God of white supremacy who called the citizens of Madison County to an illegal, but morally and religiously justified, opposition to the law of the land.

The forces of repression in Kentucky society at this time must not be underestimated. During the early months of 1860 Kentucky passed laws repealing the prohibition against importing slaves into Kentucky, laws subjecting all gipsies to arrest and fine or imprisonment, and making the writing, printing or circulating of incendiary documents in Kentucky punishable by confinement in the penitentiary. In addition a bill was passed (in March 1860) with the following provisions: "No slave hereafter to be emancipated except on condition of immediately leaving the state. Free negroes non-resident not allowed to come into the state, upon penalty of confinement in the penitentiary."[44]

During the December 17th meeting, charges brought against the Bereans included the fact that they had openly avowed their abolitionist doctrines and their intention to propagate them, the fact that their leader had proclaimed from a pulpit in New York his "sympathy for and approbation of" John Brown, saying "that we need more Browns in Kentucky," the fact that the Bereans had established a school, "free for all colors," and a church "excluding all who uphold slavery," that they had "erected machinery, built a town, the location of which, in a strategic point of view, either for stampede or servile insurrection is faultless."

Furthermore, the Bereans were charged with having an "Abolition Post Master" and a regular mail "loaded. . . with incendiary documents." The Bereans even "boast[ed] of their intention to establish an Abolition College." Berea was steadily increasing "by accessions of Northern men, all avowing the same doctrines; thus evincing a systematic and well-laid plan, not only to destroy [the slaveholders of Madison County], but in accordance with their declaration of their leader, to revolutionize the whole state."[45]

The meeting affirmed that the people of Madison had always been peaceable and law-abiding, "loyal to the Commonwealth, loyal to the Constitution, and the Union" but now they stood "wholly unprotected by law."

"We would be untrue to ourselves," R. R. Stone said, conveying the Committee's address, "and utterly unworthy of the immunities and heritage bequeathed us if the town of Berea were permitted to remain 'a standing menace' to the peace and security of our firesides."

For their security, then, the meeting adopted five resolutions which the preliminary committee had drafted. The first recommended that "a committee of 38 discreet sensible men such as the whole community may confide in be appointed to remove from amongst us J. G. Fee. J. A. R. Rogers and so many of their associates as in their best judgment the peace and safety of society may require and to this end all good men in this community will lend them support and assistance to the *utmost.*"

The second resolution directed that in discharging their duty the appointed committee should be instructed "to act deliberately, humanely. . . but most firmly and *most effectually.*" Meanwhile the present legislature should be petitioned to enact laws effecting the complete safety of the citizens of Madison County.

The third resolution defined "the true policy of Kentucky" as an effort "to bind together the domestic tie between slaves and their owners. . . . To this end they should not only worship the same God but at the same altars. . . . Separate negro preachings and ignorant negro preachers should be suppressed by law."

The fourth resolution stated that laws "for the expulsions of free negroes should be gradual, prospective and humane."

The fifth resolution called upon Senators and representatives for their "best energies" in support of the Madison County resolutions of December 17.

The committee was appointed—a roll call of prominent citizens once again. John G. Fee's first circular addressed to the citizens of Madison was read, as was a letter Rogers had written to the editors of the *Messenger* and *Mountain Democrat* (both Richmond papers). The appointed committee was instructed within ten days to "wait upon" Fee, Rogers and all others "that the said committee may think inimical and dangerous to our institutions, our interests, and our public safety and tranquility." The Bereans were to be informed that they had to leave the county and the State, being outside the limits of the county with ten days of receiving "said notice." If they should be found within the county after the ten-day limit the committee was directed by the meeting "to take such steps as they deem right and proper in removing the said Fee, Rogers & co. from the county." Major Squire Turner and Col. William H. Caperton, Thomas Bronston and other prominent citizens addressed the meeting.[46]

Meanwhile, in Berea praying continued. On the 18th, a Sabbath, James Scott Davis preached "upon not fearing him that can only kill the body & fearing Him who can destroy both soul & body in hell." Rogers also spoke that day. "The lord enabled me," he wrote, "to fearlessly & faithfully exhort the brethren." That afternoon the community held a prayer meeting at Fee's house. That night another one: "The Holy Spirit sweetly and solemnly present at the prayer meeting," Rogers stated, "Myself & others expressed a solemn purpose to labor personally for the salvation of some on the morrow."

In a final burst of self-justification the slaveholders of Madison County set the following story loose in the Kentucky press: "Sharpe's Rifles—we hear that a box, directed to Jno. G. Fee, was landed at Cogar's Landing on the Kentucky river, a few days since; and suspicions being aroused by its great weight, it was opened and found to contain Sharpe's Rifles." The story was, of course, utter nonsense—the Sharpe's Rifles were in reality Rev. John F. Boughton's crate of candlemolds.[47]

On the 22nd of December John A. R. Rogers spent the night in prayer.

"They were terrible days," Lizzie Rogers wrote, "I remember one night hearing the merry voices of young people shouting as they coasted down a hill nearby, taking advantage of the little snow squall which so seldom came to Kentucky, and I wondered how any one could be merry; and I wondered too . . . if life and property were safe, was there anything else that could cause great anxiety? My vision was narrow. The two Kentucky years had sobered me pretty fast."[48]

Christmas was coming; "nearer and nearer grew the threats," Lizzie wrote, "I thought I had known danger before; I had lain awake at nights trembling at every noise, and I had stood terror stricken before the drunken crowd who used to swagger up and down our streets, but there was a more savage element than ever before in the threats toward us."

"We almost forgot it was Christmas [time]," she wrote, "How could we hear the 'Peace on Earth, goodwill to men' when the nearer voices were so loud in their hatred?"[49]

December 23, 1859, a Friday—the day was bright and cold. "A slight snow had fallen and the men came up so quietly that their approach was not noticed." Some 60 men on horseback drew up "in a wedge shaped array, the point of the wedge at the front of the [Rogers'] house." The family, including the Davises and Rogers' mother, had just sat down to eat their noon meal. Someone said, "They have come."[50]

EXILES

The First Exile (December 1859)
"Brother and sister I have seen many trying times as you both know but my eyes have never seen such a sight as this—sixty three lawless men riding up to mens houses and warning them to be gone in ten days or suffer the penalty and for what—no crime more than this, standing up and preaching the truth as it is on record." Martha Stapp Wright to John G. and Matilda Fee.

In his journal for December 23, 1859, John Rogers wrote one sentence: "Sixty three men from various parts of Madison Co. called on me & 10 others & warned us to leave the State in 10 days on pain of expulsion."

John and Lizzie and their little son Raphael, then three years old, stood in the doorway of their house to receive the committee. In his report to the AMA, Rogers emphasized that the committee members had behaved well, using "no harsh or personally direspectful language." Many years later Rogers characterized the event almost as a social call, testifying to the courtesy of the visitors and their gentlemanly manners, as if such marks of breeding somehow exonerated them. He was never able to write anything unpleasant, but his narrative of this particular day in his life seems careful to the point of spinelessness.[51]

Lizzie Rogers' accounts give a very different picture. Her summary view directly contradicts her husband's: "We were met with every mark of disrespect that could be shown."[52]

"Sixty armed men full of whiskey look like so many fiends," she wrote, ". . . it seemed as if all the powers of Hell were let loose. Slowly I scanned those faces, and found among 'Kentucky's best sons' not one I could trust or look up to for protection."

The leader of the group, Reuben Munday, gave Rogers a letter which ordered him to promise to leave the State within ten days.

"Gentlemen, let me speak a word," Rogers said, "If I have failed to keep your laws, I am willing to be tried by law; for what am I called in question?"

"We consider you a gentlemen, but you are from the north and you must go."

Lizzie said, "Judging from appearances, gentlemen in Kentucky are scarce; you had better let him stay."

Munday again demanded that Rogers promise to leave. "I have but one Master to serve," Rogers replied, "I cannot promise."

Some angry men rushed forward, but Munday wheeled in front of them and said, "Not now, boys, come back in ten days and do your worst." According to Lizzie's account the committee fell into a drunken fight among themselves on the way back to Richmond, several being killed or wounded, although their numbers were quickly replenished. It certainly seems as if John and Lizzie Rogers were present at two different occasions; he had an interesting visit with some pleasant gentlemen performing an unpleasant duty, while she was threatened by incarnate devils from Hell. Whom should we trust? Perhaps we ought not overlook the possibility that gentlemen can behave like demons.

The committee paid a call that day on ten other people—some of them representing families, some single men; included were Matilda Fee, John G. Hanson, John Smith, Rev. John F. Boughton, Charles E. Griffin, A. G. W. Parker, Swinglehurst Life, E. T. Hayes, J. D. Reed and W. H. Torry. (James S. Davis, who was included in this exile, was staying with Rogers and so not counted.) The committee's official visits were over in about two hours. But two more of their "calls" became material for local legend. The committee

> found Mrs. Boughton at home in her husband's absence. After receiving their written warning, she said, "Dismount, gentlemen, and I will get you some dinner." One of the committee then said, "I am afraid you want to pizen us." "No," said she, "I wouldn't play such a trick as that." . . . Her offer was not accepted.

W. H. Torry, the Irishman from Tennessee, received his visitors in a more bellicose spirit; "he engaged in a fight with one of the committee and his wife came to his assistance. To an overactive Berea imagination this afterward seemed "the first battle of the rebellion."[53]

The Bereans agreed to meet that evening to pray and consult about what to do. At the meeting John Hanson read the 37th Psalm ("Fret not thyself because of evil doers"). This rather ferocious psalm, comforting the oppressed through promises of retribution for the wicked, impressed all who heard it read that night. Many accounts mention the exact psalm Hanson chose and everyone seems to have been exalted by it. On December 23, 1859, the people of Berea believed that the committee were evildoers and workers of iniquity, rather than Kentucky gentlemen courteously performing an unpleasant duty.[54]

At first, Rogers was in favor of staying in Madison County to put the burden of removing the Bereans upon those who wished to get rid of them. Others were convinced that to stay would mean certain death. Rumor had it that Rogers was destined to be hanged to the tree nearest to his house, and the town burned.[55]

On December 24, the people who had been warned to leave met and arrived at a consensus that they should go. But the group decided to appeal to the governor of Kentucky for protection. Rogers composed a petition which eleven men signed; then J. D. Reed and Swinglehurst Life rode to Frankfort and presented the document to Gov. Beriah Magoffin personally. He said it was impossible to do anything for their protection, but he received the bearers of the petition "courteously," advising them for the sake of preserving the peace of the state to leave it. "He said the public mind was deeply moved by the events in Virginia, and that until the excitement subsided, their presence in the State would be dangerous." He did promise that they would be safe while they were departing and that their property would be protected.[56] (See Appendix 3 for the full text of the Bereans' Petition to the Governor)

Ironically, Fee wrote to Jocelyn on December 24 concerning his intention of starting for Berea on Christmas Day. He thought there would still be time—that he might go "and improve . . . [the] time and then come away peacefully—not stubbornly. . . . I suppose," he added, "it is best to come away." Fee's friends in Cincinnati prevented him from going into Kentucky even for a short time. Hamilton Rawlings had written Fee that he would certainly be killed if he returned to Berea.[57]

A committee of local friends advised the Bereans that all should go; although some of the men of the neighborhood were willing to defend Berea, it seemed hopeless to try to stand against the whole state. Martha Wright, the wife of the postmaster (daughter of William Stapp) was so upset by the departure of the Fee family that she wrote a letter to them on Christmas day. In it, she expressed what many Bereans must have felt:

> I feel like standing up and pleading for. . . the poor and oppressed not only the white man but all who are made in god's image. Brother and sister I have seen many trying times as you both know but my eyes have never seen such a sight as this—sixty three lawless men riding up to mens houses and warning them to be gone in ten days or suffer the penalty and for what—no crime more than this, standing up and preaching the truth as it is on record. They themselves feel the power of this truth and want to crush it out, but truth is might and will prevail. I don't know, brother and sister, that I may even see you any more, I feel like standing the test if hanged on a tree, or burned at the stake. I wish would incourage my dear husband to stay [but] he feels it is best for us to go. I am willing to stay here and endure many trials and privations of this this [sic] if I can do it all for Christ's sake and his poor. I feel that there has not been any labor spent here in vain.

Receiving this letter, John G. Fee and his wife probably felt that their labor had, indeed, not been spent in vain. Mrs. Wright's heroic stand, couched in her semiliterate language, gives eloquent testimony to the power of Fee's ministry in Berea. He had inspired in the hearts of many ordinary people a fervent vision of social justice. Martha Wright's love and courage may not have been typical (her husband and father, for example, backslid from their early support of Fee and eventually repudiated Berea's ideals altogether), but even if she were an isolated instance her attitudes indicated the depth of John G. Fee's achievement.

"And now my dear friends," she wrote in closing,

> I may never see you any more on this earth but I want your prayers assend up in to Heaven for my family and all Around Berear. I have one request to make of you both if I should Suffer the penalty of death I want you to make provisions for my little ones who are nearer than life I breeth. I say to you please take my little babe yourselves . . . .

She signed her letter, "respectively yours, Martha A. Wright."[58]

On Christmas Day 1859, the Bereans heard farewell addresses from those warned to leave Kentucky. The next day Rogers began to settle his debts. On the 27th George Candee arrived from McKee and advised the Bereans to go.

The people remaining behind grieved at losing their leaders and the school on which they had set their hopes. William B. Wright gave a farewell dinner for the exiles on the 28th of December, 150 people attending. "It was more like a funeral than a feast," Lizzie Rogers wrote, "yet it was a beautiful thing to do." Rogers was less receptive: "Did not enjoy the occasion," he stated, characteristically taciturn.[59]

The day of the feast Rogers composed his official report to the AMA, explaining what had happened and what decisions had been made. "There is but one mind," he reported, "as to the wisdom of leaving which we shall do to-morrow. We go sorrowing yet rejoicing," he added, "We have been able to take joyfully the sacrifice of much of our property. We sorrow to leave those so dear to us. I part with great reluctance from many of the slaveholders & their families. We rejoice believing that by leaving we are giving a more public testimony for Christ & truth than we could in a long time if we remained." A recognizable martyrdom for Rogers had come at last!

Rogers suggested that if the exiles had chosen to stay civil war might have resulted; but if the Governor had provided protection the group would certainly have remained. The little band proposed to spend a few days in Cincinnati "counseling for the future." Rogers urged the Association not to give up on Kentucky. "My sympathies," Rogers stated, "are strongly toward every class—the slaveholder with his fine bearing and more generous impulses—the slave in his degradation and the nonslaveholder great . . . with his undeveloped powers." The slaveholder with his "more generous impulses" was fully represented in an article in the *Daily Commonwealth* of Frankfort, December 28, 1859, which stated: "Rev. John G. Fee and other noisy and incendiary abolitionists in this county should be driven from it."[60]

Meanwhile, Lizzie Rogers was packing the trunks, although there was little to pack. Furniture had to be left behind, because large crates from Berea could never make it safely through the state. "Our valuables were few," Lizzie wrote, "and could easily be crowded into the trunks which had only four short years before held our wedding garments."

Matilda Fee had to make her preparations in her husband's absence, with three of her four children, Burritt Hamilton, 10, Howard Samuel, 8, and Tappan, 3 years old. (The eldest child, Laura Ann, then 14, had accompanied her father on his Eastern tour.) At some point before Christmas, Mrs. Fee had gone to Cincinnati to meet her husband and warn him not to enter Kentucky. (While she was in Cincinnati she had caught her clothing on fire in a domestic accident; Fee burned his hands putting out the fire.) By the 29th of December, Matilda Fee had returned alone to Berea.[61]

Some 36 people in all prepared to leave Berea. John and Lizzie Rogers and their children, John Raphael and William Norris (their elder son three years old and the baby not yet a year old); James Scott Davis and his wife Amelia, with a little girl named Amelia and an infant, Samuel, both children under two. Rogers' mother, Elizabeth (Hamlin) Rogers, was among the travelers, but since she was only visiting was not 'officially' counted; John G. Hanson and his wife Ellen, with their infant child William Gregg, less than a year old; John Smith and his wife Olive, both in their seventies; A. G. W. Parker with his wife and two or three children, probably all under ten. In addition the fourteen colonists already named formed part of the first exile group.

With the Rogers family some twenty people planned to travel together to Cincinnati; the others, perhaps a dozen in all, dispersed to various places.

On December 29, the exodus began. All the people met in front of Rogers' house. "A drizzling rain was falling, the snow had melted and everything," Lizzie said, "was as dreary without as our hearts were within. [John Smith] sat in an open wagon with his arm around his aged wife. Mrs. Fee drove her own carriage full of children; the bride and groom, Mr. and Mrs. Griffin, sat in another carriage; a few of the men were on horseback. There was "a great white covered wagon which carried . . . trunks"; a lady or two sat in that vehicle waiting for Lizzie and her babies. "We were not a dangerous looking crowd," Lizzie Rogers remarked ironically, "and it would take a vivid imagination to understand how we could be so 'dangerous to Kentucky's best interests.'" Neighbors and friends, many weeping openly, gathered about to say goodbye. George Candee led the assembly in prayer, committing the travelers to the guidance of God.[62]

"The doors of our little home were closed to us," Lizzie Rogers wrote, "all my romantic fancies, my dreams had a rude awakening. I have never clothed a home with such romance as I did that one, and with the going out from its doors went out from me much of my youth, and I believe those long, sad months changed me from a child wife to a woman. With scarce a backward look, I took my place under the rude shelter of the wagon, and the word came to move on."[63]

At Silver Creek the procession found that an ordinarily small babbling brook had been transformed into a roaring torrent by heavy rains and melting snow. The covered wagon in which Lizzie rode was chosen to cross the stream first since it was the heaviest vehicle. The driver, although fortified with Kentucky bourbon, noticed that the women in his vehicle were visibly frightened. "With a roguish wink," he said, "Now, ladies, you do the praying and I'll do the driving." Lizzie gathered her babies in her lap and sat bolt upright to demonstrate a courage she did not feel. All the wagons crossed safely. In the ride to Richmond Lizzie noticed that her husband "deliberately sought a prominent seat," because their journey was closely watched: if there was danger he wanted to be at the forefront to meet it.[64]

The little group spent the first night in Richmond, although they felt some anxiety about how they would be received in the county seat of Madison. One of the hotels opened to them and the Kentuckians kept their word—since the ten-day limit was not up, the Bereans went unmolested. One of the local merchants, Col. William Holloway granted Rogers a few weeks' grace on paying his bill and even offered to lend him money. Some of the citizens of Richmond had not participated in the committee work, or condoned it.[65]

On the day of the exodus Fee was writing to Tappan: "The possibility of being shut out from a work so dear to my heart almost crushes me. We may not be able to go on with out school, but we will try to pay for our land—that will not run off."[66]

The next day the Bereans reached Lexington, where they dined in one of the best hotels without any trouble, although everyone knew who the travelers were. "I doubt if Barnum's circus could have produced among the older folk, greater curiosity," Lizzie wrote. In Lexington the exiles boarded the train to Cincinnati. "I was glad of every mile behind me," Lizzie recalled, "rejoicing that every hour was carrying us toward the North Land, the old feeling of safety came back and when at last we reached the Ohio side, I could have knelt and kissed the dust of her streets."[67]

The next morning the Berea exiles woke to find themselves famous. Frontpage headlines in major newspapers blazoned the news of Kentucky's injustice to the citizens of Berea. For the next few days, in a clamor of publicity, the Bereans were much in demand to speak at churches and lecture halls in Cincinnati. Prominent Ohioans denounced the Berea Exile as "an unparalleled outrage."[68]

Fee met the exiles who had traveled to Cincinnati; there the little group divided again—some remaining in Cincinnati, some moving on. Lizzie Rogers and her children departed for Pittsfield, Ohio, while her husband accompanied Fee to Bracken County to confer before Rogers returned to Ohio. On New Year's Day Rogers spoke in Bracken County about Berea and the exile; beginning on January 2, he spent a week filling various speaking engagements in Cincinnati and working on his address to the People of the United States in defense of the Berea exiles. J. B. Mallett, an Oberlin student teaching in Bracken County, marvelled at the good spirits of Fee, Hanson, Griffin and their families.[69]

Fee, like Rogers, spoke in Bracken County on New Year's Day. Some members of Fee's family had not arrived with the other exiles in Cincinnati (they had evidently come with John G. Hanson who was a day behind the others, for some reason.) Mallett's account describes an unexpected meeting:

> As Mr Fee concluded the reading of the morning lesson two of his sons aged 9 & 11 respectively entered the church and walking down the aisle fixed an affectionate look upon him which seemed to say Father, is that you? He paused and the deep emotions of the father meeting his exiled children after a separation of several months were seen . . . . He quietly stepped down from the pulpit

and embraced his sons for a moment. A tear stole down his careworn cheek, while he resumed the exercises by a prayer. In this prayer he spoke of the pain caused by the separation of the parents from their children and the pleasures afforded in a reunion. He prayed that the time might come when there should be no laws to separate wife from the husband, the child from the parent, thus destroying the most sacred ties of humanity, that the gospel might triumph and universal freedom reign. He prayed for the slaveholders of Madison County and besought God to show them the truth and save their souls. . . . [70]

On the evening of January 2, Rev. John F. Boughton, accompanied by J. D. Reed, addressed the 1st Congregational Church (Unitarian) in Cincinnati, describing his own experience in arriving as a prospective colonist at Berea. There he had found, he said, "a few faithful, noble souls, suffering many privations, destitute, yet cheerful, hopeful, and happy, laboring to educate the people; then looking over the condition of the people . . . he resolved within himself that there was a proper field for him in which to labor. He sent for his goods and family." Boughton acknowledged that the arrival of his own household goods "which were cumbrous" [the famous candlemolds] had frightened people in the region, as had frequent visits of friends from the North and "the constant receipts of sums of money." The immediate cause of the expulsion had, of course, been "the knowledge of Fee's absence and the report of remarks made by him in the eastern States."[71]

While Madison County citizens were registering their horror at John G. Fee's supposed remarks in Brooklyn, they must also have been noting that if Fee was in the East, Berea was without a leader. No one ever assumed that any of the other men associated with Berea had the power that Fee had. What would have happened had he been at home when exile was threatened? Of course, we will never know. But we may be sure that the task of expelling the abolitionists was deliberately undertaken while Fee was gone.

Boughton's summary of the slaveholders' motives for acting when they did is probably accurate, as far as it goes. The slaveholders themselves put forward the reasons Boughton mentions, along with their own studied misinterpretations. In another passage of Boughton's speech he mentions facts that may have had more to do with the slaveholders' decision to expel the Bereans than those 'facts' the committee acknowledged. Boughton said,

> The children of many slaveholders were attending the school [at Berea], and the prospects of business around were improving; the land was looking up in price, and many facilities for a comfortable life were being introduced as a result of the labor of the few who were engaged in this work. . . . Men from the North were obtaining a favorable recognition as men of enterprise and real worth.[72]

"The steam mill of Mr. Hanson was doing well until he was constrained to abandon it," Rogers wrote, "The school of Mr. Rogers was in a flourishing condition, having nearly a hundred pupils during the last term, a great portion of them the children of slaveholders. Kentucky cannot afford to drive beyond her borders the men who build mills and academies." Rogers' analysis is naive—abolitionists who built successful mills and academies were precisely the ones who could not be tolerated in Kentucky. As soon as it became evident that Berea might succeed, the village of the abolitionists had to be destroyed.[73]

Boughton believed that the people who had been forced out of their homes at Berea had left a powerful testimony behind them. "The church, the rough houses and the few vacant acres of land," he said, "[have] a tongue to speak louder than could any of the exiles." Fee wrote to the AMA on January 16, asking that both Reed and Boughton be sent $20 apiece for their work in Berea, although he emphasized that Reed had done the most good and also needed the money more than the prosperous Boughton.[74]

Fee said that all his books and things were still in Berea; Matilda Fee would probably go back long enough to sell some items. He himself had been sick earlier and now was sicker than ever. "I am quite feeble," he wrote, "exhausted. I thought to rest here & preach a few months then go possibly to a free state & lecture until October." He considered going to Cincinnati or someplace in Indiana. Finally, he reviewed what had happened in Madison County. "The people there," he said, "were not able to give protection to the brethren because of the defection of [Cassius] Clay. If he had been willing to stand by [George] Candee said 100 men would have come from Jackson & stood by the friends." The people in Jackson County had been willing to protect Candee and he was still in central Kentucky, the only AMA missionary left in the area—soon he would be the only

244

one in the whole state. Fee wrote, with some foreboding, that he feared he would be driven out of all slave states unless the people were willing to protect him.[75]

Of those exiled from Berea in December 1859, only members of three families ever returned: the Fees, the Hansons and the Rogers. The rest of the colonists—ministers, carpenters, two trustees (Davis and Smith)—went their separate ways. The Boughtons returned to Oberlin where Rev. Boughton died in1871; Ezekiel Timothy Hays also returned to Oberlin, serving as a soldier in Co. C, 7th Ohio Infantry during the Civil War.[76]

When the 1860 Federal Census was taken (June 1860), J. D. Reed and his small family were living with the Fees in temporary residence in Cincinnati; at the same time, Swinglehurst Life had found lodgings in a Cincinnati boarding house run by Levi Coffin—eventually Life returned to Oberlin where he married an Oberlin student and became a shoe merchant. Old John Smith and his aged wife Olive returned to Ohio too, spending their last years in the home of their married daughter near Columbus.[77]

Mobs and Committees
"So much the greater peril to society when men of property and standing will consent to disregard law and order." John G. Fee.

The distinction between mobs and committees was one of class. A group of local roughnecks coming together to attack abolitionists was a mob; a group of Kentucky gentlemen joined for the same purpose—and much more effective in realizing its goal—was a Committee. Actually, most of the bands of Kentuckians who had molested Fee or his helpers had been committees, at least in the sense that they had planned their action together: they had not entered upon it spontaneously or by accidental conjunction. Frequently, these group signed petitions or other documents to constitute themselves as committees. In this way a committee had been formed in Rockcastle County in 1853 to denounce Fee and Clay; this group had tried to drive A. G. W. Parker out of the county within ten days and prevent Peter H. West from distributing tracts, and so on.

The mob which had whipped Robert Jones in 1859 had a military-style organization, with officers in charge—that was, in fact, the usual 'committee' arrangement, since many of the men had been soldiers, frequently having served together in the Mexican War. Officers in the regular army became officers in committees; after all, an important aspect of 'committee work' was the deployment of troops. Fee described the retreat of the whipping mob as "ludicrously orderly. The Captain ordered all to march away in double file. The column was quite long and imposing." Committees resembled vigilante bands, and a few years later some committee members may have moved quite naturally into the ranks of the Ku Klux Klan.[78]

The Madison County committee of 1859 had both kinds of structure. The planning committee members were bound together by signing a petition; the committee for executing plans—mostly the same people as in the earlier committee—signed a document and also maintained a quasi-military organization under the leadership of Col. Reuben Munday.

Who were the members of the committee that tried to destroy Berea? When Rogers walked out his front door to face them what did he see? A disreputable mob of local ruffians?—practiced cuttroats? Drunken swaggering bullies?

No, he saw something much more frightening. Some of the committee men may have been drunk—a few of them may have shed blood; but to characterize them as men of violence, on the assumption that they were part of a criminal element, is to misread them entirely. They were men of property, social standing, wealth, prominence, education—respectable men, well-known, and, in some cases, popular in the community: they were the elite slaveholders who belonged to the first, the founding families of Richmond; in short, the social cream of Madison County Bluegrass—planters, wealthy farmers, lawyers, army men, legislators, bankers, professional politicians. As Fee remarked, "So much the greater peril to society when men of property and standing will consent to disregard law and order."[79]

What gathered in Rogers' yard on December 23, 1859, was the essence of power in Madison County: big money, great political influence and social standing. Simple hoodlums would have been easy to deal with in comparison, but who could prosecute these men? Who would defy them? Not even Governor Magoffin himself dared stand against them, although, of course, he did not have any desire to do so—insofar as he was a successful pro-slavery politician he had to be *one of them*. If he had been a Madison County citizen the Bereans might have reasonably expected to see *him* out in the yard that morning. Everyone who was anybody was there!

The committee represented a whole society which had turned in various organized and respectable ways to the repression of civil rights, a society which had persisted in the defense of one injustice by more and more overwhelming oppression of dissenters. The committee was a good representation of the slavery system; in a way, the whole South came to Berea in December 1859, determined to snuff out one small flame in the enormous night of the peculiar institution.

In 1860 slightly over 100 individuals in Madison County owned as many as 15 slaves or more; 24 of those slaveholders were themselves committee members. At least 26 more were close relatives of committee members—so the Exile committee of 1859 represented the prominent Madison County slaveholders very directly, and they certainly represented no one else. All the committee members were themselves slaveholders. The 24 already mentioned owned approximately 520 slaves; if the numbers of slaves that committee members and their relatives owned in Madison County were computed the figure would run into the thousands: probably more than half of the slaves in Madison County were owned by the committee men and their relatives. It comes as no great surprise, of course, to find that the people most concerned to maintain the institution of slavery were those who themselves owned most of the slaves. The same people—a relatively small group out of the total white population of Madison County—also monopolized political power in the region, although nonslaveholders outnumbered slaveholders.[80]

Most committee members were descended from one of a few founding families of Madison County—Harris, Miller, Woods, Kavanaugh, Gentry, Maupin, families which in some cases had been interrelated and allied to one another for almost a hundred years by 1859; they had originally been settlers of Albemarle County, Virginia, and virtually all of them had come to Madison County between 1786 and 1795.[81]

For example, at least 10 committee members were direct descendants of one founding family—the Harris clan. Many other committee members were related to one another and were descendants of the Madison County founders from Albemarle county. In fact, it is clear from the "address" of the Madison County committee that its members were well aware of their descent and prized it highly as one of their primary marks of status; virtually all of them were connected in some way to the Virginians who had fought in the Revolution and claimed land in Madison County, Kentucky, where they settled, bringing their slaves with them.[82]

Some 60 men rode in the committee, representing a very small proportion of the total population, but a very large proportion of the county's wealth, power and heritage. They regarded themselves as the natural and rightful leaders in their world; their background, as well as their prosperity, supported their claims. They were gentlemen. Their fathers, literally from Thomas Jefferson's Virginia (he was born in Albermarle County), had established and hallowed the United States of America and the slavery system within it. Their fathers had fought and died for freedom.

In the not-too-distant future many of the members of the committee would be fighting in another war; ironically, they would be fighting each other; some of them became soldiers for the Confederacy, others fought for the Union. As much as they had in common, the prominent citizens who banded together to oust the Bereans did not constitute a monolithic group. Their common enmity toward abolitionists held them together only briefly. If Lizzie Rogers is accurate in her account, the committee was not capable of riding 15 miles—from Berea back to Richmond—without violence erupting among its members.

The Second Exile—James Scott Davis from Lewis County

Driven out of Madison County, James Scott Davis returned to Cabin Creek, where he intended to continue as minister of the church Fee had founded. On the 21st of January 1860, 75 pro-slavery men from Mason, Lewis and Fleming Counties held a meeting at Orangeburg which adopted resolutions and appointed a committee of seven to inform Davis that he had to leave the state within seven days.[83]

The committee arrived at Davis's house, only six miles from their meeting place, the same afternoon and delivered their notice to Amelia Davis, her husband being absent on a preaching appointment 30 miles away. When Davis returned, his friends in Lewis County told him they would defend him if he chose to stay, but some of the older men were convinced that he should go.

Among this committee's resolutions were statements of their approval of the Madison County action and their conviction that no abolitionist had the right to establish himself in a slaveholding community. Basically their resolutions demanded that they be "let alone" for their "own peace, and the good of the slaves." One resolution identified Rev. James S. Davis as a co-worker with John G. Fee—a relationship sufficient to incriminate anyone. A number of rumors had been circulated about Davis, including one which reported that he had urged a slave man to steal a bag of corn and a horse from his owner. In addition, Davis had received a shipment of Hinton Rowan Helper's *Impending Crisis of the South*, a book which the committee considered "dangerous"—so dangerous, in fact, that on "January 25 [before Davis had left the county], he was called to give up [a] large number of copies of [Helper's book]; but finally, by way of compromise, burnt them in the presence of the persons who had called."[84]

In February, Davis, who by that time had taken refuge at the home of his wife's parents in Pittsfield, Ohio, wrote in the *Congregational Herald,* "My own opinion was and is that a skirmish at any point on our field would have provoked a contest which would have swelled into a civil war." So he had decided to go.[85]

At first Davis and his wife and two children found refuge with some of the other exiles in Cincinnati, but by early March he had gone home to Galesburg, where he was a hero among his relatives, neighbors, schoolmates and former teachers. "From the pulpit of the original colony church he related how the apostles of anti-slavery Christianity had been driven out of Kentucky, and his audience contributed a substantial sum for 'relief of the Kentucky exiles.'[86]

In March, Davis visited Broad Oak, in Pope County, Illinois, where his former colporteur, James M. West of Fleming County, had been living for four years. At first West had been persecuted in southern Illinois, in a district where most of the population was from Tennessee, quite as much as he had been in northern Kentucky. But by 1860 a number of antislavery people had gathered around him.[87]

Davis may have been attracted to this field in Illinois while he visited West in March, but he still wandered for awhile: back to Pittsfield, Ohio, in June; when the 1860 census was taken, Davis and Rogers and their families were all living with John Cornwall Rogers near Oberlin, a large household. Both Davis and Rogers listed their occupation as 'lecturer.' Also in June, Davis attended the Republican convention in Chicago as a member of the Kentucky delegation, although he could not list a specific residence on the roster; a number of his friends from Kentucky served on the same delegation.[88]

Through most of 1860, Davis lectured in Illinois and Ohio on the work in Kentucky, but by the fall he turned his attention to the mission field in southern Illinois, settling in Little Egypt. In October 1860 he met Abraham Lincoln, found him "lively and chatty." All Lincoln's visitors, Davis wrote, seemed to be mentally exclaiming, "Why, he is just like one of us!"[89]

Soon Davis was promoting the cause of a Christian colony at Hoyleton, Illinois; it had been established in 1857 by Avery Bent, a brother-in-law of Jonathan Blanchard. James S. Davis's brother Southwick, printer and newspaperman, had settled there, along with some other Galesburg colonists. After a visit to Hoyleton, Davis wrote, "It was a treat . . . to hear, in Egypt, the familiar tones and tunes of New England; and find men earnestly alive to the interests of freedom and righteousness. . . . This is a glorious place for a Christian colony."[90]

Davis would never return to Kentucky.[91]

Reactions to the 1st Exile

"Emancipation has been indefinitely postponed; and human misery—if servitude is misery—infinitely increased by the officious intermeddling of blind and bigoted men [abolitionists] with that which they were unable to comprehend, and in which they had no legitimate concern." Cincinnati Enquirer.

Reactions to the first exile from Madison County, Kentucky (December 1859) were most vehement, of course, in the newspapers of Kentucky and Ohio, especially Cincinnati. The *Cincinnati Enquirer* for January 5, 1860, commented at length on the Berea incident.

The Berea exiles were charged only with active abolitionism. "Prejudice and the peculiar excitement of the time acting upon a people not remarkably intelligent, have probably produced the result." The *Enquirer* maintained that the act of expulsion was unjustifiable, but went on to ask, "Why do the people of Kentucky rise against those of their fellow-citizens who are suspected of entertaining anti-slavery sentiment, and expel them from their midst?"

Kentucky was the state with the first abolition society in the United States, and once many of her citizens had "zealously enlisted in the cause of emancipation." What changed the situation? According to the *Enquirer* "the answer is easy and the fact is notorious. Emancipation in Kentucky died under the influence of Northern Abolitionism." Antislavery men of Kentucky ceased their own efforts because of Northern interference. "Emancipation," claimed the *Enquirer*, "has been indefinitely postponed; and human misery—if servitude is misery—infinitely increased by the officious intermeddling of blind and bigoted men with that which they were unable to comprehend, and in which they had no legitimate concern." Naturally, the abolitionists were expelled from the State of Kentucky, but not before they had blindly, naively, with the best of intentions, done incalculable "mischief."

The *Enquirer* editorial urged a direct causal connection between the work of abolitionists in the South and the arrival in Cincinnati (simultaneously with the Berea exiles) of crowds of freed blacks from Arkansas, legally expelled from that state in the winter of 1859-60. The *Enquirer* predicted that these miserable people, penniless, starving, homeless, would be only the first of such innocent victims of abolitionist meddling. Free blacks would pour into the North where white citizens would be faced with the question of whether to receive the "defenseless and generally inoffensive but unprofitable people," or to force them back into slavery. This terrible dilemma, said the *Enquirer*, was brought about by the Northern Abolitionists, "men [who] have added weight to the bonds of the slave and forged fetters for the free man." The editor concluded by labeling all such philanthropists as "monsters of cruelty."[92]

This argument is reminiscent of the claim set forth by Madison County slaveholders in their "Addresses," in which abolitionists were blamed for increasing the misery of slaves: after all, the slaveholders had been forced to sell many of their bondservants down the river to prevent them from hearing or responding to the dreadful doctrines of abolitionism. We are asked to pity the poor unfortunate owners who had to be cruel because of the wicked demands for justice which reformers persisted in uttering. Perhaps Fee was right in assuming that slavery was a sin so all-pervasive that it spoiled everything it touched. It is certainly true that most people who wrote about the issue before the Civil War revealed a moral bankruptcy that has scarcely been equaled, even in our own age.

On January 7, 1860, the *Maysville Daily Press* reported the news of Madison County's action in driving out Fee and his followers. Maysville, seat of

Mason County, was the largest Kentucky town near Fee's birthplace: a region where people knew him well personally. In fact, the writer of the *Daily Press* account of the exile was a schoolmate of Fee's, acquainted with him since boyhood. In a way, the Kentucky paper presents a more sympathetic story than the Ohio one, although its attitude too is basically condemnatory toward abolitionists.

The *Daily Press* allows that there may exist two opinions of the Berea Exile: it may be condemned "as an unwarrantable and indefensible interference with the freedom of speech and opinion." On the other hand, the action of Fee's neighbors may be seen as "rendered necessary by urgent consideration of prudence and self-preservation." After all, the *Daily Press* points out, "the population of Madison [County] is one of the wealthiest and most intelligent in the State [unlike the same people, who were "not remarkably intelligent" from a vantage point on the other side of the Ohio River], and would not be likely to resort to a measure of this extreme character, without urgent necessity or at least great provocation." Even though freedom of speech is important it is clear that "the public mind has been so wrought upon by the interference of Northern fanatics with a purely domestic institution, that the people are no longer in a condition to listen. . . . " Abolitionists should not want to remain in the South, inflaming the people, even by their very presence. "The slaveholding States is [sic] no longer a fit place for abolition propaganda. They ought not to desire to remain among us."

The *Daily Press* avers that abolitionists must surely suffer from the unpleasantness of their situation in Kentucky anyway; social ostracism and suspicion must follow them everywhere. Ministers of the gospel are in an especially difficult position, since their commitment to abolition doctrines must destroy their usefulness no matter how fervent, sincere or pious they may otherwise be.

Finally, the *Daily Press* describes Fee himself—a passage of particular interest since it is written by one who knew him as a boy. "He was, if we mistake not," the writer says, "even then [in boyhood] somewhat noted for the fervor of his religious convictions, and for an enthusiasm of disposition which has since become intensified into fanaticism. He is a fanatic in the true sense of that word, and capable, we believe, of going to great lengths, and making great sacrifices in obedience to his convictions." Fee "is undoubtedly honest and intends not harm to anyone. But he is a man of *one idea* and such are always dangerous."

Fee is, the writer states, "a man of most estimable character" in private and personal matters—and would be highly respected if not for his "unfortunate notions." His family is one of the most respectable in this county, and are all "staunch pro-slaveryites and some of them extensive slaveholders."

The writer concludes: "We are glad that he has left the State, and we hope he will stay away."[93]

The *Maysville Daily's* account, genuinely sympathetic to Fee but not to his 'notions,' nevertheless condemns him. His respectability, his estimable character, his acknowledged piety, count for nothing. The Maysville writer knows Fee, 'understands' him, probably likes him—nevertheless, he is as insistent as any enemy that Fee's exile is necessary, even desirable. Somehow the open hostility of most Southern accounts of the Exile is less frightening than this revelation of respect, regard and knowledge which must be sacrificed to the cause of slavery.

With the disappearance of ordinary decency toward the people whom one knows, every violation of human rights becomes possible. Fee had been driven from Berea, where he had lived for some five years, but many people in Madison County still regarded him as an alien, an interloper, after that length of time. When he returned to Bracken County he sought the shelter of his own birthplace, his family, his friends, people who had known him all his life, many of whom welcomed him. But the citizens of Bracken County drove him out of Kentucky.

The Third Exile—Fee and Others from Bracken County
"Church building in Kentucky is over. . . . I can understand now why the Savior wept over Jerusalem. . . . The giving up of property, home & all earthly considerations are not so painful as the idea of giving up these churches & the privilege of laboring directly with & for the people of Ky. How shall I go away & give up this work? I cannot give it up." John G. Fee.

The committee which resolved to drive the Bereans out of Madison County had met in Richmond on December 17, 1859. The committee to drive James Scott Davis out of Lewis County met the following January 21 in Orangeburg (Mason County); two days later, a meeting at Brooksville, county seat of Bracken County, took measures to drive John G. Fee, John G. Hanson and "others of like sentiments" from the State. This committee's resolutions began:

WHEREAS John Gregg Fee and John G. Hanson, lately expelled from Madison County, Kentucky, are now in Bracken County, preparing to make it their home. And whereas, that both Fee and Hanson are enemies to the State, dangerous to the security of our lives and property, we, the citizens of Kentucky, deem it our duty to protect our lives and property from enemies at home as well as abroad, do now solemnly declare the said John G. Fee and John G. Hanson, must, by the 4th day of February next, leave this county and State.[94]

Other men were named as enemies: J. B. Mallett, native of New York, a schoolteacher who had been teaching at Locust Academy since the winter of 1857, and G. R. Holman, who had been teaching because of poor health; both men had been educated in Grand River Institute, Austinburg, Ohio, and Mallett had studied at Oberlin as well. Wyatt Robinson was also named in the Committee's resolutions, but he seems to have left the county before the mob had a chance to call on him.[95]

Two men unnamed in committee resolutions were nevertheless invited to leave Kentucky: Charles Griffin, Rogers' friend, who had decided to settle in Bracken County after being exiled from Berea, and Oliver Grigson, a member of Bethesda Church who had worked as a colporteur for James S. Davis.

The *Augusta Sentinel* reported, "This meeting bore not the slightest resemblance to a mob: it was the people rising in their sovereign capacity to rid themselves of an evil for which there was no remedy given in the statutes." John Gregg Fee, the *Sentinel* stated, was "personally known to almost every man in the county."[96]

A committee of 50 local citizens was appointed to deliver the usual warning to Fee and his supporters. Chairman of the committee was Dr. J.[oshua] Taylor Bradford, a kinsman of Fee's (Fee's paternal grandmother was a Bradford). The *Cincinnati Weekly*, in an account sympathetic to Fee, mentioned the "astonishing amount of pomposity" with which this committee proceeded to its work. The group passed through a local tollgate and told the keeper that "this company paid no toll."[97]

The committee called first at the house of John Humlong, where J. B. Mallett resided. Mallett had been mobbed two days earlier in Germantown; he had been in the company of Leander D. Gregg and William Humlong when a crowd of some 80 people set upon him. Gregg and Humlong attempted to defend him, but to no avail. Mallett was carried bodily into a dark alley and surrounded by men armed with revolvers, pistols and knives. Mallett asked, "What is this for?" The reply was, "For your d—d villainous sentiments." The mob then began removing Mallett's clothing, until he was partially nude. Again he asked, "What is this for?" The answer: "For your d—d Abolition sentiments."

People were crying, "Hang him!" and "Shoot him!" "An iron vessel containing nearly a gallon of tar was brought . . . nearly or quite, boiling hot." The timely intervention of one Dr. John A. Coburn, an old and respected citizen, and some others, saved Mallett from further harm.[98]

When the committee called upon him so soon afterward, Mallett was understandably reluctant to approach them. "The chairman, Dr. Bradford, called out in a stern voice . . . , "Walk this way, Mr. Mallet; don't have any fears, we don't intend to hurt you." Mr. Mallett replied, "No, he expected not; he was in the company of gentlemen, he supposed." After the resolutions were read to him Mallett was asked if he intended to leave and he said he did, but asked for the privilege of making a few remarks; the committee refused to listen to him.

The next visit was paid to the residence of Greenbury G. Hanson, where his son John G. Hanson was notified to leave. Hanson, like Mallett, asked for a hearing, but the committee again refused, although some of Hanson's relations were part of it. Next, the committee visited the house of Vincent Hamilton, Fee's father-in-law, where the resolutions were read to Fee. Asked if he intended to go Fee replied that he did, but not because he recognized any right of the mob to have him leave. He stated, "I make no pledges to surrender God-given and constitutional rights to any man or set of men. . . . " He also asked to address the people, but Bradford ordered them on. As one of the committee members was passing him Fee held out his hand and said, "Do you approve of this action?" "Yes, I do." "Well," Fee said, "we took vows together in the same Church. I expected different things of you." The man Fee addressed was an Elder in the Sharon Presbyterian Church, and Matilda Fee had boarded with him during her school days. He had known both the Fees from their childhood. His final words to Fee were, "It is not worthwhile for us to talk."[99]

"In that mob," the *Cincinnati Enquirer* reported, "were school-mates, parents of school-mates and life-long acquaintances [of Fee's]."

Next stop—the residence of John D. Gregg, where G. R. Holman, in feeble health, received his notice.

When John G. Fee was planning to return to his native Bracken County in January 1860, he wrote, "This is a trial, but yet I must rejoice in it. . . . Many are ready to laugh at the supposed failure & friends do not like to pay for a 'dead horse' & so Moses endured—I am not a Moses by a long ways. I am what I am by the grace of God & intend to be more—endure to the end." At first Fee had thought he would not go from Bracken County, and had even said so. He had taken "every step to avert expulsion" from Bracken County, every step he thought "consistent and right." He visited prominent men and talked to the people—all his friends advised him to go. He had been very sick—from exposure and exertion— eventually suffering pneumonia. He did not even have a horse of his own; his illness alone would have made his leaving at this time a terrible hardship. But two members of the church in Bracken, his cousin John D. Gregg and John Humlong, both loyal to him, said, "Our first impulse was to take our rifles and stand with you, but others warned to leave decide to go, and we find that we will be utterly overwhelmed by the opposing power, and if you stay we shall be driven out."[100]

On Saturday January 28, Fee, Hanson, and most of the others left their homes; they missed their boat to cross the Ohio River, and, while they were stranded at Smith's landing, the daughter of a riverboat captain "made the first hours of exile pleasant with her unsurpassed music." By Monday, Fee, Hanson, Griffin, Holman, Mallett and Grigson had arrived in Cincinnati.

Fee's reaction to this exile was more intense than to the earlier one. The whole affair, conducted on a larger scale, was more frightening but even more personal than the Madison County exile had been. Eight hundred to one thousand people attended the meeting to oust the abolitionists. And, of course, Fee was to be driven, as he put it, "from relatives, from the dear brethren and & sisters in the church & friends around." Bracken County was Fee's last vestige of work in the State of Kentucky. Despairingly he wrote, "Church building in Kentucky is over . . . . I can understand now why the Savior wept over Jerusalem." He mourned being "shut away from any direct labor for the poor slave & poor white children— I have no language," he said, "to describe this weight of feeling when I knew that the friends looked to me. . . . "[101]

If the Madison County exile had been painful for Fee, the Bracken County one was sheer agony. He said leaving Bracken County was the greatest trial of his life; at times he thought his "feelings would overcome" him. "Oh how I wish I could be with you," Fee wrote to Jocelyn, "to tell the anguish of my heart for others—and to plan for the future. The giving up of property, home & all earthly considerations are not so painful as the idea of giving up these churches & the privilege of laboring directly with & for the people of Ky. How shall I go away & give up this work? I cannot give it up."[102]

Years later, Fee confessed to Cassius Clay that he had broken down in 1860, apparently suffering a complete mental and physical collapse. "I felt then almost ready to[,] in the language of Elijah[,] 'let me lie down & die.' I desired not that [but] I felt the bitterness of death."[103]

J. B. Mallett returned to his home in Sheridan, New York; he could not go back into Bracken County, where the citizens believed a rumor that he was raising an army to burn Germantown. "It is the severest trial of my life that I cannot go on with my plans of building up an academy in Bracken co.," he wrote, "It has almost unmanned me." From New York in May 1860 he wrote to the AMA; he had lots of time on his hands, he said. A few days earlier he had been to the residence of John Brown, Jr., finding at home only Brown's wife and his brother Owen, who had escaped from Harper's Ferry. "On visiting them," Mallett wrote, "I was completely taken aback. I expected to find them somewhat severe in spirit but to the contrary—amiable, kind, lovely, intelligent, generous-souled folks, and add to this a far-reaching faith which looked away into the future & surely saw the day of universal freedom." Echoing a now famous speech, Fee's sermon in Beecher's church, Mallett said, "I would be like the Brown's in spirit of consecration yet differ widely in plan."[104]

Charles and Anna Griffin, exiled twice within two months, never returned to Kentucky, never renewed their connection with Berea in any way. In fact, the Griffins were among the few exiles who landed on their feet. By July 1860, Griffin had written Fee several times, never complaining of "want of means"; Griffin's father was able to help the young man, who spoke of building, presumably in his former home in Roseville, Illinois.[105]

Matilda Fee, in spite of the danger, believed she could reach Berea and get their household goods out of Kentucky. Driving a carriage, accompanied by her eldest son Burritt, "she started and on the third day, after overcoming severe difficulties, reached . . . home." There she boxed up their goods and shipped them to Cincinnati, then returned to her father's house, where the remainder of the children were staying, and from thence, Fee wrote, "she came to me."[106]

CHAPTER SEVEN

CLAY, HANSON AND "WAR" IN MADISON COUNTY; MORE EXILES

Cassius Clay and the Exiles
"Well, I am no Don Quixote to go forward and fight the battles of every man who may venture an opinion on the subject of slavery. . . . " Cassius M. Clay.

Throughout the ordeal of the exiles, Cassius M. Clay attempted to divorce himself from the proceedings. In spite of all his efforts (or perhaps because of them), he was still connected in the public mind to John G. Fee; now that Fee was in trouble—or, let us say, in *more* trouble than usual—Clay, whose repudiation and withdrawal had already done incalculable harm, redoubled his efforts to "stand aloof." He apparently did not consider keeping silent on the matter: that form of aloofness was never part of his approach.

The week before the first exile an article had appeared in the *Mountain Democrat* of Richmond representing Clay as opposed to the Bereans, and "as saying they *ought* to be driven off." On December 26, 1859, George Candee warned Clay that the report of his remarks about the Bereans would do him (Clay) great harm with the Jackson County constituency, for all the citizens of Jackson were in sympathy with the Madison County exiles.[1]

Immediately after the first exile, Clay spoke in defense of the Bereans on the Capitol steps in Frankfort; in his speech he said that driving Fee out was "lawless and unjustifiable." He also claimed that he had written to the Madison County papers before the Exile stating that Fee had no Sharpe's rifles, that Fee had never approved of John Brown's actions, and so on. Unfortunately, his defense of Fee had been delayed; it "had not been allowed to reach [its] destination in time to disabuse the public mind. . . . " Indeed, finding that his article had not been published before the Exile actually took place, Clay went to the *Messenger* office and "took it away, as the occasion for its publication had passed." Thus he forestalls anyone suspecting that the article was never given to the *Messenger* in the first place.

In his own defense Clay had written that his "whole connection with the Radicals at Berea" had consisted of being "all the time against their doctrines; all the time for the peace and safety of the community." His Frankfort speech was more in defense of himself than of Fee, in any case. He opened his address with a long presentation concerning his own courage, although he said, "Those who know me, know full well I am not in the habit of speaking of my courage." But speak of it he did, saying, "The brave are always generous—always!" claiming he had no fear of Kentuckians because of their bravery. Perhaps he protested too much in his claims for himself and for his fellow citizens, who were being particularly craven just at that time.[2]

His self-defense continued with an explanation of his abandonment of Fee, based on their Fourth of July disagreement at Slate Lick Springs. Fee had taken the ground of the radical abolitionists—and, Clay said, "As I was a constitution- and law-loving man I argued to him that I could not and should no longer stand with him. . . . Well," he added, "I am no Don Quixote to go forward and fight the battles of every man who may venture an opinion on the subject of slavery . . . . "

In spite of his unwillingness to "stand" with Fee, Clay described him by saying " . . . he is as pure a man as ever I knew. . . . " Clay's actual defense of Fee was eloquent and forceful. The real loss with the exile of Fee and his friends, Clay stated, would not be to Fee but to the Commonwealth of Kentucky, especially to those ill-educated citizens of the mountains. Then he spoke of Fee's actual invasion of Kentucky: not "with Sharpe's rifles, pistols and bowie knives . . . but with the New Testament, the school-house, the church and the saw mill." Fee had been accused of introducing a "New God"—not so, Clay said, rather he introduced " . . . the same God who before the long centuries created the heavens and the earth, who based His Throne upon the eternal principles of justice, and draped it in the undying beauty of harmony, liberty and love."[3]

Clay was caught in a very dangerous position: he feared that the Madison County slave power would turn on him next, and drive him out of Kentucky simply because he had once supported Fee, but he was equally afraid he would lose all his political support in the region if he sided with the slaveowners. Those people who still counted as followers of Cassius Clay had a disconcerting tendency to sympathize with John G. Fee. It may be unjust to assume that Clay deliberately attacked the Bereans until they were driven out, then defended them (quite eloquently and ineffectually, of course) after they were already gone. But I doubt it.

It is certainly not unfair to Clay to recognize that the departure of the Bereans was an enormous relief to him. Since the Slate Lick Springs debate one of his goals had been to get rid of Fee and Fee's followers. Clay had not attempted direct action against the Berea community, but he had openly presented the opportunity to Fee's enemies: he had deliberately encouraged the attitude that Fee was a revolutionary and insurrectionary, and he had withdrawn all support and protection in the most public way. The Exile was simply the climax of Clay's own policy—but he had miscalculated; he had thought Fee would leave of his own accord, long before matters came to such a pass, long before there was any risk that Clay himself would be included in the reaction of the Madison County slavepower. So Clay may have been glad that Fee had been driven out, but he was also fearful that he might share the same fate himself.

John G. Fee, writing to Clay from Cincinnati in February 1860, still regarded him as a friend. "I have just rec'd your kind & frank letter of 21 inst.," Fee wrote,

> I love you for it. I love principle so do you. I have a desire to be faithful spoken. If I had not you could not have respected my fidelity or felt that I was faithful. We do not need to part—I do not part with a man because he differs when I feel he is honest. Moreover you have uttered sentiments as radical as I and I am glad of it. . . .

Fee reproached Clay only very briefly: "You had power to protect me," Fee said, "if I violate no law I ought to be protected." With that single sentence Fee concluded his personal recriminations against the friend who had done most to endanger Fee's life and ministry. "I wish I could see you as you return," Fee wrote, "I would love to see you. I have the kindest of feelings toward you. Shall rejoice in your welfare."[4]

Nevertheless, Fee had repudiated Clay's leadership forever—and, although Fee apparently forgave his friend personally, his estimation of Clay's character was henceforth low indeed. Clay "is sceptical and wicked," Fee wrote, "& it may be God will not in the work in Ky have his help." From now on, Fee indicated, he would no longer follow the leadership or ambitions of Cassius Clay, instead he would "follow Christ."[5]

In March 1860, when John G. Hanson returned to Madison County in defiance of the committee's orders, Cassius Clay found himself once again in an untenable position.

Hanson's Return

"I have left the county, my business & my house & have fled to these mountains as if I had been a Ravening beast. . . ." John G. Hanson.

John Gregg Hanson, son of Greenbury Griffith Hanson and Rebecca Gregg, was born January 13, 1834, in Bracken County, Kentucky, first cousin of Matilda Hamilton Fee, first cousin once removed of John Gregg Fee. Hanson's father was himself a native of Bracken County, having been born there in 1806; Greenberry G. Hanson, descendant of Maryland slaveholding families, owned no slaves himself, although he was rich and prominent in his community. He had, Rogers wrote, a "fine house with . . . broad porches . . . not more conspicuous than were its occupants for every good word and work." Greenbury Hanson was an early member of Fee's Bethesda Church.[6]

Of all Fee's Gregg connections, John Hanson was the most committed to his cousin's work; before he turned 20, Hanson became a member of Fee's Bethesda church. Fee's doctrine and example influenced the younger man enormously. On May 15, 1858, in Bracken County John G. Hanson married Ellen J. Sholes, an Oberlin student, with Fee performing the ceremony. Having agreed to teach at Berea the next fall, the young couple arrived in Madison County in October. Soon Hanson was an integral part of the Berea project—although he taught only one term, he soon became a member of Berea's first board of trustees, serving as secretary (a position he held for many years), and on the Prudential Committee. By July 1859, his circular sawmill was in operation: his contribution to "the cause of Christ." His first mill was located at the mouth of Log Lick Hollow Branch on Old Slate Lick Road, in a small settlement he called Glendale, about a mile south of the district schoolhouse. Before the December exile Hanson's mill had been in full operation.[7]

About the 3rd of March 1860, Hanson returned to Berea "to saw out some 300 logs left at the mill" and to try to sell the mill itself unless he saw some chance of coming back permanently. He arrived on a Saturday; the following Monday was a court day at Richmond.[8]

Hanson had not been the only exile to return. A. G. W. Parker, Fee's former colporteur, who had been ordered to leave at the same time, had gone away—but some of his northern friends had given him money and, apparently in sheer bravado, he had come back and commenced drinking and carousing. The day after Hanson's arrival Parker had used "rough" and threatening language to a local citizen and had attracted a great deal of public attention to himself; on Monday court day a call was issued for the committee to assemble at Glade Church a week later and take steps to expel Parker *and* Hanson.[9]

Friends warned Hanson to be gone by Saturday. He had not found a buyer by Friday at noon, when he was told "that a company of 150 would be out the next day. . . ." In haste he boxed his goods for shipment, said goodbye to his friends and started as if he were bound for Cincinnati. Actually, he stopped and spent the night with a friend in the mountains; but his friend's cabin was not a suitable hiding place, too near the road that committee members would be taking to reach the Glade Church.[10]

The committee, only some 30 or 40 men, met on schedule, stayed together about 24 hours, and drank—it is reported—a great deal of whiskey. The group spent some time talking about the American eagle, a cast iron ornament which Hanson had placed on top of one of his mill buildings. Two committee members volunteered to go take the eagle down, for reasons which were probably as clear as anything else in their drunken condition. Since the eagle was replaced the next day, one may assume that sobriety revealed its removal as basically pointless.

Forty armed men—or the rumor of 40 armed men—pursued Hanson, who fled to Rockcastle County. From his hiding place there he wrote,

> [I] have left the county, my business & my house & have
> fled to these mountains as if I had been a Ravening beast & here had
> wandered to-day not dareing to see the face of a fellow man, lest he
> betray me into ruthless hands, & while I write I reflect on my doom,
> my conscience quick responds What's my crime? What have I done
> that I should flee & to these mountains, as a beast, to be hunted as a
> partridge of the mountains & again I cry what [have] I done &
> against whom. Or am I accursed because the Omnipotence of
> reason—that god like attribute of man, & with conscience dares to
> play the parts known & freedom & freeman—if so know this that its
> a gift from God.

Hanson's letter, growing more incoherent as it proceeds, attests to his condition by its very breakdown of style. On the side of the letter he had written "Supplantation of His own hand, then Curse God & let me go free." Only God knows what he meant.[11]

WAR IN MADISON COUNTY! (First with rifles, then with words)
"They shot in all I think twenty five times." David Preston.

Hanson composed an Appeal to the People of Madison co. which appeared under the date March 13. Meanwhile, the committee reported that Hanson had left the region, although many people knew that was not true; eventually Hanson returned to Berea, where his friends were very surprised to see him. On the Sabbath he preached there twice, and he decided to stay in the region. "I am here," he wrote, "& still own property & want to do what God directs." Meanwhile, some of his Richmond enemies still planned "to pounce on him unawares and hang him. . . ."[12]

On the 24th of March, Cassius Clay went to Berea accompanied by his friend John Hamilton Rawlings, and there "used all [his] influence" to persuade his Republican friends not to identify themselves "at all in any manner with Hanson." Clay told his friends to ask Hanson to sell his mill and move from the State "as his presence would be a continual source of discontent and might possibly involve the Republicans in conflict, when innocent men might be killed." On his way home through Berea the next day Clay was stopped by Hanson, and Rawlings introduced the two men; then Hanson asked Clay about the public attitude toward him. Clay told Hanson "that the feeling of bitterness against him was greater than ever on account of his return," and advised him to leave the state for his own sake and also "to avoid the possible fight between [Clay's] friends and the committee." Hanson replied "that everyone must stand on his own convictions; and that 'every dog has his day,'" or words to that effect. (Clay reported at the time that Hanson had said 'every tub must stand upon its own bottom.'; both remarks seem equally inappropriate, but quite within Hanson's eccentric range.)[13]

His interview with Clay frightened Hanson, as it was intended to do. "Under an apprehension of danger [he] left [town] and travelled around some three miles, so that no one at Berea should know where [he] was." He spent a night of anxiety with Thomas J. Renfro, and planned to finish sawing his logs, leave someone to run the mill, and get out the next day. On Monday morning, however, Hanson found his plans drastically altered. "I had just put on my hat and coat, after breakfast," he wrote, "to go to the mill, when a neighbor [Benjamin Kirby] ran in, and told me, the mob, some 25 in number, were then at Berea." They had already searched his boarding place, and had announced that they intended to hang him. Hanson hid under Renfro's board pile when the mob came in quest of him, then fled to the woods in Jackson County, hiding "up in high cliffs and caves" in the mountains during the day and staying in a friend's house at night. A reward of $100 was offered for him on published handbills. Nevertheless, many citizens of Jackson County invited Hanson to stay with them and pledged their protection.[14]

The committee's renewed action was, according to Clay, a direct result of his visit to Berea over the weekend; in fact, he said, the mob had come to Berea expecting to take Clay there by surprise. The men found neither Clay nor Hanson, but their behavior makes it clear that Hanson was their intended victim.[15]

The mob—to use Hanson's designation for them—had a very busy day on March 26 "scouring the country." At six o'clock in the morning, 24 armed men from Richmond arrived at Hanson's boarding place, which happened to be John G. Fee's house, occupied by Jerusha Preston and her children. The men searched the house and insulted and threatened its inmates; failing to find Hanson, they dashed off to intimidate many other local citizens. At John Preston's they "presented a pistol at him saying that if he did not confess where Hanson was they would kill him." From there they proceeded to the residences of Willis Green Haley and Franklin Bland, where they insulted "the wives of these gentlemen."

They then visited William B. Wright and "threatened to take him out and paint him," presumably with tar.[16]

Near Hanson's mill the mob visited James Walters (or Waters), cuffed him, "pulled his hair, drew pistols, talked indecently to his wife, and. . . attempted to provoke him to a fight," shooting many of his chickens "for sport."

After searching Hanson's mill, the mob went to the house of George West, a mile south, where they jumped their horses over the yard fence. West's eldest daughter "was closing the back [door], when they broke it down upon her, and entered the house, over the door, she being under it." Inside they found George West in bed, propped up with pillows, in the last stages of consumption. "Putting their pistols to his breast, [they] demanded where Hanson was" and struck him two or three times. Meanwhile, the daughter managed to scramble out from under the door, but one of the men "put his pistol against her breast, and pressing her back against the cupboard, told her she ought not to have shut the door against them." The mob also said they would "bring out a buck nigger" for her benefit.

Still they had not found Hanson; so the mob rode into Rockcastle County to the house of Josiah Burdett, where they found only Mrs. Burdett and her five daughters. Once again the men burst into the house, threatening the women with death, "putting their pistols to Mrs. Burdett's and her daughters' breasts." Two or three men cocked their guns and went upstairs, where they tore up the beds. They also ripped away part of the underpinning of the house and searched for Hanson for quite a distance in the nearby woods and mountains. Later, some of the men reported that they had seen Hanson escape from the Burdett house in disguise. According to Hanson, this story arose because "one of the elder daughters ran down to a little thicket below the house, to bring up her two little sisters, who had gone there to hide, and were crying bitterly. As she passed, a drunken wretch cried out, 'There he goes in woman's clothes.'"

On their way home, when they neared Slate Lick Springs, the committee, who had so far encountered no resistance, met a band of Bereans, headed by Green Haley, armed with rifles and shotguns. According to the Richmond band, there were 30 irate abolitionists in this little army; according to David Preston, there were only 12, although 3 more came along as the battle was joined. But it was not much of a battle, by any account.

Preston, who was actually present, described the encounter in a letter written only three days later:

> . . .Twelve of us, friends of Hanson, went to seek for him. We had gone two miles when we met the mob. When we were fifty yards from them they began to shout and came toward us and when within twelve yard [sic] they fired on us. They shot three or four times. Some of them said they wanted peace, other still continued to fire. I walked forward & began to talk to [Reuben Munday]. He asked me if we came to fight. I told him that we did not intend that they should hurt Hanson. He said if we wanted a fight to go at it. I raised my gun when he threw up his hands and asked me not to shoot. By this time one company were some fifty yards off. Then a man came within steps of me & fired twice at me with a repeater another fired at me with a shot gun. Some cried out shoot him. I then made off. They shot in all I should think twenty five times.[17]

Soon, very contradictory accounts by various pro-Berea and pro-Richmond authors began to appear in newspapers and journals. Each side claimed the other fired first; each claimed the other had acted like cowards. Both sides denied that any one of their number was injured or killed.

A typical pro-Berea narrative runs something like this:

"What in hell are you doing with your guns?" asked the armed men from Richmond, apparently shocked. The Bereans replied, "We are going to defend our families from violence." The mob "bore down on them in full gallop," yelling, "Shoot, shoot!" The leader of the Bereans told them to hold their fire. Part of the mob dismounted, made "a breast work of their horses and commenced the attack by firing some fifteen or twenty shots." The Bereans made ready a second time, but obeying orders, did not fire. Seeing that a fight was inevitable, twelve of the Bereans now moved a short distance to a high point of woodland, and determined to resist to the last. Three remained, and as the mob came up, two fired and then ran to join their comrades on the hill. The mob fired several shots at the three as they retreated.[18]

The standard pro-Richmond story claimed:

> The leader of the committee, Col. Reuben Munday, rode forward and asked if the [Berea] party were for peace or war. The answer was that they understood that the committee had Hanson under arrest, and that they intended to rescue him. The party drawn across

the road immediately fired at the committee, who dismounted, hitched their horses and returned the fire. After the first fire, the opposite party commenced a drawback movement, retreating to and taking refuge in, a house, forming it into a temporary fort. The committee followed them closely and returned their fire, until having housed them, and their ammunition giving out, they retired. Some three or four rounds were fired by each party, with intermediate discharges from the weapons of parties on either side.

Two of the opposite party are known to be wounded, perhaps more. We heard a report on Monday night that one man was known to have been killed, but could trace it to no responsible source. On the side of the committee not a scratch was received.[19]

Cassius Clay, convinced that the mob had been searching for him, had another version of the affair:

So soon as the Committee heard I was at Berea on Saturday and Sunday, they raised a terrible clamor, accused me of [trying] to bring on a war, mustered the forces, and made a night expedition of the most desperate men, all the moderates being left behind, expecting to take me by surprise and put me to death. This was told me by a friend in the Revolutionary Committee. They, however, did not reach Berea before daylight, armed with shot guns and pistols. They searched all the houses, insulted the women and our friends, and at last were so violent . . . to West and his daughter (a Republican) that our party would stand it no longer, went in defense of West, when the parties met, and a battle took place, in which three of the mob-ites were wounded (an old Mexican companion-in-arms confessing to me in private, shot in the thigh), and at last defeated.[20]

In Lexington's proslavery *Kentucky Statesman* a report maintained that

Shots were exchanged and no lives lost, though the yells elicited from the abolitionists, by the fire of the citizens, gave reason to believe that some were wounded. The Freesoil men retreated through the brush and disappeared.[21]

After threatening to return the next day, "hang the Bereans and burn their houses," the mob returned to Richmond for reinforcements.

. . .The excitement [there] raged to fever heat, and every one commenced preparing for a brush the next day. Rifles, shot guns, pistols, powder, buckshot, and lead were in request, and from all portions of the town was heard the bustle of preparation.

Two hundred and nineteen armed men arrived in Berea on Tuesday morning, searched every house and possible hiding place for miles around, found no enemies, "tore the roof off and log out of a dwelling house [Waters]," and the roof off a meat house; then, as Cassius Clay put it, they "killed Hanson's sawmill." Before returning to Richmond, the committee assembled in front of the Berea Postoffice and "gave orders to the people of Berea to leave in ten days."[22]

Hanson, who believed "no one was hurt on either side," was most concerned about the destruction at his mill. "They. . . tore off the roofing," he complained, "pulled down a smoke stack, broke all the wheels of the mill, and cut a hole in the top of the boiler, leaving all a complete wreck." [23]

So the incident was over, except for the flurry of stories about it, many of which have survived as legends to the present day. A Cincinnati news report poked fun at the committee which had believed it necessary to recruit 219 men from the Bluegrass to fight 15 Bereans. This Ohio version reduced the entire battle to nothing:

> The meeting with the mob party was by accident. Both parties at first proclaimed for peace, but as soon as the mob could dismount and arrange their horses before them as a barricade to their own persons, they commenced firing. Their firing, however, had no effect, and was not returned except by two men who fired but once. The Bereans quietly went along about their own business, and the mob-ites returned to Richmond to report the commencement of the war.[24]

No doubt this point of view was more amusing before the Civil War.

After Willis Green Haley and Franklin Bland fled to Cincinnati, they were interviewed by reporters and stated that accounts of the Madison County incident appearing in Richmond and Louisville papers were almost wholly erroneous. They gave their own version: The initial encounter involved 24 committee men on horseback against 12 antislavery men on foot. The committee fired first, Bereans returned the fire and wounded five of the Richmond band—only one severely. The next day a party of several hundred men came seeking Bland and Haley, who had sensibly gone into hiding—after ten days the two men had made their way into Ohio.[25]

From these accounts one may gather that the skirmish in Madison County was fought to defend the insulted families of various Bereans, or over John G. Hanson or over George West or Bland and Haley or possibly Cassius Clay, that the Vigilance Committee behaved bravely and wounded several cowardly Bereans, that the Bereans behaved bravely and wounded several craven committee members, that someone was killed, that no one was killed; that very little happened although the committee returned to Richmond in such an hysterical state that everyone in Richmond became hysterical too. In addition, one may choose among a wide variety of estimated numbers of people.[26]

Certainly the Richmond Committee ordered a cannon from Lexington, with a p. s." "If you send us two or three of your boys who know how to load and shoot, and are competent to direct the piece, etc. . . . We have no one who has been accustomed to loading or shooting a cannon and would like for some one to come who is convenient."[27]

Hanson Flees Madison County
"When I reflect what my course of life and my labors have been, what I had at heart and wished to do for my countrymen in Kentucky, and think of what I have received at their hands, it makes me weep and love them more." John G. Hanson.

Hanson, who had been hiding in Jackson County, left on April 3, walked all night, going past his mill and his home, "now desolate and ruined." Near Kirksville (in Madison County) some of the original committee pursued him on horseback, caught him and searched him for weapons. They found none, since he never carried any. They had expected him to be loaded down with guns and knives, like the incendiary he was supposed to be. Nevertheless, they headed toward the county seat with Hanson, assuring him, "You must now go to Richmond and pull rope." But en route Hanson's surprisingly sympathetic captors, convinced that he would never leave Richmond alive, decided to let him go, giving up the $100 reward they could have claimed for delivering him.[28]

Still enemies pursued Hanson—"three times during one night they passed so near him, while he lay concealed, that he could hear them talking about him, and the reward offered for him." Travelling by night, he made his way through "plowed fields, and along the line of a rail road." One day he walked fifty miles and rode fifty more, hiding in box cars. Finally, he made his way to Cincinnati, arriving on the night of the 12th of April, "in tolerable health," although "for three previous nights he had not slept in a house." He had traveled 125 miles on foot, "part of the time without food." From safety Hanson wrote,

> When I reflect what my course of life and my labors have been, what I had at heart and wished to do for my countrymen in Kentucky, and think of what I have received at their hands, it makes me weep and love them more, as they show by their madness that they 'know not what they do,' and are tending fast to eternal sorrows. In the course I have followed, I have done nothing that I regret. Trusting in God, I shall still labor that so good a land, filled with many generous spirits, and many wailing slaves, shall yet be free.[29]

Cassius Clay Takes Precautions after the "War"
"You may drive these men into the mountains, you may burn their houses; you may hunt them down like wild beasts; till the last one falls by superior force; but their cause is the cause of American liberty, and of the noblest instincts of human nature. Their martydom will light up the fires of civil war. . . . " Cassius M. Clay.

In the wake of these events, Cassius Clay took every conceivable precaution. On the 27th of March he gave a speech in Richmond at the courthouse in which he disclaimed any connection with Hanson or his doctrine and maintained that he (Clay) had told Hanson that "any man advocating the doctrines he held, could not live peaceably in this community." On the same day Clay had written to New York papers saying,

> The mob increases in violence; I lie upon my arms awaiting an attack; my family absolutely refuses to retire, saying they will run bullets and aid as in 1776. If driven into the woods, I shall attempt to hold my position as long as possible, standing on the Constitution, the laws and my right. I will defend them or die. The cannon at Lexington is sent for, and the Governor aids. Is this my cause only, or that of the American People? It is to be vindicated in this way and now? Shall I stand or fall alone? May God defend the right! [He added a postscript:] My daughters are as true as I, and Mrs. C.[30]

The *Kentucky Whig* at this time published a story claiming that the revolutionary committee had turned their attention to Clay. The *Whig* editor remarked, "They are on the right track now," maintaining that the committee in

Madison County should either invite Fee and his men to return or else exile Cassius Clay along with them, since it was pointless to get rid of Fee and allow Clay to remain.[31]

On the 29th of March, Clay wrote the *Louisville Journal*, attempting once again to disclaim all connection with Fee and his doctrines. But he said he knew he was himself included in the violent intentions of the Madison County committee; he considered any action against him unjust because he had cut himself away "from the revolutionary doctrines of the 'Radical Abolitionists,'"—as he put it—" in good faith."[32]

Once again Clay wrote to a New York paper (the *Tribune*). The committee was to go to Berea that day to see if their orders had been carried out. "If some are killed," Clay said,

> God only knows the end! We will at once take to the woods and the mountains and defend ourselves to the last.
> If we had fifty or one hundred Sharpe's rifles, it would give us immense power in the mountain recesses where cannon could not touch us . . . . God knows we don't want the scenes of Kansas again re-engaged—first disarming us and setting our foes upon us![33]

On the 31st of March, Clay composed his "Appeal to the People of Madison County," published in newspapers and distributed also as a handbill. In it, Clay identifies himself as a free citizen of a Constitutional Commonwealth and as such "solemnly" protests "against any power on earth but the legal and regularly constituted authorities of [his] country to decide in any manner upon [his] "life, liberty or property."

At the same time, he reiterates his repudiation of Fee and Hanson, and his refusal to defend them. "My reasons for this," he writes, "are these: I regarded the radical doctrine that 'there is no law for slavery' as revolutionary." Even as he announces his unwillingness to protect or defend John G. Fee, Clay proclaims his ardent desire to defend the people who fought against the committee. "You may drive these men into the mountains," Clay says,

> you may burn their houses; you may hunt them down like wild beasts; till the last one falls by superior force; but their cause is the cause of American liberty, and of the noblest instincts of human

nature. Their martyrdom will light up the fires of civil war, which will pervade the Union, and be extinguished only by the downfall of one or the other of those great powers, Liberty and Slavery, forever! Men of Madison, <u>I stand by those men</u>![34]

Clay's 'boys' were still a part of his program, although Fee and Fee's supporters definitely were not. Clay intended to return to the plans he had formulated for Berea before Fee had taken the reins from him.

In addition to his published self-justifications, Clay made other, more active provisions for his own safety. He "anticipated violence and prepared for it." Convinced that he and his family would be the next exiles, he dispatched Hamilton Rawlings "posthaste" to Jackson and Rockcastle Counties "to gather together enough loyal friends to protect him in his home in case of armed attack." He placed the two cannons from the office of the *True American* at "advantageous points" and set his wife and children to work moulding lead balls for the cannons and bullets for rifles. "Rollins [sic] returned from the mountains with a horde of stout-hearted men of the hills." They established a camp in tents and in the outbuildings of White Hall, completely surrounding Clay's house. Men stood picket duty every night.

Meanwhile, Clay fed the men, some 100 "expert riflemen," but the committee did not appear. On April 4, escorted by his men Clay gave another speech in Richmond. From that point on he heard no more of expulsion and "in a few days disbanded his armed guard and bid [sic] them Godspeed with an eloquently expressed gratitude for their loyal support and friendship."[35]

In a speech at the Republican State Convention of Kentucky, Clay once again defended his desertion of Fee, this time on purely political grounds: they had been, he said, "political comrades up to such time as [Fee], in his wisdom and what he conceived to be his duty to his God and his country, felt in conscience bound to separate himself from the Republican Party." Having shifted the grounds of Fee's offense altogether to party politics, Clay concluded in the same vein, asking if Fee has "any more right to my physical and personal sacrifice of limb or of life than the Democratic Party or the Union party in this Commonwealth? I say he has not."History does not record if Clay paused after his rhetorical question in case someone in the audience wanted to give it the resounding 'Yes' it deserved.[36]

Clay was criticized harshly for his stand against Fee during the Exile, and his political image in the North was badly tarnished. A Cincinnati paper reported that before Rev. John G. Fee became an exile from Madison County, Cassius Clay had been asked "if he would not use his influence to prevent the expulsion of Mr. Fee. . . . Mr. Clay, on this occasion, showed a bitterness towards Mr. Fee rivaling that of the mob itself. He refused assistance in any shape or manner, adding that *Mr. Fee ought to have left Kentucky long before.*" Clay later boasted that he had advised John G. Hanson to leave the state.

> Had Mr. Clay, instead of notifying the public that he had *advised* Fee and Hanson to leave, proclaimed in ringing words that these men had violated no law, and that, therefore, they had the same right to live in Kentucky that he or any other man had, his position would have been far better, and he would have stood infinitely higher in the estimation of true Republicans.[37]

The *Chicago Press and Tribune* also protested Clay's stance:

> We do not like Cassius M. Clay's Appeal. It is . . . not what we had a right to expect, from that courageous and self-sacrificing friend of human rights. By implication . . . it sanctions the lawlessness of the mob that despoiled the peaceful church at Berea, and drove John G. Fee and his brethren out of the state. . . . [Fee] believed that human slavery has no foundation in law; and that theoretical conviction was [his] offense. For it he was driven off. Mr. Clay says he could not defend him. We ask why not. . . ?[38]

The Radical Abolitionist Convention at Syracuse, New York (August 29-30, 1860) framed a resolution which pronounced Clay's actions "in perfect keeping with his baseness."[39]

Such criticisms from abroad may have been easier for Clay to face than some he received from much closer to home. Rev. George Candee wrote to Clay on April 24, 1860, from McKee in Jackson County, and pulled no punches. "You were grieved," Candee writes,

> because of the demonstration made here to 'sustain Hanson.' This 'surprises' me. What! a 'real Republican' grieved to learn that there is one county in the state of Ky[.] where 50 responsible men will pledge all their earthly interests to give legal protection to an innocent man—a very respectable native citizen—a faithful Christian in the enjoyment of his constitutional rights against lawless mobs! It is much more surprising that you, who are yourself exposed to a

like persecution should be grieved to learn of a place of reffuge [sic] where you could be protected by the civil authorities not because you are a better man than Hanson, nor because your doctrine is more acceptable than his; but because like him you would have a just claim on each citizen. . . . Now how can you be grieved by this law-loving demonstration in Hanson's interest unless you are regardless of his rights. Is it patriotic to protect only such as agree with you?

Candee asserted that Fee's work had secured many friends for Clay and made him no enemies. "Your recent acts toward him, however," Candee said,

have made you enemies. The poor have regarded the Berea Exiles and their work as friendly to their interests, and when you take so much pains to separate from them, many look upon you as an enemy to their interests.

You say "Converts made here before Fee came, are now exiled! Is it fair to come among us and destroy us thus?" Nearly all the native exiles are Fee's converts. Let me ask in behalf of those wronged exiles, is it fair for you to encourage Fee to come here, as you did, giving him land and money to build with, then cause him to be exiled and degraded before the world, as I consider that you have done, for fear of personal harm?

Finally, Candee charged that Clay had "an overly anxious desire for self-preservation."[40]

Perhaps Clay was less concerned about his own personal safety than Candee suggests Basically, Clay was fighting for his political life, as is evidenced in his determination to *publish* every detail of his actions, reactions and policies concerning Fee's exile. People who are merely trying to survive do not have so much time and energy to devote to writing about their plight for the newspapers.

Clay had cultivated his relationship with Fee for political purposes, but at Slate Lick Springs the politician had begun to see the preacher as a terrible liability. For years thereafter Cassius Clay tried to shake off John G. Fee, who clung to his "friend" and supporter like a cocklebur. Unable to discourage Fee—whose publishing habits were as aggressive as Clay's own—Clay attempted to put his former disciple in harm's way. If Clay could not rid himself of the increasingly vocal radical that he himself had introduced into Madison County, maybe the other powerful citizens in the region would do it for him. So Clay announced that Fee no longer had his support and protection: it was like saying, 'Go get him. I won't try to stop you.'

Still Fee persisted, expanding his work, bringing in more people, proposing more and more ambitious projects: not fleeing for his life, but digging in to stay and persistently claiming that Cassius was wronging him by denying him the protection that had been promised. For a man interested in political office—of any kind, much less the highest office in the land—John G. Fee was not an asset. If Fee could claim that Clay's withdrawal of support had endangered Fee's divine mission, Clay could equally well maintain that Fee's behavior had cost him his political career. They would continue to argue these questions with one another for the rest of their lives.

The Committee's Final Report
"The whole proceeding of this committee have been characterized by the greatest moderation, patience and forbearance, under circumstances of the greatest and most trying provocation." Madison County Committee Report.

The final report of the Madison County committee, submitted April 3, 1860, summarized all the actions the committee had been involved in since its initial proceedings in December. Concerning the battle between committee members and Bereans, the committee reported:

> To justify this treacherous and dastardly attack, it is now alleged that the attack was made on account of the mistreatment by some of the committee of Mr. Geo. West, indecent language was used in the presence of his daughters, and the rude and unauthorized searching of the houses of the Bereans. Mr. West is in poor health, and is of opinion that he has but a short time to live, and has sent us two messages, requesting us to deny the statement, not wishing the sanction of his name to be appended to so huge a fabrication, but states on the contrary, that those of the Committee who came there behaved like gentlemen.[41]

George West signed his will (witnessed by Thomas J. Renfro, Reuben Kirby and Harrison Burnam) on April 6, 1860; he must have died very shortly thereafter, for the Mortality Census of 1860 records his death in March—some of his family evidently having mistakenly believed that he died late in that month rather than early in April. Whether he denied the committee's allegedly outrageous behavior at his house or not was probably beyond any mortal's power to ascertain by the time the committee wrote its report.[42]

> The Committeemen, who are men of undoubted veracity, deny that they searched or even entered any house without the owner's express permission with one exception, and that the house from which Hanson is believed to have fled, disguised in woman's clothing and from which house a shot had been fired at them; and there they offered no insult or aggravation of any kind. The committee state that the worst language used, if not the worst they ever heard used for obscenity and profanity was used by some of the women of that place.

On the following day, according to the committee's statement,

> no violence of any kind was perpetrated, except to break Hanson's mill, so as to render it for the present, useless, in which they believed themselves justified. The whole of the attacking party have been notified to leave except one old man, who being very penitent, was excused.
> The whole proceeding of this committee have been characterized by the greatest moderation, patience and forbearance, under circumstances of the greatest and most trying provocation. The Committee have been sustained and supported in their action by the citizens of the county, with a unanimity heretofore unexampled. . . . The meeting on Monday April 2d when all the recent acts were reported, was one of the largest we ever saw convened at the court-house, and the approval was unanimous. Many of the charges against the Committee such as design to assassinate citizens and excite civil war, are too absurd and ridiculous to require denial, much less refutation.[43]

The 4th Exile: Natives of Kentucky
"I los all my things on the road to Indiana and i cant hear of them i was sick all the time when I was there but too weeks and then I cum back to Ky and i am well." Benjamin Kirby, Exile, to John G. Fee & John G. Hanson.

The headline in Cincinnati read: "Fifty more Bereans Expelled from Kentucky," but the article said only, "Several families numbering about fifty persons have just left the Berean settlement and gone to the free States, having been ordered out of the State by the pro-slavery mob-ites." End of story. Accounts in Kentucky newspapers were scarcely more expansive. An article in the *Kentucky*

Statesman reported that "the whole of the attacking party" was ordered to leave with the exception of one "penitent" old man. When the news appeared, two people, Green Haley and Franklin Bland had already left Kentucky for Indiana.[44]

Willis Green Haley, known as Green, and Franklin Bland had been the leaders of the local band which had fought the committee near Berea; he and Bland had been organizers or 'captains' of Fee's supporters for several years. (Descendants of Franklin Bland maintained that he had been Fee's closest guard, accompanying the minister on trips to protect him, even being mobbed with him in Augusta, Kentucky.) One account of the little "war" in Madison County spoke of the "army . . . under [Green Haley's] command." Before the actual shooting encounter, the committee had heard rumors that Haley "had used very blustering language as to what he and others intended doing if the committee ever visited that way." Riding in search of Hanson, committee members seized Haley, questioned him and elicited from him a denial that he had ever used such language, but when they met him again, he was heading a band of armed men. After Haley and Bland fled to Indiana, the *Kentucky Statesman* commented, "These men have been the main disturbers of the peace of the county, and they are now gone[;] it is hoped all will again be quiet."[45]

Many of the Madison County exiles traveled to Cincinnati to ask John G. Fee what to do, and where to go. On April 5, 1860, William Kendrick met some of them as they arrived in Ohio, having fled a mob "who threatened death." Among these travelers was Joel Todd, Sr., better known as Uncle Joel, an old man at the time of his exile, born in 1799 in Madison County. He had been "in the affray" and stated that none had been killed, "as he knows of." According to Todd, John Hanson was being "hunted with greatest anxiety to put him to death," and "Bro Candee [would] be killed or kidnaped & moved out of the state."[46]

At this point, Fee, burdened with responsibility for numbers of poor Kentucky exiles, was suffering such bad health some of his friends thought he was going to die. But more exiles kept coming. On the 9th of April, Fee reported that he was feeling somewhat better, although Matilda Fee and his son Tappan had severe colds and influenza.[47]

To add to his trials, the Preston family, Jerusha and her children, arrived in Cincinnati to find shelter with him; they had been occupying Fee's house in Berea before they were driven out. If they had been poor before, they were much more so now; "they had not more means," Fee reported, "than would barely take them out of the state." After spending three days on the roadside without shelter, they crossed the Ohio River, and David Preston, the eldest son, "went to work for bread." They were accompanied by George Adams, husband of Jerusha's daughter Martha, and by a cousin Reuben Preston, "a young man of excellent habits," according to Fee. They were all going to a small house and three acres of ground the Preston family owned in Decatur County, Indiana. "All look to me," Fee wrote, "I feel the need of means."[48]

The Preston family had been among Fee's chief supporters since the beginning of his ministry in Madison County. Jerusha Preston (or the Widow Preston, as she was usually called) had been especially supportive of his work—to put it mildly. The Widow Preston was surely one of the bravest people connected with antislavery movement in Kentucky. The AMA missionaries were able to find refuge at her house even when others were too fearful to associate with abolitionists. When Fee was "walked" out of Rockcastle County by a mob, Jerusha Preston walked beside him. (In 1860, John Rogers referred to her "most remarkable heroism" on this occasion "some years since.") When Otis Waters visited Jerusha Preston in 1858, she was then living with her son-in-law [George Adams], who had been "one of the prominent actors in . . . the mob," although Jerusha and her daughter, "the man's wife, were strong friends to Brother Fee." Jerusha had persisted

> though in feeble health, in walking [Fee] more than a mile, unmindful of the abuse and reckless excitement of the company. Her son-in-law coarsely assailed her with the taunt, 'Well, mother, I didn't think you would go the whole hog.'

Waters found his time with Jerusha Preston well-spent, more encouraging than anything [he] had experienced for a long time. The Widow Preston's kindness and religious fervor impressed him deeply.

> She said she had never until within a few months learned the value of prayer, although she had prayed all her life. 'Oh, how good it is,' said she, 'to be in liberty, not to hold one's life dear; to have no fear of death or of anything men can do.'

In his *Birth of Berea,* Rogers extolled Jerusha Preston for her courage during the Exile: "Greater heroism was not manifested in the days of the American Revolution by mothers or daughters than by this widow and her children during the anti-slavery persecution. . . . "[49]

After Jerusha Preston and her family had found other lodgings, Fee reported that James Walters (whose names is sometimes given as Waters) and his family, who had settled in Macoupin County, Illinois, needed aid. They had never been very prosperous, for Fee had once described Walters as totally unfit to be a colporteur, even though he was one of the "antislavery friends," because his "only qualification [was] that he [had] not strength nor capital to make much at anything else." The Walters family's plight grew so much worse that in August Fee suggested that $30 which had been donated for Benjamin Kirby should be divided with Walters. "James Walters," Fee wrote, "is in much distress. All sick with chills, life not expected to one child. They are *suffering*. Kirby is poor but not sick."[50]

Kirby was certainly among the poorest of the poor, as his experience during this exile testifies. A young man with almost no education, Kirby was banished because he had warned Hanson of the approaching mob. Both Benjamin Kirby and his wife Nancy were natives of Kentucky, and he was an orphaned son of a very poor woman. The Kirbys wrote a joint letter to Fee and Hanson soon after their exile ended. This document, the only first-hand account of the Exile as it was experienced by the common people of Berea, provides an amazing picture of what the group as a whole may have suffered in their silence. The Kirbys' notes are written in almost illegible scrawls, the handwriting childish and unformed.[51]

Der frendes I take my pen in hand to in forme you that I am well at present time and family friende I am come back to Madison Ct. Ky. the mob is dis banded and Says that all them may come back to ther homes if they chuse. Some has come back. Haly and Blan and son have come and Tine [Valentine] Willames has come and Shady Robbers [Shadrach Roberts] is come back to his home.

My frinde I in forme you that I am in trubble I loste all my plunder [possessions] on the roade When I wente oute and I hant [haven't] hearde frome them I hante gote no bede and and [word missing] withe us to goe to house keaping on, & I would be glad if you can see your frends and you and send me some money John G. Fee I be sure that you will helpe me now trye you frendes and see whate tha [they] will do fore me & fambly

I los all my things on the road to Indiana and i cant hear of them i was sick all the time when I was there but too weeks and then I cum back to Ky and i am well. Now I hope you will help me sum if you can form [from] Benjamin Kearby to John G Hanson and John G. Fee yor frend benjamin Kearby John G fee and Hanson god bee Withe all you Willam Wright he has joined the mob party which i think he has lost all his frends on both sids [sides]

Miss Nancy L. Kerby

To my Dear Frens I take my pen in [hand] to inform you all we are well at present and hopeing at the same [time] that these few lines may find you all enjoying blessing of health we walk to indiana and Sent our boxs on the cars and never got them and walked back to ky Madison couty I send my best love and Respects to you all.[52]

From Madison County to any point in Indiana is well over 100 miles. Benjamin Kirby was 22 in April 1860, Nancy Kirby was 17; their first child was not yet two years old. Nancy had another baby sometime in 1860, so she must have been pregnant when she took her 200-mile walk.

At least 60 people were exiled early in April 1860, a sizable group to be put out of their homes and their state on a week's notice. Virtually no protest was heard in their favor; their hardships received little or no notice in the press. Why not? Because these exiles were poor mountain people, defenceless in relationship to the wealthy men who wished to expel them. They were ill-educated; they could not speak publicly for themselves, and their chief defenders, Fee and his abolitionists, were already gone. Clay had been expected to defend them; in fact, he had promised he would. But somehow he did not appear. J. B. Mallett asked, "Where is he? 13 families have been driven [out] this week. . . . Clay attempts to defend himself by *not* defending others."[53]

However, the most nearly complete record of the exiles from Madison County is a list (dated 1860) in the handwriting of Cassius Clay, giving the name of each exile who was head of a household and the number of persons in his or her family. Clay's List is headed "No. of individuals ordered off from the vicinity of Berea by the mob."—the first ten lines name the people exiled in December 1859; the next fourteen, although no distinction is made in the document itself, identify the exiles of April 1860.[54] (See Appendix 4: Clay's List of Exiles)

Their expulsion from Kentucky represented the oppression of poor people by rich people, of non-slaveowners by slaveholders, of mountain whites by

Bluegrass planters. The exiles of 1860 were *all* citizens of and almost all natives of Kentucky, most of them of Madison County; virtually all of them were poor; not surprisingly, all had some demonstrable connection with the work of Berea before their involvement in the local battle. Many of them had sent their children to the Rogers school; some were members of one of Fee's local churches; some had done construction work on Rogers' house; some were employed at John Hanson's sawmill. They were not citizens of the Glade District, but a very scattered community of families, all interrelated with one another, who lived in the mountains south of Berea near the Rockcastle County border. Hanson's mill was the center of the episodes leading to this exile; most of the people involved lived nearer to Hanson's settlement than to Berea, and many of them owed their primary allegiance to Hanson, rather than to Fee, even though they were virtually all members of Fee's Union Church or else his church in the Cummins neighborhood.

Almost all of them returned to central Kentucky because their roots were there; unlike the Northern 'interlopers,' these people had lived in the same place for years, sometimes for generations. Although none of these exiles ever wrote down such a sentiment, it is clear from their later actions that the committee's threats only increased their determination to live near Berea and support Fee. The Exile formed a community of people with their lives bound into the antislavery project; in fact, few events in the history of Madison County made more friends for Berea's work than the 1860 exile. Many years later, when Fee returned, these same people supported his school and his church again, more strongly than ever. Beginning in 1866, a great number of native Kentucky exiles cooperated in Fee's scheme for interracial education in an integrated school, which did—after all—require white people as well as black ones. For some, sending their children to school with former slaves was a chance to thumb their noses at former slaveholders who had driven them out of their own homes.

Business in Berea; Fee's Influence Persists

Although they were living in Ohio, Fee and his abolitionist friends continued to conduct business in Madison County, mainly transactions related to plans for Berea College; in January 1860, Fee sent Thomas J. Renfro $625 to pay

John Woolwine for land bought for the school—he mailed the letter to the Big Hill postoffice because it would arrive "sooner and safer." On the 16th of January, William B. Wright traveled from Berea to Germantown to deliver mail to the Fees.[55]

In April 1860, William B. Wright and Thomas J. Renfro wrote to Fee in Cincinnati, both using the same sheet of paper. Wright's note described the game of musical chairs people were playing with land and houses in Berea. The Prestons had been forced out of Fee's house, which Wright immediately occupied. "The grand cause of my mooveing [sic] to your House," Wright explained, "was to take care for very soon there would not have been a notion there." He had rented his own house to Dr. Ephraim Preston. "I intend & expect to be able to take such care of your interest here as will extort from you that good expression well done thou good & faithful tenant. . . ." In a postscript Wright added, "My family is well except my self. I have been quite unwell for some days—Martha says it is fear."[56]

Wright was in a peculiar position when he composed (and dictated) this letter; his house had been searched and he had been threatened by the exile committee, but he was *not* in exile. No, he was safely located—without the owner's permission—in Fee's house, which the loyal Prestons had been forced to vacate. Even Fee may have not have been surprised to learn a few months later that Wright had joined the mob party—his wife had rightly diagnosed his illness.

Renfro's note dealt mainly with money matters, for a reason which he made abundantly clear: he was "scarce of money," even "left minus," because he had remained behind as a "Trustee"; even though no institution existed for him to be trustee of, all the debts for Berea's pre-Exile boom were coming in for him to pay.[57]

In the meantime, school in Berea was still going on—in a way. When John Rogers and the others were driven out, Elizabeth Rawlings, Hamilton's daughter—described in the *American Missionary* as "a Southern lady, combining amiability with great decision of character"—had "announced that she would continue the school on the same principles. Accordingly she went into the schoolroom after a few days, with a little band of small scholars. . . ." She kept it up "perseveringly" well into 1860.

On her behalf, Fee applied to abolitionist friends in England for financial aid. Elizabeth had planned to prepare as a teacher, but the Exile had wrecked her chances. "This noble and brave-hearted young woman is about twenty-two years of age," Fee wrote, "has a very vigorous mind; acquires knowledge very rapidly; is very modest; and is . . . a true believer in Christ." He asked for money to pay for her schooling for one year; at the same time he requested assistance for his own daughter Laura, who also desired to become a teacher. "I once had a small patrimony," Fee explained, "but expended it in freedom's cause, and now live on the small salary of a Missionary." The people in England responded by sending money across the ocean for the benefit of the two young American women.[58]

In the district school, after Humphrey Marshall returned to Cabin Creek, Margaret West, daughter of Peter H. West, taught for a term in 1860. Then her elder brother Granville took her place; both had been among Rogers' advanced pupils. Shadrach Roberts, an 1860 exile, taught the school during its third term. These people kept alive the songs and some of the spirit of the Rogers school. Education in the region was still going on, and Fee's project was still influencing it, even though he was far away.[59]

By July 1860, Green Haley and Franklin Bland and their families had come back from their exile; by August most of the Prestons had returned as well. Presumably many other of the native exiles were living around Berea again before winter set in.[60]

In August 1860, Renfro queried Fee again about finances; he detailed how much money was due Woolwine for the college land and described other transactions, reporting by the way that Elizabeth Rawlings had received her tuition money. Other developments were not so positive: "W.B. Wright will move to the lower part of the Cty [county] or Garrard," Renfro reported, without further comment—although by this time both Fee and Renfro were well aware why Wright was leaving. There were more defections to report: "I understand Dr. [Ephraim] Preston said in your house he hoped to God you never would come back, his wife we believe is for you. I hear Some others, Speak not much better, that seem your friends (Esq. Stapp, perhaps) [parentheses in original]." Then Renfro cautioned, "These last lines keep in your own breast, lest I should be abused for truth." Wright, Ephraim Preston and William Stapp had simply saved their own skins by cooperating fully with the enemy, betraying Fee and his friends—who were also their friends *and* relatives. Wright showed his colors by fleeing the county; Ephraim Preston's true allegiance had already emerged: he and his son Reuben were both ordered out of the state, but while the son left, accompanying Jerusha Preston and her children, "the father contrived to stay at home."[61]

Other business dealings concerning Berea took place in Ohio, where Fee, Rogers and Hanson were all living in exile. They comprised the Prudential Committee (James S. Davis, although not a member of the committee, was present by invitation), which met in Fee's residence near Cincinnati on February 5, 1861, and resolved to request that John G. Woolwine make a deed to the Trustees to be held in trust by them for the use of the institution. Fee was authorized to borrow $280 from David F. Newton, one of Berea's primary financial supporters in the early years. In addition, to pay present debts, Fee was empowered to mortgage to Newton all the land purchased from Woolwine as security. The committee resolved to prepare a full statement of money received by Fee on his big, ill-fated fund-raising trip to the East and collected by Lewis Tappan, and to present the statement to the AMA. Much of those funds had only been subscribed; but Fee and his colleagues conducted their business as if it would be simple, as if collecting pledges for a hypothetical school planned in a hostile region where none of them could live would be easy.

At times it is hard to imagine what would have daunted Fee and his cohorts.

George Candee and College Plans in Jackson County

George Candee was not driven into exile in December 1859, but he and his companions, Rev. William Kendrick, an Oberlin seminary graduate whom Candee had invited to Kentucky, and colporteur Robert Jones, were seized by a mob in Laurel County. "They then had their hair and beard shaved, and their heads and faces covered with tar." Kendrick reported that the mob said they were "a committee sent to request us to leave, and not preach any more." The incident occurred when all the Madison County abolitionists were threatened with expulsion or death. "The probability is that all the brethren at Berea will be killed or driven out. They intend to kill Mr. Fee if he should come to Ky." (Fee was out of state on a fund-raising trip.) Kendrick and Candee were virtually prisoners in Jackson

County, afraid to go beyond its borders, making appointments only in McKee and Station Camp. No hero, Kendrick pointed out that Candee could deal with those places by himself and asked to be assigned some place in the North, or to be allowed to go "to Missouri for the winter."[62]

Therefore, from January 1860, when Fee and others were driven from Bracken County, to April 1861, when he and his family also fled the state, Rev. George Candee was the only AMA missionary working in Kentucky. For awhile, Jackson County, with its seven slaves in 1860 (the smallest number of any county in Kentucky), was a stronghold of safety for him—his neighbors in the mountains showed themselves willing to protect him; but, for the most part, he needed no protection, at least in early 1860. He was so poverty-stricken, so apparently insignificant, that, practically speaking, he attracted no attention to himself at all—as long as he stayed in Jackson County.[63]

In January 1860, replying to an official AMA inquiry about his finances, Candee wrote, "We are rich. We have a very rich Father. He has never let us get hungry yet, and more than that we expect he never will, unless it is to feed our souls more sumptuously with the bread of Heaven." The year before, he and his wife had spent several weeks with nothing to eat but "a little cornbread (wet up with water) and blackberries"; now they were faring slightly better. Anyway, all their friends were also impoverished, and the Candees dispensed hospitality. They lived in "a log house without partitition, ceiling or windows—a rough log stable," he called it—with about three acres of cleared land around it. The only financial need Candee foresaw was enough money to pay interest on what was due on the land. He owned one chicken and "a young nag."[64]

The Candees were indistinguishable from their neighbors in most respects; few ministers can have gone farther to identify themselves with their people. George Candee had also, inadvertently, camouflaged himself—bought with his poverty one year of grace in the mountains of Jackson County.

William Kendrick, Candees's sometime co-worker, had left Kentucky for Hamilton County, Ohio, by January 1860. He had not been driven out, he claimed, but left to stay with his sick mother in Cleves. At that time, he did not think Candee would be expelled even though his labors were "very much circumscribed." Candee was forbidden to go into Madison County "under penalty of threat of death." But Kendrick had preached at Berea shortly before leaving

Kentucky—"to the mourning forsaken ones who were left behind." He reported that school in Berea was going on and prayer meetings held on a regular basis. Cassius Clay, with considerable inconsistency, voiced his intentions of protecting Candee, who was fully as radical and religious as Fee, but had voted Republican while he was in Ohio. Candee, reporting "glorious meetings now in Station Camp" in February 1860, said himself he did not think he would have to leave Kentucky.[65]

In fact, at the end of March, he told Kendrick, "I came home yesterday from Station Camp where I had one of the largest & one of the best meetings I have ever had there. The Sabbath before I preached at Bro. Nichols on the subject of slavery to an audience of 80 or 90 attentive sympathetic hearers where I have never before had over a dozen besides his family." The Exile, it seems, had converted some "avowedly proslavery" citizens into "the wildest abolitionists."[66]

Even the explosive events near Berea in March and April 1860 left Candee and his region unscathed. In fact, Candee informed the AMA in March that "the Bereans [in exile would] soon receive a formal invitation to come to the mountains where they [could] be protected and where they [could] probably do as much good as anywhere else." Robert Jones, now under Candee's supervision, was still riding as a colporteur. On April 20, Jones filed a report in which he mentioned another candidate for colportage, Bro. William Mobley, a Methodist preacher and abolitionist. By June, Jones had stopped laboring as a colporteur for the summer, because he wanted "to make a corn crop." Soon Mobley took his place. It all sounds so normal, so very like Fee and his colporteurs before the big troubles began. In Jackson County, Candee reported, all was quiet, with no sign of molestation.[67]

In Berea, where Candee had recently visited, the situation was different; there he had found himself surrounded by a mob "pretending to be on the search of Haley and Bland"; still the people did not bother Candee. He had preached in Rockcastle County where he found the mountaineers disgusted with the Madison County mobbings. About the same time Candee heard Clay speak in Richmond, where Clay was challenged and insulted by the man who had "abused Geo. West so badly." But the man's friends took him away—perhaps to avoid having Clay kill him.[68]

Candee was following with interest a political race in Jackson County, a race in which the candidates for sheriff represented totally opposing views. One candidate, John Stephens, had interrupted John G. Fee's Fourth of July speech the previous year; the other, John Reese, had helped rally support for John G. Hanson when he returned to Madison County. Clearly, the outcome of this election might determine Candee's position in his own mission field.[69]

Miss Pratt's School and Peniel College
"It seems to be utterly impossible to give such a description of our work and surroundings, as to enable you to approach the character of our field." George Candee.

As the excitement of the exiles died down, Candee's ministry returned to normal—or, at least, he found himself able to be preoccupied with the same problems he had had to deal with before. On June 22, 1860, he wrote to John A.R. Rogers, thanking him for locating a teacher willing to come to McKee; undoubtedly, Rogers had located her at Oberlin where she was an academy student from 1858 to '60. Her name was Maria C. Pratt; she was from Boston, probably a kinswoman of Rogers, who had many Pratt relations. "Have her come by all means," Candee instructed, "though we have no house for her to teach in, still if she was here, her presence would be an incentive to action. . . . The most of the people here would oppose her as she would teach the Griffin children &c. [the Griffins were mulattoes], but many will send if she starts a school."[70]

Candee was sanguine about Miss Pratt's prospects; he thought she might be hired for the district school if she arrived in the fall, but she could surely have one at Station Camp, in any case. Eliza Candee, planning a trip East, would be able to escort Miss Pratt to Jackson County on her return; the Candees would, of course, board the new teacher, and she could assist them in the Sabbath School. Her presence, George Candee thought, might even help stamp out prejudice. People would not attend his church in McKee, which they called the 'nigger' church, although his congregations elsewhere in the county were as large as any preacher in the region could secure.[71]

Candee was beginning to see prospects of all kinds opening up; he had invented a new water-power device he wanted to patent. (Unfortunately, patent men in Cincinnati pronounced Candee's patent valueless, but that must not have daunted him—he was still working on his invention some 60 years later.) His plan involved using his new gadget to harness the streams in the local mountains, opening up factories in Jackson County. By August 21, 1860, it had occurred to him that the school project which had just failed in Madison County might work in Jackson. The other missionaries were gone, perhaps forever; by September, Candee was actively promoting "an excellent school in the mountains."[72]

When Maria Pratt arrived she reported to the AMA that she had anticipated a dark field of labor, "but not just such a darkness as I find." She announced later that Jackson County was worse than the Sandwich Islands. But by November, Miss Pratt's classes were in progress, conducted in Candee's one-room log cabin, and Candee was overwhelmed by a vision of bigger things to come. He wanted advice and consent from those in exile, trustees and a charter.[73]

Maria Pratt had 18 students in her new school, six of whom were black; two of her students came from Berea; one, who had been a teacher himself, protested the presence of the blacks, but continued to attend anyway. Another problem seems to have created more difficulty in Jackson County. "One day during school session," Miss Pratt wrote,

> the tobacco question came up. I remarked that, of course, none of my scholars would use it when they knew that I disapproved of its use, regarding it as decidedly pernicious; also a sin. Shortly after I missed from his place, a poor sickly boy about twelve years of age; as he was much interested in his studies, I sought the occasion of his absence. He said he desired "to get learning very much," but he could not give up tobacco.
> Thus for miles around, "Miss Pratt's school" has the fame of being not only "anti-caste, but anti-tobacco!" Several whom I know are disturbed from coming to school on this account, and wish to make a compromise with me; but I feel that if education is not worth more than tobacco, it is not worth seeking.[74]

As 1860 drew to a close, Candee saw more and more exciting potential in his Jackson County ministry. William Mobley, colporteur, preaching at McKee, and in Laurel (his native county) and Clay, encountered no resistance, even in the very place where Candee had been mobbed. Mobley considered prospects particularly good in Clay County and at Pond Creek in Jackson. In fact, he was finding more places to preach than he could supply. Candee himself reported that everyone was being very friendly to him, even though opposition to the 'nigger' church continued, and the anti-caste school gave "more offense than everything else combined." Candee felt that the fear of eminent civil war diverted the attention of leading men in Jackson County, else his mission would have been "interrupted."[75]

The black students at Maria Pratt's anti-caste school came from two Jackson County families. The Griffins, William and Stephen, probably brothers, mulattoes, born in Kentucky, may never have been slaves; William's wife Elizabeth was also a mulatto, but Stephen's wife Sabra was apparently white. John (or Jack) Drew, a member of Candee's South Fork Church, was a mulatto from North Carolina, but his wife Isabella was a white woman. All these people were among those whom Candee identified as the Jackson County radicals. Although they suffered persecution, these families were able to live in Jackson County in relative safety, in spite of domestic relationships which would have endangered their lives in any slaveholding community—the combination of black man and white woman being the most inflammatory, of course.[76]

Probably the Griffins and the Drews were black only by the legal fiction that made one drop of blood sufficient to determine race. Candee seems to have taught some of their children in his first school without realizing they were supposed to be black. In any case, the fact remains that there were enough tolerant or indifferent citizens in Jackson County to make the residence of the Griffins and Drews possible—and their church membership and school attendance as well.

On January 9, 1861, Maria Pratt happily reported that a new schoolhouse was being built, and the Candee's first daughter, Vena, had been born on January 3. Candee prepared to settle in earnest; by the 4th of February, he wrote that he had "organized a board of trustees to found an Institution of learning in this county. Have adopted in the main the constitution of Berea College." The new college was to be called Peniel College; its trustees: George Candee, Maria C. Pratt, Robert E. Nichols, Robert Jones, L. J. Robinson, William Blanton, Morgan N. Faubus, Elisha H. Harrison, Isaac S. Fowler, I. L. H. Young, Hardin Cox, Amos Metcalf and William Mobley. L. J. Robinson (or Robertson) of Grey Hawk was to serve as Treasurer, Maria Pratt as Secretary.[77]

Most of these individuals were local citizens. Among them, Candee's most important supporter was Robert Emmit Nichols, better known as "Radical Bob," who lived on Moore's Creek. A native of North Carolina, Nichols had been living in Rockcastle County as early as 1835, and in Pulaski by 1844. He was an outspoken abolitionist, who read all the latest antislavery literature and "taught his sons to answer the question, 'Who are you?' by saying 'I'm Bob (Jr.) or Tom [as the case may be] Nichols, abolitionist, a patriot and a lover of my country.'" Nichols owned enough land in Jackson County that he could afford to be generous for the abolitionist cause. He offered 200 acres for Peniel College, to sell "to all friends for half price [$2.00 per acre]"[78]

Of the remaining trustees, Robert Jones had been Fee's most faithful colporteur, while William Mobley was Candee's colporteur in the field when Peniel College was being chartered. The other eight men all lived in Jackson County, but their backgrounds were diverse. L. J. Robinson was a South Carolinian; Morgan Faubus, of an influential Jackson County family, was a native of Tennessee, while L. H. Young hailed from Ohio. Some of the trustees—William Blanton, Isaac S. Fowler and Elisha Harrison, for example—lived on Station Camp Creek where radicals were particularly numerous.[79]

All the trustees but Candee and Pratt were local, established citizens. Candee had found his requisite 10 Kentuckians to sign a college charter! Almost all of the Peniel trustees belonged to one of Candee's churches, and virtually all of them were—according to Candee's definition—radical abolitionists. Some (Jones, Young, Harrison) had certainly known and respected John G. Fee. Robert Nichols, in fact, named one of his sons John G. Fee Nichols (born May 23, 1858). However, the Peniel project, with all its affinities to Berea, was basically Candee's plan, not Fee's. Candee personally held the enterprise together and it had no life without him.[80]

In February, Maria Pratt's school continued to do relatively well ("Considering all circumstances," she wrote, "the school has proved a complete success."), although its 'prosperity' must have been a great hardship to the Candee family, who were boarding Miss Pratt and nine students in two rooms (evidently, a partition had been installed). However, Candee explained, three of the boys roomed "in the school room." Four or five more boarders were expected to arrive. Among the new students were "children of strong pro-slavery parents." Miss Pratt pointed out that the school was open to the sky, with the roof not entirely on; in addition, the windows—without panes throughout the month of December—had to be covered with newspapers "which neither let the light in nor kept the cold out."[81]

The main problem of the school, however, as it existed in the early months of 1861, was simple. No one in McKee, where it was located, was willing to be associated with it, either by sending or boarding students. Unlike the citizens of outlying areas, settlers in McKee had secessionist sympathies. For that reason Candee had decided the school should be removed to an area where all the friends could settle together; many of the members of his churches sent their children to Pratt's school in McKee, although they lived miles away. Nichols' offer of 200 acres seemed a perfect solution.

Candee proposed that James S. Davis, expelled from his own field in Lewis County, should come to Jackson County. (As it turned out, Davis did not go.) Already Candee had support from some who were in exile: John Rogers had amassed $174.62 for Candee's new schoolhouse (over $100 of this sum was collected at Plymouth Congregational Church in Rochester, New York). "It may be a gleam of light before a mighty tempest," Candee wrote, "but I feel more hopeful for this field now than ever before." His hopes had very little time left.[82]

On March 4, he reported, "Our stay here is barely tolerated. At McKee our religious meetings and Sabbath Schools are regularly attended only by our own family and one colored family." Candee felt that he could not adequately convey his situation to his Northern audience. "It seems to be utterly impossible," he said, "to give such a description of our work and surroundings, as to enable you to approach the character of our field."[83]

Few of the people had courage enough to espouse unpopular positions, and fewer still enough to act upon such convictions. But Candee was encouraged by Nichols' willingness to have a colony established on his land; the presence of supporters banded together in some numbers would be enormously strengthening. Candee was also encouraged by changes in Nichols himself. Although he had earned a reputation as a "fist and skull" fighter, "Radical Bob" had begun to soften under Candee's influence. He had signed the temperance pledge before he had any idea of his land being the center for Peniel College. "And though a profane swearer," Candee wrote, "[Nichols] advocated & voted for a resolution that would expell him from the Board of Trustees for profain [sic] swearing and pledged himself not to violate it." Nichols' daughter Mary Ann, boarding with the

Candees, had recently been converted, and Candee saw signs that the father was close to conversion himself. Nichols had promised to build a good house on his land for the church and the school.[84]

Contributions for Peniel College continued to come in—from Oberlin and other places. John C. Rogers, father of Berea's teacher, made a small contribution, and Grandison Fairchild, father of the Fairchild brothers who became presidents of Oberlin and Berea, sent $5.00. Rev. John F. Boughton donated $30; Candee had invited Boughton to colonize at Peniel as soon as the panic should be over. "We hope to do so," Boughton wrote, "but when is the panic to be over?"[85]

Candee's Exile
"The storm was gathering dark around us." George Candee.

On April 1, 1861, Candee, who had just turned 30, wrote his last letter from McKee. He had been to visit Berea quite recently to send John F. Boughton's goods to him (returning the famous candlemolds!). "There is a gloomy prospect there," Candee said, " I have no thought that the exiles will ever be allowed to return there, while slavery lasts." The Civil War began April 12, 1861, with the firing on Fort Sumter.[86]

Twelve days later, Candee was driven from Kentucky by a drunken mob; his wife and babies with Maria C. Pratt, followed him into exile on the 25th, David Preston escorting them to Cincinnati. John G. Hanson wrote his parents on April 28: "I was somewhat surprised to find Mrs. Candee and Miss Pratt from McKee, Ky. at our house [in Middletown, Ohio] last evening Exiles from Ky oweing to the strong opposition rising in their Co. among the drunken rowdies. Bro. Candee's life was not considered safe & it was thought best that they leave."[87]

Hanson may not have been surprised, but Fee was shocked when Candee abandoned his field. Even though Candee's life had been threatened, Fee felt that the younger missionary should have stayed in Jackson County. He had had less "direct or personal opposition than any of his friends [the other missionaries]. Yet it may be best that he is out," Fee wrote grudgingly, "I cannot tell." Fee's ruthlessness with the lives of others is fully revealed in this remark.[88]

For Candee, Fee's disapproval must have been the final straw. He had done so much to try to please the older minister, even imitating him with a church-school-colony plan of his own. Now Fee was displeased with him. Perhaps Candee's imitation had been too close for comfort; Fee may have felt his own plan had been virtually plagiarized by the younger minister.

To the AMA, Maria Pratt defended her own and Candee's flight. For some time past, she said, they had "been troubled with threats of violence, but thinking they were used to frighten us from post of duty, we took little notice of them." Then "the threats . . . became serious realities." About a week before they left they were very unsafe at night, watch was kept around their house, "while bonfires were made and guns and pistols shot by the whole town which constituted a mob." The schoolhouse was hit with rocks several times. One night Candee heard rocks striking the schoolhouse, which was at some distance from the house, and he went down to find out who was doing the throwing. They asked him his name and as he passed on "they stoned him and shot at him and when the next day he asked for protection of town officers it was denied and [he was] warned to leave immediately."[89]

Candee himself confessed to Jocelyn that he had not been "expelled," but "the storm was gathering dark around us." He described the stoning and shooting incident as an evident attempt to assassinate him. "It was painful to part from those we so much love & leave them in so great peril. All our colored brethren have been ordered to leave and have probably gone, some of them at great sacrifice."[90]

While the mob's primary purpose had been to frighten Candee away, other citizens of Jackson County were threatened, including Robert Nichols, John Casteel (brother of Hiram Casteel), the Griffins, Jack Drew, L. J. Robinson, Elisha Harrison and many others; some people of Laurel County, including William Mobley, Linsey Robinson and Levi Buckels, were included in the mobs' effort to sweep the mountains clean of abolitionism. Mobley had been threatened with tarring and feathering, and with hanging.[91]

It was rumored that Judge Faubus himself was chairman of the mob committee, so that it partook of the respectability of the Madison County committee. As a matter of fact, the Madison County group had threatened to 'invade' Jackson County at one point; they sent George Washington Maupin to McKee to talk to Judge Isaac S. Faubus and Jeff Morris about the possibility. The reply to "Wash" Maupin's message is not on record, but it is reported that he "most ran his horse to death getting back down Big Hill." Early in 1861, a drunk rode into McKee with the rumor that the Madison County committee was on its way. Candee sent word to Radical Bob Nichols and L. J. Robinson, who arrived at two o'clock in the morning with twelve armed men who guarded Candee's house until everyone was sure the drunk's report had been a rumor.[92]

The reaction of Jackson County citizens to threats of exile was not at all like the reaction in Madison. Nichols, John Reese, John Casteel, Elisha Harrison and others banded together to protect all victims of mob violence. The Griffins and the Drews, among the first families ordered off because of their African descent, were visited by John Reese, the Republican candidate for Sheriff beaten by the mob clan, who "guaranteed protection and counselled [them] not to leave." And they stayed. Many of the Jackson County radicals signed a petition demanding that Faubus execute the law since the town constable, Jack Morris, had stoned one of the black men in McKee in the presence of the judge.[93]

At any rate, the radicals of Jackson County stuck together; in fact, the Jackson County mob was "right much embarrassed," according to Mobley, by the movement against them. He believed that the mob party was in more danger of attack than the Jackson County "exiles." Candee's friends had soon "gained the ascendancy" and actually "routed the pro-slavery Judge and others who were ringleaders in driving off Bro Candee." All the men who had avowed secessionist principles were intimidated; McKee, the proslavery town in antislavery territory, was virtually abandoned. Fee had been right; Candee's flight had turned out to be unnecessary.

By June 1861, members of Candee's churches were already writing to him (he was in Lucas County, Ohio), begging him to return. But he had suffered a complete nervous breakdown and felt himself incapable of sustaining the work any longer. William Mobley wrote in July:

> Wherever I go the friends express themselves anxious for the time when bros. Candee & Fee and the Berean exiles can safely return to their homes in our hills and their labor of love, but it is the general opinion that it would not be expedient for them to do so until the close of the war. This is the general sentiment among them in Laurel, Jackson, Rockcastle & Madison.

By July the threats had died down, and those who had remained in Jackson County seemed to be completely safe.[94]

Late in July, Candee shared a letter he had received from Elisha Harrison with the AMA. Harrison, a magistrate in Cavender District, the primary stronghold of radicalism in Jackson County, a member of Candee's South Fork Church, had been a delegate to the Republican convention in Chicago. Another friend, WIlliam[son] Coyle, had sent greetings to Candee; Coyle, a noted Republican, had aided in building the schoolhouse, paid workhands out of his own store, and run the risk of receiving [apparently at the postoffice] Candee's aid from abroad. Candee could not have doubted the support of his Jackson County friends, either while he was living in McKee or afterwards.[95]

Elisha Harrison's letter was both encouraging and affectionate. He reported that all Jackson County was for the Union. On a more personal note, he said, "We have a very fine son. Born on the 6th June we call him Isaac F. If the Lord's will I want to prepare Him for Peniel College." He continues with a kind of native eloquence: [only the errors which might mislead are designated]:

> write [sic] to Miss M.C. Pratt. Tel [sic] Her that we have no language fit to express our Love and Admiration of her, of one so brave and of such generous sympathies as to pass by all the refinements of Good Society and come here, to bear the insults of the heathens here at McKee; all for the sake of Educating our children and making men and women of them; Tel here [sic] that we have nothing to good to Sacrafice for her protection not even Life Itself, and you My Dear Brother and Sister in Christ, when I think of the Insults and Abuse that was heaped upon you I allmost Conceive a Spirit of Desperation, but Blessed by [sic] God for his Mercy: He said we Should not be Tempted above that we are able to bear, and again He has said Revenge is mine and I wil [sic] repay Saith the Lord; we believe that same Good Spirit that passed by the nature of Angles [sic] and took upon Himself the seed of Abraham Directed you all here and strengthened and Guided you In this heathen Land; and May God ever bless and Comfort you all; while in this wilderness—May it pleas [sic] Him to Bring us all toGether again in This Life and help up build up Penial College. . . . [96]

In March 1862, Harrison wrote to Candee again; this time both Isaac S. Fowler and William Mobley were present when he composed the letter, and Harrison spoke for all of them. They believed Candee would be safe to locate at Station Camp or anywhere else in Jackson County. McKee seemed "destined for desolation"; the primary opposition to Candee was simply disappearing. "There is such grate call for you here that we believe that God will prosper you here," Harrison said, "We want you to bring with you a teacher for ignorance is one of the pillows [he means pillars!] that Sustains this Rebelion here in the South and we don't want rising generation brought up In the same School the present one was."[97]

By the end of May 1862, Candee did visit Jackson County, taking with him John A.R. Rogers. At that point, Candee seems to have been eager to return, probably with Rogers as Peniel College's first teacher. Rogers noted his and Candee's journey to central Kentucky, where they had found "very much to encourage" them. They spent the days from May 26 to June 9 visiting and preaching before they returned to Ohio.[98]

But Peniel College had missed its moment; George Candee would never live in Jackson County again. A war that was to stretch on and on changed everyone's plans—soon Rogers, Fee and Candee himself would be involved in work no one could have foreseen for them, Rogers with an entirely new school in Decatur, Ohio; Fee and Candee with contrabands. The Bereans, returning to Kentucky years later, had no particular affinity with Jackson County. Fee himself was not attracted to a colonizing site on Robert Nichols' farm. When Candee finally returned, he settled not in McKee but in Berea where many of his Jackson County parishioners were relocated themselves.

Nevertheless, Candee's project had very nearly made it into existence. If the timing had been just a little different what is now Berea College would probably not exist: the funding and support of the AMA would have gone to Peniel College, which would have drawn Berea's students and attracted Berea's workers, since it was beginning with Berea's ideals and program. Colony, church, college, antislavery, anti-caste, anti-rum . . . even if Peniel College had started and lasted as long as five or six years its existence could have effectively blocked the way to a similar institution 25 miles away in Berea.

Some foundation stones of a building on Pond Creek may provide the only physical evidence that Peniel College was ever planned. In another sense, however, Candee's college came to a full realization in Berea. Elisha Harrison and many, many other citizens from Jackson County turned to Berea College after the war; in fact, many of the families of Jackson County, became, along with the native exiles of Madison County, the most faithful supporters Berea ever had. The foundations of their loyalty, a crucial aspect of Berea College's relationship to Appalachia, were laid in the ministry of George Candee and his abortive plans for a college in the mountains.

CHAPTER EIGHT

MISSIONARIES IN EXILE

Lecturers: "Scattering the Much Needed Light"

As soon as the first group of exiles arrived in Cincinnati, friends urged them to inform the American public of the injustices they had suffered. They were advised that those who were strong in public speaking should be employed for months in Pennsylvania, New York and points east, "scattering the much needed light." Rogers, Fee, Boughton and others followed this advice almost immediately. And almost immediately, financial contributions for those in exile began pouring in. People who had not sympathized with abolitionists before became interested in the groups whose civil rights had been so openly violated—even a few slaveholders and Democrats lent them some support.[1]

Early in January 1860, Fee lectured in Cincinnati—as did Rogers, Hanson, Boughton and Reed. One sabbath they all spoke in different places in the same city. By the 12th, Rogers had presented "the interests of Ky" at Oberlin and Pittsfield and was planning a trip to Cleveland. A meeting had been arranged for the exiled abolitionists in Oberlin; meanwhile, Professors Morgan and Fairchild advised their former student to lecture for some months on the subject of Kentucky and the Exile.[2]

Boughton, who arrived in Oberlin while Rogers was still there, had spoken at the Free Presbyterian Church near Chillicothe, Ohio, where the congregation had offered his wife and daughter, then desperately ill, shelter for the winter. (The little girl's illness Boughton ascribed to the "overdoing, excitement, exposure" of the exile journeys. On January 23, Lizzie Rogers wrote Anna Shailer Griffith that

Libbie Boughton was quite sick, probably dying. Raphael Rogers was also seriously ill at the same time.) Boughton reported that the whole company of Bereans had incurred expenses of about $150 in their flight. He and Rogers planned to publish a tract about the Exile, although that project was never realized.[3]

Later in January, Rogers and Boughton held joint meetings in Cleveland and Collaman. Rogers found his lecture tour somewhat trying at times—during his last speaking engagement in Cincinnati, he said he had been "mortified," adding "It was what I needed. The moment I crossed the Ohio river I felt my old pride & ambition rising & found that it required far more grace to obtain a victory over the same than the fear of death." In any case, he planned to speak in Willoughby, Painesville, and at James A. Thome's church in West Cleveland, before leaving for New York.[4]

Boughton, now traveling alone, intended to lecture at the significantly named Berea, Ohio, but he was prevented by a smallpox epidemic there. He had collected some $40 at other recent meetings. He regarded his position as Exile lecturer as a powerful one: on January 27, he wrote that he expected James S. Davis to be expelled from Kentucky, but stated, "If he is he will thereby be furnished with a sword with two edges instead of one."[5]

Briefly, Boughton teamed up with Hanson, who had spoken at several churches and at Lane Seminary, and the pair began a speaking tour in Indiana, while James S. Davis, now in exile too, added his efforts to the lecturing enterprise by speaking in Wakeman, Ohio, Chicago and Galesburg, Illinois. Rev. Joseph E. Roy of Chicago, a graduate of Knox College, suggested to Davis that he tell his story in various parts of Illinois before settling down. (Davis collected $16 from a Wakeman congregation for clothing for A. G. W. Parker's family.)[6]

Meanwhile, Boughton and Hanson enjoyed considerable success with their tour. One Indiana paper described them:

> Their appearance is prepossessing—that of Christian gentlemen—and is alone sufficient to demonstrate to an unprejudiced mind, that they would be any thing rather than disturbers of the peace or best interests of any community which they might select for a residence.

The pair attracted a large audience at a Methodist church where Boughton spoke of the last sabbath at Berea, describing "their parting with their parishioners, who were overcome with grief and dissolved in tears at losing their best friends." Then Hanson delivered "a stirring appeal to the Northern people to do more constantly their whole duty, in effectually divorcing themselves from all support of American slavery, and in steadfastly opposing not merely its extension, but the institution itself."[7]

Fee was in great demand—with "hundreds of congregations now desiring [him] to come," but for awhile his health would not permit him to travel. However, on the 16th of March 1860, Fee reported to the AMA that he had received $90 for the benefit of the exiled brethren; he also listed his expenditures for the exiles, which included $4 for J. D. Reed, who had recently "buried a child." Fee had himself been on tour in Ohio, although he said, "My head is at this time hurting me much." A few days later he received a $25 gift from the Ladies' Anti-Slavery Society of Dover, New Hampshire, for relief of the exiles.[8]

The refugees from Kentucky were celebrities throughout the world of abolitionism, widely in demand for their lectures and generously supported. The AMA administered an Exile fund, with contributors from all the New England states, New York, Pennsylvania, Michigan, Wisconsin, Iowa, Minnesota, Indiana, North Carolina, East Canada and France. Expenses from all the different exile-periods were covered: Fee sent Tappan an accounting which included expenses for the first and second exodus, payment to Levi Coffin for board for the exiles, emergency funds for Parker, Grigson, Davis, etc. Eventually, this money was also applied to the needs of Bracken County citizens and natives of Madison County who were exiled later.[9]

J. B. Mallett, schoolteacher from Bracken County, joined the lecture circuit, and, according to Fee, performed very well. Another "lecturer," A. G. W. Parker, collected some $60 in Indiana on the strength of being an exile, returned to Berea, "displayed his money, [boasting] what the North had done for him, [and] represented them as ready to go to any length in their opposition to slavery." His trip to Berea coincided with Hanson's return, and he seems to have precipitated the retaliations which eventually imperiled Hanson—so Parker's post-exile work, like his whole colportage career, was a doubtful achievement.[10]

Fee continued to travel and speak in spite of ill health. On one trip he was "greatly chilled riding" and "in great distress of body & head," but he still lectured in Moscow, Manchester and Ripley, Ohio. Shortly afterward, Mallett wrote that

Fee was "very weak & must rest or die. I never saw him look so feeble." Eventually, all the lecturers concluded their labors; James S. Davis, who had traveled in Illinois, Ohio and Michigan, was still sepaking about Kentucky in July 1860, but Rogers remained on the circuit longer than any of the others—until September 1860. In his journal Rogers wrote on September 3: "I have spent the past seven months lecturing on behalf of Southern missions in New York City & vicinity[,] Massachusetts & Connecticut. The Lord has been with me & greatly blessed me though I have often yes continually grieved Him." The *American Missionary* reported in October 1860 that the exile lecturers had awakened "an interest in thousands, in the missions in the slave States." But, inevitably, the exiles had to relocate, find permanent work, stop talking about Kentucky and stop living as if a return there might be possible next week or the next. . . . .[11]

On January 16, 1861, Hanson had just suffered *another* forcible expulsion from Kentucky. He had been in Bracken County for weeks as his wife had been confined there, and he stayed longer doing some work for his father. In addition, Oliver Grigson's wife had returned to visit some friends and Grigson himself crossed the river for a few days. A meeting of the committee was called, precipitated simply by the presence of two exiled abolitionists—and then another meeting, which directed members to warn Greenbury Hanson, Vincent Hamilton and others against harboring any exiles, Fee or Hanson, or any "Northerners." Hanson and Grigson had to flee Bracken County again.[12]

Anonymous letters circulating in Bracken at this time spread a rumor that Fee was raising a band of men to invade the county. A former committee member remarked to a friend who scoffed at such a foolish tale: "It is hard to tell what a man will do who has been treated as he (Fee) has been." Fee's friends in Bracken County were understandably depressed. And so was Hanson, thwarted in all his desires. He was in most trying circumstances again—"driven from home & property in Madison—driven from his father's house & from his wife and children—from employment."[13]

Rogers in Exile

In August 1860, John Rogers attended a meeting of the Kentucky exiles at Oberlin, coinciding with commencement exercises. Davis, Boughton, and their wives, E. T. Hayes and Swinglehurst Life, were all present, along with Maria Pratt, who was on her way into Kentucky at the time. Mrs. Boughton was a little "cast down," but all the rest were described as hopeful. Rogers wrote that Whipple had "cheered & strengthened" the exiles on this occasion. By September, Candee had invited Rogers to join him in Peniel Colony—and Rogers had said he would be "happy to go to Jackson county." [14]

Meanwhile, Lizzie and the two little boys were staying with Rogers' parents in Pittsfield. She was pregnant again; in the midst of his lecture tour, she begged her husband "to find [them] a home, if it was only a shanty, [she] was so homesick." [15]

In January 1861, his lecturing days effectively over, Rogers expressed a willingness to preach at some church or churches under the auspices of the AMA, but he asked for a "thoroughly established" church, so he could leave it at any time and go back to Kentucky. He had been collecting money for Candee's Peniel Colony, which was now ostensibly Rogers' goal as well. [16]

On January 23, Rogers received a letter from his sister Amelia Davis describing the attack of a mob upon the family with whom the Davises were boarding in Southern Illinois (Broad Oak); three days later she arrived in Pittsfield for a visit, and for some relative safety as well. From her, Rogers probably learned that James S. Davis wanted him to join the Davises in the settlement at Hoyleton, Illinois. At the same time, Rogers was planning to meet the next week with Davis, Hanson and Fee to settle Berea business, and a Free Presbyterian church in Decatur, Ohio, invited Rogers for a trial visit. Rogers had so many options at this point he must have been paralyzed trying to choose! [17]

Soon Rogers received a call to the church in Decatur and—after some of his usual reservations and soul-searchings—eagerly accepted. Decatur was about 10 miles north of Maysville, Kentucky; the church would leave Rogers free to travel half the time as an evangelist and missionary, and he could easily reach Bracken and Lewis Counties, where he was already known, in a day's journey. Davis and

Hanson advised him to locate in Decatur, but Fee thought it might better for him to go out as a Christian laborer without any church connections. One might suspect that Fee's opposition was the deciding factor: Rogers decided to do precisely the opposite of what the older minister suggested. "It was so near the Ohio River," Lizzie Rogers wrote, "we could almost see the Kentucky shore, and it made a good tarrying place until the troubles died down, and we could resume our work again, for we never for one moment gave up the thought of returning to our Kentucky home." Soon after locating, Rogers became interested in working in two black settlements, both destitute, 15 miles away. Rogers, of course, plunged instantly into his pastoral duties at the Free Presbyterian Church in Decatur, multiplying his own labors as much as he could, since overwork was a necessity of his moral life. But he did not forget Kentucky; Lizzie's claimed that they never gave up the thought of returning, although going back was a very difficult prospect for many reasons.[18]

Lizzie Rogers was ailing: unwell during her pregnancy, slow to recover after delivery. The Rogers' third son, Joseph Morgan Rogers, was born in March 9, 1861. On April 19, Rogers wrote that his wife was still "very feeble" and might have to remain quiet for weeks. It was difficult for them to settle in; they had no home of their own until the middle of March, and their possessions, such as bedclothing, were still arriving from Berea in April. But in May, Rogers was already writing enthusiastically about returning to Kentucky. Seven of the "respectable & wealthy [Exile] committee" were dead by that time, one having been recently "cut to pieces in an affray." "God has said," Rogers quoted, "Vengeance is mine I will repay." All the Kentucky missionaries wanted to go back, he added, cheerfully.[19]

In July, Rogers received an invitation to the chaplaincy of the 8th Ohio Regiment. He declined, as he thought the post not as favorable to his "life work in the South," as the ministry he held. As the war progressed, Rogers was repeatedly asked to be a chaplain for the Army (or, in one instance, for the Navy), "but the old call to Kentucky stood in the way. . . . Each year," Lizzie wrote, "he hoped to find himself back in his chosen field of labor." Her father and brother were both soldiers, so she experienced much anxiety and fear during the war years. The Rogers themselves were relatively safe in Decatur, although their location was so close to the Kentucky border that they could sometimes hear battles and marauding bands of rebels passed nearby.[20]

Despite all his other options, Berea still retained its place in Rogers' plans; he invited his good friend Charles C. Starbuck, a fellow Oberlin graduate, then missionary in Jamaica, to come to Kentucky to join the workers there. Starbuck agreed, but Rogers had recruited him for a labor that was no more than a receding memory of the past and a faint hope for the future. When Rogers himself received a letter (April 24, 1862) from Rev. Mr. Simeon S. Jocelyn proposing that he should go "speedily" to Kentucky, Rogers was "tried in [his] temper." He was certainly not eager to go at that time, not at the command of someone in New York City—maybe not at anyone's 'command.'

His primary reservation was the continuing influence of Fee in Berea. Rogers confided to Whipple and Jocelyn his concerns about Fee's Kentucky free churches, which he said were being educated into right doing, rather than into Christ. He said he did not hold the same opinion about Candee's churches, a clue that he objected to Fee's position on baptism more than any other issue, since Candee and Fee held identical antislavery, anti-caste beliefs. Fearing legalism in Fee's congregations, Rogers claimed he was glad of the Exile because the Berea missionaries might return to start on a different footing. He hastened to add that he intended no disloyalty to Fee; "I love & honor [him] the more, the more I know of him." But, clearly, he had no desire simply to revert to the service of Fee's insistent vision. He wanted to return to Kentucky, but not to John G. Fee.[21]

In May, Rogers and Candee visited Kentucky together, going first to Bracken County, where Rogers was sick at Hanson's house; on the 29th the two preachers arrived at the residence of Hamilton Rawlings, who provided them with hospitality, and on June 1 they began to preach: Rogers in the morning on the bread of life, Candee in the evening. Both men were very much encouraged by what they saw in Berea. Rogers was especially heartened to learn that "almost all householders in the Berea area kept muskets and were sworn to use them to protect law-abiding Union men," an observation more practical than pious—and not at all in his usual vein.[22]

On his return to Decatur, Rogers asked his wife about returning to Berea in August. "She did not seem to feel it wise," Rogers wrote on the 11th of June, "Though a trial I leave it with the Lord." The next day his journal entry read:

"Lizzie is quite willing to go to Ky." He does not explain what pressure he applied—if any—to change her mind.

Rogers and Fee visited one another several times in the summer of 1862, and spent one session riding around Decatur discussing—you guessed it!—baptism. When Rogers returned from this trip the plastering in his house fell on his head, but he did not interpret the incident as a sign. On August 11, Rogers recorded a "refreshing interview with Bro Fee concerning Ky," but that night he was unable to get to sleep because he "was tempted to be jealous." He fails to specify of whom for what. Presumably, he meant Fee, but it is difficult to see anything enviable in Fee's precarious position at this time. Nevertheless, the relationship between Rogers and Fee had undergone a great shift. They would work together again, but never in unison, never in basic agreement and perhaps never in harmony or affection.

During this period Fee himself was experiencing doubts about relocating in Berea on the bases of infertility of soil and immorality of the people around. Rogers argued Fee down, saying "Better barren Plymouth than fertile Carolina," pointing out, as Fee himself had done, that "the historical associations that the [Bereans] have with the past are of no little value." The Berea exiles had already seen how valuable Berea's troubles were for raising money—"for the place had assumed national importance." Rogers was enjoying his work in Decatur, but he wrote, "I feel a longing to be at work in Kentucky & shall hasten there as rapidly as possible."[23]

He insisted that Peniel and Berea would not conflict, and, even though his Ohio friends opposed his going, and his family could not accompany him, he determined to go to Berea. His name had just been enrolled in Ohio as subject to the draft—so he had to hurry if he was to keep control of his own future.[24]

Rogers' Return to Berea

On August 18, 1862, Rogers packed his goods to go to Kentucky; on the 22nd his journey began. He drove a buggy pulled by his horse Rosa, even though the trip was some hundred miles. He stopped first in Augusta, Kentucky, to pick up Matilda Fee and Laura and Burritt, who were to travel with him. Rogers preached at Bethesda Church on Sunday; then on Monday the 25th of August, the little party sat out in a buggy and a carriage; they spent the first night at Millersburg, and passed through Lexington the next day. On the 27th they met the Union Army at Richmond and with some difficulty persuaded Union pickets to allow them to go on to Berea.

In Berea, Rogers continued writing cryptically in his journal in spite of the magnitude of the events afoot in Madison County: Rebel invasion of Kentucky and the Battle of Richmond.

> 29th While removing roof from house heard firing of cannon. 30th Battle near Richmond. A solemn day. 31st A very brief meeting. Most of the people go to the battlefield. Sept 1st Remove roof. Work at house for two or three days & leave it.

Roger's preparations on the house, as he labored to make it comfortable for the return of his family, seem to have distracted him almost altogether from the Battle of Richmond, "one of the hardest fought and most disastrous to the Union forces of any of the battles of the war." It was also the battle which would result in the Confederate Army gaining control of most of Kentucky; now Mrs. Fee and her children and John A. R. Rogers were trapped behind enemy lines.[25]

Lizzie Rogers was supposed to follow her husband to Berea, but on the day of her departure, even as she donned her hat and cloak to leave the house, news came that Kirby Smith was in Kentucky. She wanted to go anyway, but her neighbors and friends would not permit it. War excitement was high in Ohio at this time; Confederate troops were approaching Cincinnati, which was under martial law. Lizzie was in the seventh month of her fourth pregnancy. Years later, she described her feelings to her children: "Sadly I turned back to the deserted home to take up my lonely life as best I might. I had little hope your father would escape the enemy." As the days passed she received no letters, but newspapers were full of dire reports. Ohio towns along the Kentucky border, especially Cincinnati, grimly prepared for invasion by Rebel forces. "I learned then," Lizzie wrote, "how long a day could be, and the nights were longer still. It sometimes seemed as if to know your father was quietly sleeping the sleep of death would have been a comfort. I feared only the worst. I grew old and sick at heart."[26]

No one was receiving any direct news from Berea—neither Lizzie Rogers nor John G. Fee. Hoping against hope, Fee reported to the AMA (September 29, 1862) that Rogers' school would be in progress by that time. But Rogers was certainly not teaching school when Fee filed his report. Kirby Smith's Confederate troops were encamped in the Glade, and pickets were observed on the main street of Berea, "one of them frying slices of raw pumpkin, while another had his shirt off and wrong side out looking for 'gray back' lice." Rogers' journal, beginning at October 8, gives a detailed account of his experiences in Berea:

> Oct 8th. From Sept 1st a reign of terror. I remained at Berea with the exception of a week spent in the mountains of Jackson co. strengthening the members of Bro. Candee's churches. During this reign of terror I was brought to view death as at hand. Though at times I suffered from fear whenever I came very near to my Lord he removed fear & greatly comforted me. Twice I slept out once in the woods—once ran from the rebels. Otherwise except as I twice read for two hours in the woods I remained at home (Bro. Fee's) or visited from house to house.[27]

Many Union men had to flee from their homes after the battle, "like the partridges in the mountains," Rogers said, echoing John G. Hanson's imagery. "Some grey-haired men in our vicinity," he wrote, "to keep out of the way of the rebels, left their homes and spent their time in thickets and mountain fastnesses for weeks, sleeping in the open air, in caves, and getting food as they could from friends." Rogers himself was threatened with hanging by some former residents of Madison County who had enlisted in the Rebel army.[28]

When Rogers hid in the woods he was accompanied by Teman Thompson, also on the run. Although Rogers escaped from Berea, Thompson was captured there and sent to Libby Prison in Richmond, but it was rumored that he had been hanged with 15 others at Cumberland Ford. (Thompson was safely back in Berea by February 1863.) It is baffling that Rogers fails to mention his fellow fugitive in the journal account—particularly given the kind of details he does mention:

> I studied Nordhumer's Hebrew Grammar and "Aids to Faith" &c. learned anew or rather as never before in reading Christ's Atonement an article in Aids to F. that Christ died for man's sins. I thought of starting homeward sooner than I did but waited the Lord's direction. I learned what Christ meant when He said to his mother at Cana "My hour has not yet come." This morning Oct 8th I started for Decatur not having heard a word from my family since I

> left Decatur. Arrived at Lewis Cox's & spent the night. 9th David Preston left me here neither of us thinking it wise for him to come on. At Mr. Wiseman's received a cordial welcome. At Irvine was closely eyed & was glad to get away. Was stopped on the road by a rebel citizen. Saw a man shot by the rebels. Arrived at Mr. Blevins' on the Red River where I spent a sleepless night.

The Blevins family had been recommended to him as willing to shelter a Union man, but were otherwise unknown to Rogers. "The Emancipation Proclamation had recently been made and at supper the woman of the house said, 'When you get to Ohio tell everybody we want to cut Lincoln's heart out for freeing the niggers.'" (Lincoln's preliminary Emancipation Proclamation was issued September 23.)[29]

Rogers replied, "Lincoln has done right."

The woman lifted her hands in horror and stated, "If you had said that anywhere else, your life would not be worth a straw." Actually, Rogers concluded his life was not worth a straw right then and there, and "spent a sleepless night."[30]

> 10th Went throught highways, byways & fields to Henry Reed's avoiding Rikes & Mt. Sterling. Ran among rebel infantry, got lost, came in sight of rebel Cavalry from whom & from all other dangers my good Lord delivered me. After dark, wet & weary I arrived at Mr. Howe's where I received a most cordial welcome. O Lord how great was thy goodness. 11th Lay too late in the morning & grieved my Lord. Came near running into rebel cavalry, went a long circuit & arrived at Maysville at 10 p.m. finding all my family well.

Rogers had to swim his horse across the Ohio River at Maysville, and did not arrive at his home until about midnight, "a safe and happy man." The fortunes of war were turning again, and by October 13, the day after Rogers reached Decatur, the Confederate army was retreating from Kentucky into Tennessee, although there were skirmishes near Paint Lick and Big Hill later on in the month. By early November, Confederates were being hanged in Rockcastle County.[31]

Rogers in Decatur, Ohio

The Rogers' fourth son, Lewis Fairchild Rogers (named after Rogers' professor at Oberlin), was born November 4, 1862, in Decatur. Lizzie Rogers, as usual, had a difficult labor. Probably she had been very fortunate that the war had prevented her from joining her husband in Berea, where medical treatment would have been impossible to procure. She did not leave her room until the 18th of November. For obvious reasons, the family gave up the idea of returning to Kentucky at this time.

Rogers' church work continued, and he was teaching now as well. The Rogers family were enjoying a very busy social life; in his journal Rogers recorded dozens of visits with church members and parents of students: the Decatur Church was a growing concern, apparently with a large membership—at least, much larger than any of the Kentucky churches Rogers had pastored. Some of the people in Decatur became very friendly with Rogers, including the Snedakers and Robes (names that would become very familiar in Berea a few years later).

Rogers' school suffered an upset on April 22, 1862, when two black girls, Berilla and Julia Hines, began attending it. Their presence "caused a great excitement" and several students left the school: there was much prejudice against Negroes in Rogers' region, and their children were banned from public schools. The next day Rogers received a letter from James H. Fairchild asking him to serve as agent for Oberlin College. Later on, in the summer of 1863, Rogers assisted James Mercer Langston, a black lawyer (Oberlin graduate), in recruiting black soldiers for the first Negro regiment from Ohio. In addition, during this period, Rogers was appointed examiner for Marietta College and also for Lane Seminary. His reputation as an educator and reformer was growing rapidly.[32]

In his Decatur church, Rogers raised the questions of tobacco as a sin and of anticaste. He had intended to go to Berea again, but a young man from his church who was with the army in Kentucky came home and urged Rogers not to go. Rogers had a "triumph" with the anticaste question in Decatur—and with anti-tobacco as well; at his big revival the preacher was James M. West, former Bracken County colporteur, now a minister himself in a church near Decatur.[33]

In June 1863, Rogers visited Candee in St. Louis where the latter was ministering to contrabands. At the Freedman's Sunday School at Zion Church, Rogers met "Robert Wade a colored man of great simplicity of heart to whom [he] taught a part of the alphabet & told of Jesus' love. . . . " This journey marked Rogers' first real contact with black people as subjects for missionary work. He visited sick soldiers, converting one 16-year-old who "promised to trust the Lord with all his heart." He spoke to the freedmen at the Missouri Hotel, preached at the Second Colored Baptist Church, and went with Candee on the latter's various assignments—in barracks, hospitals and churches.

When he returned to Decatur, Rogers went as a militia soldier to Ripley, expecting a fight with Morgan's Raiders. Excitement was high, but Rogers saw no actual combat, even though Morgan passed within two miles of Rogers' home, "robbing & plundering." Rogers' work in Ohio, already very demanding and engrossing, increased. On August 3, 1863, his school officially became Decatur Academy, with Rogers himself serving on the board of trustees and Prudential Committee. Unavoidably now, he was drawn into a work that rivaled the claims of Berea on his life. His ill-fated trip to Kentucky had confirmed him in the belief that he could not simply wait.

The first session of Decatur Academy began September 1, 1863. Laura Fee, one of the early students at this institution, may have attended the first term. The school seems to have been a success from the beginning, although Rogers worried about it. The school board voted on September 11 that the Academy would admit black students. On September 13, Rogers recorded this entry: "Saw that I had been anxious about the Academy & had been afraid that colored students would attend. I humbled myself." A couple of months later, still troubled by the admission of black students, Rogers discussed the issue with his sister-in-law, Sallie Embree, who urged him "to be very bold."[34]

From the time of the opening of his academy, Rogers stops referring to Berea in his journal. His Ohio friends, especially his students, receive all his attention. One of the latter was William Robe (later a student and teacher at Berea College); on December 9, Rogers wrote, "Talked and prayed with Willie Robe who is about to go to the Army."

As trustee and teacher at Decatur Academy, the name of which was changed to Ohio Valley Academy in February 1864, Rogers found himself more and more drawn to the new work. Kentucky, however, still had a hold on him. He had begun preaching in Bracken and Lewis Counties from time to time, since Decatur was so close to Fee and Davis's old fields. But in June, Fee, at Rogers' suggestion, wrote to Oberlin and Hillsdale, looking for a new principal for the school at Berea. At that point, Rogers himself was apparently not planning to return to Kentucky, and Fee, clearly enough, did not want him back.[35]

By February 1865, however, Fee having failed to find a replacement, Rogers decided it would be wise for him to go soon to Berea. In fact, he wanted to return immediately while Fee still needed him desperately. On February 20, Rogers wrote to Whipple, "I have always felt since leaving Berea that my life work was to be there. Bro Fee and myself can work together happily and harmoniously though doubtless he would be very glad if I were an immersionist." At a meeting of the Ohio Valley Academy board of trustees, however, all the members urged Rogers to "give up going to Kentucky for the present." He wrote sadly, "The indications of God's spirit and providence are that I should remain here for another year." Fee had informed Rogers by this time that he had a teacher for Berea anyway and no house for the Rogers family.

In April, Rogers visited Berea, traveling by boat to Cincinnati, by rail and stage to Richmond, and on foot the last fifteen miles to Berea, after which, as he confided in his journal, he "Was weary." He saw "the wondrous change in five years in slavery" and observed "some patrolled rebel soldiers on stage for Richmond." The 'wondrous change' had begun in Berea too: the Prudential Committee planned to open the school the next March; a school building was to be constructed and the town laid out. Rogers settled the final business with John Woolwine for the college tract and then rode with Fee to Camp Nelson before returning to Ohio.[36]

Reporting this visit Rogers was most sanguine:

> The church [at Berea] is receiving new life and is hopeful. The Trustees of the Lit. Inst. [Literary Institute: the new school, not yet a college] at Berea, have arranged to erect a desirable building for the growing wants of the school. A town planned before the rebellion has been more fully laid out, machinery is being introduced, and new desires are being enkindled in the minds of the people. With God's blessing it will not be many years before mighty streams of influence for good will go forth from Berea in every direction. The seed sown will yet bear fruit an hundred fold.

Fee's labors with contrabands at Camp Nelson, Rogers said, were "abundantly blessed. Through his untiring efforts hundreds of lives have been saved, their physical comfort greatly increased and fuller provisions made for their spiritual wants." He had founded a church and schools. For some time, Fee had been considering centering his own mission at Camp Nelson rather than Berea: it was possible Rogers might have Berea to himself.[37]

Meanwhile, Rogers was finding more opportunities to work with black people himself. One hundred ex-slaves from Kentucky had settled near Decatur, and Rogers had established a Sabbath school for them—and he had plans for establishing a day school soon, since Ohio law made it impossible for blacks to enter public school if a single white householder objected.[38]

At noon on November 30, 1865, after two weeks of travel, Rogers and all his family arrived at Berea to take up residence again, almost six years after they had been driven out. The house they had been building before the Exile was uninhabitable; so the Rogers family was forced to share a house with new staff members Willard W. and Ellen Wheeler. "Outward comforts not abundant," Rogers wrote on December 2, "Favorable weather." On December 3, a Sunday, Rogers preached on the text: "Let us arise and build for God will prosper us."

His wife, writing years later about their return, recalled, "At the first glimpse of the Kentucky hills, [his] eyes began to glisten. Once more he was on his own ground. Then I knew why the offers of prominent church or position, during the war, could not tempt him from his chosen work. In all the years of our absence I had seen no such look on his face."[39]

Fee's Tragedy: Problems and Persistence
"The cup is a bitter one—but my Heavenly Father will overrule it for my good."
John G. Fee.

After being twice exiled from Kentucky, Fee settled with his family in Ohio, "one mile below Cincinnati," very close to the Kentucky border. Rev. J. D. Reed and his family, in dire financial straits, rented part of the house with the Fees. On April 29, 1860, when the families had barely moved in, Fee's youngest son Tappan died of typhoid.[40]

Fee's announcement of his son's death, composed only three days after the event, measures the depths of his despair and the even deeper foundations of his faith.

In this labor of moving & gathering together things in the stead of that lost scattered by ·the [sic] in consequence of the

Madison mob our little boy was probably [last word crossed out] somewhat exposed, took a fever, which soon assumed a typhoid form; settled early upon the glands of his throat, which became swolen [sic] & putrid, baffling all skill & nursing. After some two weeks sickness developed evident marks of death. These appeared last Sabbath morning, his throat swelled rapidly & the blood receded from the extremities. At 20 minutes past 8 ocl. P.M. he was manifestly [word omitted] He remained very sensible up to the last hour. At 20 minutes past 8 p.m. was manifestly struggling for breath & looking up at me very earnestly he extended his hands to me and with his little hands clinging to mine he died. None but the bereaved can know what we as parents felt when we looked upon the lifeless & livid form.

On Monday we gathered up the dear body and brought it to this county [Bracken], the place of our birth, the home of our relatives, and the field in which for years we spent part of our gospel labors--from which we had recently been driven [last two words crossed out] retired because of then excited state of the populace. In the little graveyard attached to the Free Church here we prepared a last resting place for the body of our boy.[41]

A large crowd attended the funeral; Fee preached the sermon himself. "We think that good was done," he wrote,

which will yet be seen. Nature feels the loss—the loneliness oh how great. Nothing but the consolations of the gospel—the consideration that Christ has become his teacher & guardian instead of myself. . . .

The cup is a bitter one—but my Heavenly Father will overrule it for my good. I shall as never before be able to sympathize with the bereaved & to see the goodness of God in the gift of children and to realize the terribleness of sin as never before. The wages of sin is death.[42]

Fee was not easily resigned to the loss of his child; later he would confess that in his affliction he had been "seriously anxious and troubled." The calling upon which he had staked his life had been taken from him; he had lost his work, his home, his possessions and now his child. When Tappan died he was not quite four years old, "bright and promising." In response to a letter of condolence from Lewis Tappan, for whom the child had been named, Fee wrote, "I loved the child greatly. . . . Oh it would have been to me a great pleasure to have had him where you & sister Tappan could have seen him—you will see him—Bright boy, oh my bright boy. Jesus wept & he can sympathize with me."[43]

Fee buried his child in Bracken County, Kentucky, to "strengthen [his own] purpose to return," to confirm his claim upon his native soil and his field of labor. The body of his dead son became Fee's symbol of the covenant he had made years before, his sign that he would never give up the work in Kentucky. In the face of discouragement which would have deterred almost anyone else, Fee resolved anew to return to his God-given mission—a resolution which in the next few years would appear more and more impossible to fulfill.[44]

Soon after the funeral, Fee returned from Ohio to Bracken County bringing with him head and foot stones to erect in the cemetery. When he left the boat at Augusta he was "surrounded by a mob, a gathering of citizens, many of whom considered themselves respectable people"; they detained him for awhile, but their "mere hostility to . . . a known abolitionist" could not be sustained, for the "outrage [was] too gross." Eventually, they let him go on his way to perform his sad errand. He preached one more time at Bethesda Church and returned to Ohio.[45]

He began preaching at a new church in Jacksonburg, Ohio, near Cincinnati, sharing the work with Jacob Emerick, But Fee was greatly debilitated, unable to do much studying. He found, he wrote, "the excitement of attending meetings" sometimes brought on "that pressure on my brain as if your hand were on my head." Constantly tired and usually in pain, he began a schedule of preaching every Sunday, although he was not being paid. Tappan's funeral expenses had depleted his funds, and he was unable to pay the physician who had attended the dying child.[46]

Prospects did not improve. Like Fee, Reed was in utter poverty, without one dollar, and could not pay his share of the rent, which the landlord demanded. Several of Reed's family had been sick, one of his children had also died, he was in feeble health himself and had been disappointed in promised work. At one point, Reed was reduced to exchanging gooseberries and apples for other foodstuffs.[47]

Still Fee had loaned $12 to George Candee, in Ohio for a series of meetings, leaving himself with exactly $1.50 "in pocket." Fee and Candee spoke jointly on June 19, "urging Federal action in abolishing the cause of the war," which they identified as slavery. The juxtaposition of crushing poverty and lofty missionary zeal is characteristic in the lives of both Candee and Fee.[48]

Adding to his problems, Fee suffered a hernia and had to be fitted with a truss toward the end of June. "This affliction," he wrote, "will I fear be a great trial to me." The Madison County exiles, who had begun arriving even before Tappan's death, were a continuing burden for Fee. He had promised David Preston $5 in June, and needed more money for the impoverished Walters family. Although the Exile fund reiumbursed Fee for much of the money he supplied to refugees, he was kept continually short by fulfilling their immediate needs. The fund, after all, was in New York City.[49]

Meanwhile, he had still been working to collect money for the land that had already been bought as a site for Berea College; during this painful period of his life he succeeded in raising the funds to pay for the tract which is the center of Berea College now. He had somehow transformed his personal grief into a motivation to continue the work in his native state, although he could not be sure he would ever be able to return.[50]

And it had been no easy matter. Fee had received dozens of subscriptions for the new school on his ill-fated fund-raising tour, but the money had simply been promised. Collecting funds for a school which no longer had an assured prospect of coming into existence was very trying. In the midst of the exile period (December 29, 1859) Fee received a check from Tappan for $628.50, a first installment from the subscriptions, but Fee undertook at that point to collect the remaining money himself. "I do not want that you shall have the trouble to write to those who have subscribed for a school. . . . Yet I have no resting place—much care—my family scattered. . . . "[51]

Concerning the next installment, Fee wrote frantically to Rogers: "Soon another payment will be due Woolwine. What shall we do? Can the money be raised—or shall we sell the land & buy elsewhere—I think we had better try to raise the money." Rogers, on his speaking tour in the East, was in the position to meet many of the former subscribers and ask them personally to fulfill their pledges. The fact remained that he and Fee were requesting funds for a school in a place where they could not even set up residence.[52]

The last installment was difficult to come by. Fee wrote, "I know not how we shall make last payment on land bought for our school—due last of this month [May 1860]."[53]

On May 25, Hanson informed Rogers that the notes to John G. Woolwine for $735.62 were due, but subscriptions paid through Tappan and Jocelyn at the AMA would arrive in time. Perhaps this payment was delayed (or mistakenly called the 'last'), for Fee stated in a letter (written July 12) that he thought Rogers should stay in the East and solicit money to meet the last payment on the 15th of August. Meanwhile, Fee himself was writing to various subscribers. "I carry fifteen letters to day to the post office," he complained, "This does not relieve my head much." He had just received a paid subscription from the reliable David F. Newton.[54]

Fee now wanted to return to Berea; reports were good from Madison County in July 1860, but Fee was reluctant to go at just that time because "there [would] be drinking & excitement until after election & probably until after inauguration of President." A little later he wrote, "The mob have disbanded—divided—are killing one another—a proposition was made by Mr Clay on 4 of July to have all come back & first one that violates law all parties join in enforcing law against him. . . . If the way shall open for me to go back, I shall go." Fee was disappointed in the new president, Abraham Lincoln, whose positions on the Fugitive Slave Act and "Negro Equality" were inadequate in Fee's view.[55]

By the end of July, six or eight exiles had returned to Berea and others intended to do so. But Fee's own plans to return were destroyed when he visited Bracken County in August 1860 to visit his son's grave. The vigilance committee in Bracken County detained Fee, his wife, daughter and mother-in-law in the public street for more than an hour. Since he was supposed to visit Lewis County during the same period, Fee thought it best to leave Kentucky and cross over into Cabin Creek from Ohio, rather than travel through his native state.[56]

Shortly, he began a tour through several counties in Indiana, and in September opened a protracted meeting at his and Emerick's church in Jacksonburg, Ohio. He expressed a desire to attend the AMA meeting in Syracuse, but also spoke of going to Canada to see "the free Negroes." "Yet this is not really necessary," he said, "I know that freedom is right."[57]

The AMA having asked Fee if he always preached on the subject of slavery, he replied that he did not and enclosed a clipping describing one of his meetings in a Baptist church in Middletown, Ohio. Fee "is a very pleasant speaker, easy and graceful in jesture [sic] and manner, and not arbitrary in his peculiar doctrines, in fact, saying little or nothing of them in his sermon."[58]

He continued to aid Emerick, who had proposed that Fee move to Middletown to be closer to the work. But Fee was reluctant to leave Cincinnati, where he desired to found an integrated church. In addition, he did not want to become a regular preacher because he would then be unable to return to Kentucky. It continued to be a time of great hardship for him and his family. "We are living without any hired help," he wrote, "My wife doing all her work, washing, ironing, sewing, &c. My children are in school. I try to economise [sic], yet I am out of money."[59]

In December 1860, Fee still felt that forming a free church in Cincinnati would be worthwhile. "There is a strong conservative influence in this city. I do not know a single church here that treats the colored man practically as the gospel requires." Berea was quiet by this time, but Fee was convinced it would not be if he or Rogers attempted to return. "My unsettled life is a trial to me & family," he said.[60]

In January 1861, Fee tried to gather all the Christian ministers in Cincinnati into an organization regardless of color—he found only five who were willing to participate: this experience strengthened his desire to start an anticaste church in the city. But Jacob Emerick was still imploring Fee to locate in Middletown. Now Fee was reluctant to settle there since the area had no school, and he feared he would have to be the teacher himself for the sake of his own children.[61]

This question was resolved by default in March when Fee, ill "from continual labor . . . exposure, bad weather, cold beds etc.," found his family, friends and himself evicted. "Do not know which way I will turn," Fee wrote. John G. Hanson had settled in Middletown to work as a carpenter, and Fee decided to follow his cousin in April.[62]

In the spring of 1861, Fee, in Cincinnati on business, stopped to see his friend Levi Coffin, as he usually did when he was in that city. Since the onset of war a number of regular prayer meetings had been established in many churches of the city "to pray that the rebellion might be put down and the awful calamities of war averted." Coffin had become disillusioned with these meetings—particularly the union prayer meeting for business men which was held at a central church in the heart of the city—since, as he said, "the real cause of the war [was] not alluded to; the poor slaves [were] not remembered in their prayers, and the sin of slavery [was] not mentioned." Coffin shared these sentiments with Fee, and the next morning the two men went together to one of the "business men's prayer meetings."

Coffin's account of this occasion reveals John G. Fee in rare form; the meeting

> was largely attended; many prayers and short speeches were made, and every sin but that of slavery was mentioned. Toward the close of the meeting John G. Fee rose and spoke of the real cause of the war—slavery, that great and crying sin of the nation, to which no one had alluded. The chairman of the meeting at once brought down his mallet, as a signal for him to stop, but Fee continued to speak, for a few moments, with great earnestness and power. His words seemed to create a stir and uneasiness with many in the meeting. When a few more sharp taps of the mallet had been given, he took his seat, but immediately kneeled in prayer, and prayed with such earnestness and power that he was not interrupted, although he brought before the Lord the sin of slavery and alluded to it as the cause of the terrible judgment that was hanging over us. At the close of the meeting, Horace Bushnell, a minister and a warm friend to the slave, came up and taking Fee by the hand, said: "Brother Fee, you drove in the nail and clenched it, and they can't get it out."[63]

Fee in Middletown, Ohio: A Brief Respite
"We must still cry, 'Let my people go.'" John G. Fee.

By April 1861, Hanson wrote his parents from Middletown to say, "Cosin [sic] Gregg will locate here as he had taken a house here & has his Goods now here & opened & has his Garden plowed. I think about as good a place as he could have gone in some respects." In May, John and Matilda Fee wrote a joint letter to her aunt Rebecca Hanson (John's mother, John G. Fee's first cousin); in this communication with a near relation, whose sympathy they could count on, both the Fees revealed some of their deepest feelings.[64]

Matilda confided,

> My spirits have been very much pressed ever since I left Ky rather more however since the prospect of war grows stronger [indecipherable] of you all in Ky & wonder where your lot will be cast.

Moving beyond her own troubles, she shared her thoughts concerning the great national turmoil.

> The north in my estimation as a mass are little less guilty than the south & all will suffer greatly if they get to battling in earnest. The north has the men & money & is pouring them out like water, but I think she will not be so skillful in war as the south many of whom have been reared in the school in tyranny. Our prospered nation has become to [sic] proud & will shurely [sic] be humbled.

In her postscript Matilda asked her aunt to find out if "the nice rose" lived that Rebecca Hanson had given her to plant on Tappan's grave. " I so much rejoice," the bereaved mother wrote, "to hear that the Sabbath School is in progress. Tis pleasant to know that faithful ones attend that sacred place where my precious boy is laid if we can go no more."[65]

Fee himself wrote only briefly; this letter seems to be the only one from this period of Fee's life which is wholly personal:

> Mrs. R. Hanson—Dear cousin and friend, I thank you for your kind letter. Oh how I wish it were words from loving lips. "The friendship of kindred minds is like to that above." Many are my trials—perhaps most now through needless care. I need to be quiet—rest in the Lord.
>
> I am here in a very conservative democratic place—Cousin John is here. He is doing well. I know many did not think he did right this last winter—I believe he acted in the fear of God—got much useful knowledge—will yet succeed I think there are but few who will trust as he does. God will yet prosper him. Think you will all see it so. J. G. Fee[66]

Fee's removal to Middletown was a mixed blessing. His worries about a school for the children turned out to be needless—and he found it cheering to be near Emerick and Hanson, so they could help one another. But the moving itself turned out to be "all most surprisingly tedious—attended with impaired health and much depression of spirit." The Fees "landed in an old building" because they had to take what they could get after a two-week delay. The neighborhood was hostile, the region was unhealthy and Fee was stuck with the house for 10 months.[67]

To add to Fee's worries, Candee suddenly arrived (May 1861), having left his work in Kentucky. Fee could hardly believe in the necessity of Candee's exile, which he (Fee) viewed as virtually self-imposed. Although Candee's life had been threatened, Fee said there had been "no open & associated opposition" to him, "no county meetings," as if only a public organization could take a human life! Candee had feared that the state would secede and leave him stranded.[68]

In September, Fee undertook a speaking tour in Ohio; while he was away from home, a severe illness confined him to his bed for a week and to his room for even longer. His lectures now were devoted to support of John C. Fremont's Proclamation, an early act of emancipation which President Lincoln had immediately revoked. In an open letter to the President, Fee wrote, "If the rebel's life, his horse, his ox, may be taken why not his slave?" He urged permitting slaves to join in putting down the rebellion—he was convinced that they would, and that the war would then come to a speedy conclusion. He called for a National Convention in Cleveland to demand "enforcement of Fremont's Proclamation," and "extend it to all slaves in rebel states."[69]

Fee's health had improved somewhat by October, and he expressed growing interest in "arousing the North to demand that the slaves in rebel states go free." Still he was not well enough to resume a lecture tour. "Oh this is a crisis," he exclaimed, "Once passed—the nation refuse to release the slaves what scenes of blood—what Judgements. . . . "[70]

In the course of the war, conditions in Kentucky changed repeatedly, as armies moved and power bases shifted in the state. (A battle was fought in Rockcastle County, October 21, 1861.) On December 4, 1861, Fee wrote to Jocelyn from Lexington, Kentucky. He and his wife were on their way to spend a few weeks in Madison County, before returning to Ohio by way of Lewis County. On December 21, Fee reported that he had spent three consecutive Sundays in Berea, which he found quiet and relatively safe; people were able to assemble with some security and many more were willing to listen to him than before; he conducted an antislavery meeting near the Jackson County border.[71]

On Christmas Day 1861, Fee reported to the AMA: he had been preaching constantly for months, part of the time at Jacksonburg. Friends in Kentucky were urging him to return, but he said he was not ready to fight for slavery under so-called Union men. "I consider labor & blood lost," he wrote, "until the government shall proclaim freedom at least to slaves of rebels." Matilda Fee and Burritt had, at her father's urgent request, gone to Bracken County, where the Hamiltons were feeling much oppressed. Having paid for his wife's trip Fee now had no money for winter clothing and wood.[72]

The AMA—or rather Jocelyn—sent Fee $75 to relieve his present misery, and he was duly grateful. In a letter written immediately after the New Year began, Fee evaluated his position: in his Middletown location he felt out of sympathy, since he did not approve of Republicans (they were not radical enough for him) with whom he was surrounded, nor did he want to identify himself with sects—and all the local churches were, of course, denominational. He wanted to aid Emerick with a church and school, but Emerick himself regarded the plan as too uncertain. Fee was all-too-obviously apt to leave for Kentucky on a moment's notice. Concerning his own speaking engagements Fee was becoming doubtful: "I sometimes think the work of freedom is in the hands of the military," he wrote, "and my lecturing will not reach them—that we will have to wait the logic of events. . . . " He was still glad to be "in the exciting field of antislavery," but he thought that its outcome had passed into other hands.[73]

During January, Fee, nevertheless, spoke in two villages in Ohio, then traveled to Lewis County, to preach a funeral service for all those who had died since he had been there. By this time his Kentucky friends had changed their minds and urged him to delay his return to the state. Matilda Fee commented, "Mr F is very anxious to resume his labors there soon. Be assured that Mr Fee will make no permanent engagements to labor elsewhere."[74]

Fee and the officers of the AMA had a doctrinal dispute in the winter of 1862, over a matter which would cause even more contention at Berea a few years later: Fee had been fellowshiping with Unitarians who did not believe Christ was very and eternal God. Fee himself maintained that "Christ [was] God manifest in the flesh," but he insisted that he might have fellowship with Arians and Unitarians since he found good men among them. Jocelyn indicated that Christians might as well fellowship with slaveholders—but Fee maintained "some men are better than their theories. . . . It seems to me that goodness—love to God & man is to be fellowshiped—Such men have candid consciences and can be reached by power of truth."

In the same letter, he said he was "oppressed in head," because of his "undecided state." He feared now he would not be able to return to Kentucky until the war ended, since people would not go there nor give money for a project there.[75]

On a visit to Tappan's grave in Bracken County in March (1862), Fee encountered no violence, but much opposition to antislavery agitation. There would be no free speech, Fee suggested, until slavery was overthrown. He had heard an antislavery man say it might be a duty to return a fugitive slave. No, Fee said, we must strive for "obedience to God's higher law even to the neglect sometimes of the enactments of ungodly men." And, he wrote, "we must still cry, 'Let my people go.'"[76]

Fee Attempts to Return to Kentucky: Mobs Again
"In my native place, they hate me more than [in Cincinnati]." John G. Fee.

By May, Fee felt it safe to go either to Lewis or Jackson Counties, but he wanted to go to Berea, because that was the place from which he had been expelled. Sometimes his motivation to return to precisely that spot seems merely an index of his stubbornness. Also, he obviously thought Jackson rather insignificant with its 13 slaves to Madison's 5,000 (a comparison of figures which Fee used himself, and a clear indication of his actual preference for head-on collision with slavery). Slaves were still being bought and sold in Richmond, where on May 5, 1862, 11 blacks were auctioned at an average price of $296 apiece. Fee was thinking strongly of going to Newport or Covington, but he was unwilling to go into any of the "sects," as Rogers had with Presbyterians in Decatur. Fee had been visiting the wounded at the hospital in Covington, and saw a chance for useful work there. But no matter how many possibilities he considered, he kept returning to the memory of Berea. In any case, he needed a new horse to go anywhere; the old one was 20 years old. On his speaking engagements (as in Dayton in May) he was still urging that people demand freedom for the slaves and not leave the matter to Abraham Lincoln.[77]

In June, Fee received a request to move to Iowa and work among former slaves there. A. M. Thome, younger brother of James A. Thome, invited Fee, having been acquainted with him when they were both teenagers in school together. Apparently, Fee did not seriously consider this offer. He made a successful trip to

Berea in July, even though Morgan's guerilla band passed through Madison County while Fee was there. Fee, writing on the roadside, saw "many indications of good," but does not specify them. He had already tried to make some preparations for a return, calling upon a freight house in Lexington to arrange the forwarding of his goods. The proprietor refused to do business with Fee, however, even though he was a former customer, and stated, Fee reported, "he would rather have hung me."[78]

Nevertheless, Fee continued with his arrangements, even though the committee in Bracken ordered him out of his native county again while he was there. "In my native place," Fee wrote, "they hate me more than here [Cincinnati]."[79]

On August 25, 1862—two days after the Battle of Big Hill, only a few miles from Berea (but, of course, news traveled slowly in those days)—Matilda Fee started across country in a carriage accompanied by John A. R. Rogers and her two eldest children. They reached Berea only with great difficulty, since the area was full of both Union and Rebel soldiers, "each scrutinizing closely every person, horse and carriage."[80]

Fee himself had to go to Cincinnati to get a tract published before he made his way to Berea; his son Howard, then the youngest, accompanied him. The delay in Fee's journey proved most unfortunate, for the war was shifting again, with Rebel lines now located between Richmond and Berea. Fee managed to rent a single horse in Richmond, which he and his son rode double. About halfway home, near Kingston, they met Union forces retreating before the Confederate invasion. It was impossible to reach Berea that day, so Fee returned to Richmond to await another opportunity. But the Battle of Richmond changed the whole state of Kentucky overnight.

Fee narrates the events of the next day:

> Early that morning an engagement came off between the Union and Confederate forces. I obtained another horse and went to the scene of the conflict. To me it was a sad sight. The Union forces were small and badly managed. Soon they were outflanked on both sides. Overpowered and continually decimated, they were compelled to retreat, again and again.[81]

By evening the Confederates were surrounding Richmond. Fee and his child accompanied the Union forces as they fell back to the Kentucky River and then to Lexington. "I saw flocks of slaves escaping in the direction our army was retreating when the retreat began," Fee wrote, "I suppose they were surrounded by the rebel forces & delivered up. I do not think we will begin to succeed until we begin to free the slave & obey God." By the evening of the next day the Union Army was vacating Lexington. In the Battle of Richmond, beginning August 30, 1862, the Confederate Army lost 450 killed and wounded, but Union forces lost 1,050 killed or wounded and 4,000 taken prisoner. "It was one of the most dramatic victories of the war and at one stroke caused the evacuation of all Kentucky east of Louisville and south of Cincinnati." With incredible suddenness a Union state had come under Confederate rule, and Berea was in the middle of enemy territory. Lexington, at this point, had become a Rebel recruiting station.[82]

With his son, Fee made his way across country to Bracken County, where he left Howard with his grandparents, the Hamiltons. Fee himself continued to Augusta, intending to take a boat for Cincinnati, and proceed from there to Berea, where his wife and other two children were stranded. By this time it was September.

While he was waiting for the boat, about ten o'clock at night, Fee was seized by another mob and taken to the office of Dr. Joshua Bradford, his kinsman—a relative on his father's side—and former schoolfellow. Bradford professed loyalty to the Union, as many Southern sympathizers had to do in Kentucky, but his treatment of John G. Fee revealed his real allegiance.[83]

Fee describes the scene:

> In an enclosed room and with other mobocrats around him, he demanded of me the pledge that I now leave the county, my native county, and never return. Of course I declined any such pledge.

Bradford and others decided to put Fee across the Ohio River and warned him not to return again. Bradford said, "I will hang you if it is the last act of my life." Fee replied, "Do what you conceive to be your duty and I will try to do mine." Bradford and his henchmen took Fee to the riverside, with a crowd following. Some of the mob tried to get into the boat which had been procured for Fee's passage, but they were pushed away by the crew. The leader of the mob turned to go for other boats, saying, "We will whip him like hell."[84]

Fee was soon landed on the Ohio shore; but his enemies were crossing at the same time to continue pursuit. He escaped by clambering up the river bank and leaping a fence into a cornfield. Eventually, he achieved the top of a high hill from which he could see his pursuers passing up and down searching for him. "I saw them abandon pursuit," Fee writes, "and cross the river. As I sat on the brow of that hill my emotions were mingled. I looked up and said, 'God is good; man only is vile.'" All around him was beauty; it was early September, the air soft, the sky clear and the moon shining brilliantly.[85]

He could see the moon reflected in the river. On the Kentucky side lay the town of Augusta. "Prominent among its buildings," he says, "were the old college building, within those walls I had studied. . . . Oft in my youth I had walked the streets of that town, with hopes of a happy future. There, too, my wife, in girlhood days, had gone to and fro from the little brick schoolhouse, standing yet before me." In the peace of that moment on the hill, Fee realized fully his own situation: "Now I was an exile," he writes,

> for no other offense than that of pleading in my native land, for the liberty and equal rights of all men. My wife and two little ones were one hundred and forty miles in the interior of a slave state, and in the very midst of rebel bands. Mine, then, was sorrow in the midst of mingled beauty.

And so, ironically, at this crisis in his life Fee once again stood in Ohio, looking across the symbolic river into his native state.[86]

The next day Fee boarded the first boat to Cincinnati, and crossed to a Union camp on the Kentucky side. From there he traveled to Oberlin for a meeting of the AMA, then back to Bracken County, determined once more to reach Berea. Again his son Howard accompanied him. Railroad communications were cut, because the bridges had been burned—so the father and son went to Washington, in Mason County, hoping to find a stagecoach there.

While waiting for the stage to arrive, Fee stopped at the house of a Presbyterian minister, Rev. Mr. Conditt, whom he had known for years. The minister was not at home when Fee arrived, but on the man's arrival he made it clear Fee was not a welcome guest. "I am sorry you are here," he said, "Do you see those men gathering?" Fee had not noticed them "They do no intend to let you pass." Soon the minister's yard was full of men, the house surrounded.[87]

Escape was impossible; Fee and his son were borne along down into the town, the crowd increasing. Some debate was held about what to do with Fee: the men decided to take him back to Augusta, where he had already been mobbed twice.

By this time it was night; Augusta was 15 miles away. The captain of the crowd ordered a slave to go fetch horses and a wagon, but the slave was gone a long time—long enough for the captain to enter a nearby bar and fortify his courage.

Eventually, the slave returned with a team and wagon. Fee's son, Howard, stood quietly by during all this, "hearing each word and watching every action." One young man, not a member of the mob, only a spectator, was touched by the sight of the little boy; he determined to protect the child and save the father from the proposed outrage.

The young man quickly found three others who were willing to aid him in his plan. When the team was ready he and his men offered their services to the captain and stepped into the wagon.

At the crossroad, instead of allowing the captain to turn toward Augusta, the young man seized the reins and said, "No, let's take him to Maysville and deliver him up to Judge C."

> This, to the drunken owner of the team, seemed like 'business.' He yielded. [The young man] kept the reins and soon [the party was] in Maysville and in the room of Judge C. The Judge, having over [Fee] no jurisdiction, after a friendly [handshake] took the young drunken man aside and told him what might be the serious consequences of his action.[88]

Fee and Howard thanked their rescuer and walked away, crossed the Ohio and spent the night in a quiet hotel. The next morning they returned to the Kentucky side, and Fee conferred with friends in Maysville. Fee was told he could not travel safely in Kentucky (rather obvious information at this point!), and advised "that [his] family was safer without [him] than with him." Many of the

Union soldiers left around Berea had been carried off into Rebel territory, others were hiding in the caves and mountains.[89]

Fee had been separated from his wife and other children for almost ten weeks; he was aware that they had little to eat and must be suffering greatly—there was no possibility of his communicating with them or their with him. "They will get along," Fee wrote, "My wife has great endurance & will work & plan. The people will doubtless share to some extent but they are poor & wars around them have nearly eaten up the country." Still, he thought they were really better off without him.[90]

In fact, Matilda and the children *had* been enduring hardships of their own. She had returned to "a destitute home in a destitute region." She had been stopped on the road by Union pickets, who suspected her of being a Rebel spy, but a Union flag painted on her carriage saved her. When she arrived home, she "constructed a bedstead, filled a tick with straw, borrowed a blanket to sleep under, lay down with her two children and slept." The next day while she was out reclaiming some cooking utensils she had loaned to neighbors two years earlier, Rebel soldiers entered the house and stole her blanket, combs, dress shoes, Burritt's hat and the carriage harness.[91]

With some other women, Mrs. Fee visited Kirby Smith's encampment to see the Confederates. An officer asked her about the politics of the region. "My home is nearby," Matilda said, "and as for politics we are for the Union, and believe slavery is wrong, and that the rebels are fighting for a lost cause."

"Madam, ain't you from the North?" the officer asked.

"No, this is my home and my native State."

He asked derisively, "Madam, are you an Abolitionist?"

"I am," she replied.

"Well," he said, "I have seen some men who were Abolitionists, but I never before this saw a woman who was."[92]

Rebel officers visited the Fee's house, asking for food, which she gave them, though the family's own supplies were low, only to discover that other soldiers were in the potato patch, "grabbling her potatoes." She walked out to the patch and confronted the thieves.

"Men, I have fed your officers," she said, "and now you are taking the last potato I have; this is no credit to you."

One young fellow looked up pertly and said, "Madam, credit has gone up long ago." The soldiers took the potatoes.

Matilda Fee and her children endured "privation, anxiety and toil from . . . day to day" during this period. At one point, Morgan's Raiders passed within a mile of Fee's house.[93]

Fee's mother-in-law, Elizabeth (Gregg) Hamilton, believed she could rescue her daughter more safely than Fee could. At the end of October, all alone, driving a horse and carriage, she went to Berea and brought Matilda Fee and the children to the Kentucky border, arriving presumably early in November. Reunited again, Fee and his family settled on the banks of the Ohio River, at Parker's Academy in Clermont County, Ohio.[94]

Fee at Parker's Academy: "Immediate Emancipation" and Contrabands
"The history of these contrabands reveals the deep wickedness and meaness of Ky in a light little known or understood. . . ." G. P. Reily.

Parker's Academy, where the Fee family resided from the fall of 1862 to March 1864, was founded by J. K. Parker in 1839; a coeducational school located above New Richmond, Ohio, it was supported by abolitionists of that region, including the wealthy and prominent Donaldson family from England. The Donaldsons had supported the Lane Rebels and, when James G. Birney had found it impossible to publish his abolitionist paper, the *Philanthropist*, in his native Danville, Kentucky, the Donaldsons invited him to base his operations in New Richmond, where they defended him boldly. Fee, also invited to locate near the Donaldsons, took no permanent work in New Richmond, or anywhere, during his exile, because he wanted to hold himself ready to return to Berea. He preached for the Academy every Sunday, and baptized several students who were converted under his influence.[95]

At this period Fee rested his hopes almost wholly on emancipation—the slaves would be freed, and, fighting in the Union Army, help bring the war to a speedy conclusion. Fee campaigned vigorously for emancipation on those grounds. New Richmond became the new base for his activities: there he preached regularly, but made weekly forays to lecture about the wisdom of freeing all slaves immediately. His health improved and his anxieties seemed to be allayed. Secretary Salmon P. Chase urged Fee to continue lecturing in Ohio.[96]

After a few months in New Richmond, Fee took his family again to Bracken County and made a personal *reconaissance* through several counties on horseback, returning again to Berea. The outcome of the war was still completely unsettled. So the Fees returned to Parker's Academy, where the children again entered school, and where their new son, Edwin Sumner, "a very promising boy," was born March 13, 1863.[97]

In April, Fee accepted financial help from the Freedman's Aid Society for his speaking engagements. But he assured Whipple that he had no intention of leaving the AMA: "I still feel that Ky. is my field," he wrote, "and that I have the one thing or important thing—& that is to help build there a school, church & colony." There was no hope for Fee's project at that time, however—the work there now, Fee thought, was to move for emancipation.[98]

In June 1863, Fee received a letter from a soldier named G. P. Reily; the subject—contrabands. Reily's regiment was located in Louisville, Kentucky, where he had been rounding up contrabands—that is, slaves, not legally freed, who were no longer in their masters' possession. The war had produced thousands of them, homeless, frequently without occupation or means of support; thousands of blacks were now in a legal no-man's land, without rights, without lawful status of any kind. "The history of these contrabands," Reily wrote, "reveal [sic] the deep wickedness and meaness of Ky in a light little known or understood by the north." Reily reported that hundreds of contrabands had accompanied Buel's army to Louisville in the fall. There they had been thrown in jail until all the jails were full, to be left eight months and then sold, as the law provided. It had become necessary to send them to jails in other portions of the state; to ease this burden the Kentucky legislature changed the law and made it possible for the imprisoned slaves to be sold after only 30 days. By that time more than one hundred contrabands had already died. "The water they had to drink was so filthy and loathsome," Reily wrote, "that it was their poison, they were sold out and went abroad to tell the simple little story of their wrongs and it had its effect."[99]

The Union Army had begun turning many former slaves loose; some 20 had just been brought to Reily's camp in Louisville to work on fortifications, and he was expecting more. Reily's letter was simply a report to Fee in his capacity as a known friend of the enslaved, an appeal to him to use his influence however he could to help in the contraband situation.[100]

Fee immediately apprised Whipple that he wanted to go into Kentucky or down the river to Memphis to the freedmen. "To visit the Freedmen will be the greatest relief to my head." He had been speaking on emancipation—but would soon be able to journey more widely since school was closing at Parker's Academy the next week. Reproached by the AMA for his single-track ministry (or one-track mind), Fee wrote, "I am preparing a discourse in reference to the colored people—I wish never to be regarded as fanatical; but it does seem to me there are reasons why the colored people of this nation—the freed men offer one of the most promising fields for good now open to missionary effort." In addition, he felt that blacks would themselves exhibit "their willingness to contribute to the spread of the gospel."[101]

Invited back to Berea, Fee visited Madison County in the last week of June 1863. There he found the mobs played out. But he could not stay—he had to go on a speaking tour in Indiana with Levi Coffin for the Freedman's Aid Society. Later, in July, he spoke at Sardinia in Brown County, Ohio, but more and more he was occupied with his campaign to have contrabands from Kentucky enlisted. He was working also to obtain freedom for some slaves who had been sent back to their owners after having fled to the supposed protection of the Union Army. In July he had an interview with the Governor of Ohio in Columbus concerning black soldiers in Ohio. In addition, he corresponded with friends in Kentucky about setting up Emancipation Societies there. When he returned to Parker's Academy in August he was seriously ill again.[102]

By August 14, over 100 contrabands had been sent to Cincinnati, where General Dolson Cox (Rogers' friend; Finney's son-in-law) wanted to form a regiment and add slaves from Kentucky, "for whose liberation," Fee wrote, "I have been working for a month past." Slaves would become free by enlisting as soldiers.[103]

Later on that year, in September, Fee paid another visit to Kentucky, passing through Lewis and Mason Counties, where he held meetings on immediate emancipation. But he was intensely ill by September 27, scarcely able to write, certainly unfit for travel.[104]

Nevertheless, he would not rest; by October 6, he reported having held two emancipation meetings in Mason County, although he had been sick for the past eight days with bilious fever. He could scarcely sit up and was unable to study. But he wrote of plans for taking a boat to Memphis, Vicksburg and New Orleans to work with freedmen. He was casting about in every direction to be "useful" to slaves emerging from their bondage; he was frantic to have his efforts count now that freedom was coming in a virtually undreamed of way.[105]

He was literally tearing himself apart. On October 13, his daughter Laura wrote for him, since he could not perform the task for himself: "Pa is in bed—a continued attack of intermittent fever—and wishes me to write for him, saying that probabilities for entering upon the agency are small." Fee suggested Candee to take his place. Shortly afterward, he had a relapse but was still planning to return to Berea. But by November 13, he was on his way to Lewis and Mason Counties to urge people to go to a border state conference in Missouri. He planned to return to New Richmond and then go to Madison County. But he had a relapse again, and in his illness wrote that he feared Kentucky would go for "gradual emancipation." "Perhaps Egypt must feel the effects of another judgment," he said, "before they will let God's people go."[106]

Fee was in Berea again by December. He found there more friends than at any previous time: he was able, he said, to visit thousands with freedom; he requested Bibles for the slaves at work on the roads and boxes of tracts for the local citizens and soldiers. He wrote, "The people are very destitute—both armies have passed through here again & again—many will suffer this coming winter— provisions are very high & very scarce."[107]

Fee returned briefly to his role as supervisor of colporteurs and other workers in the mission field. He conveyed his opinions of John Drew and William Mobley, whose work had been primarily for the now absent George Candee. Their labors as preachers had evidently been effective. Mobley reported (December 14, 1863) average attendance at meetings: 125 at Berea, 55 at South Fork, 25 at Little Clover.[108]

Drew Fee regarded as a "good man, sensible & industrious"; Fee thought he might be a better preacher than Mobley, although Fee had never heard him "attempt to preach." Mobley, on the other hand, was a case of *deja vu*. He was terribly lazy. "Since he has commenced riding as a colporteur," Fee wrote, "he has grown very fat & therefor commenced the use of tobacco to deplete [reduce]. He will quit tobacco rather than lose his commission." Mobley, Fee said—in another of his efforts to make the Southern situation understandable in the North—was used to preachers who thought it fulfilled their appointments to "go to houses of friends, eat a big dinner & talk." "He is terribly lazy," Fee complained, "He will go to house of a friend in mid day pile up in bed & there sleep for hours."[109]

William Mobley, faced with the implacability of John G. Fee, appealed rather piteously to the AMA. His friend John Drew had already quit drinking and smoking, but Mobley had a more difficult time of it. He said he had gone from 170 pounds to 206 when he quit smoking the last time, and he had only started again because a friend had advised him to resume. But he promised to quit if he had to. Whenever John G. Fee was back in town, people knew it.[110]

On January 9, 1864, Captain T. E. Hall of Camp Nelson in Jessamine County, Kentucky, wrote to George Whipple, asking the help of the AMA. Some 600 contrabands had come into the camp and the number was increasing. Some of the abolitionists in central Kentucky shared the new concern for former slaves. Mobley sent to the AMA (on February 2, 1864) a list of donors for the freedmen. The names included his own, Elisha H. Harrison, William Blanton, Mrs. Elizabeth Blanton, Isaac F. Fowler, Robert Jones, Robert E. Nichols, John Drew, William Griffin, M. L. Robinson and others.[111]

In February 1864, Fee convened an "immediate emancipation" meeting at Berea, where he delivered two lectures; the audience, large and orderly, provided a "bountiful basket-dinner" and elected six delegates to attend the Border-State Emancipation Convention at Louisville (February 22). Some slaveholders were present, but "past dissensions and persecutions were forgotten." Later, Fee preached at a camp of soldiers six miles away from Berea; he was so well-received, both at home and at the camp, that he became convinced the door in central Kentucky was wide open again.[112]

Fee Returns to Berea
"I have kept myself for this field ready. I believed it would come. I am here ready—God is in it." John G. Fee.

In March 1864, Fee was in Bracken County, working at the Bethesda Church; having left Parker's Academy, he was ready to return to Berea. On April

24, 1864, the school there reopened with Matilda Fee and Fee's son Burritt in charge, although Fee also taught one class himself.[113]

"Nothing but an experience where there has been the desolution of war and that carelessness which slavery & war engender," Fee wrote, "could enable you to comprehend the difficulties. House, garden, well, fencing, stables every thing to repair." To make matters worse, Fee had lost a wheel from his only carriage when it fell off in the Licking River. Rebel raids were still expected; so Fee, because of the uncertainty of the war, was afraid to import female teachers from abroad to take a subscription school.[114]

Along the road near Berea, which led through the Cumberland Gap, passed the fighters and the victims of the war. Soldiers and guerilla bands, and "flocks of women and children in most destitute condition on their way to some other part of the state or to free states." But the school at Berea was started and people there had regular preaching from Fee again. In addition, he continued to address soldiers in their camps.[115]

In spite of the war, or perhaps because of it, Fee's work in Berea prospered. Congregations were increasing, the number of students at the school increasing too. "There are some good men in Jackson county," Fee reported, "who now purpose to purchase lots and go to Berea. They believe Jackson county is so mountainous & poor that community cannot be concentrated so as to sustain a colony or good school." Thus Fee pronounced the last word on Peniel College, without ever mentioning its name.[116]

Fee himself was toying with the idea of relocating his own school project, but, he said, "Now there is no point in merely finding a mere 'stand point' in a slave state." Soon other changes would be open—the colony and school might be located any place in Kentucky. "Money has been expended at Berea & friends have purchased there or I would not now select that place," Fee said. "I would hunt for one where the soil is richer and the water free from chalyclicate taste." Land was available at Berea that "poor men can have homes within their reach." His final reason for staying at Berea was simple: "The immediate locality is poor in soil but rich in moral principles."[117]

Fee was prosperous enough in June 1864 to send $30 to James Snedaker for board for Laura Fee, who was attending John A. R. Rogers' new academy in Decatur, Ohio.[118]

The slaves, Fee wrote on June 4, were leaving Madison County "without let or hindrance." (Ironically, slaves were still being sold in the Lexington slave market as late as the summer of 1864.) On June 6, Fee reported to Jocelyn from Richmond, where he had been talking to black men anxious to enlist if they could have freedom and pay. "Hundreds of these colored men know me," Fee wrote, "& would have confidence in what I would say to them." He considered going elsewhere for the sake of black people. "I desire much to be quietly at the work of building up the school, & congregation & bringing in men into the Colony at Berea, but perhaps I ought to go to the camp at Louisville."[119]

At the end of June, he wrote, "Last week near three thousand [black soldiers] were in camp at Camp Nelson about 35 miles from my house. I feel that I ought to go and preach to them—distribute tracts—get suitable chaplains for or missionaries with them." John Drew could preach in Berea until the last of August, when school would have to begin—unless it was interrupted. John Rogers had been preaching at the Bracken and Lewis County churches, Fee's other "obligation" in Kentucky. He was free to travel, free to explore potential mission fields again, eager to turn his attention from the problems of slavery to the challenges of freedom.[120]

In his *Autobiography* Fee describes the most crucial decision of this period in his life:

> . . . whilst sitting in my study, thinking of the political and social condition around me, these words came to me with wonderful force, "Prepare thy work without, and make it fit for thyself in the field; and afterwards build thine house." Prov. 24: 27. I did not remember to have seen the text before; but of course I had, in general reading, though at that moment I was not reading my Bible. The text came to me in such manner and with such force, that I could not but regard it as from the Spirit of God; and therefore a call to the work indicated. The thing indicated to me was this: Until the work on the battlefield shall be first settled, there will be no permanency, or marked progress in your work here, either in school or church;—go do your part. That part, as I then believed, was moral, religious; rather than physical,—the actual bearing of arms. I had hitherto no confidence that the government would succeed, until it began to "break every yoke and let the oppressed go free"; until it began to enlist men as men,—and not merely as white men. I also knew that just at that time colored men were being enlisted in Kentucky. I believed . . . there were reasons why I could instruct,

comfort and encourage them,—reasons why they would hear me. . .
.121

"I am glad to live. I bless God for this day," Fee exclaimed to Jocelyn (June 1864). "I was severely anxious & troubled at time of our expulsion & loss of my son four years since. My health is now good. I feel that a glorious door is opening." The black people were not to be sent to Louisville, but to Camp Nelson, close at hand. "I have kept myself for this field ready," he exulted, "I believed it would come. I am here ready—God is in it."122

Reverend John G. Fee would start all over again.

EPILOGUE

In 1844, at the beginning of his antislavery career, John G. Fee asked
Cassius M. Clay how slavery would be ended: by politicians urging the economic
disadvantages of the institution; by preachers employing "moral suasion"; or by
revolution? Twenty years later it was clear to everyone—the peculiar institution
was ending in the disaster of war. Lincoln's Emancipation Proclamation signaled
the eminent demise of the whole Southern system. Theoretically, Kentucky's
slaves remained in bondage until the adoption of the 13th Amendment (which
Kentucky never ratified), but, actually, slavery in Kentucky simply disappeared, as
more and more black people walked away from their "owners"—into other states,
into the Union Army, into camps for contrabands. As former slaves became
contrabands, antislavery missionaries became *former* abolitionists; they no longer
had slavery to oppose.

In promoting the antislavery cause, Fee and many of his fellow workers
had lived two lives of exile: exiles *in* Kentucky, they had endured as persecuted
abolitionists in the midst of slavery; then, turned away from their chosen work and
their established homes, they had lived five more years in exile *from* Kentucky.
Their sacrifices for the abolitionist cause had been real and deeply painful to them.
But how did their mission affect the final outcome? Some might argue that the
efforts of the abolitionists, on a nation-wide basis, were merely quixotic, ultimately
without influence. Some people asserted (and still assert) that abolitionists, by
their determined opposition, had aroused an equal reaction from slaveholders, thus
extending the life of the slavery system, especially in Kentucky. On the other
hand, the abolitionists' work may have hastened slavery's collapse: they had
convinced many citizens that slavery was sinful and dishonorable; they had insisted
on *immediate* emancipation, and, as it turned out, the granting of freedom to black
people was not gradual. Certainly, evangelical abolitionist ideals supplied many of
the aims of Radical Republicanism during Reconstruction.

But it is all speculation: in 1865, no one could say with confidence what
would have happened if the war had never taken place. Neither can we. Would the
abolitionist movement in Kentucky ever have worked? Would the slavery system

in the state have been completely overturned? In the absence of such a large-scale victory, would the abolitionists have achieved anything worthwhile? Would they have persisted in their work, making tiny advances against ferocious opposition? Would their efforts in education have undermined Kentucky's slave power? Ironically, slaveowners themselves feared that all these questions would have been answered 'Yes!' For us, however, the questions must remain unanswered.

Nevertheless, one result of Fee's abolitionist mission in the midst of slavery is quite clear: it laid the foundation for the second of Berea's reforming missions. Characteristically, Fee never looked back to estimate his own achievements in the antislavery battle, but turned immediately to a new mission: fighting for political and social equality of the races. His campaign against prejudice and injustice began in his sojourn at Camp Nelson, where he defended human rights of contrabands who had no legal rights. In its second birth in 1866, under Fee's leadership, Berea pioneered interracial education with an integrated school, community and church. The citizens of the Glade District supported this radical project in their midst; black settlers poured into the District, many of them from Camp Nelson, where Fee had befriended them; Appalachian settlers from Jackson County, former congregations of George Candee, moved to Berea as colonists; from the North came other settlers, many of them friends and relatives of John and Elizabeth Rogers. Within five years (by 1870), Fee, the Rogers, Candee and Hanson had all returned to the Glade; Berea College had been established with a fully integrated student body and an integrated board of trustees (eventually, the faculty was integrated as well); Fee's church had reorganized, with black and white members communing on an equal basis; land in and around Berea was available to all—former slaves, Kentucky mountaineers and Yankees living side by side in a system of ownership Fee called interspersion.

For almost 40 years, in spite of many difficulties, failures and even tragedies, Berea conducted a unique experiment in interracial living. In 1904 with the enactment of Kentucky's Day Law—which made it illegal for black people and white people to study together in any educational institution in the state, public or private—the experiment ended. . . .   And began again in 1950 when Berea College opened its doors to black students for the first time in almost 50 years. At present, John G. Fee's mission—although altered almost beyond recognition in some respects—continues: interracial education is a central commitment at the college he founded in the town he founded.

Although he did not succeed in reforming the world in some ultimate way, he left a visible mark on it. If John G. Fee were to look at Berea College, at Berea, at Kentucky, at the United States today—would he consider his work so many years ago a failure? The question would be irrelevant to him: if he were alive he would be ready to begin all over again.

APPENDICES

APPENDIX 1: FEE'S CHILDREN

John G. Fee's children played an important part in the development of Berea throughout his lifetime. His eldest child, Laura Ann, born September 15, 1845, in Bracken County, Kentucky, began her education in Rogers' school at Berea before the Civil War; during the exile period, she studied under Rogers again at his Decatur Academy, boarding with the James Snedaker family (Eliza Snedaker, one of Berea's first teachers was James Snedaker's daughter). In Decatur Laura met William Norris Embree, who came to live with his brother-in-law and sister, John and Lizzie Rogers, at the end of the Civil War; Embree and Laura Fee were married September 12, 1865, in Berea by her father, with John G. Hanson, James West and W. W. Wheeler witnesses. Toward the end of the Exile (1865) Laura taught in the Berea school before it was officially reopened, and retained her teaching post through 1866-67. She and her husband sold out in Berea in 1870, and eventually moved West, but she returned to live with her parents after Embree's death in 1891. She was a member of the Berea College Ladies' Board of Care (Council of Dean of Women) from 1866 to 1872 and from 1895-1902. During her last years in Berea, she was her father's chief support, especially after Matilda Fee's death in 1895. In his will Fee designated that Laura should continue to occupy his house in Berea after his death if she should then be unmarried and "desire to remain here as a Christian worker." One-fourth of Fee's estate was "set apart for the education of hopeful, Christian young women who shall be found willing to help themselves." He appointed Laura Embree as chairman of the committee in charge of this fund: a clear sign of Fee's estimation of his daughter's trustworthiness. She survived her father by only two years, dying in Berea, July 30, 1903. *Madison County Will Book 2,* pp. 326-28.

Burritt Hamilton Fee, born May 1, 1849, in Lewis County, Kentucky, was, like his sister, a student in Rogers' pre-Civil War school; during the Exile he attended Parker's Academy, while the family was living in New Richmond, Ohio. Before he was 16 (by February 21, 1865) Burritt was teaching black soldiers in his father's school at Camp Nelson. There the young man became seriously ill—and continued to suffer very poor health for the rest of his brief life. But when the Berea school reopened in 1866, Burritt, then an Academy student, was part of everything: one of the charter members of the reorganized church, he began immediately serving on committees—the finance committee (September 22, 1866), committee on collections (November 6, 1866), the committee to meet with the Prudential Committee of the college to arrange matters concerning joint ownership (November 14, 1866). By June 4, 1868 (then barely 19) he was elected deacon, but he declined renomination to that office March 6, 1869. He became a colporteur for the college in 1867 and was elected vice-president of the Berea Temperance Society in January of that year and again in June, signing the pledge October 10, 1867. He was active in all campus organizations, especially the Phi Delta Society, which was initiated in 1868.

He was one of four students in Berea College's first graduating class in 1873; the same year he entered Oberlin Theological Seminary to prepare for the ministry, working as a teacher while he was still a student. He stayed in seminary until 1875, but by then he was desperately ill with tuberculosis, and moved to Texas under his father's care, both remaining there at least a year. The case was hopeless—Burritt returned to Berea to die, October 10, 1876 [his tombstone in the Berea Cemetery has the date 1877, which is obviously incorrect since Fee received a letter of consolation for Burritt's death on October 24, 1876—Lincoln to Fee, in BCA]. Fee to Rogers (from Selina, Texas) 15 Mar 1875 BCA; Sophie Hodges to Fee (in Texas) 16 Jan 1876 BCA.

Howard Samuel Fee (born August 25, 1851, in Lewis County, Kentucky), student at Berea before the Civil War, in Parker's Academy during the Exile, at Berea again from 1866 to 1874, when he was one of four Berea College graduates. He joined the Berea church February 24, 1866, and was elected Secretary and Librarian of the Sunday School, June 4, 1868. He married Charlotte Elizabeth Chittenden (sister of Berea faculty member Henry Reed Chittenden) August 25, 1875, and became Principal of Ariel Academy in Camp Nelson, Kentucky, the same year, but he held the position only briefly. By 1880, he had emigrated to California, where he became a rancher; he died October 15, 1904, in Whittier, California: the very day he moved to that town).

Tappan Fee (born May 14, 1856, in Berea; died April 29, 1860, in Cincinnati), buried in his grandfather Vincent Hamilton's plot in Bethesda Cemetery, Bracken County, Kentucky.

Edwin Sumner Fee was born March 13, 1863, at Parker's Academy in New Richmond, Ohio. Student at Berea from 1870 to 1882, he received an Honorary Degree from Berea in 1917; he served on the board of Lincoln Institute, the school founded for blacks when Berea College was forced to cease interracial education. Married to Enrie Jane Hamilton (grad. Oberlin 1875), a music teacher at Berea from 1881-82, on September 11, 1883, in Clarksburg, Indiana, Howard Fee lived most of his life in her hometown (Clarksburg), dying there December 14, 1934. He was the only one of Fee's children whose longevity almost matched his father's.

Elizabeth Hamilton ("Bessie") Fee, born April 1865, probably in Berea, died unmarried January 9, 1886. She joined the church in 1876 and was a student at Berea from 1873 to 1885.

Howard Samuel Fee obit., *Berea Citizen*, 17 Nov 1904; Golden Wedding Anniversary Notice, Mr. & Mrs. Edwin Fee, *Berea Citizen*, 21 Sept 1933; Edwin S. Fee obit., *Berea Citizen*, 20 Dec 1934; Laura Fee obit., *Berea Citizen*, 6 Aug 1904 & 13 Aug 1904.

APPENDIX 2: COLPORTEURS' APPEAL TO THE AMA

The following petition, obviously composed by John G. Fee himself, contains his typical style, doctrines, opinions and a very characteristic error in spelling. A very clear presentation of the goals of the abolitionist movement in Kentucky at this time, the document was signed by most of the local men who supported Fee initially in his Berea mission.

Appeal [March 1854] (from AMA 43245)
To the members and friends of the American Missionary Association

You seek by your efforts under God to convince the American people and especially the southern portion of them, of the sinfulness of slaveholding and the duty of non-fellowship with this and other sins. In this work you have to contend with fifteen hundred millions of dollars invested in slave property. You have to contend with a moral sense stultified by habit and long established association—with a public sentiment educated by the popular press, ministers and other speakers to believe that slavery is instituted by God[,] at least tolerated by Him. You have also to contend with a public sentiment prejudiced against the antislavery movement by distorted facts and exaggerated tales concerning antislavery men and associations.

These errors must be corrected, as they may be, by the press, the ministry—the living speaker & the talking friend. All these have their relative advantages.

By printed tracts or documents we can have access to thousands who cannot be reached by the public speakers. These documents correct error, remove prejudices, and awaken under God in many strong desires to hear for themselves and thus they advance the cause of truth. Here in the interior every organization has been preceded by the scattering of antislavery documents. They are the great harbingers of reform.

There is another encouraging fact. It is this. The continual agitation of the subject of slavery politically and ecclesiastically has awakened in the minds of the people an <u>increasing desire</u> to read and understand for themselves. The great mass of them, especially in the nonslaveholding districts are not only willing but <u>desirous</u> to read. This is God's providence. Shall we [improve?] it? Avail ourselves of the opening and obey the call? If not, awakened desire will grow weary with disappointment and give up the struggle, and aversion will follow present negligence.

Now is the time for action.

Another fact—the circulation of these documents is followed by increasing calls for free church organizations and ministers to supply them.

Now, in the infancy of our movements, and sparseness of men and means, we must look to the friends of humanity and righteousness abroad for aid in our struggle. Send us aid—documents showing the political, the social, and especially the moral wrongs of slavery, and the great error of fellowshiping the sin in church relations. Send us such as you have been sending us—tracts carefully written, full of facts and arguments and touching appeals. We have here colporture [sic] and other zealous friends who take great pleasure in judiciously and actively circulating them.

Under God we hope, we expect to succeed. Help us. (signed by 25 persons) [parenthetical note in original; signatures have been omitted]

APPENDIX 3: THE BEREANS' PETITION TO GOV. MAGOFFIN

To his Excellency, the Governor of the State of Kentucky

We, the undersigned, loyal citizens and residents of the State of Kentucky and County of Madison, do respectfully call your attention to the following facts:

1. We have come from various parts of this and adjoining States to this County, with the intention of making it our homes, have supported ourselves and families by honest industry, and endeavored to promote the interests of religion and education.

2. It is a principle with us to "submit to every ordinancy of man for the Lord's sake, unto governors as unto them that are sent by Him for the punishment of evil doers and the praise of them that do well," and in accordance with this principle we have been obedient in all respects to the laws of this State.

3. Within a few weeks evil and false reports have been put into circulation, imputing to us motives, words and conduct calculated to inflame the public mind, which imputations are utterly false and groundless. These imputations we have publicly denied and offered every facility for the fullest investigation, which we have earnestly but vainly sought.

4. On Friday the 23rd inst., a company of sixty-two men, claiming to have been appointed by a meeting of the citizens of our County, without any shadow of legal authority, and in violation of the Constitution and Laws of the State and United States, called at our respective residences and places of business, and notified us to leave the County and State, and be without this County and State within ten days, and handed us the accompanying document, in which you will see that unless the said order be promptly complied with, there is expressed a fixed determination to remove us by force.

In view of these facts, which we can substantiate by the fullest evidence, we respectfully pray that you, in the exercise of the power vested in you by the Constitution, and made your duty to use, do protect us in our rights as loyal citizens of the State of Kentucky.

J. A. R. ROGERS,	SWINGLEHURST LIFE,
J. G. HANSON,	JOHN SMITH,

I. D. REED,   E. T. HAYES,
JAS. S. DAVIS,   CHAS. E. GRIFFIN,
JOHN F. BOUGHTON   A. G. W. PARKER
          W. H. TORRY

BEREA, Madison Co., Ky. Dec 24, '59

From *American Missionary,* Vol., IV, no. 2 (Feb 1860), p. 40.

APPENDIX 4:   CASSIUS CLAY'S LIST OF EXILES

No. of individuals ordered off from the vicinity of Berea by the mob.

J. G. Fee and family	6
J. A. R. Rogers and family	4
_____ Bougton & family	3
Jno. Smith & family	2
J. G. Hanson & family	3
Charles C. Griffin & family	2
J. S. Davis and family	4
S. Life & Reed & Shoals & Hays.	4
Torry & family	5
A. G. W. Parker & family	5
G. Haley & family	6
F. Bland & family	5
Widow Preston & family	7
Jesse Preston & family	4
J. Waters & family	5
George Adams & family	2
Wesley Dobs & family	2
Joel Todd & family	3
Ben. Kirby & family	3
Joseph Williams & family	6
John Williams & family	6
Silas Williams & family	4
Widow Williams & family	2
R. Preston	1

94

A manuscript note in Cassius M. Clay's handwriting in BCA.

APPENDIX 5: NATIVE KENTUCKIAN EXILES

"G. Haley & family   6" [each quoted heading is an item from Clay's List]

Born 1824 or '25 in Madison County, Green Haley was the son of Coleman Haley and Eleanor Renfro (and through his mother a cousin of Berea trustee Thomas J. Renfro). Green's grandfather, Barnabas Haley, a native of Virginia and a Revolutionary War soldier, had settled in Rockcastle County, where he was a small-scale slaveholder, as early as 1805. Most of Green's family lived in Rockcastle County, where many of them, including his mother, were members of Scaffold Cane Baptist Church; Haley himself seems to have been a Madison County resident.[1]

Green Haley had four children living at home at the time of the Exile, one of whom was a pre-Civil War student at Berea. Rogers' account book shows Haley paying for school books in August 1858 and paying tuition in July 1859. Rogers bought a cow and calf from Haley in April of the same year.

Throughout the late 1860's Haley continued to have business dealings with Berea people. George Haley, probably his son, was a student at Berea from 1867 to 1878; America and Adeline Haley, probably his daughters, were students at Berea from 1866 into the 1870's.

"F. Bland & family 5"

Franklin Bland was born 1805 in Madison County where his parents had been married as early as 1791. He owned a 40-acre farm on Silver Creek in 1854; entries for him occur in Rogers' account book for 1859. Bland and his second wife Nancy Parker, widow of Matthew Powell, were married September 2, 1858, by John G. Fee. Bland's daughter Mary became a member of Union Church in Berea in 1866, a student at Berea in 1867 and a member of Fee's Madison County Temperance Union the same year.[2]

Several of Bland's grandchildren attended Berea in the 1860's and '70's, children of his daughter Catharine, who married Harvey Walkup, and of his daughter Julia, who married Granville Galloway.

"Widow Preston & family   7"
"Jesse Preston & family   4"
"R. Preston   1"

Jerusha Preston, or the Widow Preston, as she was usually called, is mentioned by many of the early Bereans, including Fee and Rogers, both of whom emphasize her poverty and her piety. Of her children, the names of five are definitely known: Elizabeth, Clara, John H., Ellen and David—her sixth child, a daughter, was the wife of exile George Adams, and probably named Martha.

Born in Kentucky in 1810, Jerusha [maiden name unknown] was the daughter of Kentuckians; she married John Preston, uncle of Reuben and Jesse Preston, who were also exiles, but he died before 1858. She and her children lived in the Cummins neighborhood of Rockcastle County until 1860, when they moved to Berea.

John G. Hanson was closely connected with the Jerusha Preston household; he boarded with her when he returned to Berea from exile, and Jerusha's daughter Elizabeth became Hanson's second wife in December 1866; they were married by John G. Fee with Arthur Hanson and Franklin Preston witnesses.[3]

Rogers' account book contains several references to Jerusha and her children; the Widow Preston was a covenant member of the Berea Church when it re-opened in the Summer of 1865, and a charter member of the Madison County Temperance Union. All her children, but Mrs. Adams and John, attended Berea, and he became briefly a member of the board of trustees of Berea College. Elizabeth ("Lizzie") Preston studied at Berea before the war in the term ending July 8, 1859 (Rogers paid her for making clothes that year); David Preston also attended Berea before the Civil War and worked chopping wood, helping build Rogers' house in 1859 (David was paid 25 cents for one half day's work chopping wood February 16, 1859). His letter provides one of the first-hand accounts of the skirmish in Madison County in March 1860. Clara Preston, student at Berea in the term ending July 5, 1859, married another exile, Valentine Williams, in 1861. Ellen (Alice or Elsy Ellen), the youngest of Widow Preston's children, became a student at Berea Academy in 1866; her children by Alva Allen Cooper—Clara, Bessie and Maud—entered Berea a generation later.[4]

Jerusha Preston's son John H., born August 1842 in Kentucky, was a member of Berea's board of trustees in 1866-7; like his mother and sister Clara, he was a charter member of the Madison County Temperance Union (October 10, 1867).[5]

Jesse Preston, another Preston on Clay's List of Exiles, was the son of another Widow Preston, namely Eliza, whose husband's name is unknown. A native of Kentucky, born 1832, Jesse married Charity Ann Owens in 1856 in Rockcastle County, where the couple settled permanently. In 1860, when he suffered exile, Jesse had two children; his son John A. was three and his daughter Mary E. no more than one.

Reuben Preston, a single man at the time of the 1860 Exile, was born September 10, 1840 in Rockcastle County, the son of Ephraim Preston and Elsie Cummins (member of the Cummins family whose neighborhood in Rockcastle County has been mentioned so often). Reuben settled in Madison County about 1856 and eventually found work in John G. Hanson's sawmill. An early member of Fee's Glade Church, Reuben married Zerelda Moore, a pre-Civil War student, daughter of a slaveholder. All six of their children attended Berea.[6]

Although the Prestons went into exile in April 1860, many of them had returned by August the same year. Descendants of these Preston exiles continued to support Berea for many generations; for decades Berea College was never without a Preston in the student body.[7]

"J. Waters & family   5"

James Waters (or Walters) was born 1821 in Kentucky and lived in the northern part of Rockcastle County, very close to the Madison County border. His wife Amanda was a Renfro, first cousin to the Berea trustee; she was a charter member of Fee's Glade Church in 1853, although her husband apparently never joined. The couple had three children before they left Berea for good: Peter M. (born 1843), Lane (born 1848) and Mary A. (born 1853); one of their children was a pre-Civil War student at Berea, for James Waters paid tuition July 8, 1859.

In April 1860, James Waters held a note for $29 on John G. Hanson, who must have been his close neighbor, as the mob tore the roof off Waters' house the same day they destroyed Hanson's mill. By 1868 Waters and his family were living in St. Clair County, Missouri; they never returned to Berea after the Exile.[8]

"George Adams & family   2"

George Adams was paid for seven and one-half day's work in October 1859, according to Rogers' account book; probably his labor was in helping to build Rogers' house, as in the entry for November 7. Adams was bondsman for the marriage of Valentine Williams and Clara Preston in 1861 and witnessed Jerusha Preston's consent. Adams is mentioned in conjunction with David Preston in a letter written in August 1860; at that time he had returned from exile. He was married to Jerusha Preston's daughter by the time of the Exile, but they had no children: Clay's List shows two people in his family. He may have been the George Adams shown living with his wife Martha in Rockcastle County on the 1880 Federal Census.

"Wesley Dobs & family   2"

Wesley Dobbs (possibly John Wesley) was born in Kentucky in 1817, the son of William Dobbs, a native of Tennessee, and his wife Mary. In 1858 Rogers paid him for some potatoes; Elisha and John Dobbs, Wesley's brothers, were excluded from the Scaffold Cane Baptist Church in the summer of 1853 for joining one of Fee's free churches. The name of Wesley's wife is unknown. Both his brothers had children who became Berea students soon after the war.[9]

"Joel Todd & family   3"

Joel Todd, Sr., was born in 1799 in Madison County, son of John Todd and Martha ("Patsy") Collier; his first wife, mother of all his children, also a native of Madison County, was Nancy R. Lee, whose father owned a large amount of land on Brushy Fork of Silver Creek. Although many of Joel Todd's relations were slaveholders in both Madison and Rockcastle Counties (his cousin John Todd was the slaveholding deacon of Scaffold Cane Baptist Church), Joel's sympathies lay with the abolitionists; in 1854 he signed a petition to the AMA asking for antislavery tracts to distribute. Some of his children married into slaveholding families, but his daughter Lucinda, as wife of Silas Williams, was herself an exile.[10]

The only one of Joel Todd, Sr.'s many children who was living at home in 1860 was Joel, Jr., a student at Berea before the war, many of whose numerous children attended Berea in later years. Joel, Sr., was living in exile—apparently with John G. Fee's household—near Cincinnati in April 1860, but he returned to Madison County, where in the late 1860's and early 1870's he performed a great service to Berea: selling land to colonizing black families.[11]

"Ben. Kirby & family   3"

Benjamin Kirby and his wife Nancy had one young child, Martha A., born in 1858 or '9, at the time of the Exile. The couple had married in 1857, when Nancy Kirby was 14; eventually they had 12 children. Although the Kirbys returned from exile and settled again in Madison County, none of their throngs of children ever attended Berea, although he had relatives who did both before and after the war.

"Joseph Williams & family   6"
"John Williams & family   6"
"Silas Williams & family   4"
"Widow Williams & family   2"

As is clear from the heading, the Williams family, 18 of whom were sent into exile, made up almost one-third of the whole group. The Widow Williams was Martha ("Patsy") (Stutz) Williams, whose husband Abraham Williams (born 1799 in Kentucky) died before 1858. All the other Williams family members were her sons. Her daughter Celia was wife of Elisha Dobbs, brother of still another exile.

The Widow Williams is unique among the exiles, for she was a slaveowner at the time; herself a native of Virginia, she had imported a slave, a gift from her father Abner Stutz, from that state for private use by 1850 (it was illegal at that time to bring slaves into Kentucky to sell); she still owned the slave in 1860. One of her sons, Valentine Williams, was living at home with her at the time of the Exile; he had been a student at Berea in 1858. By July 1860, he had fled Berea and returned—a few months later he married Clara Preston, daughter of Jerusha; his second wife Margaret Martin was the mother of most of his children. He had at least 11, many of whom became Berea College students, as did a host of his grandchildren a generation later.[12]

Joseph Williams, born 1816 in Madison County, was one of the trustees of the 1858 Berea school, and probably the Williams who distributed tracts for Fee in 1857; by his wife, Patsy Kimbrall, also a native of Madison County, Williams fathered six children, two of whom, Howard and Joseph, were pre-Civil War students at Berea. Howard Williams had become a teacher himself by 1860, when John Rogers visited his former students' exhibition.[13]

John Williams, like his brother a native of Madison County, married Keziah West, daughter of George West, whose alleged mistreatment at the hands of the committee caused so much trouble; John's sons Samuel and WIlliam entered the Berea school in 1866.

Silas Williams and his wife Lucinda Todd, daughter of Joel, Sr., became covenant members of Fee's church in the summer of 1865; one or more of his children attended school before the war, as Silas paid tuition in October 1859; after the war his son Joseph was a student in the intermediate department from 1867 to 1870.[14]

Through the years Williams descendants at Berea College have been (practically speaking) too numerous to count. This family, like most of the 1860 exiles, formed a tenacious loyalty to the institution, a loyalty which lasted many generations.

Shadrach Roberts [an exile, but not on Clay's List]

One family known to have been exiled is not included on Clay's List. Shadrach Roberts (better known as "Shade," "Shady" or "Shay"), a native of Madison County, was in his late 20's at the time of the Exile; his wife, Susan Jane West, was another daughter of the ill-fated George West. In April 1860, the couple probably had two children. Shade Roberts, who was remembered as one of Madison County's old-time teachers, taught the district school in Berea while Rogers was still in exile in Ohio. Like many others, Shadrach Roberts had been in exile and returned by July 1860.[15]

Wrights, Burdetts & Wests [not exiled, although they were likely candidates]

Three families which had been both abused and threatened by the mob were apparently not exiled: the Wrights escaped that fate by the easiest route, when he became a turncoat, while the Burdetts, who certainly remained loyal to Fee, may have simply defied the committee—the family was noted for its courage. The Wests may have escaped persecution simply because widower George West died, but his eldest daughter Susan Jane (wife of Shadrach Roberts) was included among the exiles, as was his daughter Keziah Williams. His other three children, Elizabeth Ann, Eliza Ellen and George Branceford (only three years old in 1860), left orphans, were living with their grandfather George G. Woolwine in 1860. (Eleanor West, George's wife, was a Woolwine, sister of John G. Woolwine, from whom Berea College purchased the central part of the campus.)

NOTES FOR APPENDIX 4:

[1] *Minutes of Scaffold Cane-Silver Creek Baptist Church 1802-1859,* TS [copied by Frances Moore from original in possession of Clyde Linville, Mt. Vernon, Ky.]; Manshardt books in KHS; Haley Chapter in W. Wayne Rogers, *Gone to Texas* (Bloomington, Ill., 1978).

[2] UCMB; *Minutes of Berea Temperance Society,* in BCA.

[3] Mont Hanson to Ernest Dodge 19 Aug 1903 BCA.

[4] UCMB; *Minutes of Berea Temperance Society;* David Preston to John Rogers 27 Mar 1860 AMA 43860.

[5] John H. Preston obit., *Berea Citizen,* 8 Apr 1915.

[6] Reuben Preston obit., *Berea Citizen,* 10 Sept 1903.

[7] UCMB; Fee to Jocelyn 10 Sept 1859 AMA 43511; Fee to Whipple 12 May 1854 AMA 43238.

[8] Renfro to Fee 20 Apr 1860 BCA; *Madison County Deed Book 16,* p. 292.

[9] *Minutes of Scaffold Cane-Silver Creek Baptist Church.*

[10] Todd Genealogical Records in possession of James T. Todd, Kansas City, Mo.; Petition May 1854 [signed by citizens of Madison and Rockcastle Counties] AMA 43245.

[11] Kendrick to Jocelyn 6 Apr 1860 AMA 109485; Elizabeth (Todd) Gay obit., *Berea Citizen,* 21 Feb 1918.

[12] Benjamin Kirby to Fee & Hanson 13 July 1860 AMA 43876; *Madison County Deed Book 5,* p. 116.

[13] Berea School Leaflet, 19 Aug 1858 AMA 43396; Fee to Jocelyn 10 Sept 1859 AMA 43511.

[14] UCMB; Silas Williams obit., *Berea Citizen,* 31 Jan 1901.

[15] Galatha Rawlings, "Still More Old History," *Berea Citizen,* 20 Oct 1927; AMA 43876.

NOTES

CHAPTER ONE

[1] Fee to Whipple 1 Nov 1853 in AMA Correspondence (on Fisk University microfilm in Hutchins Library, Berea College), Item no. 43193: all subsequent references abbreviated as AMA, followed by an item number. Fisk to Whipple 5 Jan 1853 AMA 43146; John G. Fee, *Berea: Its History and Work* (published in *Berea Evangelist*, Jan. 1, 1885-June 10, 1886), TS, p. 2: this work is located in the Berea College Archives, hereafter abbreviated as BCA. Cassius M. Clay, *The Life of Cassius Marcellus Clay: Memoirs, Writings, and Speeches* (1886; rpt. New York: Negro Universities Press, 1969), vol. I, pp. 570, 571. The second volume never appeared; therefore, the volume reference is omitted from all subsequent notes.

[2] Clay, pp. 570, 571; Fee to Whipple 26 Aug 1853 AMA 43175. *American Missionary* (1853), p. 70 (typewritten copy in BCA); this collection of excerpts contains most of the articles about or by John G. Fee in the *American Missionary*—I have used this version *only* in numbers before 1857, when I could not consult actual volumes of the magazine (Hutchins Library, Special Collections, has the original *American Missionary* beginning from 1857); in subsequent references the copy will be identified as typescript (TS). Fee to Whipple 18 June 1853 AMA 43171.

[3] Fee to Whipple 12 May 1854 AMA 43238; Fee, *Berea,* pp. 2, 3; John G. Fee, *An Autobiography* (Chicago: National Christian Association, 1891), p. 91.

[4] AMA 43238. Besides giving Fee land, Clay also contributed to the building of his house. Clay recorded this payment in his diary, 29 Mar 1855. Clay, p. 571. Raphael Rogers said Clay's "munificent gift [of the land] was probably worth from twelve to fifteen dollars." John Raphael Rogers, "Pioneering in Berea," p. 5, pamphlet dated 31 Sept 1931, BCA.

[5] Fee, *Autobiography*, pp. 26, 89; Fee to Clay 18 Sept 1849 BCA "Vincent Hamilton," a contemporary wrote [4 June 1851], "has set Jim free and pays him wages for his work." Kendall, p. 245.

[6] Fee to Whipple 12 May 1854 AMA 43238.

[7] Fee, "Biographical Sketch", p. 7. Fee, Autobiography, pp. 75-78, 83. In Berea College's collection of books from Fee's private library those concerned with baptism outnumber those dealing with all other subjects put together, including abolitionism. Fee's idea of baptism changed drastically, for in 1849 he wrote, "A church may administer the ordinance of baptism either by sprinkling or immersion, allowing liberty of conscience as to the mode which the convert may honestly believe the Bible to teach." Mode of baptism, he indicated, was not "any fundamental principle of Christianity," but one of the non-essential doctrines. Fee, "Nonfellowship with Slavery the Duty of Christians (New York: John A. Gray, 1855), p. 29.

[8] Fee to Clay 22 June 1854 BCA; Fee to Whipple 1 Aug 1854 AMA 43255.

[9] Fee, *Berea*, p. 6.

[10] Clay to Arthur Tappan 24 Oct 1852 AMA 43141; Fisk to Whipple 5 Jan 1853 AMA 43146.

[11] Fee, *Berea*, p. 24; Elizabeth Rogers, "Personal History," pp. 14, 15; Galatha Rawlings in *Berea Citizen*. Rev. David Rice's abolitionism may have influenced local families who later belonged to his Paint Lick Church: they included Rawlings, Best, Burdette and Burnam families. Forrest Calico, *History of Garrard County, Kentucky and its Churches* (New York: Hobson book Press, 1947), p. 426. For an account of Rice's antislavery views and activities, see Lowell Harrison, *The Antislavery Movement in Kentucky* (Lexington: U. Press of Kentucky, 1978), pp. 18-23.

[12] Rawlings in *Berea Citizen; Garrard County Will Book L (1844-48)*, pp. 487, 488; *Madison County Deed Book X*, p. 353. Lizzie Rogers described Amanda (Rawlings) Sayers as a typical "mountain mother." "No doubt," Mrs. Rogers wrote, "her mountain farm aided her some, and her needle was always ready to help those who could afford to pay for her services, yet I can but wonder how she managed to live and keep her children in school." Amanda Sayers had inherited a slave girl Ruth from her father and she retained her bond servant until Emancipation. Thus Mrs. Rogers' poor mountain woman was a slaveholder; as stereotypes, these two characters are never combined, but in real life the conjunction did occur. A "mountain mother" might be the daughter of a slaveholder from Baltimore, careful to maintain her own status in that class, even in the depths of poverty. At the same time, her brother, a "true Southerner," with all the accoutrements of a Kentucky gentleman, might refuse to countenance slavery. Elizabeth Rogers, p. 15; *Garrard County Will Book L (1844-48)*, pp. 487, 488; *Madison County Slave Census 1860*.

[13] Green Clay, *Cassius Clay: Militant Statesman, Moses of Emancipation 1810-1903*, p. 109: in Dorris Collection, Crabbe Library, EKU; see, for example, Fee to Jocelyn 26 Apr 1858 AMA 43613.

[14] William Still, *The Underground Railroad* (1871; rpt. Chicago: Johnson Publ. Co., 1970), p. 622.

[15] Clay, pp. 570, 571. Cassius Clay's popularity in the Glade and its immediate vicinity is amply attested by the number of children who were named after him and his kin—for example: Cassius M. Rawlings, Green Clay Renfro, Cassius Clay Stapp [nephew of William], Cassius Clay West, Clay S. Todd, Cassius Cornelison, Cassius M. Clay Cummings and Cassius Clay Moody, all born between 1832 and 1859.

[16] Clay, p. 245. " . . . I have told my boys to retreat, leaving their wives and children at home. . . . If some are killed, God only knows the end! We will at once take to the woods and the mountains and defend ourselves to the last!" Letter from Cassius Clay, *Kentucky Statesman*, 13 Apr 1860, in Lexington Public Library.

[17] Fee, *Berea*, p. 1; John Wesley quoted by Fee in *The Sinfulness of Slaveholding*, (New York: John A. Gray, 1851), p. 10.

[18] *American Missionary* Vol. IV, no. 2 (Feb 1860), p. 43; "Speech of Cassius Clay at Frankfort, Ky., from the Capitol Steps, 10 Jan 1860," pamphlet, p. 3: in BCA.

[19] In May 1853 Wiley Fisk reported 11 members of Glade Church; at Scaffold Cane 6, at Boone's Fork 4—Fisk to Whipple 30 May 1853 AMA 43167; Fee to Whipple 3 May 1853 AMA 43164; Andrew Hill, Deposition, 5 June 1916, Founders & Founding: Fee, BCA.

[20] *Union Church Minute Book*, MS, BCA—hereafter abbreviated as UCMB; *Madison County Tax Book 1855*, Kentucky Historical Society; Hiram K. Richardson, *Memoirs of Berea* (Berea: Berea College Press, 1940), p. 13. Among the citizens who lived in the Glade District, John Burnam, Sr., William Stapp and Thomas Jefferson Renfro, charter members of the church, later to be among the first trustees of Berea College, were the oldest, most respected members of the community—prosperous, non-slaveholding farmers, belonging to very old and prominent families in Madison County; Teman Thompson and John Hamilton Rawlings (usually called

'Ham') were also community leaders, although their roots were in Paint Lick. On the Ridge where Berea College now stands only two families resided: William B. Wright (Berea's first postmaster, son-in-law of William Stapp) with his house in Stapp's woods near the site of the present postoffice, and James Maupin, a widower with many children, located at what is now known as Van Winkle Grove.

Some families in the neighborhood were smallscale slaveholders: Moores, Ruckers, Todds, Harrison Burnams, Elders, Ballards, others. The smallscale slaveholders in the Glade District and nearby seldom owned more than 10 slaves. In 1860, for example, Jesse Denham owned 9, Jeremiah Rucker 4, Fergusson Moore 7, Mossiah Moore 2; Madison Todd, on the other hand, owned 17 (although he had only 2 in 1850). William M. Ballard owned 1 slave in 1850, 1 in 1854, and 3 in 1860. William Stapp and John Hamilton Rawlings had been slaveholders, but had sold all their slaves long before John G. Fee moved to Madison County—probably as part of their commitment to Cassius Clay. Madison County Slave Censuses 1850, 1860; *Madison County Tax Book 1854.*

[21] *Kentucky Statesman,* 29 Nov 1859, in Lexington Public Library. J. Winston Coleman, Jr., "Lexington's Slave Dealers and Their Southern Trade," *Filson Club History Quarterly,* Vol. 12, no. 1 (Jan 1938), p. 16; J. Winston Coleman, Jr., *Slavery Times in Kentucky* (Chapel Hill: U. of N. C. Press, 1940), p. 315. Lewis Collins & Richard H. Collins, *History of Kentucky* (1874; rpt. Berea: Kentucke Imprints, 1976), II, 260, 261. The slave population of Kentucky in 1850 was 210,981 out of a total population of 982,405.

[22] Fee to Whipple 9 Jan 1851 AMA 43093; Fee to Whipple Mar 1851 AMA 43098. In 1870 Fee wrote that the Church at Berea "is known simply as a Church of Christ." It was not named "Union Church" at that time. *American Missionary,* Vol. XIV, no. 1 (Jan 1870), p. 2.

[23] UCMB; John A. R. Rogers, "Speech on 50th Anniversary of Berea," *Berea Citizen,* 18 June 1903. The original church book of the Glade congregation was destroyed in 1862; however, the Minute Book which the church began keeping in 1864 records the following nine people as the "covenanted association" of 1853: "Thomas J. Renfro & Frances Renfro, his wife, William Stapp, John Burnam, Sr., Jemima Tatum [2nd wife of William Stapp; they married in 1853], George West, Nancy west his wife [actually, her name was Eleanor, and she had been a Woolwine; her nickname was Helen, not Nancy], Wiley B. Fisk, & _____ Walters [Amanda (Renfro) Walters or Waters—the surnames are usually interchangeable—wife of James Waters]." John A. R. Rogers in his speech on the 50th Anniversary of Berea (1903) mentioned all the names listed in the Minute Book, correcting Mrs. West's name to "Helen," supplying Mrs. Walter's first name, "Amanda," and adding two more names: William B. Wright and his wife Martha. Fee may have counted himself and his wife as original members, even though he had not removed permanently to Berea when the church organized, in which case all of the original 13 are accounted for. In any case, every person on the list was to play a role in subsequent developments—all except Wiley Fisk. See Will Frank Steely, "The Established Churches and Slavery 1850-1860," *Register,* Vol. 55, no. 2 (Apr 1957), pp. 97-104, for an account of the established churches in Kentucky when Fee was most active in his church-founding work.

Minutes of Scaffold Cane-Silver Creek Baptist Church 1802-59 [typescript of original minute book in possession of Clyde Linville, Mt. Vernon, Ky.], pp. 72, 73; Fisk to Whipple 1 Sept 1853 AMA 43178. Certainly Scaffold Cane Baptist Church was not the place to protest slavery; one of its deacons, holding the office, it is said, for fifty years, was John Todd, owner of 13 slaves in 1850. Georgia Ann (Todd) Kinnard obit., *Berea Citizen,* 28 Oct 1926.

[24] Fee, *Berea,* pp. 4, 5. It is quite likely that Fee moved his church and center of operations up to the Ridge when his relationship with Wiley Fisk and those who favored Fisk was at its lowest point. Fee and Fisk were supposed to share the ministry of Glade Church and others, but Fisk's supporters certainly included slaveholders and Fee was appalled when he returned to Madison County and found how the church had backslidden under Fisk's careless ministry. Fee

spoke of Fisk as the "Apollos" of Berea—one, that is, who was the occasion of factionalism. So Fee found "the place for the church and *co-operation with working friends*" [my own italics] was on the Ridge. The move was another example of Fee's "coming out." Fee, "Biographical Sketch," p. 8.

[25] UCMB; *American Missionary* Vol. III, no. 5 (May 1859), p. 114; Lowell H. Harrison, *The Antislavery Movement In Kentucky* (Lexington: U. Press of Ky., 1978), Chap, 1; *Kentucky Messenger,* 23 Dec 1859 in Exile File, BCA; Sidney E. Ahlstrom, *A Religious History of the American People* (Garden City, N. Y. : Image Books, 1975), Vol. II, "Churches," Chapter 42; Harrison, p. 15; Fee, *Autobiography*, p. 60.

[26] Louis Ruchames, *The Abolitionists: A Collection of Their Writings* (New York: G. P. Putnam's Sons, 1963), p. 177; George P. Rawick, *The American Slave: A Composite Autobiography* (1941: rpt. Westport, Conn.: Greenwood Publ. Co., 1972), XVIII, 180 ("Kentucky Slave Narratives," p. 3).

[27] Fee, *Autobiography*, pp. 60, 61.

[28] *American Missionary*, Vol. II, no. 2 (Feb 1858), pp. 42,43; Vol. II, no. 5 (May 1858), pp. 114, 115.

[29] *Ibid.*, pp. 114, 115.

[30] David L. Smiley, *The Lion of White Hall: The Life of Cassius M. Clay* (Madison: U. of Wisconsin Press, 1962), pp. 33, 34.

[31] *Ibid.*, p. 163.

[32] *Ibid.*, p. 144.

[33] Fee to Whipple 28 July 1851 AMA 43103.

[34] Collins & Collins, II, 772; Clay, pp. 17, 22, 25. See my entry on "Green Clay" in *The Kentucky Encyclopedia*. Lexington: U. Press of Kentucky, 1992.

[35] Clay, pp. 25, 27. When Cassius Clay looked at the mulatto slave girl, "her features finely cut, quite Caucasian," and his brother Sidney, he may have seen more resemblance than "equal agony" in their faces. Of Green Clay, his son wrote: "In the discipline of women, my father knew, as every sensible man knows, the strength of the sexual passions. Nature ever tends to the preservation of the races of animals. Opportunity, notwithstanding all the sentimentalism about innate chastity, is the cause of most of the lapses from virtue." Clay used this same observation when he argued against interracial education of both sexes at Berea College. Clay makes it clear that the mulatto girl Mary was born at White Hall; maybe she was his half-sister. Clay, p. 45.

[36] *Ibid.*, p. 28.

[37] *Ibid.*, pp. 56, 57. Clay biographer David Smiley suggests that Clay's Yale 'conversion' by Garrison was "out of character," a "romanticized story" concocted at a much later time for Clay's memoirs. Perhaps Smiley does not allow for the rather familiar distance between the views of an idealistic college student and the opinions of the same individual struggling in social and political arenas a few years later. Smiley, p. 238.

[38] Smiley, p. 30; Eric Foner, *Free Soil, Free Labor, Free Men: The Ideology of the Republican Party before the Civil War* (London: Oxford U. Press, 1970), pp. 61, 62.

[39] Smiley, pp. 53, 54.

[40] *Ibid.*, pp. 56-58; [*Anti-Slavery Bugle* 30 Jan 1847 quoted in Jane H. Pease & William H. Pease, *Bound With Them in Chains* (Westport, Conn.: Greenwood Press, Inc., 1972), p. 76; Foner, p. 58. Clay's grandson, in a biographical account of Cassius Clay, wrote that General Clay "was not misguided by a misconception of the Negro's capacity and character. He was not, like the northern abolitionists generally, a victim of the delusion that the black man differed from the white only in the color of his skin, and needed but the removal of the oppressors' yoke to blossom into a noble race of citizens." He perceived well before Emancipation "that the freed

slave would be a danger and a charge to the nation. . . . " Francis Clay, "The Political Significance of the late C. M. Clay," *Filson Club History Quarterly*, Vol. 33, no. 1 (Jan 1959), pp. 47, 48.

[41] Smiley, pp. 47, 56, 81, 238. The "inferiority of races" exists: "the Caucasian is the superior race," Clay said, in his address at Philadelphia (14 Jan 1846), "of a larger and better formed brain; of a more beautiful form and more exquisite structure," although that is not "a good basis for enslavement." Cassius M. Clay, *The Writing of Cassius Marcellus Clay* (New York: Harper and Bros., 1848), p. 531.

[42] Smiley, p. 238.

[43] *Ibid.*, p. 36.

[44] *Ibid.*, pp. 94; Clay, p. 235. In 1862, Clay said, "I have never been, and am not now, an 'abolitionist' in the strict sense of that word. . . ." Hans L. Trefousse, *The Radical Republicans* (New York: Alfred A. Knopf, 1969), p. 18.

[45] Fee to Clay, 4 Apr 1844 BCA.

[46] Fee to Clay, 18 Sept 1849 BCA.

[47] H. Edward Richardson, *Cassius Marcellus Clay* (Lexington: U. Press of Ky., 1976), p. ix.

[48] Clay, pp. 572, 573.

[49] Fee to Tappan 2 May 1853 AMA 43155; Fee to Clay 17 Aug 1849 BCA.

[50] *American Missionary* (1847), TS, pp. 23, 24; Fee to Clay 18 Sept 1849 BCA; Fee to Whipple 15 July 1853 AMA 43172. On March 7, 1853, Fee begged William Goodell to come to Kentucky to edit a newspaper Clay would approve and support. It is doubtful that Clay felt any particular enthusiasm for Goodell, for Clay warned Fee: "Beware of Goodell's abstractions in politics—we cannot stand on them in the South." Clay to Fee 8 July 1855 BCA.

One reason Clay gave up the *True American* was to serve in the Mexican War. Fee objected to that too, protesting that Clay was "doing evil that good might come." Clay, it seems, felt military glory would revitalize his political career in Kentucky. Fee, *Autobiography*, p. 127.

[51] Fee to Tappan 2 May 1853 AMA 43155; David L. Smiley, "Cassius M. Clay and John G. Fee: A Study in Southern Anti-Slavery Thought," *The Journal of Negro History* Vol. XLII, no. 3 (July 1957), p. 208; Clay, p. 576; Fee, *Autobiography*, p. 46.

[52] Fee, *Autobiography*, p. 55.

[53] Fee, *Berea*, pp. 7, 8.

[54] *Ibid.*, p. 9. Some of Fee's efforts to obtain justice through civil courts had been successful in his earlier locations—in Lewis County, for example. (See Fee, *Autobiography*, p. 45, and Victor B. Howard, "Cassius M. Clay and the Origins of the Republican Party," *Filson Club History Quarterly*, Vol. 45, no. 1 (Jan 1971), p. 59.) In 1855 after Fee had been attacked Lewis Tappan sent him a gift of $50 from himself and Gerrit Smith and advised Fee to use the money for the comfort of his family, not to spend it on lawsuits, "unless you can find some precept in the Gospel authorizing you to go to law . . . better rely on moral force" and leave the assailants in God's hands. Evidenty, Fee found the appropriate Gospel precept, because he certainly ignored Tappan's advice. Tappan to Fee 3 Apr 1855 BCA; Fee to Gerrit Smith 18 May 1855 in Syracuse University Library, quoted in Carleton Mabee, *Black Freedom* (New York: Macmillan Co., 1970), p. 237. See Fee, *Autobiography*, p. 101.

[55] Richardson, p. 76; Howard, p. 59; Pease & Pease, p. 84; Asa E. Martin, *The Antislavery Movement in Kentucky* (1918; rpt. Westport, Conn.: Negro Universities Press, 1970), p. 123. According to John A. R. Rogers' *Birth of Berea College; A Story of Providence*, Otis Waters wrote that Clay's famous ultimatum was delivered in Mount Vernon, in Rockcastle County. John A. R. Rogers, *Birth* (1904; rpt. Berea: Berea College Press, 1933), p. 41.

[56] Fee, *Berea*, p. 9; Harrison, *Antislavery Movement*, p. 73.

[57] *American Missionary* (July 7, 1855), TS, p. 78. Clay says the 4th of July meeting for 1855 took place at the Glade, Fee says in Rockcastle County. Both these reports appear in contemporary accounts. Perhaps the two men appeared in both places on the same day. Howard, "Clay," p. 60.

[58] Clay to Fee 8 July 1855 BCA.

[59] Fee to Clay 26 Oct 1854 BCA. Ironically, many years later, William E. Lincoln was to write that he *had* given abolitionist tracts to slaves while he was working at Berea, but Fee probably did not know about Lincoln's action, and would not have permitted it. Lincoln, p. 35.

[60] Clay to Fee 8 July 1855 BCA.

[61] Howard, "Clay," pp. 60, 61. Harrison, p. 73. *Cincinnati Daily Gazette*, 23 July 1855, quoted in Howard, "Clay," p. 61. Cassius Clay respected John G. Fee's courage, even though it was so different from his own. William E. Lincoln recalls Clay saying, "Fee has more courage than any of us; we go into danger with our pistols—knives & friend-helpers; he goes alone with no one; trusting in God." William E. Lincoln, "Memoirs" (letter to President Frost 18 Oct 1909), p. 28: in BCA.

[62] Clay to Fee 18 Dec 1855 BCA.

[63] Fee to Clay Apr 1856 BCA.

[64] Fee, *Berea*, p. 10.

[65] John G. Fee to Editor, 4 July 1856, *Newport Kentucky Weekly*, Aug 25, 1856, clipping in Clay-Fee Correspondence, BCA.

[66] *Ibid.*

[67] Fee, *Berea*, p. 11.

[68] Davis to Jocelyn 29 July 1856 AMA 43392; Davis to Jocelyn 1 Aug 1856 AMA 43394.

[69] Both Clay and Fee published installment of their argument in newspapers from 1856 to 1860; clippings of these letters are in Correspondence between Clay in Founders and Founding: Fee, BCA.

[70] Fee, *Berea*, p. 11.

[71] Clay to Davis Oct 5, 1857 BCA.

[72] Fee to Clay 17 Apr 1857 BCA.

[73] Fee to Clay 22 May 1857 BCA; Fee to Jocelyn 15 July 1857 AMA 43485.

[74] *American Missionary* (1857), TS, pp. 211, 212; Fee to Clay 28 July 1857 BCA; Fee, *Autobiography,* p. 107. From other evidence it appears that the widow who walked with Fee was Jerusha Preston, matriarch of a family which later became well-known in Berea. Fee does not name the woman in his accounts.

[75] Fee, *Autobiography,* p. 109.

[76] *Ibid.*

[77] Fee to Clay 28 July 1857 BCA.

[78] Fee to Jocelyn 29 July 1857 AMA 43492.

[79] Fee to Clay, 27 Aug 1857 BCA; Fee to Clay 3 Aug 1857 BCA.

[80] Fee to Jocelyn Aug 1857 AMA 43503; Fee to Jocelyn 10 Sept 1857 AMA 43511.

[81] Fee to Jocelyn 27 Mar 1858 AMA 43596.

[82] Fee to Jocelyn 10 Sept 1857 AMA 43512; Clay, "Notes from Gen. Clay," pamphlet, 28 Mar 1898, BCA. Clay claimed that Fee "was reinforced by adventurers using force." Fee had been "at first a non-resistant," Clay wrote, "but, further along, allowed his friends to use force." Clay does not point out that the same men who armed themselves to protect Fee were accustomed to bearing weapons to defend Cassius Clay. Clay, p. 77. For a full discussion of the issue of

violence in Fee and Clay's relationship and work, see Stanley Harrold's "Violence and Nonviolence in Kentucky Abolitionism," *The Journal of Southern History* Vol. LVII, No. 1 (Feb 1991), pp. 15-38.

[83] Fee to Clay 17 Sept 1857 BCA.

[84] Fee to Tappan 17 Dec 1857 AMA 43535.

[85] Fee to Clay 19 Jan 1858 BCA.

[86] Fee to Clay Apr 1858 BCA.

[87] Fee, *Autobiography*, p. 126.

[88] Fee to Jocelyn 28 July 1858 AMA 43650.

[89] Fee to Clay 12 July 1858 BCA.

[90] Fee to Clay Apr 1859 BCA.

[91] Candee to Jocelyn 29 June 1859 AMA 43775; Fee to Clay 1 June 1859 BCA.

CHAPTER TWO

[1] John Gregg Fee's birthplace would have been located in Mason County in 1792; since Bracken County was partly formed out of Mason in 1786, it is possible that Fee and his father were born in the same place and only the county had moved. The house where John G. Fee was born, located on the road between Germantown and Augusta, has been placed on the National Register of Historic Places. Fee, *Autobiography*, p. 9; Charles B. Heinemann, "*First Census of Kentucky" 1790* (Baltimore: Genealogical Publ. Co., 1976), p. 34; Fee, *Biographical Sketch*, p. 1; Collins & Collins, II, 776; Family Record in Fee's Cut Bible; *Bracken County Will Book B*, p. 281. The chief sources for genealogical information on the Fee family (all in BCA) are Ralph Emerson Pearson, *A History of the Fee Family* (no date), Vol. I; Col. Robert Arthur, *The Fee Family and Its Gregg Connections* (New Orleans, Apr 1959); and Anne Pirkle, *The Fee Book*, a compilation of genealogical charts, which corrects many errors in the other two books. Ms. Pirkle, great granddaughter of Fee's brother James, donated her work to Berea College while I was engaged on the present history and graciously spent a day discussing the Fee family with me.

[2] Fee to Whipple 17 Sept 1850 AMA 43086; Fee, *Autobiography*, p. 10. The most reliable source for Gregg genealogy is Hazel May Middleton Kendall, *Quaker Greggs* (priv. printed, 1944). Unfortunately, the Hutchins Library does not have a copy of this relatively rare book, which I discovered in the Virginia State Library in Richmond.

[3] Ivan E. McDougle, *Slavery in Kentucky 1792-1865* (1918; rpt. Westport, Conn.; Negro Universities Press, 1970), p. 53; Coffin, p. 471; Coleman, *Slavery Times*, p. 101.

Harriet Beecher Stowe uses the Ohio River symbolically in one of the most famous passages in all of Western literature: Eliza crossing the ice in *Uncle Tom's Cabin*:

> An hour before sunset, Eliza entered the village of T——, by the Ohio river, weary and foot-sore, but still strong in heart. Her first glance at the river, which lay, like Jordan, between her and the Canaan of Liberty on the other side.
>
> It was now early spring, and the river was swollen and turbulent, great cakes of foating ice were swinging heavily to and fro in the turbid waters . . .
>
> [Trapped by her pursuers (a slave trader and his assistants) on the Kentucky shore Eliza seizes her child and flees to the river.] In that dizzy moment her feet to her scarce seemed to touch the ground, and a moment brought her to the water's edge. Right on behind they came; and nerved with strength such as God gives only to the desperate, with one wild cry and flying leap, she vaulted sheer over the turbid current by

the shore, on to the raft of ice beyond. It was a desperate leap—impossible to anything but madness and despair . . .

The huge green fragment of ice on which she alighted pitched and creaked as her weight came on it, but she staid there not a moment. With wild cries and desperate energy she leaped to another and still another cake—stumbling—leaping—slipping—springing upwards again! Her shoes are gone—her stockings cut from her feet—while blood marked every step; but she saw nothing, felt nothing, till dimly, as in a dream, she saw the Ohio side, and a man helping her up the bank. Harriet Beecher Stowe, *Uncle Tom's Cabin* (Garden City, N. Y.: Doubleday & Co., Inc., 1960), pp. 78, 79.[7]

Stowe's famous story was purportedly based on an actual incident: a Kentucky slave woman named Eliza carried her infant across the frozen Ohio with slave hunters close on her trail; she was rescued by John Rankin, a Presbyterian minister at Ripley, Ohio, only a few miles down the river from Fee's home; Levi Coffin, the Quaker "President" of the Underground Railroad and one of Fee's friends later in his career, also aided in Eliza Harris's escape. The Underground Railroad was so successful along the Ohio that slaveowners reckoned their property had "depreciated by twenty per cent in all counties bordering the Ohio River from the facilities offered fugitive slaves by the organized societies." Page Smith, *The Nation Comes of Age: A People's History of the Ante-Bellum Years* (New York: Hill Book Co., 1981), IV, 629; Levi Coffin, *Reminiscences of Levi Coffin* (Cincinnati: Western Tract Society, 1876), pp. 147-9; *Lexington Observer and Reporter*, 10 Nov 1838, quoted in Coleman, *Slavery Times*, p. 235. For a complete account of runaway slaves in Kentucky see Marion B. Lucas, *A History of Blacks in Kentucky*, Vol. I, pp. 61 & foll.

[4] Coleman, p. 92.

[5] Fee, "Biographical Sketch," p. 1; Fee to Whipple 15 Oct 1851 AMA 43112.

[6] Ohio was no paradise for black people: the state's Black Code was notoriously oppressive; fugitives frequently headed for Canada, because even the northern United States was a hotbed of prejudice and discrimination. (See William H. Pease & Jane H. Pease, *Black Utopia: Negro Communal Experiments in America* (Madison: State Historical Society of Wisconsin, 1963), pp. 5-7 and foll.)

[7] Fee, *Autobiography*, p. 17.

[8] Fee, "Biographical Sketch," p. 1; Marshall E. Vaughn, article on organization of Sharon Church, *Berea Citizen*, 30 Nov 1933; Fee, *Autobiography*, pp. 11, 12.

[9] Fee, *Autobiography*, pp. 10, 11.

[10] Fee's diploma from Augusta College BCA; Walter H. Rankins, *History of Augusta College* (Frankfort: Roberts Printing Co., 1957), pp. 16, 17.

[11] Fee to Clay 4 Apr 1844 BCA; Lawrence T. Lesick, *The Lane Rebels* (Methuchen, N. J.: Scarecrow Press, 1980), p. 126; Fee, "Biographical Sketch," p. 2; Fee, *Autobiography*, pp. 10, 11.

[12] Lesick p. 142.

[13] Fee, "Biographical Sketch," p. 2; *General Catalogue of Lane Theological Seminary 1828-1881* (Cincinnati: Elm Street Printing Co., 1881), pp. 20, 21. James C. White spent most of his long life as a minister in Ohio—in Cincinnati, Cleveland and Dayton. Fee, *Autobiography*, p. 15.

[14] Fee, *Biographical Sketch*, p. 1, 2; Fee, *Autobiography*, p. 14.

[15] Fee, *Autobiography*, p. 14.

16 Ahlstrom, I, 561-63; Marshall E. Vaughn, article on organization of Sharon Church, *Berea Citizen*, 30 Nov 1933.

17 Fee to Whipple 15 Oct 1851 AMA 43112.

18 Fee to Badger and Hall 23 Jan 1845, U. of Chicago Microfilms; Fee, *Autobiography*, p. 23.

19 Fee to Badger and Hall 23 June 1845; Fee to Badger & Hall 2 Apr 1845: both on U. of Chicago Microfilms.

20 Ahlstrom, I, 513, 514; Cross, pp. 22, 23.

21 Goodell to Josiah Cady, 14 Sept 1850 in Founders & Founding: Fee, BCA.

22 Harold M. Parker, "The New School Synod of Kentucky," *Filson Club History Quarterly*, Vol. 50, no. 2 (Apr 1976), pp. 79-80. Fee wrote, "Whilst [the American Home Missionary Society] manifestly, for some reason desired to help sustain one anti-slavery church in the South, they were at the same time sustaining fifty-two slaveholding churches in the South." Fee, *Autobiography*, p. 42.

23 Fee to Badger and Hall, 27 June 1848 and 29 Aug 1848: U. of Chicago Microfilms; Fee to Whipple 10 Oct 1848 AMA 43104.

24 Barnes & Dumond, I, 50.

25 Fee to Goodell, 29 May 1850; Nonfellowship with Slaveholders," p. 52; Fee to Goodell 23 Aug 1850 BCA.

26 Ironically, late in his life Fee, in a storm of controversy, would withdraw from the AMA and even from the church he himself had founded in Berea. Even later, he virtually repudiated Berea College as well. Once John G. Fee started "coming out," he never stopped!

27 Fee, "Biographical Sketch," p. 3; Fee, *Autobiography*, pp. 18-21. In marrying his cousin Fee was following the custom of his mother's family: Greggs married Greggs in incredible numbers. See Kendall, Quaker Greggs.

28 Fee, "Biographical Sketch," pp. 3, 4. *Bracken County Marriage Register Book 1*, p. 45.

29 Fee, *Autobiography*, p. 22.

30 Collins, II, 258-261, 464; Fee, *Autobiography*, p. 23, 24.

31 Fee, *Berea*, p. 2; Fee to Badger & Hall 23 Jan 1845, U. of Chicago Microfilms; Fee (1st year's report) to Badger & Hall 1 Apr 1846, U. of Chicago Microfilms.

32 Fee to Badger & Hall 1 Apr 1846, U. of Chicago Microfilms.

33 Fee, *Autobiography*, p. 29. Fee, "Biographical Sketch," pp. 4, 5;

34 Fee, *Autobiography*, p. 29; Fee, "Biographical Sketch", pp. 4, 5; Clara Degman Hook, "John G. Fee's Work in Lewis Co., Ky.," in *Lewis County Herald*, 5 Mar 1931, clipping in BCA.

35 List of Donors to Bethesda Church, 29 Aug 1851, in Founders and Founding: Fee, BCA; Fee, *Autobiography*, p. 58.

36 Fee's report in *AMA 4th Annual Report, 1850*, pp. 34, 35.

37 *Bracken Circuit Court Order Book H*, p. 473, Sept 17, 1850, quoted in Coleman, *Slavery Times*, p. 322.

38 Fee to Whipple 10 Oct 1848 AMA 43014.

39 *AMA 4th Annual Report*, 1850, p. 35.

40 Fee to Whipple 7 Sept 1851 AMA 43109.

41 Harrison, p. 70; Fee, *Autobiography*, p. 58. List of Donors; *AMA 6th Annual Report, 1852*, p. 44.

[42] Fee to Jocelyn 16 Sept 1859 AMA 43794; Marshall E. Vaughn undertook to prove that Fee's father did not disinherit him. See his article on John Fee's will in *Berea Citizen*, 14 Dec 1933.

[43] Fee to Jocelyn 16 Feb 1857 AMA 43442.

[44] Fee to Jocelyn 16 Sept 1859 AMA 43794; James T. Norris, Autobiographical sketch, p. 4 (xerox copy of TS in BCA); Fee to ? June 1858 AMA 108409; Fee to (Lincoln?) 21 June 1858 AMA 108404. When the Union Army was occupying New Orleans James Fee's house was taken by Gen. Benjamin ("Beast") Butler for his headquarters.

[45] Fee, *Autobiography*, p. 61, 66.

[46] Sarah Fee's will in *Bracken Co. Will Bk. O*, p. 251.; Norris Ms., p. 4.

[47] Fee, *Autobiography*, p. 68.

[48] Fee to Gerrit Smith 21 Feb 1854 (letter in Syracuse U. Library), quoted in Mabee, p. 236.

[49] Kendall, p. 19. Greenbury Griffith Hanson, father of three Berea College trustees, was born March 26, 1806, near Germantown, Bracken County, Kentucky, and died in the same place October 10, 1894. A member of Fee's Bethesda Church, Hanson was an early abolitionist although his own parents, John Hanson and Averilla Hollis, both of Harford County, Maryland, had belonged to slaveholding families. (Some of Greenbury Hanson's Hollis relatives were slaveowners in Bracken County.) John and Averilla Hanson settled in Bracken County by 1799, when his name appears on a tax list. Greenbury Hanson married Rebecca Gregg April 11, 1833, in Bracken County, Kentucky. See Gaius Marcus Brumbaugh, *Maryland Records: Colonial, Revolutionary, County and Church* (1928; rpt. Baltimore; Genealogical Publ. Co., 1967), II, 168-74, which comprises a Census of 1776, Harford Lower Hundred, Harford county; Obit. notice of Greenbury Hanson in Founders and Founding: John G. Hanson, BCA.

Vincent Hamilton, who married Rebecca Gregg's sister Elizabeth (March 24, 1821) was also born in Bracken County, March 12, 1799. His parents, Samuel Hamilton and Dilly (or Dolly) Donovan, were natives of Pennsylvania and Maryland respectively. Vincent Hamilton actively supported his son-in-law, John G. Fee's work, joining Bracken Church, freeing his own slaves, and contributing to the AMA. He died in Bracken County in 1879 and is buried in the Bethesda Cemetery. His children seem to have been generally sympathetic to abolitionism; his daughter Laura sent a son to Berea College, while his son Edwin Stanton was a student at Oberlin Prep. 1853-56.

[50] Fee, *Autobiography* p. 10; ADD 1st par. of her OBIT in *American Missionary* (Oct 1872)

[51] Fee to Whipple 15 Feb 1853 AMA 43150. In a letter dated June 4, 1851, a friend wrote, "Old Misses Gregg [Mary DeMoss Gregg] has set Henry free and pays him for his work— That is the honest way of doing business." Kendall, *Quaker Greggs*, p. 245.

[52] John F. Gregg, "Ed Mofford," MS in Founders & Founding: Fee, BCA.

[53] Goodell to Cady; Fee to Tappan Sept 1853 AMA 43183.

[54] Fee to Jocelyn 3 Dec 1856 AMA 43415.

[55] Elizabeth Rogers, *Personal History of Berea College*, p. 9.

[56] Rogers, p. 35. Fee, *Autobiography*, p. 41.

[57] Fee, *Autobiography*, pp. 41, 99, 100; Rogers, 35; Fee, *Berea*, pp. 14, 15. Fee, *Autobiography*, pp. 44, 45. Miss Tucker was probably Sarah A. Tucker, student in Oberlin Academy 1857-58.

[58] Elizabeth Rogers, p. 9.

[59] Fee, *Autobiography*, p. 121.

[60] Matilda Fee to Jocelyn 17 Oct 1856 AMA 43406.

[61] *AMA 11th Annual Report, 1857*, p. 64; Fee to Jocelyn 17 Oct 1856 AMA 43405.

[62] Fee, *Autobiography*, pp. 19, 20.

[63] Elizabeth Rogers, p. 9.

[64] *American Missionary*, Vol. III, no. 4 (Apr 1859), p. 92; Harrison, *The Antislavery Movement*, p. 74.

[65] *American Missionary*, Vol. II, no. 3 (Mar 1858), p. 67; *American Missionary*, Vol. III, no. 8 (Aug 1859), p. 187; Ronald G. Walters, *The Antislavery Appeal* (Baltimore: Johns Hopkins U. Press, 1976), pp. 97, 107. See Chapter 6 on "Families," pp. 91-110.

[66] Fee, *Autobiography*, p. 86; Fee to Jocelyn 2 May 1860 AMA 43864. See Appendix: Fee's Children.

[67] Walters, pp. 91, 92.

[68] Hermann R. Muelder, *Fighters for Freedom* (New York: Columbia U. Press, 1959), pp. 30, 34.

[69] Fee to Badger & Hall, 23 Jan 1845; Fee to Hall 15 May 1846; both these letters are on U. of Chicago Microfilm (John G. Fee's letters to the American Home Mission Society, Jan. 1845-Sept. 1848).

[70] Fee, *Autobiography* pp. 42, 43, 56.

[71] Fee, "Colonization," p. 21.

[72] Donald W. Dayton, *Discovering an Evangelical Heritage* (New York: Harper & Row, 1976), p. 15.

[73] Charles G. Finney, *Lectures on Revivals*, quoted in Lesick, p. 86.

[74] Dayton, p. 17.

[75] *Ibid.*, p. 18.

[76] Whitney R. Cross, *The Burned-Over District* (Ithaca: Cornell U. Press, 1950), "New Measures," Chap. 10, pp. 173-84.

[77] Dayton, p. 16; Ahlstrom, II, 96n.

[78] *Letters of Theodore Dwight Weld, Angelina Grimke Weld and Sarah Grimke 1822-1844*, ed. Gilbert H. Barnes & Dwight L. Dumond (Gloucester, Mass.: Peter Smith, 1965), I, XXV.

[79] Fee, "Colonization: The Present Scheme of Colonization Wrong, Delusive, and Retards Emancipation" (Cincinnati: American Reform Tract and Book Society), pamphlet, p. 1.

[80] *American Missionary Association 6th Annual Report, 1852*, p. 45; *American Missionary Association 7th Annual Report, (1853)*, p. 59; *American Missionary* 1853, TS, p. 78.

[81] *American Missionary Association 8th Annual Report, 1854*, p. 74.

[82] *American Missionary*, Vol. C (Nov 1855), p. 6; *American Missionary* (1847), TS, p. 23; *American Missionary Association 7th Annual Report, 1853*, p. 59; *American Missionary* (1853), TS, p. 78.

[83] Fee, "Colonization", p. 19, 22, 27.

[84] Fee to Editor in *The True American*, 15 July 1845 Lexington Public Library.

[85] Thomas, p. 126, 174; Fee, "The Sinfulness of Slaveholding," p. 21. Fee's "Cut Bible," with all references to slavery cut from it, is often displayed in the Hutchins Library on the Berea College campus with a note implying that Fee excised the offending passages in abhorrence of slavery. Of course, he did abhor slavery, but he did *not* abhor the Bible; he had dealt with all the passages in such a way that none of them could have 'offended' him. It is likely that he cut the Bible to produce for himself a complete collection of biblical references to slavery—perhaps to use as an aid in composing "The Sinfulness of Slavery."

[86] Smiley, "Clay and Fee," p. 203; Fee, *Autobiography*, pp. 69, 70; Fee to Jocelyn 15 July 1857 AMA 43485.

[87] Fee, *Autobiography,* pp. 139-140.

[88] *American Missionary* Vol. II, no. 4 (Apr 1858), pp. 88, 89; Fee to Whipple [undated] AMA 45322. In this letter, Fee seems to be referring to Francis Hawley, who was traveling with him at the time, as a negative example: the kind of judging, damning minister not needed in the South. Hawley, a disciple of Theodore Weld, had contributed an essay to *Slavery As It Is.*

[89] Ahlstrom, I, 145; Muelder, p. 288.

[90] Robert Samuel Fletcher, *A History of Oberlin College* (Oberlin: Oberlin College, 1943), I, 259.

[91] Lesick, pp. 6 & 189.

[92] *Ibid.,* p. 190.

[93] See Chap. 15, "The American Missionary Association," in Bertram Wyatt-Brown, *Lewis Tappan and the Evangelical War against Slavery* (Cleveland: The Press of Case Western Reserve U., 1969), pp. 287-309; Tappan to Fee 20 July and 13 Aug 1855 Ltrbk, Wyatt-Brown, p. 333. See Carleton Mabee, *Black Freedom* (New York: Macmillan Co., 1970), p. 237.

[94] Wyatt-Brown, p. 293; Swint, *The Northern Teacher in the South* (New York: Octagon Books, Inc., 1967), p. 155.

[95] Lesick, p. 191; Barnes & Dumond, I, 51n; Swint, p. 169.

[96] Fee to Jocelyn 16 June 1855 AMA 106919; Fee to Jocelyn 21 June 1855 AMA 106932. Fee's address to the student body in Oberlin (1855) was undoubtedly an important occasion for the future of Berea: in his audience would have been John A. R. Rogers, his sister Amelia (later wife of James S. Davis), Elizabeth Embree, her brother Joseph and sister Sallie, Eliza Ogden and her future husband George Candee, William E. Lincoln, Otis B. Waters, William Kendrick, John M. McLain, Frances Estrabrook, and John W. White. Almost all these people made some significant contribution to Berea later.

[97] Fee to Jocelyn 26 Sept 1855 AMA 107078.

[98] Fee to Jocelyn 10 dec 1857 AMA 43528.

[99] *AMA 8th Annual Report, 1854,* p. 71; Fee to Whipple & Jocelyn [undated] AMA 45319.

[100] Asa E. Martin, *The Anti-Slavery Movement in Kentucky Prior to 1850* (Louisville, 1918; rpt. New York: Negro Universities Press, 1970), pp. 130, 131, 137; Wallace B. Turner, "Abolitionism in Kentucky," *Register* Vol. 69, no. 4 (Oct 1971), p. 321.

[101] Fee, *Autobiography,* pp. 27, 28; Fee to Editor, *The True American,* 15 July 1845, Lexington Public Library; see articles in DAB for Salmon P. Chase, Elihu Burritt and George W. Clark.

[102] Muelder, p. 279; also see the account of Christian Conventions in William Goodell, *Slavery and Antislavery* (New York: William Harned, 1852), p. 492. Fee at Christian Anti-Slavery Convention, Cincinnati, 1850, noted in Founders & Founding: Fee, BCA. The convention of 1850 was attended by a black student from Oberlin who introduced a resolution. Fletcher, I, 264.

[103] Goodell letter; Muelder, p. 279.

[104] *American Missionary* (May 1850), TS, p. 77-78.

[105] Muelder, p. 280; Fletcher, I, 264; Christian Anti-Slavery Convention, noted in Founders & Founding: Fee, BCA. On his way to Chicago Fee had stopped at Galesburg to give the commencement address at Knox College, where one of the graduating seniors was James Scott Davis, a young man whose future was to be intertwined with Fee's and with the work of Berea College.

[106] Notice for Antislavery Convention in Cincinnati 27, 28, 29 Apr 1852 AMA 105400; Mabee, p. 203. See articles in DAB on Frederick Douglass, Charles Lenox Remond, Samuel J. May and George W. Julian.

107 Pease & Pease, *Antislavery Argument*, p. XXXVI; Cross, pp. 217, 280, 281. Also see the note on William Goodell in Dwight L. Dumond, *Letters of James Gillespie Birney 1831-1857* (New York: D. Appleton-Century and Co., 1938), I, 128; Louis Filler, *The Crusade Against Slavery 1830-1860* (New York: Harper & Bros., 1960), p. 63; and Gerald Sorin, *The New York Abolitionists* (Westport, Conn.: Greenwood Publ. Corp., 1971), pp. 57-62. Fee and Gerrit Smith, sometime sponsor of John Brown, corresponded from 1855 until Smith's death in 1874. In 1856, Fee sought Smith's advice about founding a school and two years later asked the wealthy philanthropist for five hundred dollars. Smith sent Fee twenty instead. Apparently he donated some $10,000 later on. See James M. McPherson, *The Abolitionist Legacy* (Princeton: Princeton U. Press, 1975), p. 158: Ralph Volney, Gerrit Smith: *Philanthropist and Reformer* (New York: Henry Holt & Co., 1939), p. 232. For a brief biography of Smith see Sorin, pp. 26-38.

108 Muelder, *Fighters*, pp. 223, 275-276.

109 *A Debate on Slavery Held in the City of Cincinnati on the First, Second, Third and Sixth Days of October, 1845 . . .* (Cincinnati: William H. Moore & Co., 1846), pp. 78, 81. Fee's personal copy of this book, with his annotations, is in the Berea College Archives.

110 *Ibid.*, p. 206.

111 *Ibid.*, p. 229.

112 *Ibid.*, pp. 46, 305, 306, 309.

112 *Ibid.*, p. 239.

114 Thomas, p. 127; Pease & Pease, *Antislavery Argument*, p. XXXVII. J. Horace Kimball, editor of the *Herald of Freedom* at Concord, N. H., was a co-author of Thome's *Emancipation*. After Weld and Thome conceived the idea of studying the conditions of emancipated slaves, Thome and Kimball spent six months in the West Indies collecting first-hand information. But Kimball died, aged 26, soon after his return, so Thome wrote up their findings and Weld took on the job of editing and rewriting Thome's manuscript. Thomas, pp. 127, 128.

CHAPTER THREE

1 Fee to Whipple 25 June 1852 AMA 43130; Fee to Jocelyn 24 Oct 1854 AMA 43280. Fee to Jocelyn Aug 1857 AMA 43503.

2 Fee to Whipple 8 Apr 1852 AMA 43126; Fee to Whipple Apr 1853 AMA 43162. Fee to Benton 6 Apr 1849 AMA 43017.

3 Fee to Whipple 12 May 1853 AMA 43166; Fee to Whipple 9 Jan 1851 AMA 43092; Clara Degman Hook, "John G. Fee's Work in Lewis Co., Ky.," *Lewis County Herald*, 1931, clipping in Founders & Founding: Fee, BCA; Davis to Jocelyn 23 Sept 1856 AMA 43399. A former slave, Henry Bibb, worked part of the year (1849) collecting funds to purchase Bibles for slaves in Kentucky. *American Missionary* (1849?), TS, p. 9; *American Missionary* (May 8, 1850), TS, p. 2. *American Missionary* May 8, 1850, p. 2.

4 Fee to Tappan and Whipple 9 Jan 1850 AMA 43022.

5 Fee to Whipple 26 Mar 1850 AMA 43036.

6 Fee to Whipple and Tappan undated AMA 43050.

7 The problem of workers being thrown into prison was not confined to colporteurs. James B. Cripps, a carpenter with abolitionist views (member of Fee's Bracken County Church) and utterly dependent upon antislavery men for employment, was thrown into prison "by the slave power" in 1853; a drunkard had falsely sworn that Cripps had told him that he had helped some slaves escape. Convinced of Cripps' innocence, Fee appealed to James A. Thome for help in this case. A poor man, Cripps was held in jail for ten days and on his release found himself saddled

with a $200 debt for lawyers and expenses. In September 1854, Cripps was in Madison County, Kentucky, building Fee's house. Fee to Jocelyn 21 Sept 1854 AMA 43272; Haines to Whipple 10 June 1850 43061; Fee to Gerrit Smith 8 Mar 1855 BCA.

8 Fee to Whipple 12 June 1850 AMA 43064.

9 Fee to Whipple 13 June 1850 AMA 43065; Haines to Editor of *Commercial Cincinnati*, 15 June 1850 AMA 43068; Fee, *Autobiography*, pp. 72, 73; Fee to Whipple [1850] AMA 43070; Clara Degman Hook, article on J. G. Fee, *Berea Citizen*, 12 Feb 1931. Fee suffered much with his head in later years; his grandson Edwin Embree recalled that Fee had one visible scar from his antislavery years—a "big bump on the top of his bald head [where] an infuriated slaveholder had broken a club there fifty years before." Edwin Embree, "A Kentucky Crusader," *Brown America* (New York; Viking Press, 1931), p. 70.

10 *Ibid.*, 43070.

11 Fee to Whipple 17 Aug 1850 AMA 43081; Elij. C. Phister to Whipple 5 Sept 1850 AMA 43084.

12 Fee to Whipple 7 Sept 1850 AMA 43085.

13 Petition to AMA May 1854 AMA 43245.

14 Fee to Jocelyn 2 Mar 1855 AMA 43152; Hawley to Jocelyn 29 Sept 1854 AMA 43273.

15 AMA 43273; Fisk to Whipple 6 Mar 1856 AMA 43369.

16 Hawley to Jocelyn 20 Sept 1854 AMA 43270; AMA 43273.

17 AMA 43273 and 43369.

18 *Ibid.*

19 Fee to Jocelyn 24 Oct 1854 AMA 43280.

20 Fee to Whipple Apr 1853 AMA 43162.

21 Fee to Whipple 12 May 1853 AMA 43166.

22 Fee to Whipple 4 Jan 1854 AMA 43210.

23 Fee to Whipple 23 Nov 1854 AMA 43286; West to AMA 5 Apr 1855 AMA 43315.

24 Fee to Whipple 12 May 1854 AMA 43239.

25 West (Report) to Whipple 13 May 1854 AMA 43240.

26 West to Whipple 23 Dec 1853 AMA 43202.

27 West to AMA 5 Apr 1855 AMA 43315.

28 West to AMA 20 Feb 1857 AMA 43444; Fee to Jocelyn 14 Apr 1857 AMA 43460.

29 Fee to Jocelyn 29 July 1857 AMA 43492. Fee to Jocelyn 10 Sept 1857 AMA 43511.

30 Fee to Whipple 12 May 1854 AMA 43239; Hawley to Jocelyn 29 Sept 1854 AMA 43273; Fee to Jocelyn 4 Jan 1854 AMA 43209.

31 AMA 43209 & 43273; Fee to Jocelyn 30 Nov 1855 AMA 43348; Fee to Jocelyn 14 Feb 1856 AMA 43366.

32 Shearer's Return 28 Oct 1853 AMA 43188.

33 AMA 43209.

34 West to Whipple 13 June 1854 AMA 43248.

35 Fee to Whipple 23 Nov 1854 AMA 43286.

36 Fee to Whipple 5 Jan 1854 AMA 43210.

37 Hawley to Jocelyn 20 Sept 1854 AMA 43270.

38 Fee to Jocelyn 24 Oct 1854 AMA 43280.

39 Fee to Whipple 5 Sept 1853 AMA 43179; Fee to Whipple Apr 1853 AMA 43162; Fee to Whipple 12 May 1853 AMA 43166.

40 West to Whipple 1 Sept 1853 AMA 43177. Also see *American Missionary* 5 Sept 1853, p. 99.

41 AMA 43177.

42 Fee to Whipple 5 Sept 1853 AMA 43179.

43 Fisk to Whipple 6 Mar 1856 AMA 43370.

44 Fee to Jocelyn 17 Oct 1856 AMA 43405.

45 Fee to Jocelyn Aug 1857 AMA 43506. Fee to Jocelyn 15 Nov 1858 AMA AMA 43681. Fee to Jocelyn 4 Dec 1858 AMA 43685.

46 Fee to Jocelyn 9 Feb 1859 AMA 43717; Parker 's Report Apr 1859 AMA 43745.

47 Jones's Report Feb 1859 AMA 43725.

48 Fee to Jocelyn 8 Apr 1859 AMA 43749.

49 Parker's slave report June 1859 AMA 43766.

50 See data on the Madison County Jones family in Miller, *History and Genealogies* (Richmond, Ky., 1907); George Candee, "Reminiscences," *Berea Citizen*, 16 Oct 1913.

51 Jones family information in the possession of a descendant of Robert Jones, Brenda Harrison of Berea.

52 McLain to Jocelyn 13 Aug 1857 AMA 43496; Fee to Jocelyn Aug 1857 AMA 43503.

53 AMA 43503. Fee to Jocelyn Aug 1857 AMA 43506; Fee to Jocelyn 4 Sept 1857 AMA 43509.

54 Jones' Report Oct 1857 AMA 43519.

55 Waters to Jocelyn 19 Jan 1858 43564.

56 Jones' Report 14 May 1858 AMA 43628; Fee, *Autobiography*, p. 119.

57 "From Rev. Geo. Candee," *American Missionary* Vol. II, no. 5 (May 1858), p. 113.

58 Jones' Report Feb 1859 AMA 43725.

59 Fee to Jocelyn June 1859 AMA 43777.

60 Kendrick to Jocelyn 13 Dec 1859 AMA 43823; George Candee, "Reminiscences," *Berea Citizen*, 25 Dec 1913.

61 Lincoln to AMA 26 June 1856 AMA 43387.

62 Fee to Jocelyn Oct 1854 AMA 43276.

63 Fee to ? 23 Nov 1854 AMA 43286.

64 Fee to Jocelyn 24 Mar 1855 AMA 43308. In 1854 Fee's total property in Madison County was assessed at $770 (32 acres on Silver Creek $300; one town lot $400; one horse $70; a buggy $100; gold, watches, clocks, etc., $30). *Madison County Tax Book 1855*, p. 20 in Kentucky Historical Society.

65 Fee to Jocelyn 23 June 1855 AMA 43321. Fee to Jocelyn 30 Nov 1855 AMA 43348.

66 Fee to Jocelyn 22 June 1854 AMA 43213.

67 Fee to Jocelyn 7 June 1855 AMA 43325.

68 Elias S. Hawley, *The Hawley Record* (Buffalo: Press of E. H. Hutchinson, 1890), p. 477 [a rare book in Sterling Library, Yale U.].

69 Fee to Jocelyn 2 Mar 1855 AMA 43152; Fee to Whipple [undated] AMA 45322.

70 George Candee, "Reminiscences," *Berea Citizen*, 7 Aug 1913; Fee to Jocelyn 4 Jan 1854 AMA 43209; Fee to Whipple [undated] AMA 45319.

71 AMA 43209.

72 Fee to Jocelyn 22 June 1854 AMA 43213.

73 Fee to Jocelyn 16 Sept 1854 AMA 43268.

74 Fee to Whipple 1 Sept 1854 AMA 43263; West to Jocelyn 17 Sept 1854 AMA 43269; Candee to Whipple 19 Mar 1855 (No. missing); AMA 45319.

75 Hawley to Jocelyn 24 Oct 1854 AMA 43270.

76 Fee to Jocelyn 24 Oct 1854 AMA 43280.

77 *Ibid.;* AMA 45319.

78 Hawley to Whipple & Jocelyn 6 Nov 1854 AMA 43284.

79 Candee's letter concerning Hawley, written at Fee's urgent request, describes Holley [sic] as a good man, "as far as his intentions are concerned, but questions his "wisdom and manner and spirit." He is better qualified for some field other than Kentucky, Candee concludes. AMA 106775.

80 Fee to Whipple 23 Nov 1854 AMA 43286; Fisk to Jocelyn 32 Dec 1854 AMA 43293.

81 Hawley to fee 14 Jan 1876 BCA.

82 Fee to Jocelyn 24 Mar 1855 AMA 43308; Fee to Jocelyn 30 Nov 1855 AMA 43348; John W. White Student File, Oberlin Alumni Records; Rogers' 50th Anniversary speech, *Berea Citizen,* 18 June 1903. John White was graduated from Oberlin Seminary in 1857 and received an Honorary degree from that institution in 1870; ordained in Morrison, Illinois, 22 Dec 1858, he was minister there until 1866; he died of consumption in Pueblo, Colorado, 10 Feb 1889.

83 Fee to Jocelyn 4 Jan 1856 AMA 43358; Fee to Jocelyn 6 Feb 1856 AMA 43364.

84 White to Jocelyn 6 Feb 1856 AMA 43365.

85 Robert S. Fletcher, *A History of Oberlin College* (Oberlin: Oberlin College, 1943), I, 55; *General Catalogue of Lane Theological Seminary 1828-1881* (Cincinnati: Elm Street Printing Co., 1881), p. 9; Lecky, p. 157n. By 1859 Clark was minister of the church in Union City, Michigan, where Otis Waters' parents were members. Waters to Jocelyn 1 June 1859 AMA 108937.

86 Fee to Jocelyn 23 June 1855 AMA 43321. Fee to Jocelyn 9 Nov 1855 AMA 43343. Fee to Jocelyn 3 Dec 1856 AMA 43416.

87 Clark to Jocelyn 19 Nov 1855 AMA 43346.

88 Davis to Jocelyn 1 Jan 1856 AMA 43355.

89 Davis to Jocelyn 4 Sept 1856 AMA 43398. Fee repeated his dictum about the relative ineffectiveness of young men rather often. Ironically, the most successful minister in Kentucky, other than Fee himself, was George Candee, the youngest one of all. Perhaps Hawley was right in saying Fee was no judge of character. Fee to Jocelyn 14 June 1857 AMA 43479; American Missionary Vol. III, no. 3 (Mar 1859), p. 64.

90 Fee to Jocelyn 14 June 1857 AMA 43479.

91 Fee to Jocelyn 26 June 1857 AMA 43481; Fee to Jocelyn 15 July 1857 AMA 43484; Otis Waters to his parents 24 Dec 1857, copy in BCA.

92 Fee to Jocelyn 2 June 1857 AMA 43473; Emerick to AMA 24 July 1857 AMA 107960.

93 John M. McLean Student File [non-graduate], Box 319, OCA.

94 McLain to AMA Mar 1857 AMA 43456-43457; Fee to Jocelyn 14 Apr 1857 AMA 43460.

95 Fee to Jocelyn 15 July 1857 AMA 43484.

96 McLain to Jocelyn 13 Aug 1857 AMA 43496.

97 McLain to Jocelyn Aug 1857 AMA 43501.

98 Fee to Jocelyn Aug 1857 AMA 43503.

99 AMA 43503.

100 McLain to Jocelyn Aug 1857 AMA 43505; Fee to Jocelyn Sept 1857 AMA 43513.

101 Fee to Jocelyn 12 Apr 1856 AMA 43376; Fee to Jocelyn 1 Aug 1856 AMA 43393; Fee to Jocelyn 3 Dec 1856 AMA 43145.

102 AMA 43245; Fee to Jocelyn 2 Mar 1855 AMA 43152.

103 Fee to Jocelyn 10 Sept 1857 AMA 43511; Fee to Jocelyn 22 Jan 1855 AMA 43300.

104 Fee to Jocelyn 9 Jan 1857 43430.

CHAPTER FOUR

1 Of the six minor preachers discussed above four were from Oberlin. Chapters to follow will be peopled with multitudes of Oberlinites, including the two major preachers and their wives: James Scott Davis (grad. Sem. 1854) and his wife Amelia E. Rogers Davis (prep. 1851-2; college 1854-6), George Candee (grad. Sem. 1857) and Eliza Ogden Candee (Oberlin Prep. 1854-6, 1857-8); the first two imported teachers at Berea: Otis Bird Waters (grad. Sem. 1860) and William E. Lincoln (Oberlin Prep. 1854; college 1855-6, 1857-9; Sem. 1860-1, 1863-5) (and his wife Frances Marshall Lincoln [grad. coll. 1862], who would teach at Berea herself after the Civil War). The couple who share the honor of being Berea's most influential teachers, John A. R. Rogers (grad. Coll. 1851; grad. Sem. 1855) and Elizabeth Embree Rogers (Oberlin Prep. 1854-5; college 1855-6) were Oberlin students. John G. Hanson was not an alumni of Oberlin, but his first wife Ellen Shoals Hanson was a student in the Academy 1856-8. Many of the Northern settlers at Berea before the Civil War came from Oberlin, including Charles Griffin (Oberlin Prep. 1857-8), Swinglehurst Life (from the village of Oberlin) and Rev. John F. Boughton (grad. Sem. 1860).

For a period after the Civil War virtually the entire staff of Berea was Oberlin-connected. Berea's first president, Edward Henry Fairchild, was president of Oberlin College (1866-89) through most of the Fairchild years at Berea (1869-89). With the exception of William Stewart, Willis D. Weatherford and John Stephenson all presidents of Berea College have held degrees from Oberlin. Berea has had a president in office since 1869, and, for almost 100 years out of 120, it has been a man with Oberlin connections. (A partial list of Berea College staff to 1870 with Oberlin backgrounds appears in Appendix Two.) *Alumni Register [of Oberlin College]: Graduates and Former Students, Teaching and Administrative Staff, 1833-1960* (Oberlin: Oberlin College, 1960).

2 Fletcher, I, 208.

3 Wilbur H. Phillips, *Oberlin Colony: The Story of a Century* (Oberlin: Oberlin College, 1933), P. 15.

4 Electa F. Jones, *Stockbridge, Past and Present* (Springfield: Samuel Bowles & co., 1854), p. 204; Albert Temple Swing, *James Harris Fairchild* (New York: Fleming H. Revell, 1907), p. 18.

5 Phillips, p. 46.

6 Fletcher, I, 343.

7 Lincoln, p. 4.

8 Fletcher, II, 809; William E. Lincoln to Philip D. Sherman, March 1918, Secretary's Office, OCA—quoted in Nat Brandt, *The Town that Started the Civil War* (Syracuse, NY, 1990), p. 39.

9 Fletcher, II, 809; E.H. Fairchild to Charles G. Finney 10 July 1860 OCA.

10 *Ibid.*, II, 749; see Fletcher's Chapter, "Early to Bed,' II, 746-759.

11 *Ibid.*, II, 670, 672.

12 *Ibid.*, I, 444-6; E.H. Fairchild's Tribute to His Wife, MS in BCA; Excerpts from James H. Fairchild's memoir, "Where Liberty Lies," TS, BCA.

13 Fee, Davis, Rogers & Candee to AMA 8 Apr 1858 43609.

14 Rogers, p. 32; Herman Muelder, *Fighters for Freedom* (New York: Columbia U. Press, 1959), pp. 172, 175. All Samuel Davis's sons maintained the family tradition of

journalism. Henry Kirk White Davis assisted his father with the Peoria paper and was himself one of the founders of the *Daily Register* (1848) and *The Champion* (1st issue 1849), Peoria's second daily paper. In Bloomington he established the *Illinois State Bulletin*. After fighting in the Civil War he settled in Missouri and became publisher of the *Lexington Union* in 1863. Southwick Davis, the second son, a graduate of Knox College in 1846, edited the *North Western Gazeteer* in 1850-51 and the *Galesburg Free Democrat* in 1854-55. R. McKee Davis, also a Knox College student, edited the *Onarga Mercury* in Onarga, Illinois, in 1860, but his career was cut short by the Civil War; he died at age 26 in 1863, as a result of his wounds in the Battle of Vicksburg.

[15] Muelder, p. 187.

[16] See chapter XI, "The Family of a Female Reformer and the Freedoms of Speech and Press," in Muelder, pp. 172, 188; Jeanne Humphreys, "Mary Brown Davis: Journalist, Feminist and Social Reformer," 23 May 1939, TS, in Knox College Library; Horace Edwin Hayden, *Virginia Genealogies* (1891; rpt. Baltimore: Genealogical Publ. Co., 1979), p. 191 (also see entries on Brown, Scott and Harrison families among James S. Davis's ancestors).

[17] Muelder, p. 178.

[18] *Ibid.*, p. 185, 330.

[19] *Ibid.*, pp. 187, 280, 306.

[20] James S. Davis to Tappan 7 Mar 1854 AMA 106212; James S. Davis Student File, Oberlin Alumni Records; Amelia (Rogers) Davis Student File [non-graduate], Box 298, OCA.

[21] Davis to Whipple 7 June 1854 AMA 106322; Davis to Jocelyn 20 June 1854 AMA 106341.

[22] Fee to Whipple 1 Sept 1854 AMA 43263; Davis to Jocelyn 31 July 1854 AMA 106402; Davis to Jocelyn 15 Sept 1854 AMA 106434.

[23] Davis to Jocelyn 3 Oct 1854 AMA 43275; Davis to Jocelyn 30 June 1856 AMA 43389.

[24] Fee to Jocelyn 24 Oct 1854 AMA 43280.

[25] Davis to Jocelyn 23 Oct 1854 AMA 43279.

[26] Davis to Jocelyn 29 June 1855 AMA 43324; Davis to Jocelyn 26 Sept 1855 AMA 43336.

[27] AMA 43336.

[28] Davis letter in *Semi-Weekly Free Democrat*, Vol. III, no. 8 (21 Feb 1856), p. 1; Rye letter, 13 Dec 1855, in same.

[29] Davis to Jocelyn 1 Jan 1856 AMA 43356; Davis to Jocelyn 11 Nov 1856 AMA 43409; Davis to Jocelyn 1 Aug 1856 AMA 43394.

[30] *American Missionary* Vol. I, no. 4 (Apr 1857), pp. 77-79.

[31] Davis to Jocelyn 18 Aug 1857 AMA 43500; Davis to Jocelyn 11 Mar 1857 AMA 107827; Rogers to Whipple and Jocelyn 1 Sept 1857 AMA 108005.

[32] Davis to Jocelyn 5 Oct 1857 AMA 43514.

[33] Davis to Clay 2 Oct 1857 BCA; Davis to Fee 5 Nov 1857 BCA; Fee had written to William E. Lincoln about the same time, asking him to recall Cassius Clay's position; Lincoln wrote to Fee, like Davis in Nov. 1857, with a report which bears out Fee's own presentation of Clay's ideas. Lincoln to Fee 2 Nov 1857 BCA.

[34] Davis to Jocelyn 26 Feb 1858 AMA 43585.

[35] Candee to Jocelyn 2 Mar 1858 AMA 43586; *American Missionary* Vol. II, no. 5 (May 1858), pp. 112, 113.

[36] Davis to Jocelyn 2 May 1858 AMA 43618.

[37] Fee to Jocelyn 26 Apr 1858 AMA 43612.

[38] *American Missionary* Vol. III, no. 7 (July 1859), p. 161.

[39] Mallett to Fee 20 July 1859 BCA.

[40] John D. Gregg & John Humlong to AMA 4 Oct 1859 AMA 43807.

[41] Davis to Jocelyn 4 Oct 1859 AMA 43808.

[42] *Ibid.*

[43] Marshall to AMA 28 Oct 1859 AMA 43813; Fee to Jocelyn 20 Dec 1859 AMA 109208.

[44] George Candee, "Reminiscences," *Berea Citizen*, 24 July 1913; Candee wrote a series of about a dozen articles concerning his experiences as a missionary in Kentucky—these essays appeared in the *Berea Citizen* from 24 July 1913 to 15 Jan 1914; each story has a headline title ("Radical Bob and His Army," "Who Founded Berea College?" etc.), but the whole series is henceforth referred to as "Reminiscences." [A collection of clippings of the same materials is in Founders & Founding; Candee, BCA.] George Candee Student File (including page from "1924 Cong'l Year Book"), Oberlin Alumni Records; Charles Candee Baldwin, *The Candee Genealogy* (Cleveland, 1882), pp. 50, 93. Candee's father Asa, born in Oxford Parish, Connecticut, moved to New York, where he married Mary McAlpine, a native New Yorker. Through his father Candee was descended from a number of the oldest New Haven families.

[45] George Candee, "Reminiscences," *Berea Citizen*, 24 July 1913.

[46] Candee to Frost 8 Dec 1901 BCA.

[47] Fee to Whipple 23 Nov 1854 AMA 43287.

[48] Fee to Jocelyn 9 Feb 1855 AMA 43304.

[49] Candee wrote to the AMA describing Hawley's unsuitability for the Kentucky mission field in March 1855. AMA 106775.

[50] Fee to Jocelyn 20 Apr 1855 AMA 43316; Fee to Jocelyn 7 June 1855 AMA 43357; Fee to Jocelyn 2 Mar 1855 AMA 43152.

[51] Fee, *Berea*, p. 6; Fee to Jocelyn 4 Jan 1856 AMA 43358; Waters to Jocelyn 25 Nov 1856 AMA 43410; Candee to Frost 1901 CHECK; Fee to Jocelyn 9 Nov 1855 AMA 43343.

[52] Eliza (Ogden) Candee Student File [non-graduate], Box 40, OCA; Candee to Jocelyn 25 Sept 1856 AMA 107570.

[53] Fee to Jocelyn 3 Dec 1856 AMA 43417.

[54] George Candee, "Reminiscences," *Berea Citizen*, 11 Sept 1913.

[55] Fee to Jocelyn 24 Nov 1857 AMA 43524.

[56] Candee to Jocelyn 21 Dec 1857 AMA 43538.

[57] Candee to Jocelyn 25 Jan 1858 AMA 43569. On 22 Feb 1858 Milton Green McQuary, the widow's son, wrote her from Lucas, Iowa, to commiserate about the burned schoolhouse. He was "awe struck and astonished," he said,

> to hear that some demon in human shape had burned your school house—yes our school house—for I feel as if it composed a part of myself—for in it I received nearly the whole of my education—and in it and around it I have passed the happiest moments of my existence—but we need not give up to unavailing sorrow—the case rather makes me bite my lip than shed tears to think perhaps some lowlife tool of the popular party who never owned a Negro in his life nor never will would burn a school house or be accessory to it under such circumstances. Oh Ignorance, Thou dost uphold what will always keep thee in the dust & your nose to the grindstone!

Milton Green McQuary to Miranda McQuary and her son William, 22 Feb 1858, xerox in BCA.

[58] Rogers to Jocelyn 9 Feb 1858 AMA 43578.

[59] Candee to Jocelyn 2 Mar 1858 AMA 43586; George Candee, "Reminiscences," *Berea Citizen*, 9 Oct 1913.

[60] Candee to Jocelyn 23 Mar 1858 AMA 43493.

[61] Candee to Jocelyn 12 Mar 1858 AMA 43621. Judge Isaac Faubus's wife Lavinia ("Aunt Viny") was, unlike her husband, one of the Jackson County radicals. George Candee, "Radical Bob and His Army," *Berea Citizen*, 16 Oct 1913; Collins & Collins, II, 353.

[62] Candee to Jocelyn 12 Aug 1858 AMA 43654. *American Missionary*, Vol. II, no. 11 (Nov 1858), p. 281.

[63] Candee to Jocelyn 13 Oct 1858 AMA 43675.

[64] Candee to Jocelyn 2 Dec 1858 AMA 43683.

[65] *Ibid.*

[66] Candee to Jocelyn 29 Jan 1859 AMA 43708; *American Missionary* Vol. III, no. 9 (Sept 1859), p. 209.

[67] Taylor to Candee Feb 1859 quoted in Candee to AMA Apr 1859 AMA 43719. Candee's ministry was continually endangered, but in August 1859 an event occurred which "had a chastening influence, even upon those who had opposed the truth and threatened violence to Christ's ministers"; Candee's sister, Mrs. Fisher of Brownhelm, Ohio, came to McKee for a visit and shortly died at his home. "Her peaceful departure," Rogers wrote, was "worth more to Jackson Co. than if she had been an angel from heaven. . . ." *American Missionary*, Vol. III, no. 10 (Oct 1859), p. 234.

[68] Fee to Jocelyn 8 May 1857 AMA 43465; Lincoln, "As to the Right," BCA.

[69] Lincoln, "As to the Right."

[70] *Ibid.* In old age William E. Lincoln claimed that his prayer session with Fee marked the beginning of Berea College; in *his* old age George Candee claimed that his wood-splitting conversation with Fee was the real beginning; and in *his* old age, Cassius M. Clay claimed that he rather than John G. Fee was the founder of Berea College. Elizabeth Rogers forcefully indicated that her husband should be regarded as "the" co-founder. (Ironically, Otis Bird Waters, the man who actually initiated plans for the school, left Berea immediately thereafter and made no claims in his old age.) All these claims were made in response to the Day Law controversy, when President William G. Frost, in a totally revisionistic spirit, was actively seeking out *new founders* for Berea College to support his new goals for the institution, which were very different from Fee's.

[71] John W. Love, "William Elleby Lincoln: Biographical Material" (1 July 1957), TS, BCA; William E. Lincoln, "Memoirs," p. 1. Lincoln's "Memoirs" take the form of a 15-page handwritten letter addressed to Pres. William G. Frost on 1 Oct 1909. The MS. is in a coverless booklet in BCA.

[72] Lincoln, "Memoirs," pp. 1-4; subsequent references by author's name only; William E. Lincoln Student Files [non-graduate], Box 151, OCA.

[73] Lincoln, p. 5-8.

[74] Davis to Jocelyn 21 Mar 1856 AMA 43372.

[75] *Ibid.*; Lincoln, p. 10; Davis to Jocelyn 22 Apr 1856 AMA 43379.

[76] Lincoln, p. 8; Fee to Jocelyn 8 Aug 1856 AMA 43382.

[77] Lincoln to AMA 31 May 1856 AMA 43385; Lincoln to AMA 26 June 1856 AMA 43387.

[78] Fee to Jocelyn 1 Aug 1856 AMA 43393; Matilda Fee to Jocelyn 8 Dec 1856 AMA 43419.

[79] Fee to Jocelyn 9 Jan 1857 AMA 43430.

[80] Lincoln to Jocelyn 2 Feb 1857 AMA 43437.

[81] McLain & Fee to Jocelyn 14 Apr 1857 AMA 43461.

[82] Lincoln, "Memoirs," pp. 21-27 BCA.

[83] Fee to Jocelyn 14 Apr 1857 AMA 43460.

[84] Fee to Jocelyn 8 May 1857 AMA 43465.

[85] Lincoln to Jocelyn 27 May 1857 AMA 107900. Lincoln to Jocelyn 30 June 1857 AMA 107915. Lincoln to Jocelyn 7 Aug 1857 AMA 107944.

[86] Lincoln to Jocelyn 20 July 1857 AMA 107956. Lincoln to Jocelyn 2 Aug 1857 AMA 107977. Lincoln to Jocelyn 7 Aug 1857 AMA 107944.

[87] Lincoln to AMA 18 Sept 1857 AMA 108027; Lincoln to Whipple 21 Oct 1857 AMA 108064; Lincoln to Whipple 9 Oct 1857 AMA 43517.

[88] Lincoln to Fee 2 November 1857 BCA.

[89] Lincoln to AMA 2 Nov 1857 AMA 108084.

[90] Lincoln to Whipple 4 Nov 1857 AMA 108090.

[91] Fee to Jocelyn 18 Mar 1858 AMA 43590.

[92] Lincoln to Jocelyn 15 Apr 1858 AMA 108324. Lincoln to Whipple 18 June 1858 AMA 108394.

[93] Jacob R. Shipherd, *History of the Oberlin-Wellington Rescue* (Boston: John P. Jewet & Co., 1859), p. 11. Lincoln possessed the headlong courage he so frequently attributes to himself. One of his adventures, in Ohio not Kentucky, was a public matter and brought him praise and recognition as an abolitionist hero. He certainly did not invent his part in the Wellington Rescue of 1858. For a fully developed account of the Wellington Rescue and Lincoln's part in it, see Brandt, *The Town that Started the Civil War.*

[94] Lincoln, p. 13.

[95] *Ibid.*, pp. 13, 14.

[96] *Ibid.*, pp. 14 -16.

[97] *Ibid.*, p. 16, 17.

[98] *Ibid.*, pp. 17, 18. It is interesting that many contemporaries report the Southern practice of calling God, 'Old Massa,' as if He were conceived as the gigantic slavedriver in the sky.

[99] *Ibid.*, p. 19, 20.

[100] *Ibid.*, p. 27.

[101] *Ibid.*, p. 28.

[102] *Ibid.*, p. 34, 35.

[103] *Ibid.*, p. 35.

[104] *Ibid.*, p. 36; Brandt, p. 200. John Brown's father Owen Brown was an early trustee of Oberlin College. Brown was "more or less associated with Oberlin men in Kansas," and two Oberlin students were in his company attacking Harper's Ferry. James H. Fairchild, *Oberlin: The Colony and the College* (Oberlin: E. J. Goodrich, 1883), p. 157.

[105] *Ibid.*, p. 36.

CHAPTER 5

[1] Davis to Jocelyn 23 Sept 1856 AMA 43399. Waters to Jocelyn 30 Aug 1856 (with recommendations from George Candee and E. H. Fairchild) AMA 107526; Otis B. Waters Student File, Oberlin Alumni Records; "Rev. Otis B. Waters" [an obituary notice] in BCA; Waters to his parents, 24 Dec 1857, copy in BCA; Waters to Jocelyn 11 Nov 1856 AMA 43419.

[2] Waters to Jocelyn 26 Dec 1856 [Fee and Waters wrote on the same letter] AMA 43427.

[3] Waters to Jocelyn 4 Mar 1857 AMA 43448.

4 Waters to Jocelyn 9 Apr 1857 AM 107844; Waters to Jocelyn 29 Apr 1857 AMA 107872.

5 AMA 43488. Only one family of free blacks lived in Rockcastle County in 1850: the Gatliffs, listed on the census as mulattoes. Two Gatliff children children (Elizabeth and Henry, aged 10 and 8 respectively in 1857) were probably Waters' pupils.

6 Candee to Jocelyn 8 June 1857 AMA 107916; Waters to Jocelyn 8 June 1857 AMA 107917; Waters to Jocelyn 29 June 1857 AMA 107932.

7 Waters to Frost 25 Nov 1895 BCA; Waters to Frost 8 July 1895 BCA; Fee to Jocelyn Nov 1857 AMA 43525. Waters' Account with AMA 108470.

8 Fee to Tappan 17 Dec 1857 AMA 443535; Waters to Jocelyn 22 Mar 1858 AMA 10825.

9 *American Missionary*, Vol. IX (Dec 1855), TS, pp. 13, 14.

10 *Ibid.* ; Fee to Gerrit Smith 4 Jan 1856 Syracuse U. Library, quoted in Mabee, p. 410.

11 Fee, *Autobiography*, p. 38.

12 *American Missionary*, 1856, TS, pp. 43-44.

13 Fee to Jocelyn 30 Nov. 1855 AMA 43348.

14 *American Missionary*, XI (1857), p. 7.

15 *Ibid.*

16 Fee to Jocelyn, Whipple, Tappan & Goodell 4 Apr 1857 AMA 43458.

17 *Ibid.*

18 *American Missionary*, May 1857, TS, pp. 104-5.

19 *Ibid.*, p. 117.

20 Fee to Jocelyn 21 July 1857 AMA 43488; Fee to Jocelyn 14 Aug 1857 AMA 43498; McLain to Jocelyn 13 Aug 1857 AMA 43496.

21 AMA 43496; AMA 43498.

22 *American Missionary* Sept. 1857, TS, p. 212; Fee to Jocelyn Nov 1857 AMA 43525.

23 Fee, *Berea*, pp. 24, 25.

24 Fee to Tappan 17 Dec 1857 AMA 43435.

25 Fee to Jocelyn 8 Feb 1858 AMA 43572.

26 *Ibid.* [for both items].; Fee, *Autobiography,* p. 123.

27 AMA 43572.

28 Fee to Jocelyn 9 Feb 1858 AMA 43581.

29 "Sketch of a Great Life," *Berea Citizen*, 26 July 1906; John A. R. Rogers Student File, Oberlin Alumni Records; Edward C. Starr, *A History of Cornwall, Connecticut: A Typical New England Town* (1926), p. 103; Theodore S. Gold, *Historical Records of the Town of Cornwall, Litchfield Co., Conn.* (Hartford: Hartford Press, 1904), p. 425; Albert Temple Swing, *James Harris Fairchild* (New York: Fleming H. Revell Co., 1907), pp. 14, 15. Stockbridge was the birthplace of Mark Hopkins, later president of Williams College, where the first American foreign mission began with the famous "Haystack prayer meeting" in 1806, and, incidentally, Stockbridge was the home of the Fairchilds and many other Oberlin families before they moved to northern Ohio; Edward Henry Fairchild, first president of Berea College, and his brother James Harris Fairchild, president of Oberlin College, were born there.

30 E. R., "Full Forty Years," p. 5. Stockbridge was the birthplace of Mark Hopkins, later president of Williams College, where the first American foreign mission began with the famous "Haystack prayer meeting" in 1806, and, incidentally, Stockbridge was the home of the Fairchilds and many other Oberlin families before they moved to northern Ohio; Edward Henry Fairchild, first president of Berea College, and his brother James Harris Fairchild, president of Oberlin College, were born there.

31 Rogers, p. 48; Rogers to Frost 21 Oct 1901 BCA; Rogers Student File, Oberlin
Alumni Records; Swing, pp. 368, 369.

32 J. A. R. Rogers obit., *Berea Citizen*, 26 July 1906.

33 *Galesburg Free Democrat*, Vol. III, no. 3 (27 Mar 1856), p. 2: typed copy in
Founders & Founding: Rogers, BCA.

34 E.R., "Full Forty Years," pp. 6 & 7.

35 *Ibid.*, pp. 8-10; E. R., "Personal History," pp. 3, 4.

36 E. R., "Personal History," p. 4.

37 *Ibid.*, pp. 4, 5; E. R., "Full Forty Years,", p. 14.

38 "Sketch of a Great Life," *Berea Citizen*, 26 July 1906; John A. R. Rogers Student
File, Oberlin Alumni Records; Edward C. Starr, *A History of Cornwall, Connecticut: A Typical
New England Town* (1926), p. 103; Theodore S. Gold, *Historical Records of the Town of
Cornwall, Litchfield Co., Conn.* (Hartford: Hartford Press, 1904), p. 425; Albert Temple Swing,
James Harris Fairchild (New York: Fleming H. Revell Co., 1907), pp. 14, 15.

39 E. R., "Full Forty Years," p. 15.

40 Rogers to Frost 21 Oct 1901 BCA. 33 Rogers to Frost 2-17-1893; "Sketch," *Berea
Citizen*, 26 July 1906; Rogers to Frost et. al. 8 Mar 1901 BCA; Rogers, p. 47.

41 John Rogers joined the mission in Madison County unaware that "there had been any
thought of anything more than an elementary school." In 1901, he recollected that when he and
his wife arrived in Berea, "things looked as much and as little like a college as anything in the
Sahara Desert." Although the plan had been afoot for years, the idea had not been shared with
him, nor was it used as an inducement to attract him to Berea. The plan required teachers and both
John and Lizzie were well-qualified, but they approached their work without knowing they were
being tested for greater tasks.

In his old age, Rogers denied that the college project had been conceived before his time;
he told Berea College president William G. Frost that if such a scheme had been in existence"I
should have heard of it, but I remember nothing of the kind." And again: "When I first went to
Berea to talk with [Fee] about my plans, he said nothing about [the projected college} & I never
heard of it." Rogers was apparently not convinced that such a plan had ever existed until he read
about it in old files of the *American Missionary* magazine in 1901! There is no reason to doubt
Rogers' veracity: he arrived in Berea without prior knowledge of the college proposal, with no
intention of becoming a college teacher—his purpose was to engage in preaching and perhaps
teach part-time. Fee did not invite Rogers to participate in the big project until later, probably
because he wanted to see Rogers perform first. Fee had been disappointed in workers (preachers,
colporteurs and at least one teacher) before; by 1858 he had grown cautious—and crafty.

Many years later, Rogers' son Raphael claimed that his father had actually gone to Berea
"to consult with . . . Fee as to the establishment of a college in Kentucky." He broached the
subject of a college at Berea, only to have Fee reject the idea because Berea was not the
appropriate place. The two men then traveled to Rockcastle County, "looked around, but found
no place which would seem favorable for the establishment of a college." Rogers' own diary
entries belie this "memory," which seems to combine two different incidents into one. John
Raphael Rogers, "Pioneering in Berea," pp. 10, 11, pamphlet dated 31 Sept 1931, BCA; Fee to
Jocelyn 10 Dec 1856 AMA 43528; Fee to Tappan 17 Dec 1857 AMA 43535; Rogers to Frost 13
Nov 10-21-1901 BCA; Rogers to Frost 13 Nov 1901 BCA.

42 AMA 43528; Davis to Jocelyn 18 Aug 1857 AMA 43500; John Raphael Rogers,
"Pioneering in Berea," p. 11, pamphlet dated 31 May 1931, BCA.

43 Fee to Jocelyn 9 Feb 1858 AMA 43581. After Fee had changed his mind, he wrote,
according to Rogers' son Raphael, "commanding him in no uncertain terms to return. . . . So
peremptory was the letter that my mother and my aunt and Mr. Davis were doubtful as to whether

380

Mr. Rogers should yield to the summons." John Raphael Rogers, "Pioneering in Berea," p. 11, pamphlet dated 31 May 1931, BCA.

[44] E.R., "Personal History," p. 8.

[45] *Ibid.*, p. 9; Lizzie Rogers to Frost 23 Apr 1901 BCA.

[46] Fee to Clay June 1858 BCA.

[47] E. R., "Personal History," p. 18.

[48] *Ibid.*, p. 20; Rogers, pp. 18-20.

[49] Rogers, pp. 23, 21.

[50] E. R., "Personal History," p. 25.

[51] *Ibid.*, p. 23.

[52] *Ibid.*, p. 20.

[53] *Ibid.*, p. 24.

[54] E. R., "Full Forty Years," p. 19.

[55] E. R., "Personal History," p. 27.

[56] *Ibid.*, p. 16.

[57] *Ibid.*

[58] Term dates from Rogers' *Journal.*

[59] Leaflet advertising Berea School dated 19 Aug 1858 AMA 43396.

[60] Elizabeth Rogers, pp. 10, 11.

[61] *Ibid.*

[62] Rogers, p. 53.

[63] E. R., "Personal History," p. 11.

[64] *Ibid.*, p. 16.

[65] *Ibid.*; Rogers, p. 54.

[66] E. R., "Personal History," p. 16; Rogers, p. 55.

[67] Rogers, p. 57. Lizzie Rogers' baby, John Raphael Rogers, wrote his own account of his mother and father's combination of parental and teaching duties:

> . . . Father and mother boarded at the house of Mr. Stapp about a mile from the school house. My father brought a baby carriage with him from Illinois but there was not a path over which a baby carriage could be operated. My father, therefore, took me in his arms, and carried me every day to school with my mother following along. Part of the time a little slave girl brought up the rear of the procession and after reaching the school house, I was consigned to the care of the girl and of a Mrs. Wright, who lived near. At recess and at noon, my mother comforted me and took such care of me as was necessary. John Raphael Rogers, "Pioneering in Berea," p. 12, pamphlet dated 31 May 1931, BCA.

[68] Rogers, pp. 58, 59.

[69] *American Missionary*, Vol. II, no. 9 (Sept. 1858), pp. 232-33; Fee, *Berea*, p. 28.

[70] Rogers, p. 59.

[71] E. R., "Personal History," p. 17.

[72] Fee, *Berea*, p. 28; E. R. "Personal History," p. 18.

[73] Fee to Clay, 12 July 1858 BCA; Fee, *Berea*, p. 28. What is now the Berea College campus was (in 1858) literally in "the Bresh," as the region was locally named. "The 'Bresh' was so thick that if a person stood six feet from the road he would be invisible to a passerby on the . .

. highway, and except for a few paths it was impossible for a man to make his way through the woods without clearing his way with an ax." Rogers, pp. 51, 52.

[74] E. R. "Personal History," p. 18.

[75] Fee, *Berea*, p. 29.

[76] Rogers, p. 21.

[77] Fee to Jocelyn 19 Aug 1858 AMA 43658. Leaflet AMA 43396 [misfiled in AMA Collection].

[78] Rogers, p. 60; *Minutes of Berea College Board of Trustees*, in manuscript in the Berea College Archives, is the source for most information concerning their meetings. In most cases, subsequent references can be found by using the dates mentioned in the text.

[79] E. R., "Personal History," p. 11. No class lists exist from either Lincoln or Water's schools, and only one person, Zerelda (Moore) Preston, is *known* to have studied under Lincoln, Waters and Rogers—her obituary records that distinction. (She lived to her 90's, dying in Berea in 1929; by that time items of Berea heritage were considered precious.) Lincoln recorded the names of only two of his students (in a letter dated February 2, 1857), both of whom studied under Rogers later: Mary Jane Moore (whose father was a slaveholder) and Francis Thompson (son of Teman). Nevertheless, it is safe to assume continuity among the students of Lincoln, Waters and Rogers. Zerelda (Moore) Preston obit., *Berea Citizen*, 12 Sept 1929; Lincoln to Jocelyn 2 Feb 1857 AMA 43437.

Of the slightly more than 100 people to attend Berea before the Civil War some 105 are known. Their names have been gathered from John Rogers' account book, in which he recorded tuition payments, from his journal, maintained on a daily basis throughout the crucial years 1858-9, from various contemporary letters; in addition, Rogers published a "partial list of scholars in Berea school for spring and fall terms of 1858." Information about Berea's first students has been drawn from censuses, family records, obituaries, etc. Rogers, p. 59; Rogers' List, *Berea Citizen*, 24 July 1902.

[80] All three local trustees (Renfro, Burnam and Stapp) had at least one child or grandchild enrolled in 1858-9. Children of three of Fee's colporteurs were in attendance: A. G. W. Parker's daughters Margaret and Mary; three children of Robert Jones: Humphrey, Susan and William; and three children of Peter H. West—Granville, James and Margaret, all of whom were among Rogers' advanced students. And, of course, John G. Fee's older children, Laura, Howard and Burritt, were among Berea's first students.

Genealogical materials concerning pre-Civil war students include: files on Elder, Moore, Jones, Mitchell, Moberly, Morton, Lee and Harris families in the Madison County Family History Series (Miller Papers in the Townsend Room, Library, EKU); Helen Cornelison Shadoon, *The Cornelison Family History* (1954), TS, EKU; families files for Woolwine, Chasteen, and Renfro in the Kentucky Historical Society; Marie Gay Foster, *Denham Family Tree*, TS, in KHS; Harris and Ballard Chapters in Miller, *History and Genealogies;* Nell Watson Sherman, *The Maupin Family* (Morton, Ill. : Tazwell Publ. Co., 1962); Ruby G. Heard Maupin, *History of the Maupin Family (1969)*, in KHS; *Hughlett/ Hulett Descendants from Colonial Virginia*, ed. LLoyd J. Hughlett (Hughlett Geneal. Trust, 1981); Sadie Rucker Wood, *The Rucker Family Genealogy* (Richmond: Old Dominion Press, Inc. 1932). From private collections: Burdett and Harrison Family Records, in possession of Mary Gay Walker, Berea; Harrison Family Records, in possession of Dean Warren Lambert, Berea; Moore Family Records, in possession of Louise Scrivener, Berea; Moore Family Records, in possession of Frances Moore, Berea; Todd Family Records, in possession of James T. Todd, Kansas City, Mo.; Boatwright-Blackburn Records, in possession of James Paul Todd, Paint Lick. Amanda (Woolwine) Weaver obit., *Berea Citizen*, 30 Jan 1930. [Amanda Woolwine, born 1849, attended Rogers' school before 1860 and joined Fee's church in the middle of the Civil War. Fee performed her marriage to Will Weaver in 1870.]

[81] E. R., "Personal History," p. 11; Ann Eliza Best obit., *Berea Citizen*, 1 Dec 1927.

[82] In addition to the Maupin and Denham books mentioned above, see Marie Gay Foster, *My Father's People: The Dejarnats* (priv. printed), in KHS; Chapter 3 on "The Harris Family" in Miller. In 1860, 881 slaveholding families lived in Madison County; 110 of those families, representing 12 percent of the slaveholding population, owned 2337 slaves out of the county's total of 6118—12 percent of the population owned 38 percent of the slaves. These 110 families (not represented, of course, by 110 different *surnames*), the elite of Madison County, constituted a ruling class in a population of approximately 11,000 whites. *Madison County Slave Census 1860*.

[83] E. R., "Personal History," p. 11.

[84] Fee to Jocelyn 4 Dec 1858 AMA 43685; Candee to Jocelyn 21 Dec 1857 AMA 43538; Rogers, pp. 19-21.

[85] John A. R. Rogers' Account Book 1857-1868 in BCA.

[86] E. R., "Personal History," p. 16.

[87] *Ibid.*, p. 21.

[88] *Ibid.*, p. 14; Rogers, pp. 58, 58n.

[89] Fairchild, *Interesting History*, pp. 15, 40; E. R. "Personal History," p. 21.

[90] *American Missionary*, Vol. II, no. 11 (Nov 1858), p. 176; Harriet Beecher Stowe, in *Liberator*, quoted in *American Missionary*, Vol. II, no. 11 (Nov 1858), p. 269-70.

[91] E. R. "Personal History," p. 23.

[92] Fee to Jocelyn 4 Dec 1858 AMA 43685.

[93] *Ibid.*

[94] Fee to Jocelyn 30 Dec 1858 AMA 43693.

[95] Fee to Clay 26 Feb 1859 BCA.

[96] Fee to Jocelyn 8 Apr 1859 AMA 43749.

[97] Other families of the community supported Fee's work in various ways (and later boasted of their early loyalty—as did the Thompsons and the Rawlings). John B. Kirby (born December 1830), son of Jesse Kirby and Martha Burnam and grandson of John Burnam, Sr., was one of the oldest residents of Madison County when he died in 1914. His obituary notice states that he was always a friend of Berea College (and of Fee and Fairchild) and "during its early days stood true to the cause." He was a surety, along with Rogers, Hanson, and Embree, for a Berea College mortgage, 31 May 1867—and his wife, Elizabeth (Henderson) Kirby, supplied the Berea school (24 Jan 1866) with three pounds of butter, for which Rogers duly recorded payment. This may have been the item which Rogers describes in his *Birth of Berea*: "Butter that would not have been salable in a city market, under the cirumstances was gladly received, and if a vivid imagination was needed to make it palatable, doubtless that quality was not lacking." The local community supported Berea in *very diverse* ways! John B. Kirby obit, *Berea Citizen*, 13 Aug 1914; Rogers, *Birth*, p. 99; Rogers' Account Book 1857-1868 in BCA; *Madison County Deed Book 16*, p. 39.

[98] E.R.,"Personal History," p. 24.

[99] Fee to Jocelyn 22 Apr 1859 AMA 43755.

[100] Rogers to Frost 9 Aug 1902 BCA.

[101] Rogers, *Journal*, I, 120; Fee, *Berea*, pp. 26, 30. Rogers' entry in his journal for May 20, 1859, states that Fee had gone to Clay's. Rogers does not announce Fee's purpose, but the trip to White Hall occurred one week after the board meeting at which Berea College was organized and five days before Fee left for Boston to raise funds. In his old age Clay maintained that Fee had never offered him a place on the board of trustees of Berea College. Clay claimed he had been in St. Petersburg, Russia, at the time of Berea's organization, "and could not refuse to serve . . . because he did not know anything about it." The two men held no correspondence

while Clay was in Russia. Of course, Fee's trip to White Hall to invite Clay to serve on the board was long before Clay's first sojourn in Russia. "Notes from Gen. Clay," pamphlet, 28 May 1898, BCA.

102 Arthur J. Hanson's name appears on the copy of the 1859 constitution in the *Minutes*, but he was certainly not a trustee until 1866 (he was barely 19 in 1859); his signature is in a different ink, apparently from a fountain pen and must have been added years later.

103 John Hansel was a farmer from Oberlin; Humphrey Marshall, Jr., a graduate of Oberlin College (1842) and Seminary (1845), had also taught there from 1842-45, and joined the faculty again later on, becoming a member of Oberlin's board of trustees, although he never served in that capacity for Berea. Fairfield was a very distinguished educator, president of Hillsdale College in Michigan. See the entry on Fairfield in DAB.

On July 1, 1859, Fee had written to Oliver Grigson, member of Cabin Creek Church and colporteur for James S. Davis, inviting him to become a trustee. Apparently Grigson had refused by the 18th of July. Fee to Grigson 1 July 1859, printed in the *Sentinel* [Augusta, Ky.], 9 Feb 1860, BCA.

104 *General Catalogue of Lane Seminary 1828-1881* (Cincinnati: Elm Street Printing Co., 1881), p. 13.

105 See entries on Henry Ward Beecher, George B. Cheever & Harriet Beecher Stowe in DAB.

106 E. R., "Personal History," p. 19.

107 Rogers, *Birth*, p. 66; E. R., "Personal History," p. 26.

108 *Ibid.*, p. 24.

109 *Ibid.*, p. 25.

110 *Ibid.*, p. 26.

CHAPTER 6

1 Rogers to Jocelyn 22 July 1858 AMA 43646; Rogers to Jocelyn 19 Oct 1859 AMA 43812; Fletcher, I, 108. From Sept. through Dec. 1859, four new dwellings were erected in Berea—even John G. Fee started work on a new house of his own. *American Missionary*, Vol. IV, no. 1 (Jan 1860), p. 20; *American Missionary*, Vol. IV., no. 6 (June 1860), p. 135.

2 Fee, *Autobiography*, p. 142.

3 Rogers to Jocelyn 28 June 1858 AMA 43635; John Smith to Jocelyn 23 July 1858 AMA 43647.

4 AMA 43647.

5 Fee to Jocelyn Aug 1858 AMA 43650.

6 John Smith to Jocelyn 30 Aug 1858 43662.

7 Fee to Jocelyn 15 Nov 1858 AMA 43681.

8 Charles E. Griffin Student File [non-graduate], Box 98, OCA; Rogers' Account Book 1857-1868.

9 Rogers' Account Book 1857-1868.

10 John F. Boughton Student File, Oberlin Alumni Records; Boughton to Jocelyn 17 Sept 1858 AMA 108556; James Boughton, *Descendants of John Bouton* (Albany, N. Y.: Joel Munsell's Sons, 1890), p. 240; Boughton to Jocelyn 6 Aug 1859 AMA 109042; Waters to Jocelyn 18 Sept 1858 AMA 108557; Rogers to Jocelyn 5 Sept 1859 109082.

11 Ernest G. Dodge, "Guidebook to Berea," typescript dated 3 Sept 1903, BCA. Torry is named on Clay's List of Exiles and his signature appears on the Bereans' Appeal to the Governor of Kentucky, 24 Dec 1859. See Rogers, p. 78.

[12] Clay's List, MS in BCA. Perhaps his name was John S. Sholes; a person of that name married Catherine Thompson in Bracken County in 1863, in a ceremony which John G. Hanson may have witnessed.

[13] Wheeler to Jocelyn 6 Sept 1859 AMA 109090; Wheeler to Jocelyn 11 Nov 1859 AMA 109157; Rogers to Jocelyn 7 Sept 1859 109095; Waters to Jocelyn 6 Sept 1859 109091. Two of these interested young men intended to go to Berea, but arranged their trips too late: Charles Miles and Willard Watson Wheeler. Miles, a local preacher among Primitive Methodists in Pennsylvania, had been at Oberlin studying for the ministry about a year and a half, while Wheeler, a Christian of more than common piety, was an Oberlin freshman in preparation for the ministry. These two sought AMA commissions so they could work as colporteurs in the Kentucky mountains with Berea as their base. In November 1859, they were making their preparations, but in December John G. Fee stated it would be unwise for Wheeler to go, because of "a spirit of general hostility to the antislavery friends. . . . " Exile and war intervened before Wheeler and Miles ever arrived at their new post. Wheeler, after serving as a soldier in the war, would settle in Berea many years later. Fee to Jocelyn 20 Dec 1859 AMA 109208.

[14] Rogers to Jocelyn 3 Dec 1859 AMA 43819; Mrs. George S. [Swinglehurst] Life Student File [non-graduate], Box 151, OCA. Rogers records the exact date when Reed and Life arrived (together) in his *Journal*.

[15] Ezekiel T. Hayes Student File [non-graduate], Box 109, OCA.

[16] *Encyclopedia of American History*, pp. 220, 225. Marion B. Lucas describes white Kentuckians' attitudes toward slave rebellion in his *A History of Blacks in Kentucky*, Vol. I, pp. 59, 60.

[17] *American Missionary*, Vol. III, no. 11 (Nov. 1859), p. 257.

[18] Fee to Jocelyn, 16 Sept 1859 AMA 43794.

[19] *American Missionary*, Vol. III, no. 11 (Nov. 1859), pp. 256, 257; Fee, *Autobiography*, pp. 143, 144. Many years later Fee wrote that some of the women in the congregation had been wailing aloud and added, ". . . a series of experiences and my situation at that time all conspired to bring me more fully into sympathy with the sorrowing. I sat and quietly wept, wept with continuous weeping. I was in deep sympathy with burdened spirits." It is noteworthy that when Fee wrote of this event at the time he emphasized the happiness of the congregation and his positive sense of racial equality (blacks as talented as whites), while in later years he presented the same incident as a sad occasion, with equality primarily marked by similar sufferings common to all humanity. On this same trip Fee visited Calvin Fairbanks, a New York abolitionist in prison in Frankfort, serving a 20-year sentence for helping a Kentucky slave escape. In prison Fee preached to the assembled convicts.

[20] *American Missionary*, Vol. III, no. 11 (Nov. 1859), pp. 256-57.

[21] See entry on Beecher in DAB, or—for a full-scale account—Milton Rugoff, *The Beechers: An American Family in the Nineteenth Century* (New York: Harper & Row, 1981); Ahlstrom, II, 195; Fee, *Autobiography*, p. 146; Fee's Subscription List 12 July 1860 AMA 109681.

[22] *American Missionary*, Vol. III, no. 12 (Dec. 1859), pp. 275-77.

[23] *Ibid.*

[24] Fee was not alone in vindicating John Brown. Many of his fellow abolitionists did so: including William Lloyd Garrison, Henry Wright, Samuel J. May, Edmund Quincey, Lydia Child, Charles Burleigh, John Greenleaf Whittier, and, among Fee's personal friends, William Goodell and Lewis Tappan. Another friend of Fee's, Gerrit Smith, had, of course, helped to finance John Brown's raid. Defenses of John Brown appeared in *American Missionary*, for example, January 1860 (Vol. IV, no. 1, pp. 14-15. Lawrence J. Friedman, *Gregarious Saints* (Cambridge, Cambridge U. Press, 1982) p. 212.

25 *American Missionary*, Vol. IV, no. 2 (Feb. 1860), pp. 37-38; Fee's Notes for Sermon in Beecher's Church, MS, BCA; a full account of Fee's sermon is given in *American Missionary* Vol. III, no. 12 (Dec 1859), pp. 275-277.

26 *New York Times*, Tues. Nov 15, 1859.

27 *Louisville Courier*, 17 Nov 1859, quoted in *Kentucky Statesman*, 18 Nov 1859, Lexington Public Library. All these stories of the men who died after persecuting Fee, while omitted from the AMA summary of his sermon, were undoubtedly a part of it. Fee told these anecdotes frequently, and other recorded instances of them coincide exactly with the *Louisville Courier's* report. The AMA version undoubtedly deleted them as the rather embarrassing and tasteless anecdotes which they are, even though they are true. But the retribution stories demonstrate how accurate the *Louisville Courier could* be with some details, especially the ones that make Fee sound bloodthirsty. See *American Missionary*, Vol. II, no. 4 (April 1858), p. 89, for Fee's typical account of providential destruction of his enemies. Also see William D. ——, "Brief Sketches" (25 Feb 1885), accounts of how Fee's persecutors died untimely, unprepared deaths, in BCA.

28 *Ibid.*

29 News story from *Kentucky Messenger* (Richmond), quoted by James S. Davis in *Congregational Herald*, Vol. VII, no. 42 (19 Jan 1860), p. 1: TS in BCA.

30 Boughton to Jocelyn 2 Apr 1860 AMA 109471.

31 Matilda Fee to Jocelyn 29 Nov 1859 AMA 43817.

32 J. B. Mallett to AMA 11 Jan 1860 AMA 43835.

33 *Richmond Democrat*, quoted in *Kentucky Statesman*, 29 Nov 1859, Lexington Public Library.

34 Letter from Rogers to Frost Regarding Exodus from Berea [no date], BCA.

35 Rogers to Jocelyn 3 Dec 1859 AMA 43819.

36 *Kentucky Statesman*, 9 Dec 1859, Kentucky Public Library. The members named were Solon Harris, Wm. T. Terrill, Samuel Bennett, Arch. Kavanaugh, Geo. Parkes, R. J. White, Claibourn White, Jno. C. Terrill, Sam. Campbell, G. W. Maupin, Col. R. J. Munday, Ed. W. Turner, Col. Wm. Harris, Jas. E. Baker, Nathan Moran, J. P. Estill, C. A. Hawkins, J. R. Gilbert, Wm. M. Miller, Col. John Kinnard, W. J. Walker, Charles Oldham, J. W. Parkes, C. R. Estill, C. Field, Jr.

37 Collins & Collins, I, 81; E. R., "Personal History," p. 28; Damon to Jocelyn 9 Dec 1859 AMA 109191.

38 E. R., "Personal History," p. 28.

39 *Ibid.*, p. 27.

40 Davis to Jocelyn 11 Dec 1859 AMA 43822.

41 *American Missionary*, Vol. IV, no. 2 (Feb 1860), p. 37; Circular No. 2, 27 Dec 1859 AMA 43827; Kendrick to Jocelyn 13 Dec 1859 AMA 43823.3827.

42 *Kentucky Statesman*, Dec 27, 1859, Lexington Public Library.

43 *American Missionary*, Vol. IV, no. 2 (Feb 1860), p. 40.

44 Collins & Collins, I, 83.

45 *Kentucky Messenger*, 23 Dec 1859, clippings in Exile file, BCA.

46 *Ibid.*; *Kentucky Statesman*, 27 Dec 1859, Lexington Public Library. The prominent citizens present at this committee meeting included Thomas S. Bronston, Jr., Thomas Willis, Reuben J. Munday, Alfred Stone, Durritt White, A. J. Dudley, J. P. Estill, Benjamin Moberly, Squire Million, John D. Harris, Coleman Covington, Thomas J. Maupin, Samuel Shearer, Solon Harris, Capt. C. A. Hawkins, Henry Dillingham, Alexander Tribble, G. B. Broaddus, William Mitchell, John W. Browning, E. W. Turner, Stephen D. Walker, Thomas W. Miller, John W. Francis, Charles Oldham, Humphrey Kavanaugh, James W. Caperton, Martin Gentry, John C.

Terrill, R. J. White, Peter T. Gentry, Thomas S. Ellis, John Hagan, Willis Shumate, George Dejarnett, A. J. Tribble, Green B. Million, Thomas J. Gordon, J. R. Gilbert, William K. Hocker and R. R. Stone.

[47] *Kentucky Statesman*, 20 Dec 1859, Lexington Public Library; HRBC 1904, p. 17.

[48] E. R., "Personal History," p. 28.

[49] E. R., "Full Forty Years," p. 20.

[50] Rogers, p. 74.

[51] *American Missionary*, Vol. IV, no. 2 (Feb 1860), pp. 38-41; Rogers, Birth, p. 75. Rogers' wishy-washy account, written years after the Exile, may seem inexplicable until one learns that some of the Committee members supported Berea College *after* the war, when Rogers was composing his history at President William G. Frost's behest. Be careful not to offend a donor!

[52] E. R., "Full Forty Years," pp. 20, 21; E.R., "Personal History," p. 27. Another eyewitness of this incident, 3-year-old Raphael Rogers, recorded his memories of it many years later:

> The committee, headed by Colonel Mundy, came to Berea . . . and came first to the house of Mr. Rogers who went out to speak to them. These men were all mounted on their horses and armed. My mother, fearing violence to my father and trusting to the chivalry of Kentuckians, went out and took hold of my father's arm. The speaker at that time, about three years old, peeped between his father and his mother at Col. Mundy, who rode a white horse. This is the first distinct recollection of my life. I can still see that white horse. Col. Mundy told my father that he must leave and when my father [at]tempted some argument, he said that there was no time for speech and rode away with the committee to Mr. Fee's house, leaving a message there. Mr. Fee was in the east trying to raise money for the school. John Raphael Rogers, "Pioneering in Berea," pp. 14, 15, pamphlet dated 31 Sept 1931, BCA.

[53] Ernest G. Dodge, "Guidebook to Berea," pp. 4, 10, typescript dated 3 Sept 1903, BCA.

[54] *Ibid.*, p. 21; Rogers, p. 75.

[55] Rogers to Jocelyn 28 Dec 1859 AMA 43828; Rogers to Frost, 20-page letter concerning the Berea Exodus, [c. Sept 1893].

[56] *American Missionary*, Vol. IV, no. 2 (Feb 1860), p. 41.

[57] Fee to Jocelyn 4 Dec 1859 AMA 109220; Fee to Tappan 29 Dec 1859 AMA 109236.

[58] Martha (Stapp) Wright to Rev. & Mrs. Fee 25 Dec 1859 AMA 43825.

[59] E. R., "Personal History,", pp. 29, 30.

[60] *Ibid.*; AMA 43828; Coleman, *Slavery Times*, p. 322.

[61] E. R., "Full Forty Years," p. 22; Candee to Jocelyn 26 Dec 1859 AMA 43826B.

[62] Rogers, pp. 79, 80; E.R., "Full Forty Years," p. 22.

[63] E. R., "Personal History," p. 30.

[64] E. R., "Full Forty Years," p. 23.

[65] E. R., "Personal History," p. 30; Rogers p. 81.

[66] Fee to Tappan 29 Dec 1859 AMA 109236.

[67] E. R., "Personal History," pp. 30, 31.

[68] Rogers, p. 81. The Berea Exile was not without parallels—in the wake of Harper's Ferry other antislavery groups were driven from the South: Wesleyans from North Carolina, Quakers from North Carolina and Tennessee, and United Brethren from Kentucky and elsewhere.

Daniel Worth, an AMA commissioned worker in North Carolina, was driven from his field too—and appears with Fee and the others on the AMA list of exiles. Mabee, *Black Freedom*, p. 241.

69 J. B. Mallett to AMA 11 Jan 1860 AMA 43825.

70 *Ibid.*

71 *American Missionary*, Vol. IV, no. 2 (Feb. 1860), p. 42.

72 *Ibid.*, p. 43.

73 *Ibid.*, p. 41.

74 *Ibid.*, p. 43. J. D. Reed spoke at the same meeting and agreed with all Boughton had said. Fee to Jocelyn 16 Jan 1860 AMA 43828.

75 *Ibid.*

76 Boughton, p. 240; Oberlin Alumni Records; Ezekiel T. Hayes Student File [non-graduate], Box 109, OCA.

77 Mrs. George S. Life Student File [non-graduate], Box 151, OCA.

78 Fee, *Autobiography*, p. 119.

79 *Ibid.*, p. 117.

80 Madison County Slave Census of 1860.

81 A small sampling of the committee members reveals a great deal about who they were: Samuel Bennett, a prosperous farmer (his son married Cassius Clay's daughter); Green B. Broaddus, High Sheriff of Madison County, 1st lieutenant in Humphrey Marshall's regiment in the Mexican War; Col. James W. Caperton, attorney, President of Richmond National Bank, one of the wealthiest citizens of Madison County; Coleman Covington, a prominent man who represented the county in the Kentucky legislature in 1855-57; Curtis Field, Jr., lawyer, member of Kentucky house 1857-59; Major William Harris, common school commissioner for Madison County for 20 years, member of Kentucky house 1851-53, wealthy farmer; Humphrey Kavanaugh, soldier in the Mexican War; Thomas Woods Miller, colonel in the Kentucky militia; William Malcolm Miller, member of Kentucky house 1855-57; Green B. Million, wealthy citizen and Justice of the Peace; Col. Reuben Munday, member of Kentucky senate 1851-55; Charles Oldham, Sheriff of Madison County; Robert R. Stone, lawyer and banker; John C. Terrill, attorney at Richmond bar, later officer in Confederate Army; William T. Terrill, members Kentucky house 1850; Edward W. Turner, member of Kentucky senate; Squire Turner, member of Kentucky house 1824-26, 1830, 1831, 1839, lawyer and farmer ("amassed the largest fortune from his practice of all lawyers ever at the Richmond bar"); William Jason Walker, wealthy merchant, banker and farmer. W. H. Miller, *History and Genealogies of the Families of Miller, Woods, Harris . . . .* (Lexington: Press of Transylvania Co., 1907); Collins & Collins, II, 493; French Tipton, "The Richmond Bar," *The Lawyers and Lawmakers of Kentucky*, ed. H. Levin (Chicago: Lewis Publ. Co., 1897), pp. 520-522; James W. Caperton obit., *Berea Citizen*, 22 Apr 1909.

82 Miller; *American Missionary*, Vol. IV, no. 2 (Feb 1860), p. 40. A number of Berea students before the Civil War shared this heritage: Ann Eliza and Mary Best were Harris descendants—their mother Nancy (Harris) Best being a cousin of the committee members who bore that surname. The Maupins who attended Berea were descended from the Maupins of Albemarle County, just as committee members were. In addition to the men bearing the name (William, Solon and John D.), Harris descendants on the committee included James W. Caperton, Robert R. Stone (who delivered the address on December 17), Samuel Bennett, Durret and Richard J. White, Clifton Rodes Estill and Ambrose J. Dudley; in addition, William Jason Walker married a Harris descendant.

83 Davis to Editor, *Congregational Herald*, 16 Feb 1860, TS, BCA; Collins & Collins, I, 82.

[84] *Cincinnati Weekly,* 2 Feb 1860, clippings in Exile File, BCA; Collins & Collins, I, 82; Congregational Herald, Vol. VII, no. 47 (23 Feb 1860), p. 2. (or Filson Club Quarterly, Vol. 35, p. 207.)

[85] *Congregational Herald,* Vol. VII, no. 47 (23 Feb 1860), p. 2: TS in BCA.

[86] Muelder, p. 309; *Semi-Weekly Free Democrat* [Galesburg, Ill.], Vol. VII, no. 21 (13 Mar 1860), p. 3: TS in BCA.

[87] Davis to Editor, 31 Mar 1860, *Congregational Herald,* Vol. VIII, no. 2 (12 Apr 1860), p. 2: TS in BCA; Davis to Editor, *Congregational Herald,* Vol. VIII, no. 35 (29 Nov 1860), p. 2: TS in BCA.

[88] Muelder, p. 310.

[89] *Semi-Weekly Free Democrat,* Vol. VII, no. 80 (5 Oct 1860), p. 3: TS in BCA.

[90] *Congregational Herald,* Vol. VIII, no. 41 (10 Jan 1861), p. 2: TS in BCA.

[91] James Scott Davis Student File, Oberlin Alumni Records. Davis preached in Illinois at a number of different churches from 1860 until 1892; his last ministerial post was in Williams, Iowa, in 1893. He died in Chicago, July 26, 1896. Amelia (Rogers) Davis survived her husband by many years; in 1922, then in her 80's, she was in Australia accompanying her son George Thompson Brown Davis on a worldwide evangelistic tour. George Davis, renowned as an author and director of many revival campaigns all over the world, conducted his own world tour over a four-year period, 1921-25. Davis' daughter Amelia E. R. Davis, Berea College's only graduate in 1876, later became the wife of another Berea graduate, Rev. John H. J. Rice. *Who was Who in America* (Chicago: Marquis Who's Who, Inc., 1973), V, 172; *Berea Citizen,* 16 Nov 192.

[92] *Cincinnati Enquirer,* 5 Jan 1860, clippings in Exile File, BCA.

[93] *Maysville Daily Press,* 7 Jan 1860, clippings in Exile File, BCA.

[94] *Cincinnati Weekly,* 2 Feb 1860, clippings in Exile File, BCA.

[95] Mallett to Tappan 21 July 1858 AMA 108456.

[96] *Augusta Sentinel,* 26 Jan 1860, clippings in Exile File, BCA.

[97] *Cincinnati Weekly,* 2 Feb 1860, clippings in Exile File, BCA.

[98] *Cincinnati Enquirer,* 2 Feb 1860, clippings in Exile File, BCA.

[99] Fee, *Autobiography,* p. 151, 152.

[100] *Ibid.;* Fee to Jocelyn 9 Jan 1860 AMA 109268.

[101] Fee to Jocelyn 25 Jan 1860 AMA 43841; Fee to Jocelyn, Tappan and Whipple 2 Feb 1860 AMA 109330.

[102] *Ibid;* Fee to Jocelyn et al, see above.

[103] Fee to Clay 25 July 1886 BCA; Fee to Whipple 18 Jan 1867 AMA 44473.

[104] Mallett to Jocelyn 15 May 1860 AMA 43868; Mallet to Jocelyn 13 Apr 1860 AMA 190503.

[105] Fee to Tappan 2 July 1860 AMA 109655; Rogers to Tappan 6 Sept 1860 AMA 109802.

[106] Fee, *Autobiography,* p. 154.

CHAPTER 7

[1] Candee to Clay 26 Dec 1859 BCA.

[2] *American Missionary,* Vol. IV, no. 2 (Feb 1860), p. 43; Clay's "Appeal to the People of Madison County"—from *Louisville Journal,* 4 Apr 1860, quoted in Clay, pp. 241-47; "Speech of

of Cassius M. Clay at Frankfort, Ky., from the Capitol Steps, January 10, 1860," pamphlet, reprinted for *Cincinnati Gazette*, pp. 1-3: in BCA.

[3] "Speech," pp. 1-3.

[4] Fee to Clay 28 Feb 1860 BCA.

[5] Fee to Tappan 15 Feb 1860 AMA 109362.

[6] Rogers, *Birth*, p. 29.

[7] Ellen (Sholes) Hanson Student File [non-graduate], Box 104, OCA.

[8] *American Missionary*, Vol. IV, no. 6 (June 1860), pp. 134-6; Hanson to Jocelyn 13 Mar 1860 AMA 43855; Fee to Jocelyn 29 Feb 1860 AMA 109393A.

[9] AMA 43855.

[10] *Ibid.*

[11] AMA 43856 [part of same letter].

[12] *Kentucky Statesman*, 13 Apr 1860, in Lexington Public Library; *American Missionary* Vol. IV, no. 6 (June 1860), p. 135.

[13] *Kentucky Statesman*, 13 Apr 1860; Clay, p. 244; *Kentucky Statesman*, 6 Apr 1860, Lexington Public Library.

[14] *American Missionary*, Vol. IV, no. 6 (June 1860), pp. 135, 136; Mallett to Jocelyn 13 Apr 1860 AMA 109503; Mont Hanson to Ernest G. Dodge 18 Aug 1903 BCA; Ernest G. Dodge, "Guidebook to Berea," p. 7, typescript dated 3 Sept 1903, BCA.

[15] *Kentucky Statesman*, 13 Apr 1860, Lexington Public Library; *American Missionary*, Vol. IV, no. 5 (June 1860), pp. 134-6.

[16] The following four accounts of the events after Hanson's return are in basic agreement with one another, although each supplies some unique details; for my narrative I have combined them to give a complete composite story: Hanson's Account in *American Missionary*, Vol IV, no. 6 (June 1860), pp. 134-7; Mont Hanson to Dodge 19 Aug 1903 BCA; clipping from Cincinnati Commercial with Mallett to Jocelyn 13 Apr 1860 AMA 109503; Rogers to AMA 3 May 1860 (including transcription of D. P. to Rogers 27 Mar 1860) AMA 43860. In a report to the AMA dated May 3, 1860, John A. R. Rogers included a transcription of a letter he had himself received (dated March 27, 1860) from one D. P. (Rogers gave only initials, not names, throughout.) Undoubtedly this person was David Preston, a former student of Rogers', son of Jerusha Preston—other sources present young Preston as one of the leaders of the anti-mob forces on the day of combat. In quotations from Preston's letter I have supplied names where Rogers has initials.

[17] David Preston to Rogers 27 Mar 1860.

[18] Clipping from *Cincinnati Commercial*.

[19] Letter from C.M. Clay in *Mountain Democrat*, reprinted in *National Anti-Slavery Standard*, 14 Apr 1860 BCA.

[20] Clay to *New York Tribune*, reprinted in *Kentucky Statesman*, 13 Apr 1860, Lexington Public Library.

[21] *Kentucky Statesman*, 27 Mar 1860, Lexington Public Library.

[22] Clipping; *Mountain Democrat*; Clay to *New York Tribune*; Preston to Rogers. Whereas the Bereans claimed they had been attacked by 219 people, the Richmondites maintained that their army numbered between 150 to 160 citizens.

[23] *American Missionary*, Vol. IV, no. 6 (June 1860), p. 136.

[24] *The World We Live In*, Apr. 7, 1860, clippings in Exile File, BCA.

[25] Clipping from Cincinnati paper AMA 109503.

[26] Willis Green Haley and Franklin Bland, leaders of the Berea 'army,' explained their actions to Clay, who they regarded as their commander: "In the first place," they said, the fight

was not brought about over Hanson; but over the treatment of George West. The Committee went to his house on the hunt for Hanson. West is in the last stage of consumption, and told his daughter to shut the door; and they broke the door down, and they cuffed and abused West and his daughter; and we went to see West, with no view of seeing any of them. We met them, and I begged for peace, and did all I could to obtain it. I intended to take your good advice. Bland & Haley to Clay, 30 Mar 1860, quoted in Clay, pp. 245, 246.

In his *Memoirs* Clay expands upon the incident with West and his daughters, saying that the committee used "language to the daughter of West . . . too gross for the public eye." Clay, p. 246.

[27] Clay, p. 250.

[28] *American Missionary,* Vol. IV, no. 6 (June 1860), p. 137.

[29] *Ibid.*

[30] *Kentucky Statesman,* Apr. 6, 1860, Lexington Public Library.

[31] *Kentucky Whig,* undated clipping in Exile File, BCA.

[32] Clay to *Louisville Journal,* 29 Mar 1860, in *National Anti-Slavery Standard,* 14 Apr 1860, clipping in Exile File, BCA.

[33] Clay to *New York Tribune,* in *Kentucky Statesman,* 13 Apr 1860, Lexington Public Library.

[34] Clay to *Louisville Journal,* 31 Mar 1860, in *National Anti-Slavery Standard,* 14 Apr 1860, clipping in Exile File, BCA.

[35] Green Clay, *Cassius Clay: Militant Statesman, Moses of Emancipation 1810-1903,* TS, p. 118, 119: in Dorris Collection, Crabbe Library, EKU. Reporting this incident, Hanson gives the less grandiose figure of "8 to 10 friends who spent some two or three days at C. M. Clay's armed & much excitement." Of course, Hanson may have been giving the number of his own friends who were members of Clay's guard, not the total number. Hanson to Tappan 3 July 1860 AMA 109660.

[36] Clay, "Speech at Republican State Convention of Kentucky," clipping from *Cincinnati Daily Gazette,* 28 Apr 1860, Cassius M. Clay Papers, Filson Club, Louisville.

[37] *The World We Live In,* Apr. 14, 1860, clipping in Exile File, BCA.

[38] *Chicago Press & Tribune,* reprinted in *The World We Live In,* 14 Apr 1860, clipping in BCA.

[39] "Resolution of the Radical Abolitionist Convention" in *Douglass Monthly,* Oct 1860, quoted in Pease & Pease, *Bound,* p. 85.

[40] Candee to Clay 25 Apr 1860 BCA.

[41] *Kentucky Statesman,* Apr. 10, 1860, Lexington Public Library.

[42] Madison County Census Mortality Schedule, 1860; West's will dated 6 Apr 1860, *Madison County Will Book O,* p. 152.

[43] Committee's Report, 3 Apr 1860, in *Kentucky Statesman,* 10 Apr 1860, Lexington Public Library. The document was signed by Reuben Munday, T. J. Maupin, J. W. Caperton, Thomas S. Bronston, Jr., and Robert Rodes Stone.

[44] *Kentucky Statesman,* Apr. 10, 1860, in Lexington Public Library; Rentfro & Wright to Fee 20 Apr 1860 BCA. The "penitent" was almost certainly William Stapp, who had been "ordered to leave the state . . . but *took the risk* [my own italics] of staying at home and was not molested." After his "repentance," Stapp was risking very little by staying in Berea and cooperating with the committee. Ernest G. Dodge, "Guidebook to Berea," p. 7, typescript, dated 3 Sept 1903, BCA.

[45] *The World We Live In*, Apr. 17, 1860, clipping in Exile File, BCA; *Kentucky Statesman*, Apr. 10; 1860; Richarson, p. 14.

[46] Kendrick to Jocelyn 6 Apr 1860 AMA 109485; Mallett to Jocelyn 6 Apr 1860 AMA 109486.

[47] Fee to Jocelyn 9 Apr 1860 AMA 109496.

[48] Fee to Jocelyn 17 Apr 1860 AMA 109506; Hanson to Rogers 25 May 1860 AMA 109582.

[49] *American Missionary Association 12th Annual Report, 1858*, pp. 66-67; *American Missionary*, Vol. IV, no. 3 (Mar 1860), p. 68; Rogers, p. 19.

[50] Fee to Jocelyn 24 May 1860 AMA 109578; Fee to Jocelyn 21 Aug 1860 109764; Fee to Jocelyn 20 Sept 1859 AMA 43511; Fee to Whipple 12 May 1854 AMA 43238.

[51] Fee to Jocelyn 30 July 1860 AMA 109719.

[52] Benjamin & Nancy Kirby to Fee & Hanson 13 July 1860 AMA 43876.

[53] Mallett to Jocelyn 6 Apr 1860 AMA 109486.

[54] Clay's List of Exiles, 1860, MS, BCA. In a biography of her father, Mary B. Clay mentions having in her possession names of 94 persons who were driven from Kentucky by the Madison County mob: no doubt she is referring to the list her father compiled in 1860. The accuracy of Clay's list is attested by its agreement in every instance with facts that can be ascertained through other resources. Every person on the list has a documented connection to Berea, either before or after the Exile (frequently both); every person, but one, mentioned as an exile in contemporary letters appears on the list. In addition, the numbers for each family are in exact agreement with marriage, deed, birth and census records of Madison and Rockcastle Counties. Some families who might have been exiled, such as the Burdetts, whose house was searched by the committee, and the Wrights, were apparently not forced to leave their homes. Mary B. Clay, "Biography of Cassius M. Clay: Written by His Daughter," *Filson Club History Quarterly*, Vol. 46, no. 3 (July 1972), p. 269.

[55] Fee to Renfro 3 Jan 1860 BCA; Fee to Jocelyn 16 Jan 1860 AMA 43838.

[56] Wright & Renfro to Fee 20 Apr 1860 BCA.

[57] *Ibid.*

[58] Mrs. Anna H. Richardson [Newcastle, England], "Pamplets and Letters [1859, 1860]" in William Still, *The Underground Rail Road* (1871; rpt. Chicago: Johnson Publ. Co., Inc., 1970), p. 621; *American Missionary*, Vol. IV, no. 3 (Mar 1860), p. 68.

[59] Galatha Rawlings, "Still More Old History," *Berea Citizen*, 20 Oct 1927.

[60] Benjamin Kirby to Fee 13 July 1860 AMA 43876

[61] Renfro to Fee 28 Aug 1860 BCA; Ernest G. Dodge, "Guidebook to Berea," p. 14, typescript, dated 3 Sept 1903, BCA.

[62] Kendrick to Jocelyn 13 Dec 1859 AMA 43823; *American Missionary* Vol. IV, no 2 (Feb 1860), pp. 35, 37.

[63] Coleman, *Slavery Times*, p. 45n; Collins & Collins, II, 260, 261.

[64] Candee to Jocelyn 30 Jan 1860 AMA 43844.

[65] Kendrick to Jocelyn 10 Jan 1860 AMA 109279; Fee to Jocelyn, Tappan and Whipple 2 Feb1860 AMA 109330; Kendrick to Jocelyn 6 Feb 1860 AMA 109339.

[66] Candee to Kendrick, quoted in Kendrick to Jocelyn 24 Mar 1860 AMA 109449.

[67] Candee to Jocelyn 9 June 1860 AMA 43871; *American Missionary*, Vol. IV, no. 8 (Aug 1860), p. 185; Jones' Report to AMA 20 Apr 1860 AMA 43863.

[68] AMA 43871.

[69] *Ibid.*

[70] Candee to Rogers 22 June 1860 AMA 43872.

71 *Ibid.* Five black people had joined Candee's church in McKee by August 1, 1859. *American Missionary,* Vol. III, no. 9 (Sept 1859), p. 209.

72 AMA 43872; Candee to Jocelyn 21 Aug 1860 AMA 43878; Candee to Jocelyn 6 Sept 1860 AMA 43879.

73 Candee to Jocelyn 18 Nov 1860 AMA 43885-43887; Fee to Jocelyn 30 July 1860 AMA 109719; *American Missionary,* Vol. IV, no 12 (Dec 1860), p. 281; *American Missionary,* Vol. V, no. 2 (Feb 1861), p. 45.

74 Pratt to Jocelyn 2 Dec 1860 AMA 43888; *American Missionary,* Vol. V, no. 2 (Feb 1861), p. 45.

75 Candee to Jocelyn 1861 AMA 43893; Mobley's report 1 Jan 1861 AMA 43892.

76 George Candee, "Radical Bob and His Army," *Berea Citizen,* 16 Oct 1913.

77 Candee to Jocelyn 4 Feb 1861 AMA 43898; Jess D. Wilson, "It Happened Here," *Cooperative Spotlight Newsletter (Jackson County Rural Electric Co-op, Dec. 1982),* p. 12c; Pratt to Jocelyn 9 Jan 1861 AMA 43897.

78 AMA 43898; Wilson, p. 12c; George Candee, "Reminiscences," *Berea Citizen,* 16 Oct 1913. John G. Fee thought Robert Nichols was " a very generous noble fellow"; Nichols was an active antislavery man, according to Fee, smart and popular, who talked "incessantly" and "occasionally [swelled] his liver a little with brandy." Fee recommended Nichols to Clay to run on the State Republican ticket. Fee to Clay 26 Feb1859 BCA.

79 George Candee, "Radical Bob and His Army," *Berea Citizen,* 16 Oct 1913.

80 Wilson, p. 12d.

81 Candee to Jocelyn 4 Feb 1861 AMA 43998; *American Missionary,* Vol. V, no. 4 (Apr 1861), pp. 88, 89.

82 AMA 43898; Rogers to Jocelyn 28 Dec 1860 AMA 109970; Rogers to Tappan 7 Jan 1861 AMA 110001.

83 Candee to Jocelyn 14 Mar 1861 AMA 43902.

84 *Ibid.*

85 Pratt's Treasurer's Report to AMA 15 Mar 1861 AMA 43904; Boughton to Jocelyn 11 Mar 1861 AMA 110134.

86 Candee to Jocelyn 1 Apr 1861 AMA 43906.

87 Hanson to Greenbury & Rebecca Hanson 28 Apr 1861 BCA; Fee to Jocelyn 3 May 1861 AMA 110215.

88 AMA 110215.

89 Pratt to Jocelyn 6 May 1861 AMA 110217.

90 Candee to Jocelyn 4 May 1861 AMA 110744.

91 Mobley to Candee 18 May 1861 AMA 43907.

92 Wilson, p. 12c; George Candee, "Reminiscences," *Berea Citizen,* 16 Oct 1913.

93 Mobley to Jocelyn 18 May 1861 AMA 43908; Mobley to Candee 18 May 1861 AMA 43907.

94 AMA 43907; Mobley to Jocelyn 5 July 1861 AMA 43911; *American Missionary,* Vol VI, no. 1 (Jan 1862), p. 14; *American Missionary,* Vol. VI, no. 5 (May 1862), p. 112.

95 Candee to Jocelyn 27 July 1861 and Elisha Harrison to Rev. & Mrs. Candee 10 July 1861 [both letters together] AMA 43912.

96 AMA 43912.

97 Isaac Fowler & Elisha Harrison to Rev. & Mrs. Candee 15 Mar 1862 AMA 43922.

98 Harrison to Candee 1 Feb 1863 AMA 43963; *American Missionary,* Vol. VII, no. 2 (Feb 1863), p. 37.

CHAPTER 8

[1] Boughton to Tappan 31 Dec 1859 AMA 109241.

[2] Fee to Jocelyn 9 Jan 1860 AMA 109268; Rogers to Jocelyn 12 Jan 1860 AMA 109277.

[3] Boughton to Jocelyn 13 Jan 1860 AMA 109281; Boughton to Jocelyn 18 Jan 1860 AMA 109290A; Lizzie Rogers to Anna Shailer Griffith, 23 Jan 1860, BCA.

[4] Rogers to Jocelyn 26 Jan 1860 AMA 109309.

[5] Boughton to Jocelyn 27 Jan 1860 AMA 109311.

[6] Fee to Jocelyn 8 Feb 1860 AMA 109343; Davis to Jocelyn 14 Feb 1860 AMA 109356; Davis to Jocelyn 18 Feb 1860 AMA 109358; Fee to Tappan 7 Jan 1860 AMA 109262; Davis to Jocelyn 28 Feb 1860 AMA 190391. Joseph E. Roy, a graduate of Knox College (1848), affiliated with the AMA, became pastor of the Plymouth Church at Chicago, the "most notoriously abolitionist church in the city." Muelder, pp. 311, 312.

[7] Indiana Newspaper Clipping, "Kentucky Exiles in Indiana" AMA 109393B. The meeting may have been held in Liberty, Indiana, as Boughton reported having been there on March 8. Boughton to Jocelyn 14 Mar 1860 AMA 109425.

[8] Fee to Jocelyn, Tappan and Whipple 2 Feb 1860 AMA 109330; Fee to Tappan 16 Mar 1860 AMA 109429; Fee to Jocelyn 16 Mar 1860 AMA 109430; Fee to Jocelyn 20 Mar 1860 109437.

[9] Fee to Tappan 26 Mar 1860 AMA 109451; *American Missionary*, Vol. IV, no. 6 (June 1860), pp. 141, 142.

[10] Boughton to Jocelyn 2 Apr 1860 AMA 109471; Fee to Jocelyn 9 Apr 1860 AMA 109496.

[11] Fee to Jocelyn 30 Mar 1860 AMA 109454; Fee to Jocelyn Mar 1860 AMA 109461; Mallett to Jocelyn 6 Apr 1860 AMA 109486; Davis to Jocelyn 4 July 1860 AMA 109666; *American Missionary*, Vol. IV, no. 10 (Oct 1860), pp. 226, 227.

[12] Fee to Jocelyn 16 Jan 1861 AMA 11022.

[13] *Ibid.*

[14] Whipple to Tappan 23 Aug 1860 AMA 109766; Rogers to Jocelyn 30 Aug 1860 AMA 109781; Rogers to Jocelyn 6 Sept 1860 AMA 109801.

[15] E.R., "Full Forty Years," p. 24.

[16] Rogers to Jocelyn 28 Dec 1860 AMA 109970; Rogers to Jocelyn 7 Jan 1861 AMA 110000.

[17] Rogers to Jocelyn 26 Jan 1861 AMA 110061. James S. Davis and his family were living with James M. West, a former colporteur, when the latter's house was attacked around New Year's 1861. A mob broke the door down with an axe and threw about 50 stones, many of them extremely heavy, into the house through the windows. About a dozen people, including women and children, were present in the house at the time. The rioters then tore down the fence and returned to the house, "singing, cursing, swearing." After an hour of this barrage, the mob gave West and Davis notice that they would have to leave. West wrote his report from exile in Williamson County, Illinois, at a time when both he and Davis were planning to settle in Hoyleton, Illinois, where Davis had been called to the Congregational Church. *American Missionary*, Vol. V, no. 3 (Mar 1861), p. 61.

[18] E.R., "Full Forty Years," p. 24; Rogers to Jocelyn 13 Feb 1861 AMA 10086; Rogers to Jocelyn 19 Feb 1861 AMA 110100.

[19] Rogers to Jocelyn 11 Mar 1861 AMA 110133; Rogers to Jocelyn 19 Apr 1861 AMA 110201; Rogers to Jocelyn 3 May 1861 AMA 110219.

[20] Rogers to Tappan 2 July 1861 AMA 110282; Rogers to Jocelyn 11 July 1861 AMA 110291; E.R., "Full Forty Years," pp. 25, 26.

[21] Rogers to Whipple & Jocelyn 30 Apr 1862 AMA 110736.

[22] *American Missionary,* Vol. VI, no. 7 (July 1862), p. 164.

[23] Rogers to Jocelyn 16 July 1862 AMA 110838.

[24] Rogers to Jocelyn 8 Aug 1862 AMA 110873.

[25] Rogers, p. 85.

[26] E.R., "Full Forty Years," p. 26; Coffin, p. 599.

[27] Fee to Jocelyn 29 Sept 1862 AMA 43945; Dodge, "Guidebook," p. 11.

[28] Rogers to Jocelyn 22 Oct 1862 AMA 110978; Rogers to Jocelyn 17 Feb 1863 AMA 111179; *American Missionary,* Vol. VII, no. 1 (Jan 1863), p. 15; *American Missionary,* Vol. VII, no. 2 (Feb 1863), p. 37.

[29] Rogers, p. 86; *Encyclopedia of American History,* p. 237.

[30] *Ibid.*

[31] E.R., "Full Forty Years," p. 27; Johnston, p. 145; Collins & Collins, II, 115, 116.

[32] Fletcher, II, 872; Rogers to Jocelyn 28 Jan 1863 AMA 111160; Rogers, p. 83.

[33] Rogers to Jocelyn 22 Apr 1863 AMA 111231; Rogers to Jocelyn 4 May 1863 AMA 111240; Rogers to Jocelyn 4 May 1863 AMA 111242.

[34] Rogers to Jocelyn 11 Sept 1863 AMA 111341.

[35] Fee to Jocelyn June 1864 AMA 44005.

[36] Rogers to Whipple 20 Feb 1865 AMA 112250; Rogers to Whipple and Strieby 18 Apr 1865 AMA 112381.

[37] Rogers to Whipple 4 May 1865 AMA 112412.

[38] *American Missionary,* Vol. IX, no. 11 (Nov 1865), p. 252.

[39] E.R., "Full Forty Years," p. 30.

[40] Fee to Jocelyn 30 Mar 1860 AMA 109454.

[41] Fee to Jocelyn 2 May 1860 AMA 453864-43865.

[42] *Ibid.*

[43] Fee to Jocelyn June 1864 AMA 44005; Fee to Tappan May 1860 AMA 109551.

[44] Fee, *Autobiography,* p. 155; Fee, *Berea,* p. 38.

[45] Fee, *Berea,* pp. 38, 39.

[46] Fee to Tappan 22 May 1860 AMA 109572; Fee to Jocelyn 24 May 1860 AMA 109578.

[47] Fee to Jocelyn 19 June 1860 AMA 109622; Fee to Jocelyn 22 June 1860 AMA 109636.

[48] AMA 109622.

[49] AMA 109636.

[50] Fee, *Berea,* p. 39.

[51] Fee to Tappan 29 Dec 1859 AMA 109236.

[52] Fee to Rogers 26 Mar 1860 AMA 109450.

[53] Fee to Tappan May 1860 AMA 109551.

[54] Hanson to Rogers 25 May 1860 AMA 109582; Fee to Tappan 12 July 1860 AMA 109680; Fee to Tappan 30 July 1860 AMA 109717.

[55] Fee to Tappan 12 July 1860 AMA 109680; Fee to Whipple 16 July 1860 190692.

[56] Fee to Jocelyn 21 Aug 1860 AMA 109764.

[57] Fee to Jocelyn 5 Sept 1860 AMA 109499.

[58] Fee to Whipple Sept 1860 AMA 109841.

[59] Fee to Jocelyn 14 Nov 1860 AMA 109912.

[60] Fee to Jocelyn 26 Dec 1860 AMA 109968.

[61] Fee to Jocelyn 16 Jan 1861 AMA 110022.

[62] Fee to Tappan 22 Mar 1861 AMA 110157.

[63] Coffin, pp. 597, 598. Fee described Levi Coffin as "one of God's faithful." Coffin had lost thousands of dollars in the free produce movement and spent a great deal of money on behalf of slaves. Several of the exiled families, many of them unable to pay, lived in Coffin's boarding house in Cincinnati, while they were homeless. Fee to Jocelyn 13 July 1861 AMA 110300.

[64] Hanson to his parents 28 Apr 1861; Fee to Jocelyn 30 Oct 1862 AMA 110990.

[65] Matilda Fee to Rebecca Hanson 8 May 1861 BCA.

[66] Fee to Rebecca Hanson 8 May 1861 BCA.

[67] Fee to Jocelyn 3 May 1861 AMA 110215.

[68] *Ibid.*

[69] Fee to Jocelyn 28 Sept 1861 AMA 110443.

[70] AMA 110443; Fee to *Tribune* Nov 1861 AMA 110452-110457; Fee to Whipple 5 Oct 1861 AMA 110469; Fee to Jocelyn 8 Oct 1861 AMA 110469.

[71] Fee to Jocelyn 4 Dec 1861 AMA 43918; Fee to Jocelyn 21 Dec 1861 AMA 43919; Collins & Collins, II, 96.

[72] Fee to Jocelyn 25 Dec 1861 AMA 110571.

[73] Fee to Jocelyn 2 Jan 1862 AMA 110602-110603.

[74] Matilda Fee to Jocelyn 21 Jan 1862 AMA 110619.

[75] Fee to Jocelyn 24 Feb 1862 AMA 110655.

[76] Fee to Jocelyn 3 Apr 1862 AMA 110705.

[77] Fee to Jocelyn 6 May 1862 AMA 110746-110747; Fee to Jocelyn 10 May 1862 AMA 110756; Collins & Collins, II, 102.

[78] Fee to Whipple 16 June 1862 AMA 110798; Fee to Jocelyn 23 July 1862 AMA 110851.

[79] Fee to Jocelyn 18 Aug 1862 AMA 110886-110887.

[80] Fee, *Berea*, p. 41.

[81] *Ibid.* John G. Fee was not alone as a civilian spectator at the Battle of Richmond. A Union soldier reported that "a large number of civilians had come out to see the fight and were collected on hills in [the] rear. Some of them were killed. . . ." (*Rebellion Record*, p. 418). After the battle was over many citizens examined the battlefield. John Rogers recorded in his journal that he held only a brief Sabbath meeting on August 31 because "most of the people" had gone to the battlefield.

[82] Col. J. Stoddard Johnston, "Kentucky," *Confederate Military History*, ed. Clement A. Evans (The Blue & Gray Press), IX, 125-126; Fee to Jocelyn 16 Sept 1862 AMA 110925.

[83] Fee, *Autobiography*, p. 162; Col. Joshua Taylor Bradford, commander of the home guard, led them in the desperately fought Battle of Augusta on September 27, 1862—a few days after Fee's visit. Collins & Collins, II, 112.

[84] Fee, *Berea*, pp. 41, 42.

[85] *Ibid.*, p. 42.

[86] *Ibid.;* Fee, *Autobiography*, p. 163.

[87] Fee, *Berea*, p. 43.

[88] *Ibid.*, p. 44.

[89] *Ibid.*, p. 45.

[90] Fee to Jocelyn 16 Sept 1862 AMA 110924.

[91] Fee, *Autobiography*, pp. 169, 170.

[92] *Ibid.*, pp. 170, 171.

[93] *Ibid.*, pp. 169-172; Fee to Jocelyn 30 Oct 1862 AMA 110990-110991.

[94] Fee, *Autobiography*, p. 172; Fee to Jocelyn 30 Oct 1862 AMA 110990-110991.

[95] Bertha Hardman to President of Berea 2 Mar 1954 in Founders & Founding: Fee, BCA; *History of Clermont County, Ohio, 1795-1880* (Philadelphia: J. B. Lippincott & Co., 1880), pp. 424, 425.

[96] Fee to Whipple 5 Feb 1862 AMA 111168.

[97] Fee, *Berea*, pp. 45, 46.

[98] Fee to Jocelyn 7 Apr 1863 AMA 111218; Fee to Whipple 15 Apr 1862 AMA 111225; Fee to Jocelyn 22 Apr 1863 AMA 111233.

[99] G. P. Reily to Fee 17 June 1863 AMA 43974.

[100] *Ibid.*

[101] Fee to Whipple 8 June 1863 AMA 111262; Fee to Whipple 13 June 1863 AMA 111267.

[102] Fee to Jocelyn 15 July 1863 AMA 111287; Fee to Whipple 4 Aug 1863 AMA 111300; Fee to Whipple 6 Aug 1863 AMA 111302.

[103] Fee to Whiting 14 Aug 1863 111310-111312.

[104] Fee to Whipple 17 Sept 1863 AMA 111348-111349; Fee to Whipple 27 Sept 1863 AMA 111364.

[105] Fee to AMA 6 Oct 1863 AMA 111376-111377.

[106] Fee to Whipple 27 Sept 1863 AMA 111364; Fee to ---- 6 Oct 1863 AMA 111376-111377; Laura Fee to Jocelyn 13 Oct 1863 AMA 111385; Fee to Jocelyn 22 Oct 1863 AMA 111395; Fee to Jocelyn 13 Nov 1863 AMA 111413; Fee to Jocelyn 24 Nov 1863 AMA 111422.

[107] Fee to AMA 23 Dec 1863 AMA 111444.

[108] Fee to Jocelyn 9 Dec 1863 AMA 43983; Fee to AMA 23 Dec 1863 111445; Mobley's report to AMA 14 Dec 1863 43985.

[109] AMA 43983; Mobley to Jocelyn 16 Dec 1863 AMA 43984. Robert Smith, who had been involved in a local church controversy in Madison County years before, wrote to the AMA (apparently in Mobley's defense) to say that he had known three AMA preachers in Kentucky—Fisk, Mobley and Fee—and only one of them (Fee) had abstained from either liquor or tobacco while acting as a missionary. Smith said he had never known a preacher "in these hills" who did not use whiskey and tobacco. Robert Smith to Exec. Comm. of AMA 15 Sept 1863 AMA 43981.

[110] Mobley's report to AMA 14 Dec 1863 AMA 43985.

[111] Capt. T. E. Hall to Whipple 9 Jan 1864 AMA 43987; Mobley to Jocelyn 2 Feb 1864 AMA 43988; *American Missionary*, Vol. VIII, no. 4 (Apr 1864), p. 95.

[112] Letter from Fee dated 15 Feb 1864 in *American Missionary,* Vol. VIII, no. 4 (Apr 1864), p. 94.

[113] Fee to Jocelyn 29 Mar 1864 AMA 43990; Fee to Jocelyn 28 Apr 1864 AMA 43995; Fee, *Autobiography*, p. 173. In his *Autobiography* Fee says that his wife and eldest daughter were in charge of the school at this point, but his letter indicates that Burritt Fee, not his sister Laura, was working at the Berea school in the spring of 1864. Laura Fee was probably in Decatur, Ohio, at this date, although she was to teach in the Berea school somewhat later when Burritt was at Camp Nelson.

[114] *Ibid.*

[115] *Ibid.*; Fee to Jocelyn 11 May 1864 AMA 43996.

[116] Fee to Jocelyn 1 June 1864 AMA 43999.

117 *Ibid.*

118 Fee to Jocelyn 4 June 1864 AMA 44000.

119 *Ibid.*; Fee to Jocelyn 6 June 1864 AMA 44002; Coleman, "Lexington Slave," p. 22.

120 Fee to Jocelyn 30 June 1864 AMA 44004.

121 Fee, *Autobiography,* pp. 173, 174.

122 Fee to Jocelyn June 1864 AMA 44005.

BIBLIOGRAPHY

Abbreviations

AMA—American Missionary Association
AMAA—American Missionary Association Archives
AMAC—American Missionary Association Correspondence
BCA—Berea College Archives
EKU—Eastern Kentucky University
FFC—Founders and Founding Collection in BCA
KHS—Kentucky Historical Society

Archives and Special Collections

American Missionary Assocation Archives. Correspondence of John G. Fee, John A. R. Rogers, William E. Lincoln, Otis B. Waters, George Candee, James Scott Davis, John Wesley White, Francis Hawley, and others. Kentucky and Ohio Collections. Amistad Research Center, New Orleans, La. Microfilm in Hutchins Library, Berea College.

_____, Annual Reports of the AMA. Hutchins Library, Berea College. Microfilm.

Berea College Archives. Board of Trustees and Prudential Committee Minutes, 1858-1905.

_____, Berea College Trustees, 1858-1980. Compiled by Development Office. Typescript.

_____, Board of Trustees Annual Reports/Committees.

_____, George Candee & others: FFC.

_____, Clay's List of Exiles. Founding: FFC. Manuscript.

_____, Exile File: FFC.

_____, John G. Fee: FFC.

_____, Founding: FFC.

_____, William E. Lincoln File. Faculty & Staff Collection: Lambert-McLaughlin.

_____. John Rawlings & others: FFC.

_____. Minutes of the Berea Temperance Society. Manuscript.

_____. John A. R. Rogers: Account Book. Manuscript.

_____. John A. R. Rogers: FFC.

_____. Presidents—Edward Henry Fairchild Collection.

_____. Union Church Minute Book. Manuscript.

Burdette File. Kentucky Historical Society, Frankfort.

Burnam, Curtis Field. "Burnam Family History." Townsend Room, Crabbe Library, EKU. Manuscript.

Burnam Family. Family History Series #6. Townsend Room.

Cassius M. Clay Papers. Dorris Collection, Townsend Room.

Clay Family. Family History Series #9a. Townsend Room.

Denham File. KHS.

Kirby File. KHS.

Oberlin College Archives. Student Files [nongraduate].

Renfro File. KHS.

Letters

Candee, George. AMAC. Kentucky and Ohio Collections, AMAA.

_____. Letters and papers. FFC, BCA.

Clay, Cassius M. Clay-Fee Correspondence. FFC.

Davis, James Scott. AMAC. Kentucky Collection, AMAA.

_____. Letters and papers. FFC.

Fee, John G. AMAC. Kentucky and Ohio Collections, AMAA.

_____. Letters and papers. FFC.

Fee, Matilda Hamilton. Letters. FFC.

Hanson, John G. Letters and papers. FFC.

Harrison, Elisha. AMAC. Kentucky Collection, AMAA.

Hawley, Francis. AMAC. Kentucky Collection, AMAA.

Jones, Robert. AMAC. Kentucky Collection, AMAA.

Lincoln, William E. AMAC. Kentucky and Ohio Collections, AMAA.

_____. Letters and papers. Faculty collection, BCA.

Renfro, Thomas Jefferson. Letters. FFC.

Rogers, Elizabeth Embree. Letters and papers. FFC.

Rogers, John A. R. AMAC. Kentucky and Ohio Collections, AMAA.

_____. Letters and papers. FFC.

Waters, Otis Bird. AMAC. Kentucky Collection, AMAA.

West, Peter H. AMAC. Kentucky Collection, AMAA.

White, John Wesley. AMAC. Kentucky Collection, AMAA.

Wright, William B. Letter. FFC.

Diaries, Journals, Autobiographies and Memoirs

Candee, George, "Reminiscences." Printed serially in *Berea Citizen*. Also in FFC.

Clay, Cassius Marcellus. *The Life of Cassius Marcellus Clay, Memoirs, Writings and Speeches*. Vol. I. Cincinnati: J. Fletcher Brennan & Co., 1886.

Coffin, Levi. *Reminiscences of Levi Coffin*. Cincinnati: Western Tract Society, 1876.

Fee, John Gregg. *Autobiography of John G. Fee*. Chicago: National Christian Association, 1891.

_____. *Berea Its History and Work*. Published in *Berea Evangelist* 1 Jan 1885-10 June 1886. BCA. Typescript.

Lincoln, William E. "Memoir." FFC. Manuscript.

Rogers, Elizabeth Embree. *Full Forty Years of Shadow and Sunshine: A Sketch of the Family Life of the J. A. R. Rogers Family*. 1896. BCA. Typescript.

_____. *A Personal History of Berea College.* 1910? BCA. Typescript.

Rogers, John A. R. *Birth of Berea College: A Story of Providence.* Philadelphia: Henry T. Coates & Co., 1904.

_____. *Journal.* 2 vols. 1850-64, 1864-67. BCA. Manuscript.

Rogers, John Raphael. "Pioneering in Berea," *The Berea Alumnus* I (June 1931).

Waters, Otis Bird. "An Abolitionist Where He Wasn't Wanted," *Oberlin Students' Monthly* (August 1859). Oberlin College Special Collections.

Published Letters, Writings, Speeches, etc.

Barnes, Gilbert H. & Dwight L. Dumond, eds. *Letters of Theodore Dwight Weld and Angeline Grimke Weld and Sarah Grimke 1822-1844.* Gloucester, Mass.: Peter Smith, 1965.

Clay, Cassius M. *Speeches of Cassius Clay at Frankfort, Ky from the Capitol Steps, January 10, 1860.* Reported for the *Cincinnati Gazette.* BCA.

_____. *The Writings of Cassius Marcellus Clay, including Speeches and Addresses.* New York: Harper & Bros., 1848.

Dumond, Dwight L., ed. *Letters of James Gillespie Birney 1831-1857.* New York: D. Appleton-Century Co., 1938.

Fee, John Gregg. *An Anti-Slavery Manual.* Maysville, Kentucky: Herald Office, 1848.

_____. "Colonization, The Present Scheme of Colonization Wrong, Delusive, and Retards Emancipation." Cincinnati: American Reform Tract and Book Society, undated.

_____. *Non-Fellowship with Slaveholders the Duty of Christians.* New York: John A. Gray, printers, 1855.

_____. *The Sinfulness of Slavehold shown by appeals to Reason and Scripture.* New York: John A. Gray, printers, 1851.

Weld, Theodore. *American Slavery As It Is.* Reprinted in *Slavery in America.* Edited by Richard O. Curry & Joanna Dunlap Cowden. Itasca, Ill.: F. E. Peacock Publishers, Inc., 1972.

School Records

Alumni Register: (of Oberlin College) *Graduates and Former Students, Teachers and Administrative Staff 1833-1960.* Oberlin, Ohio: Oberlin College, 1960.

Bulletin of Oberlin College. (New Series No. 233). Alumni Catalogue: Officers and Graduates of Oberlin College. Oberlin College: 1926.

Bulletin of Oberlin College: Necrology of Alumni of Oberlin College. Oberlin, Ohio: Oberlin College, 10 Feb 1925.

General Catalogue of Oberlin College 1833-1908. Oberlin, Ohio: Oberlin College, 1 Apr 1909.

Historical Register of the Officers and Students of Berea College from the Beginning to June 1904. Berea: Berea College, 1904.

Historical Register: Officers and Students opf Berea College from the Beginning to June 1916. Berea: Berea College Press, 1916.

Oberlin College Alumni Records. Alumni Office, Oberlin College, Oberlin, Ohio.

Rogers, John A. R. "List of Berea Students 1858," *Berea Citizen,* 24 July 1902.

Church and Cemetery Records

D.A.R. Cemetery Records. Berea Cemetery. General Records Commission. 23 Aug 1969. Copied by Frances Moore, Lois Crippen Tompkins & Marguerite Sloan.

Minutes of Scaffold Cane-Silver Creek Baptist Church 1802-1859. TS Copied by Frances Moore from original in possession of Clyde Linville, Mt. Vernon, Ky.

Paint Lick Cemetery. Paint Lick, Kentucky.

Richmond Cemetery. Richmond, Kentucky.

Scaffold Cane Baptist Church Cemetery. Rockcastle County, Kentucky. Copied by the author, 12 Nov 1982.

Union Church Minute Book. BCA.

West, Donal S. *Cemeteries of Madison County, Kentucky.* Compiled at various dates. 1977. Mountain Collection, Berea College. Manuscript.

County Records

Bracken County, Kentucky. Deeds. Bracken County Courthouse, Brooksville, KY.

_____. Marriage Registers. Bracken County Courthouse.

_____. Wills. Bracken County Courthouse.

_____. Wills. Compiled by Mrs. Phillip Martin. D.A.R. BCA. Typescript.

Burnam v. Burnam. Madison County, Kentucky, Circuit Court Records. Civil Court Judgments. Box 39, Bundle 78. Kentucky Archives, Frankfort.

Jackson County, Kentucky. Marriages. Jackson County Courthouse, McKee, KY.

_____. Wills. Jackson County Courthouse.

Madison County, Kentucky. Deed Books. Madison County Courthouse, Richmond, KY.

_____. Deed Books. Madison County Courthouse.

_____. Marriage Bond Books. Madison County Courthouse

_____. Marriage Bonds. Madison County Courthouse.

_____. Marriage Bonds. KHS, Frankfort. Microfilm.

_____. Marriage Books. Madison County Courthouse.

_____. Marriage Index. Madison County Courthouse.

_____. Tax Books: 1854, 1855, 1864. KHS, Frankfort.

Madison County, Kentucky. Birth, Marriage and Death Records: Vital Statistics. Kentucky Archives, Frankfort. Microfilm.

_____. Will Books. Madison County Courthouse.

Mason County, Kentucky. Marriage Records. KHS, Frankfort. Xerox.

Rockcastle County, Kentucky. Births: 1853. Kentucky Vital Statistics. Kentucky Archives, Frankfort. Microfilm.

_____. Wills. Rockcastle County Courthouse, Mount Vernon, KY.

Scott, Sharon Elizabeth. *Marriage Records of Rock Castle Lincoln and Pulaski Counties.* Copied from Marriage Records of Martin Owens, beginning 19 Feb 1850. 1966.

Shackelford, Judge W. Rodes. "Early Marriage Records of Madison Co., Ky.," *Register* 39 (1941), and subsequent volumes.

Todd, James T. *Madison Co., Ky Marriages* [Todd]. 1982. Original in possession of James Paul Todd of Paint Lick, KY. Typescript.

Censuses

Bracken County, Kentucky. Seventh Census of the United States, 1850. Microfilm.

_____. Slave Census 1850. Microfilm.

_____. Eighth Census of the United States, 1860. Microfilm.

DeBow, J. D. *A Statistical View of the United States: A Compendium of the Seventh Census [1850].* Washington: Beverley Tucker, Senate Printer, 1854.

Jackson County, Kentucky. Eighth Census of the United States, 1860. Microfilm.

Lewis County, Kentucky. Seventh Census of the United States, 1850. Microfilm.

Madison County, Kentucky. Seventh Census of the United States, 1850. Microfilm.

_____. Slave Census 1850. Microfilm.

_____. Eighth Census of the United States, 1860. Microfilm.

_____. Slave Census 1860. Microfilm.

_____. Mortality Schedule 1860. KHS, Frankfort. Microfilm.

Rockcastle County, Kentucky. Seventh Census of the United States, 1850. Microfilm.

_____. Seventh Census of the United States, 1850. Compiled by Anna Joy Hubble. KHS, Frankfort.

_____. Slave Census 1850. Microfilm.

_____. Eighth Census of the United States, 1860. Microfilm.

_____. Mortality Schedule 1860. KHS, Frankfort. Microfilm.

Newspapers and Periodicals

American Missionary. BCA.

American Missionary Association Annual Reports. Hutchins Library, Berea College. Microfilm.

Berea Citizen. Hutchins Library, Berea College. Microfilm.

Kentucky Statesman. Lexington Public Library, Lexington, KY. Microfilm.

Mountain Democrat. Clippings in BCA.

Richmond Register. Crabbe Library, EKU. Microfilm.

The True American. Lexington Public Library. Microfilm.

SECONDARY SOURCES

Genealogy (in private collections)

Harrison Manuscript. Compiled by May Harrison Lambert. In possession of Warren Lambert, Berea, KY. Manuscript.

Harrison File. In possession of Brenda Harrison, Berea.

Jones File. In possession of Brenda Harrison, Berea.

Genealogy (published)

Arthur, Col. Robert. *The Fee Family and Its Gregg Connections.* New Orleans, Louisiana, 1959.

Baldwin, George Candee. *The Candee Genealogy.* Cleveland, Ohio: 1882.

Boughton, James. *Descendants of John Bouton.* Albany, New York: Joel Munsell's Sons, 1890.

Caudill, Bernice Calmes. *Pioneers of Eastern Kentucky: Their Feuds and Settlements.* Lexington, KY: Kentucky Images, 1969.

Genealogies of Kentucky Families. 3 vols. Baltimore: Genealogical Publishing Co., 1981.

Hawley, Elias S. *The Hawley Record.* Buffalo, New York: Press of E. H. Hutchinson, 1890.

Hayden, Rev. Horace Edwin. *Virginia Genealogies.* 1891. Reprint, Baltimore: Genealogical Publishing Co., 1979.

Hinshaw, William Wade. *Encyclopedia of American Quaker Genealogy.* 4 vols. Ann Arbor, Michigan: Edwards Bros., Inc., 1936.

Kendall, Hazel May Middleton. *Quaker Greggs.* Privately printed, 1944.

Miller, W. H. *History and Genealogies of the Families of Miller, Woods, Harris, Wallace, Maupin, Oldham, Kavanaugh, and Brown* [and others]. Richmond, Kentucky, 1907.

Pearson, Ralph Emerson. *A History of the Fee Family.* Vol. I. BCA. Typescript.

Pierce, Frederick Clifton. *Fisk and Fiske Family.* Chicago: Press of W. B. Conkey & Co., 1896.

Pirkle, Ann. Fee Family Research. BCA. Manuscript.

Smith, Zachary F. & Mrs. Mary Rogers Clay. *The Clay Family.* Louisville: Filson Club Publications no. 14, 1899.

Biography

Abzug, Robert H. *Passionate Liberator: Theodore Weld and the Dilemma of Reform.* New York: Oxford U. Press, 1980.

Biographical Cyclopedia of the Commonwealth of Kentucky. Chicago: John M. Grisham Co., 1896.

Biographical Encyclopedia of Kentucky of the Dead and Living of the 19th Century. Cincinnati: J. M. Armstrong & Co., 1878.

Clay, Francis Warfield Herrick. "The Political Significance of the Late C. M. Clay," *Filson Club History Quarterly* 33 (Jan 1959): 46-53.

Clay, Green. *Cassius Clay: Militant Statesman, Moses of Emancipation.* Dorris Collection, Crabbe Library, EKU. Manuscript.

Clay, Mrs. Mary B. "Biography of Cassius M. Clay: Written by His Daughter," *Filson Club History Quarterly* Part I, 46 (Apr 1972): 123-46; Part II, 46 (July 1972): 254-87; Conclusion, 46 (Oct 1972): 340-64.

Dictionary of American Biography.

Embree, Elihu R. "A Kentucky Crusader." In *Brown America: The Study of a New Race.* New York: Viking Press, 1931.

English, Philip Wesley. *John G. Fee: Kentucky Spokesman for Abolition and Educational Reform.* Ann Arbor, Michigan: University Microfilms, 1973. Ph.D. thesis.

Fladeland, Betty. *James Gillespie Birney: Slaveholder to Abolitionist.* Ithaca, New York: Cornell U. Press, 1955.

Harlow, Ralph Volney. *Gerrit Smith: Philanthropist and Reformer.* New York: Henry Holt & Co., 1939.

Harrison, Lowell H. "The Antislavery Career of Cassius M. Clay," *Register* 59 (Oct 1961): 295-317.

_____. "Cassius Marcellus Clay and *True American,*" *Filson Club History Quarterly* 22 (Jan 1948): 30-49.

Hill, Roger. *One Man's Time and Change: A Memoir of Eighty Years 1895/1975.* Privately printed, 1977.

Hook, Clara Degman. Articles on John G. Fee. *Berea Citizen,* 5 Feb, 12 Feb, 19 Feb 1931.

Howard, Victor B. "Cassius M. Clay and the Origins of the Republican Party," *Filson Club History Quarterly* 45 (Jan 1971): 49-71.

Humphreys, Jeanne. *Mary Brown Davis, Journalist, Feminist and Social Reformer.* Knox College Library. Galesburg, Illinois. Manuscript.

Lerner, Gerda. *The Grimke Sisters from South Carolina: Rebels Against Slavery.* Boston: Houghton, Mifflin Co., 1967.

Levin, H., ed. *The Lawyers and Lawmakers of Kentucky.* Chicago: The Lewis Publishing Co., 1897.

Loesch, Robert K. *Kentucky Abolitionist: John Gregg Fee.* 27 Aug 1969. Mountain Collection, Berea College. Bound dissertation.

Richardson, H. Edward. *Cassius Marcellus Clay: Firebrand of Freedom.* Lexington: U. Press of Kentucky, 1976.

Rugoff, Milton. *The Beechers: An American Family in the Nineteenth Century.* New York: Harper & Row, 1981.

Smiley, David L. "Cassius M. Clay and John G. Fee: A Study in Southern Anti-Slavery Thought," *The Journal of Negro History* XLII (July 1957): 201-13.

_____. "Cassius M. Clay and Southern Industrialism," *Filson Club Quarterly* 28 (Oct 1954): 315-27.

_____. *Lion of White Hall.* Gloucester, Mass.: Peter Smith, 1969.

Swing, Albert Temple. *James Harris Fairchild: Sixty eight years with a Christian College*. New York: Fleming H. Revell Co., 1907.

Thomas, Benjamin P. *Theodore Weld: Crusader for Freedom*. New Brunswick, New Jersey: Rutgers U. Press, 1950.

Tipton, French. "The Richmond Bar." H. Levin, ed. *The Lawyers and Lawmakers of Kentucky*. Chicago: Lewis Publishing Co., 1897.

Wright, G. Frederick. *Charles Grandison Finney*. New York: Houghton, Mifflin & Co., 1891.

History: Schools

Fairchild, Edward Henry. *An Interesting History: Berea College, Ky*. Cincinnati: Elm Street Printing, 1875.

Fletcher, Robert Samuel. *A History of Oberlin College From Its Foundation Through the Civil War*. 2 vols. Oberlin: Oberlin College, 1943.

Leonard, Rev. Delavan L., *The Story of Oberlin: Its Institution, The Community, The Idea, The Movement*. Boston: The Pilgrim Press, 1898.

Lesick, Lawrence Thomas. *The Lane Rebels: Evangelicalism and Antislavery in Antebellum America*. Metuchen, New Jersey: Scarecrow Press, 1980.

Muelder, Herman R. *Fighters for Freedom: The History of Anti-Slavery Activities of Men and Women Associated with Knox College*. New York: Columbia U. Press, 1959.

Phillips, Wilbur H. *Oberlin Colony: The Story of a Century*. Oberlin, Ohio: 1933.

Rankins, Walter H. *Augusta College: Augusta, Ky. 1st Established Methodist College 1822-1849*. Frankfort, Kentucky: Roberts Printing Co., 1957.

Shipherd, Jacob R. *History of the Oberlin-Wellington Rescue*. Boston: John P. Jewett & Co., 1859.

Webster, Martha Farnham. *Seventy Five Significant Years: the Story of Knox College 1837-1912*. Galesburg, Illinois: Wagoner Printing Co., 1912.

History: Local

Brandt, Nat. *The Town that Started the Civil War.* Syracuse, New York: Syracuse U. Press, 1990.

Calico, Forrest. *History of Garrard County, Kentucky, and Its Churches.* New York: Hobson Book Press, 1947.

Dorris, Jonathan Truman & Maud Weaver Dorris. *Glimpses of Historic Madison County, Kentucky.* Nashville: Williams Printing Co., 1955.

Dorris, Jonathan Truman & John Cabell Chenault. *Old Cane Springs: A Story of the War Between the States in Madison County, Kentucky.* Louisville: The Standard Printing Co., 1936.

Ellis, William, H.E. Everman & Richard Sears. *Madison County: 200 Years in Retrospect.* Richmond, Kentucky: Madison County Historical Society, 1985.

Ragan, Reverend O. G. *History of Lewis County, Kentucky.* Cincinnati: Press of Jennings & Graham, 1912.

Wilson, Jess D. "It Happened Here," *Rural Kentuckian* (April 1976): 16b-16d. BCA. Xerox.

_____, *When They Hanged the Fiddler and Other Stories from "It Happened Here."* Berea, Kentucke Imprints, 1978.

History: Civil War

Dyer, Frederick H. *A Compendium of the War of the Rebellion: Compiled and Arranged from Official Records . . . .* 2 vols. (1881 & 1901), reprint). Dayton, Ohio: The National Historical Society, 1979.

Harrison, Lowell H. *The Civil War in Kentucky.* Lexington: U. Press of Kentucky, 1975.

Johnson, Robert Underwood & Clarence Clough Buel. *Battles and Leaders of the Civil War.* Grant-Lee edition. New York: The Century Co., 1884.

Johnston, Col. J. Stoddard. "Kentucky." *Confederate Military History.* Vol. IX. Edited by Clement A. Evans. The Blue & Grey Press [no date].

Military History of Kentucky: Chronological Arranged. Written by the Federal Writers Project of the Works Progress Administration for the State of Kentucky. Frankfort, The State Journal, 1939.

Moore, Frank, ed. *The Rebellion Record: A Diary of American Events.* 1861-63. Reprint : New York, 1977.

Quisenberry, A. C. "The Battle of Richmond, Kentucky, September, 1862: A Reminiscence." Townsend Room, Crabbe Library, EKU. Xeroxed pamphlet.

Sears, Richard D. "The Battle of Richmond." Chapter 10 in *Madison County: 200 Years in Retrospect.* Richmond, Kentucky: Madison County Historical Society, 1985.

Tapp, Hambleton. "Battle of Richmond 1862," *Kentucky Pioneer* 1 (Oct 1968) 10-17.

The War of the Rebellion: A Compilation of the Official Records of the Union and Confederate Armies. Prepared by Lt. Col. Robert N. Scott. Series 1, Vol. XVI, Part I, Reports. Washington: Government Printing Office, 1886.

History: Antislavery

Duberman, Martin, ed. *The Antislavery Vanguard: New Essays on the Abolitionists.* Princeton: Princeton U. Press, 1965.

Dumond, Dwight Lowell. *Antislavery: The Crusade for Freedom in America.* Ann Arbor, Michigan: U. of Michigan Press, 1961.

Filler, Louis. *The Crusade Against Slavery 1830-1860.* New York: Harper & Bros., 1960.

Foner, Eric. *Free Soil, Free Labor, Free Men: The Idealogy of the Republican Party before the Civil War.* New York: Oxford U. Press, 1970.

Friedman, Laurence Jacob. *Gregarious Saints: Self and Community in American Abolitionism, 1830-1870.* New York: Cambridge U. Press, 1982.

Gara, Larry. "A Glorious Time: The 1874 Abolitionist Reunion in Chicago," *Journal of the Illinois State Historical Society* LXV (1974): 280-92.

Harrold, Stanley. *Cassius M. Clay on Slavery and Race: a Reinterpretation.* London: Frank Cass, 1988.

_____. "Violence and Nonviolence in Kentucky Abolitionism," *The Journal of Southern History* LVII, No. 1 (Feb 1991): 15-38.

Huston, James L. "The Experiential Basis of the Northern Antislavery Impulse," *The Journal of Southern History* LVI, No. 4 (Nov 1990): 609-40.

Loveland, Anne C. "Evangelicalism and 'Immediate Emancipation' in American Antislavery Thought," *Journal of Southern History* 32 (May 1966): 172-88.

412

McPherson, James M. *The Struggle for Equality: Abolitionists and the Negro in the Civil War and Reconstruction.* Princeton: Princeton U. Press, 1964.

Mabee, Carleton. *Black Freedom: The Nonviolent Abolitionists from 1830 through the Civil War.* New York: Macmillan Co., 1970.

Martin, Asa Earl. *The Antislavery Movement in Kentucky.* Louisville: Standard Printing Co., 1918.

Pease, William H. & Jane H., eds. *The Antislavery Argument.* New York: Bobbs-Merrill Co., Inc., 1965.

_____. Bound With Them in Chains: A Biographical History of the Antislavery Movement. Westport, Conn.: Greenwood Press, Inc., 1972.

Reynolds, Todd Armstrong. *The American Missionary Association's Antislavery Campaign in Kentucky, 1848 to 1860.* c. 1979.

Ruchames, Louis, ed. *The Abolitionists: A Collection of Their Writings.* New York: G. P. Putnam's Sons, 1963.

Sorin, Gerald. *The New York Abolitionists: A Case Study of Political Radicalism.* Westport, Conn.: Greenwood Publishing Corp., 1971.

Stewart, James Brewer. *Holy Warriors: The Abolitionists and American Slavery.* New York: Hill and Wang, 1976.

Still, William. *The Underground Railroad.* Philadelphia: 1872.

Thomas, John L. *Slavery Attacked: The Abolitionist Crusade.* Englewood Cliffs, New Jersey: Prentice-Hall, Inc., 1965.

Trefousse, Hans L. *The Radical Republicans: Lincoln's Vanguard for Racial Justice.* New York: Alfred A. Knopf, 1969.

Turner, Wallace B. "Abolitionism in Kentucky," *Register* 69 (Oct 1971): 319-38.

Walters, Ronald G. "The Erotic South: Civilization and Sexuality in American Abolitionism," *American Quarterly* 25 (May 1973): 177-201.

Woodson, Carter G. "Freedom and Slavery in Appalachian America," *Journal of Negro History* 1 (Apr 1916): 132-50.

Wyatt-Brown, Bertram. *Lewis Tappan and the Evangelical War Against Slavery.* Cleveland: The Press of Case Western Reserve U., 1969.

History: Slavery

Blassingame, John W. *The Slave Community: Plantation Life in the Antebellum South.* New York: Oxford U. Press, 1979.

_____. *Slave Testimony: Two Centuries of Letters, Speeches, Interviews and Autobiographies.* Baton Rouge: Louisiana State U. Press, 1977.

Coleman, J. Winston, Jr. "Lexington's Slave Dealers and Their Southern Trade," *Filson Club History Quarterly* 12 (Jan 1938): 1-23.

_____. *Slavery Times in Kentucky.* Chapel Hill: U. of North Carolina Press, 1940.

Gutman, Herbert G. *The Black Family in Slavery and Freedom 1750-1925.* New York: Pantheon Books, 1976.

Howard, Victor B. *Black Liberation in Kentucky: Emancipation and Freedom 1862-1884.* Lexington: U. Press of Kentucky, 1983.

Jordan, Winthrop D. *White Over Black: American Attitudes Toward the Negro 1550-1812.* Chapel Hill: U. of North Carolina Press, 1968.

Kentucky's Black Heritage: The Role of Black People in the History of Kentucky. Frankfort: Kentucky Commission of Human Rights, 1971.

Lucas, Marion B. *A History of Blacks in Kentucky.* Vol. I *From Slavery to Segregation 1760-1891.* Frankfort: Kentucky Historical Society, 1992.

McDougle, Ivan E. *Slavery in Kentucky 1792-1865.* Westport, Conn.: Negro Universities Press, 1970.

Pease, William H. & Jane H. *Black Utopia: Negro Communal Experiments in America.* Madison: The Wisconsin Historical Society, 1963.

_____. *They Who Would Be Free: Blacks' Search for Freedom 1830-1861.* New York: Atheneum, 1974.

Rawick, George P., ed. *The American Slave: A Composite Autobiography.* Vol. 16. Westport, Conn.: Greenwood Publishing Co., 1974.

History: Religion and Education

Ahlstrom, Sydney. *A Religious History of the American People.* 2 vols. Garden City, New York: Image Books, 1975.

Boles, John B. *Religion in Antebellum Kentucky.* Lexington: U. Press of Kentucky, 1976.

414

Cole, Charles C. *The Social Ideas of the Northern Evangelists.* New York: Columbia U. Press, 1954.

Cross, Whitney R. *The Burned-Over District: The Social and Intellectual History of Enthusiastic Religion in Western New York 1800-1850.* Ithaca, New York: Cornell U. Press, 1950.

Dayton, Donald W. *Discovering an Evangelical Heritage.* New York: Harper & Row, 1976.

Parker, Harold M. "The New School Synod of Kentucky," *Filson Club History Quarterly* 50 (Apr 1976): 52-89.

Steely, Will Frank. "The Established Churches and Slavery 1850-1860," *Register* 55 (Apr 1957): 97-104.

Swint, Henry Lee. *The Northern Teacher in the South.* New York: Octagon Books, Inc., 1967.

History: Kentucky

Clark, Thomas D. *A History of Kentucky.* Lexington: John Bradford Press, 1954.

Collins, Lewis & Richard H. *History of Kentucky.* 2 vols. 1874. Reprint, Berea, Kentucky: Kentucke Imprints, 1976.

Connelly, William Elsey & E. M. Coulter. *History of Kentucky.* Edited by Judge Charles Kerr. Vol. 2. Chicago: The American Historical Society, 1922.

Johnson, E. Polk. *A History of Kentucky and Kentuckians.* 3 vols. Chicago: Lewis Publishing Co., 1912.

The Kentucky Encyclopedia. Lexington: U. Press of Kentucky, 1992.